May Ellis Bolles, portrait by the well-known artist Pierre-Emile Cornillier,
spring of 1900, the year after her pilgrimage to 'Akká and meeting 'Abdu'l-Bahá

The Maxwells
of
Montreal

Early Years 1870–1922

The Maxwells of Montreal

Early Years 1870–1922

by

Violette Nakhjavani

with the assistance of Bahiyyih Nakhjavani

GEORGE RONALD
OXFORD

George Ronald, Publisher
Oxford
www.grbooks.com

*A catalogue record for this book is available
from the British Library*

ISBN 978–0–85398–551–8

Cover design: Steiner Graphics

CONTENTS

FOREWORD

At the dawn of Bahá'u'lláh's mighty Revelation, the firmament of His Cause was glittering with bright stars and blinding lights. This period of the Bahá'í Faith, which began with the Declaration of the Báb and ended with the passing of 'Abdu'l-Bahá, has been called the Heroic Age with good reason, for it witnessed the lives and deaths of some of the greatest figures to have called themselves Bahá'ís. Their brilliant services, their dazzling heroism, their acts of self-sacrifice have adorned the pages of our history and their stories are destined to inspire the whole Dispensation.

The believers in the West who rose to these heights were highly individual in character and temperament. These pathfinders and trailbreakers of the new day in Europe and America equalled, at times, their co-religionists in the Cradle of the Faith. They were iconoclastic souls with independent minds and searching hearts. They were the first to accept the Cause of Bahá'u'lláh in various cities, countries and continents, and they were undaunted by public opinion, undeterred by family opposition or social antagonism. At times they even faced persecution and their stories bear witness to the way in which they did so with a purity of spirit and a detachment that paralleled the heroism of martyrs and of saints.

This particular story is not of one person but a unit of three, which is an almost unique phenomenon in the annals of the Cause in the West. These three shining lights were members of one family, bonded in their love for the Covenant and for each other, committed through years of uninterrupted service to the promotion and establishment of the Bahá'í Faith worldwide. They were born during the Heroic Age of the Faith – the parents during the lifetime of Bahá'u'lláh, the child during the Ministry of 'Abdu'l-Bahá – and they lived to serve the Guardian of the Cause during the early decades of the Formative Age at the most critical time of his ministry. The mother was the central pivot in this wonderful triad and its driving force. The father was a noble, cultured and saintly man who had his own part to play, his unique lustre to add to their constellation. The daughter, a lovely distillation of their faith, grew up to symbolize all that was best in them. Their names were May Bolles, William Sutherland and Mary – the Maxwells of Montreal.

The story of this family was born from a verbal promise given by Amatu'l-Bahá Rúḥíyyih <u>Kh</u>ánum[1] to her mother, many years before Mrs Maxwell's death:

'One day,' she told May, 'I will write a book about your life.'

She was just seventeen years old when she made this promise. She used to say that her mother's eyes lit up like stars when she said it. Her face shone with joy.

'Will you really?' she asked her daughter. 'Will you really do it?'

Rúḥíyyih <u>Kh</u>ánum was determined to fulfil her promise. As early as 1936, she began jotting down thoughts about her mother, whenever she found a moment. But it was only after the sudden passing of May Maxwell, in 1940, that she made a deliberate attempt to write her story. On 9 December of that year, she started what she called 'Mother's Biography' in a large black leather notebook, although she hardly knew what it would turn out to be herself, at that point, or how extensive its dimensions. Due to the demands on her time, however, she did not fill many pages. Despite repeating her promise to herself and others many times, despite spilling over from the black leather binder into other notebooks where she jotted down many ideas, general thoughts, and reminders of what she wanted to cover in her mother's biography, Amatu'l-Bahá was unable to progress in writing the book.

In the mid-1980s when I had the privilege of accompanying her to the Maxwell home, now the Bahá'í Shrine in Montreal, she came to an important realization, which she herself later articulated in her notes. She came to the conclusion that if she were to write about her mother, she would have to include her father in the book, and if her father was part of the story, she could hardly keep herself out of it either. She had stated in a letter written to her mother long before,[2] that 'we are like one person with three names!' She knew that there was no way of separating the members of this family from each other. The book, as she repeated many times in my hearing, would have to be about all three of them, together.

---

1   The official name and title given to Mary Maxwell by Shoghi Effendi after her marriage to him in 1937.

2   13 October 1938.

She also realized that there was no way of truly understanding these three people except in their relation to 'Abdu'l-Bahá and Shoghi Effendi. Any life narrative of her mother, Amatu'l-Bahá knew, could not be a personal history only, but would also have to reflect the important milestones in the development of the Faith. The correspondence of her parents and herself was intimately concerned with the central figures of this Cause. The story of their three lives was linked by the centripetal force of the Covenant of Bahá'u'lláh. It was inevitable that if she undertook the writing of her family history, she would also have to write, at least to some extent, about the early history of the Bahá'í Faith as well, in both Europe and North America.

But there had to be limits to this project. Amatu'l-Bahá often stated that it would be impossible for her to write the Bahá'í history of her father and her mother at the same time as doing justice to the magnificent work of the Maxwell brothers, for example, to the artistry of William Sutherland or the architectural achievements of her uncle Edward, which remain as landmarks in the city of his birth even to this day.[3] It would even be difficult to give equal attention to her mother's Bahá'í services and her father's professional accomplishments in such a book as she was contemplating, leave alone describe all her own experiences. She was well aware that she could not hope to cover the lives of every member of the Maxwell family associated with the city of Montreal either. There was a wide range of material available about her greater family, much of it already in the public domain, which lay far beyond the scope of this project. Amatu'l-Bahá knew that she did not have the time to research her full genealogy – the Martins as well as the Bolles, the Irwins and the MacBeans as well as the Maxwells – or to analyse the rich historical and cultural background of all her relations. Aware of the limits of the project on which she was embarking, she described in her 1985 notebooks the dilemma that she faced:

If you want to place a person in history you have to have a great

---

3   Henry Yates has written a fine review of the larger family history, extracts of which are included in Appendix I at the end of this volume. An excellent summary by Nancy Yates of the artistic and architectural legacy of William Sutherland Maxwell is included as Appendix II. The achievements of the Maxwell brothers have also been analysed by Professor John Bland in *The Architecture of Edward & W. S. Maxwell* (Montreal: The Montreal Museum of Fine Arts, 1991). Since justice cannot be done to the whole story of the Maxwell clan in this selection of letters, it is hoped that a befitting biography will one day be written of this distinguished family.

many facts. After all, facts, events, are what make up a life. To even begin to procure sufficient facts concerning the lives of my father & my mother would be impossible for me at this time in my life. Details of the Maxwell family were collected by my cousin Elizabeth & her papers are in Montreal. Details of the Bolles family are with my cousin Randolph Bolles in Washington, Conn. I have no time at this juncture in world events with all their dangers & pressures, to retire for many months & study the data that may be available. So all I can do is to try & *precise* [sic] the picture of my parents & to some extent myself – so that in the future when biographies come to be written they cannot be warped out of all recognition . . .

It was with this motive and with all these challenges in mind, therefore, that Amatu'l-Bahá Rúḥíyyih Khánum returned to her notebooks and began to write the 'Introduction' to the project that she had decided to call *The Maxwells of Montreal*. It was after a break of almost forty years that she started to collect and coordinate all the facts about her family at her disposal, with the invaluable help of her devoted secretary, Nell Golden. It was a huge task, a puzzle whose pieces were scattered across eighty years.

In 1980 she had made a special trip to Montreal to do research, particularly into the life and architectural work of her father; while there she had interviews with John Bland, Emeritus Professor of Architecture at McGill University, and with her relatives including Lorne MacBean and Henry Yates. Later, in August 1986, she visited her cousins Jeanne Bolles Chute and Randolph Bolles, making extensive notes and photocopying a large number of documents.

Meanwhile, in 1981, work had begun in Amatu'l-Bahá's office on sorting the massive amount of material in her possession in Haifa – typing items, extracting data onto index cards, filing and cross-referencing. This work was done as other office work permitted, and especially when Amatu'l-Bahá was away on her many journeys. There were literally thousands of letters in her possession. Especially precious were letters from Shoghi Effendi, which had never been transcribed from the originals. And quite apart from all the correspondence between the individual members of this family – father and mother to each other and each of them with their daughter – there were also the hundreds of letters that May had written to and received from the many people she met in the course of her life, the souls she taught, the friends she made. There were also her personal notes, her attempts at writing the early history of the Faith in France and in Canada.

Unfortunately the burden of her duties at the Master's House,[4] her administrative responsibilities in Haifa, and especially her travels throughout the world, did not permit Rúḥíyyih Khánum to progress as fast as she desired on this cherished project. She continued to jot down notes, and the work of sorting continued in her office, but six or seven years before her passing she began to realize, to her deep disappointment, that she could not achieve her goal. I confess that I myself was ignorant at the time of the actual dimensions of the task she had undertaken so late in life. On one occasion, when I asked her why she did not continue writing this wonderful book, she replied, wearily, that she had no doubt others would do it in her stead. Dismayed, I asked her what others, who could possibly achieve this, and how? 'You will do it,' she replied, and then changed the subject. I understood then that I should not trouble her further by talking about the book, because she was already sufficiently saddened by her inability to finish it. When she passed away, she had filled some eighteen notebooks with entries, but the promise to her mother was, alas, still unfulfilled.

After her passing, Nell Golden and I found ourselves appointed, according to her will, as co-executors of Rúḥíyyih Khánum's Literary Estate. We were left with the daunting responsibility of dealing with the immense amount of material that came to light as the extent of her private Estate papers became known. These included Tablets of 'Abdu'l-Bahá, some written in His own hand, which retained the dates of their translations only, not the dates on which they had been revealed. In addition there were Amatu'l-Bahá's diaries and notebooks, of which there were a great many; her memoirs, with their varying discrepancies; and her private and personal papers preserved from the time of her earliest youth until her own passing. The sheer bulk and variety of this largely handwritten material was such that little could be read before it had been sorted, typed and catalogued, and nothing could be written until selections from it had been made.

Most importantly we had to decide what should be done with it all.

---

4   No 7 Haparsim Street, the house where Shoghi Effendi lived throughout his ministry, and which Amatu'l-Bahá Rúḥíyyih Khánum occupied after his passing, is referred to as 'the Master's House' in Bahá'í parlance because it was built by 'Abdu'l-Bahá Himself and was where He died in 1921.

It was an ocean. But as we embarked upon this task, I began to understand why my beloved K͟hánum had wanted to share the life of her family, and particularly of her mother, with the world. The letters were priceless; their message was timeless. And they were telling a magical tale. Since I knew how dear to the heart of Amatu'l-Bahá Rúḥíyyih K͟hánum was her promise to her mother, and how sad she had been not to fulfil it, I longed to make her dream come true. Though keenly conscious of my limitations and my presumption, I felt duty bound to pick up the pieces of the puzzle and try to complete this task for her sake.

I began, in all simplicity and with the assistance of dear Nell, by selecting letters that she had already transcribed and piecing them together, thematically and chronologically, to the best of my ability. I knew that this approach, broadly speaking, was what Rúḥíyyih K͟hánum had wanted and I also knew that it would not be anything remotely like a proper biography. I had no further aim than to share with the Bahá'í community a compilation of correspondence which, together with Nell, it was my primary task to sort through and place at the disposal of the Universal House of Justice for future reference. But what neither of us knew at the time was just how many letters and papers there actually were; what neither of us guessed was the magnitude of the task we had undertaken. As the months passed, it became clear that the Maxwell Literary Estate contained much more than we had ever dreamed.[5] As more and more letters came to light it became obvious that Nell needed assistance in identifying, transcribing and cataloguing the material. When the one book envisaged by Rúḥíyyih K͟hánum expanded into two volumes, each three times the size of my original draft, I too began to realize that I could not finish this project alone and needed help to write it. At this point Nell drew on the sterling services of Anne Banani to transfer these papers into a format that would be accessible to future writers and researchers as well as to myself, and I asked my daughter Bahiyyih to help me structure the material and link the letters into a coherent whole. And so *The Maxwells of Montreal* gradually turned into a collaborative effort.

Since Amatu'l-Bahá's own words are so precious to us, we chose to begin with her own 'Biography of Mother' taken from her 1940 notebook, followed by the 'Introduction' she later wrote in 1985. Whatever relates to a description of May Maxwell's character remains intact,

---

5   The present count is in the range of some 60,000 letters. See the note on *The Maxwell Literary Estate* for an approximate summary of the contents of this collection.

just as she wrote it in this memoir, but episodes concerning specific events have been extracted from her notebooks and inserted where they chronologically belong in the body of the text or in the footnotes. The task was rendered more difficult because Rúḥíyyih Khánum did not jot her thoughts down systematically. Some of her notebook entries have dates and others do not; some pages contain inserts and others do not; and sometimes, to indicate a break in thought, subject, and the passage of years, she turned the book around completely, and instead of adding a row of dots or drawing a line across the page, started writing from the back! She was, moreover, in the habit of using her notebooks for a wide variety of purposes including lists of linen and silverware, reminders of day-to-day household affairs, and even her personal accounts. In other words, she did what many writers do when preparing to embark upon a book project, while burdened by daily duties and obligations – she used these notebooks to think. As a result, her entries reflect a personal perspective that is not only idiosyncratic but, on occasion, irrelevant. The incongruities that may be reflected in her memoirs, moreover, are essential to an understanding of the culture and the upbringing of Rúḥíyyih Khánum; it should not be forgotten that she was a woman of her time in addition to performing a unique role in the Baháʼí Dispensation. Furthermore, the discrepancies that sometimes occur between her mother's record of an event and her own retelling of it several years later provide the reader with the privilege of echoes whose slight differences we felt it essential, even salutary, to preserve. The primary aim of this story is not only the accuracy of facts but also the adventure of their transmission through the generations.

Although we knew that we could not presume to write the book that Rúḥíyyih Khánum might have written herself, care has been taken to privilege her intentions as far as possible. We had to select from thousands of letters without her guiding hand, but our choice was governed by her wish to record the lives of her family members, to identify the historic milestones of the Faith they witnessed, and to reflect on the major events of their epoch, as candidly and as faithfully as we could. It has not been easy to avoid repetition while maintaining chronology in this selection. It has been a challenge to preserve privacy while being true to facts, as well as to steer clear of hagiography. But we hope that if readers can hear the voices, glimpse the faces, and become the recipients of the actual words written to each other by the members of the Maxwell family, some measure of balance may have been achieved.

In order to give priority to the Maxwell correspondence, we had to leave out hundreds of letters between Mrs Maxwell and the scores of souls to whom she taught the Bahá'í Faith in the course of her life, many of whom corresponded with her till the day she died. Quite apart from the restrictions of focus and of space, it has not been possible to complete the sorting, the selecting, or the cataloguing of this additional ancillary correspondence in time for publication. A few samples of letters between May and the most well-known of the Bahá'ís of the early 20th century have therefore been picked at random from a partial rather than an exhaustive selection, and priority has been given instead, in this selection, to the letters written between father, mother and daughter themselves. Since *The Maxwells of Montreal* has no pretensions of being a biography in any classical sense, it rests with others in the future to complete this secondary aspect of the task more befittingly.

The significance of capturing the lives and times of pivotal Bahá'ís through correspondence was deployed by May herself, in her earliest attempts to record the Paris days. Writing to Edith Sanderson, she confessed:

> I have tried in vain to recapture something of the beauty wonder and rapture of those early days of the dawn of our beloved Faith in the west, and to embody it in some historic form. Only by addressing it from my heart to yours can I hope to recall those events with which you are so intimately and deeply associated & to approach this precious task.

This story depends on the continuation of that 'address' from her heart to ours. It was inspired by the desire to share May Maxwell's letters with the Bahá'í world, and so, inevitably, the events of her life have served as the scaffolding for these volumes. This is how Rúḥíyyih Khánum first conceived her book, and this is how the narrative demanded to be told. Since the letters to and from May constitute the great majority of the material, moreover, it is only natural that the lives of her daughter and husband should branch out of her own. She influenced them profoundly; she was the pivot of this family, in every sense. And although she died before either of them, the critical events that marked her life provide a framework for theirs.

The story of *The Maxwells of Montreal* has been divided into two volumes, corresponding with the ministries of 'Abdu'l-Bahá and Shoghi Effendi.

Volume I (*Early Years*), which covers the years 1870–1922, is about the last decades of the Heroic Age and includes selections from all the early correspondence in the Maxwell Literary Estate. It concerns the childhood years of May Bolles and Sutherland Maxwell; their youth, their meeting in Paris and their beautiful courtship; their marriage and their first pilgrimages. It tells the story of the birth of their daughter and the historic visit of the Master to their home in Montreal just before World War I. It also describes the early development and training of young Mary, summarizes the family's activities during the war years, arrives at its climax with reception of the Tablets of the Divine Plan and ends with the passing of 'Abdu'l-Bahá. There is a note on the Maxwell Literary Estate at the beginning and two appendices at the end: by Henry Yates about the origins of the Maxwell family and by Nancy Yates on the artistic achievements of Sutherland Maxwell.

Volume II *(Middle and Late Years)*, which covers the years 1923–1952, begins with the early ministry of the Guardian and the historic pilgrimage of May and her daughter in 1923/4. It describes May's services to the Faith in the 1920s; Mary's education as a young Bahá'í, her pilgrimage during her adolescence, and the growth of the youth movement in Montreal; the sacrifices of the family during the Depression years and May's trip to Europe with her daughter between 1935 and 1937. The last part of the volume *(Late Years)* covers the life of the Maxwell family from 1937 to 1952, beginning with the marriage of Amatu'l-Bahá Rúḥíyyih Khánum to the Guardian of the Bahá'í Faith, and ending in 1952 with the death of Sutherland Maxwell in the aftermath of World War II. It includes May's heroic services before her passing in 1940, and describes her husband's remarkable architectural achievements during his final years in the Holy Land. It does not cover any aspect of Amatu'l-Bahá's personal life, either before or after Shoghi Effendi's passing.

It should be pointed out that after her marriage Amatu'l-Bahá scrupulously restrained herself from writing about any private matters in her letters related to Shoghi Effendi. In fact she may have been given specific instructions in this regard, for she never deviated from the practice, even with her family members. If she kept diaries and notebooks at this time, it was for no other reason than to record events for the future protection of the Guardian. She was not only his 'shield' against the enemies of the Cause and the defender of his personal life against intrusion, but a very private person herself. What she wanted to make public from her private diaries, Amatu'l-Bahá gave us in *The Priceless Pearl* and what she did not choose to share has therefore been excluded from these pages, in keeping with her expressed desire. Passages taken from her notebooks are relevant to the Maxwell family only and strict confidentiality has been maintained on all personal matters touching upon Shoghi Effendi. In fact, it was soon after her marriage that Amatu'l-Bahá Rúḥíyyih Khánum established the standard of spiritual etiquette required in writing about the Guardian. In a letter to her mother dated 2 July 1938 she explained that personal matters related to the Head of the Baháʼí Faith were no one's business:

> You see Mother, I cannot write freely about my particular problems because they are now largely all the same as the Guardian's problems and naturally I cannot confide those to paper anymore now than you or I could have expected to read such things in the past . . .

In compiling these letters, I have done my utmost to honour this principle. From 1937 on, Mary Maxwell became known as Madame Rabbani to the public and Amatu'l-Bahá Rúḥíyyih Khánum to the Baháʼís. Her contributions to the work of the Cause from that time on were rendered first and foremost in her capacity as the helpmate and companion of the Guardian, rather than as a member of the Maxwell family. Her work as his secretary during his lifetime, her extraordinary responsibilities at his death, and her unique position as one of his appointed Hands of the Cause during the critical interregnum years before the election of the Universal House of Justice, have no place in this book. Her vital contributions to the International Teaching Centre during her final years, to say nothing of her unparalleled journeys between 1964 and 1997 as the chief ambassadress of the Cause of God and, on many occasions, the representative of its Supreme Body across the five continents – all these deserve separate volumes and extend far beyond the scope of this project.

It would have been impossible to undertake this task, despite all its limitations, without the gracious permission of the Universal House of

Justice. I wish to thank them above all for having allowed me to come to Haifa on innumerable occasions to fulfil my obligations as the co-executor of Rúḥíyyih Khánum's Literary Estate and to continue work on the Maxwell family papers. Nor would I have dreamed of embarking on this task without the tireless support and meticulous assistance of Nell Golden, who throughout the life of Amatu'l-Bahá, and ever since her passing, has maintained the standards of integrity and fidelity which beloved Rúḥíyyih Khánum so valued.

In addition to expressing my heartfelt gratitude to Anne Banani, my dear sister-in-law, for her faithful attention to detail and discretion in helping Nell, and to my daughter Bahiyyih for her writing skills, I would also like to thank my husband Ali Nakhjavani, who provided us with his wise counsel, his encouragement, and his preliminary translations of some of the Master's Tablets. All the quotations from these Tablets of 'Abdu'l-Bahá are now provisional translations approved by the Universal House of Justice specifically for publication in *The Maxwells of Montreal*. Those requiring annotations have been provided with footnotes.

Many other friends also helped bring this work to light. In particular I wish to thank my granddaughter Mary Victoria who edited the first drafts of both volumes, and Laila Taslimi, my dear niece, whose excellent detective work enabled us to untangle the chronology of many undated letters. I would also like to acknowledge the help of the following friends for their vital work in the sorting and identifying of photographs for this precious project and for their secretarial assistance: Maralynn Dunbar, Mary Ann Gorski, Foad Katirai, Martine Caillard, Louise Mould, Sandra Briand and Dicy Hall. My particular appreciation goes to Christopher Lyons for his diligent and splendid work in improving the photographs for publication. I owe a great deal, too, to the extensive research of Kathy Hogenson concerning the details of the first historic pilgrimage in 1898. Finally I wish to express my special gratitude to May Hofman, for her unique insights and her editorial skill without which these volumes could never have been published in time for the centenary celebrations of 'Abdu'l-Bahá's journey to the West.

I know that Amatu'l-Bahá wished to share her wonderful legacy with the world. She wanted the Bahá'ís to benefit from the spiritual truths enshrined in these letters that are at the same time so full of humanity. I pray that her radiant soul may reinforce my feeble efforts to fulfil her promise. I hope she will accept my attempts to try and make her dream come true. This was her own credo: to try. 'When I die,' she used to say, 'I want just these two words engraved on the stone: "She tried."' As long as I have the strength, I would, with all my heart, aspire to that same privilege.

Violette Nakhjavani

THE MAXWELL LITERARY ESTATE

The Maxwell Literary Estate consists of a vast amount of written material, collected for over a century, from 1870 to 2000, by the three principal members of the Maxwell family: May, Sutherland and their daughter Mary (Amatu'l-Bahá Rúḥíyyih Khánum). Like the Literary Estate itself, the Bahá'í legacy left by these three individuals is immense and will only be able to be grasped in the future. As of 2010, much of this material still requires sorting and cataloguing, transcribing and annotating, but the reader may wish to have some idea of the range and scope of this collection in order to understand its relation to *The Maxwells of Montreal*. The statistics below are understandably an approximation.

There are about 60,000 items of correspondence in the Maxwell Literary Estate. Of these, around 4,100 letters were written from 1870 to 2000 between Mr, Mrs and Mary Maxwell (Amatu'l-Bahá Rúḥíyyih Khánum) and their family members. The Literary Estate also contains unnumbered thousands of letters written over this period between the Maxwells and some 500 individuals, both close friends and more distant acquaintances, as well as a wide range of correspondence conducted with administrative institutions of the Faith. The Estate also includes over 7,800 books, some 4,500 art and architectural postcards dating from the late 1890s, 1,300 handwritten notes, many newspaper articles and about 150 diaries and notebooks. Non-epistolary materials such as the art sketch books of W. S. Maxwell, over 20,000 slides, some 400 audio tapes of Rúḥíyyih Khánum's talks, videos and about 10,000 photographs are part of this collection as well.

The Maxwells of Montreal has been based on materials from the Literary Estate that are directly relevant to the years 1870 to 1952. It draws on a total of 1,600 personal letters between May, Sutherland and Mary Maxwell (Amatu'l-Bahá Rúḥíyyih Khánum) and from about 1,400 family letters which the three Maxwells exchanged with their relatives during this time. In addition to a selection of letters to and from certain of the early Bahá'ís and the Maxwells, it includes citations from the 195

Tablets, letters and cables from 'Abdu'l-Bahá, Shoghi Effendi, and the Greatest Holy Leaf to members of the family, which have never been transcribed before. It also contains extracts from Rúḥíyyih Khánum's notebooks, the memoirs of her mother, and many sketches, articles and photographs related to the period.

Although the range and richness of the Maxwell Literary Estate indicates how well both May and her daughter Mary preserved this priceless heritage, it was a habit acquired at a cost, for it appears that many important letters may have been lost in the early years. This is particularly true in the case of the correspondence in Volume I, which covers the period from 1870 to 1922. Before 1923 May wrote most of her letters by hand. Those she dictated were also handwritten and she kept very few copies. Although she tried to preserve all her incoming letters, not many of the outgoing ones, addressed to other than her immediate family members, have been located to date. Even the correspondence between May and Sutherland during this period indicates that many of their early letters and cables have sadly disappeared. More research is needed to locate whatever of this correspondence may have survived.

After 1923 and until her death in 1940, May dictated her correspondence and from then on carbon copies of practically all her outgoing correspondence as well as the letters written to her were carefully preserved. Even when travelling, she would avail herself of the hotel stenographer, and keep copies for her files. The mass of material that has resulted made it necessary to exclude from Volume II the majority of letters to and from individuals, as well as most of the correspondence related to the institutions on which Mrs Maxwell served for over twenty years. Emphasis has been placed instead on letters between the Maxwell family members themselves, which have been selected to reflect on the main events in history and their lives between 1923 and 1952. The bibliography of published works has also been kept to a minimum in order to focus on primary rather than secondary materials.

Since *The Maxwells of Montreal* includes only a drop in the ocean of the Maxwell Literary Estate it cannot pretend to offer an exhaustive summary or cover every detail in the lives of these three remarkable individuals. As future researchers and historians, writers and biographers delve deeper into this ocean in order to share its treasures with the world, there will no doubt be more facts and many more facets revealed about this unique and wonderful family, the Maxwells of Montreal.

THE MEMOIRS

of

AMATU'L-BAHÁ RÚḤÍYYIH KHÁNUM

Mother's Biography

by

Amatu'l-Bahá Rúḥíyyih K͟hánum

———— ༺༻ ————

begun December 9th, 1940

In the golden lightening
of the sunken sun
O'er which clouds are bright'ning
Thou dost float and run
Like an unbodied joy
whose race is just begun.
— *Shelley*

The author of this book makes no pretence of being qualified to write an adequate biography, either in form or style. She does not pretend to be a disinterested observer of the life of the one with whom she has to do in these pages. She does not even claim that they should be considered necessarily a complete portrait of a woman who, through her early, varied, and profound connections with the Bahá'í Faith, will find a place for herself in its glowing and wonderful history.

She is the only and beloved child of a Mother whom she adored and to whom she looked for all that is best and noblest in a woman, and in whom she was never disappointed! Her Mother was not only her physical Mother but became the Mother of her soul; gave her immortal life through imparting to her that greatest of all gifts: the knowledge of God, of His Chosen One, and of His teachings.

Life is full of love. Wherever we turn we see examples of it. The natural, warm, enfolding love of Mothers for their children, the tender, lifelong passion of married pairs; the devotion of children to parents – brothers to sisters and friend to friend. But there are some

3

great loves in the world. They are relatively few and they transcend ordinary bounds. They are not dependent directly on relationship or sex, age or opportunity. They are extraordinary and seem to have to do with something in the spirits of men placed there by their Creator.

Of such a love this book is the tender testimonial.

Some people are like gold: all gold, all pure, a noble monotone. Some like diamonds: brilliant, polished minds, clear fine characters, truly an ornament to society in every respect. But Mother was like – like a melody, like the sunlight in the country woods, like a pure venturesome, patient brook that flows on to the Infinite Sea and that offers as its right happiness and refreshment to everything that crosses its path. Her soul could rise and soar in swift, lilting strokes, upward towards its Lord, in thought and prayer, as a rising lark in the morn. She could be as worldly-wise as the greatest *grande dame*, as naive and easily overjoyed as a very small girl, as wise as any deep thinker and scholar, as all-loving and sympathetic as one to whom a heart may confess – nay feels impelled to – its heaviest and saddest load.

Wilfred Barton, in a letter to the Guardian, says: 'I came closest to Mrs Maxwell's spirit (closer than I ever had before in this life) on the day her ship stopped in Montevideo & Mr Rosenzweig and I went to meet her and Jeanne at the boat. We were all sitting at the lunch table and happened to be talking of the Guardian when impulsively she turned to me & stretched out her hand to mine in a way that brought the tears to my eyes. It was a kind of spiritual meeting . . . that was the only facet of her apparently extraordinary personality with which I have come into direct, intimate contact; but there was a great deal packed into that one moment. I shall never forget that moment.'

* * *

May Ellis Bolles came into this world in a well-bred and prosaic setting. There was nothing to make one believe her life had a right to be unique or that her destiny would be extraordinary. She was born, on the 14th of January 1870, to John Harris Bolles and Mary Ellis Martin. She was their first child and one supposes they were as proud of her and pleased about her as most young parents are over their offspring. The pleasant, old-fashioned, country town of Englewood in New Jersey was her birthplace. It lay snuggled in woods and countryside, close to those imposing palisades that skirt the left bank of the Hudson opposite New York City.

A stone's throw from the home of the Bolles was the home of the Martins, May's maternal grandparents. They lived . . . in a pleasant, homey brick mansion, smothered in ivy and set back in nice grounds [and] came of an old, respected and well-known New York family long before that city spread upward on the island and sprawled into a world metropolis. Martin was a banker. They were most devoted to their daughter and all their lives took more than an ordinary grandparents' care of their children – for 19 months later little 'May' was followed by her brother Randolph. These two were the only children of John and Mary.

Mary Bolles was a capable woman with a fine character. She had married her husband for love and he was most devoted to her in every way.

The Mother, leaning over the cradle of her first born, was often distressed to see the tiny babe convulsed by some agony of its own, the early signs of a strange malady that was to know no cure and be the greatest test in the life of the woman to come, the steel, one might say, of lifelong suffering that was to enter into her soul, be her interminable battle, help forge the beauty of her spirit.

The earliest recollections of herself which Mother had was when, at about the age of two, she was beautifully dressed in white by her Mother to be taken out somewhere (and, assumedly, shown off). On her way down the drive she discovered a large and delicious mud puddle into which she immediately went and sat down triumphantly. This, of course, brought the outing to a hectic and tearful conclusion.

On the 14th of August 1871 Randolph Bolles was born. He was the second child and became, as sons are so apt to do, the apple of his Mother's eye. All their lives 'brother' came first. And the older sister seemed from her earliest years to have accepted this with no feeling of bitterness or jealousy, rather she, too, learned to be ever ready to give up for him and never begrudged him his markedly preferential treatment.

Although this was true all of their lives, it did not prevent the sister, senior in years as well as size, for at least the earlier period of their childhood, from exerting herself in the typical subjections of child by child. She often remarked how she would mash him behind the front door as a form of punishment for insubordination, or to emphasize some dire threat!

Also they both remembered with a great deal of amusement the occasion on which little Randolph, aged six or seven, desired to climb May's chestnut tree. It seems there were two beautiful big chestnut trees on the Martin property, brother and sister each had one which was their 'house'. But that day brother wanted to come up sister's tree. 'May,' he called, looking up, 'I'm coming up your tree.' 'Don't you dare,' cried his outraged sister, 'I'll spit in your eye.' The small face of Randolph was looking up. He chose to ignore the threat, whereupon a large mouthful of saliva carefully aimed and gaining speed from a considerable height, landed square in his eye. He fled howling to Mother, and May got a first class tanning with the back of the hairbrush.

The great tragedy of Mother's life was her health. In all other respects she had a most blessed and happy life, excepting the usual salting of up's and down's to which human flesh is heir: death, poverty or disappointment, they visit every soul. From her cradle she suffered with a nervous disease which 'Abdu'l-Bahá Himself said she had been born with. No doctor ever found out exactly what it was. Organically sound in every respect – except as her heart became affected in later life – she yet was the large proportion of her life an invalid. I have never been for a walk with my Mother a greater distance than two blocks. She just could not do more. Her back and legs would be exhausted, though she was in no way crippled or deformed and would walk about as briskly as any normal person in the house. At the age of 21 she had her first major illness. Until that time she had been a dynamo of youthful energy. She often told me she would swim in the morning, play three sets of tennis in the afternoon and dance till midnight!

If to be a Bahá'í is to be one whose deeds exceed their words a thousand fold; one who at all hours, in all states of mind and health, is ever ready to proffer the divine chalice of the knowledge of God to whosoever seeks it; one whose love shines tenderly on friend and foe, on the important and the least of human riff-raff; one whose friendship is an abiding security, uncorrupted by time or separation; one whose word was honest and kept; one whose purse and home alike were ever open to those in want; one of whom it can truly be said she was a refuge for the hearts of those who turned to her – then May Maxwell was a true Bahá'í.

And if to be a lady is to be modest and self-effacing; to be ever sensitive to the feelings of others; to put all, rich and poor alike, at ease; to be cognizant of and careful of the niceties and refinements of person, home and hospitality – then she was indeed a very noble lady.

All my life no beggar went empty-handed from our door. Often she herself would go down into the kitchen and see that they had food and a hot drink, if they were ready to eat when they came to our home – if not, a sandwich to take away or some food for their family. She often gave money but preferred to give food or aid as so many beggars go and buy drink, but then she would say, 'Poor soul, I guess if I were in that state I might drink too to get warm and to forget!'

She had the most marvellous interest in everyone. One could best say she was a lover of her fellow-men. She truly loved them. It was not affected or sanctimonious at all. For example, one day she was standing out in front of our house and she saw a shabby looking man walking up and down the street. Our next-door neighbour came out of his house, had a look at the man and went in again. A few moments later he came out again, this time with his son, and they both had a look at him and on evident consultation on the matter, Mother deduced they were suspicious of such a dreg of society in their neighborhood and intended to do something about it. So when they went in she beckoned to the man and told him she thought he had better disappear as she suspected they were going to send for the police! He thanked her most gratefully for the tip and promptly made himself scarce. As I remember he had some inoffensive reason for being there – apart from the fact that he was a free citizen. Sure enough, a few minutes later a couple of policemen appeared and nosed about in vain for the 'suspicious character'! This was typical of her intense comradeliness with everyone, more particularly with the downtrodden. She would never have aided and abetted a criminal, but she saw no reason why the well-to-do should abuse the poor.

To really know a person you have to live with them, and that for a long time. I lived 25 years with my mother and she was always the same. No meanness existed in her nature. That is a much more important statement than it would at first glance seem to be. Nearly all of us, in some way, be it ever so small, are mean. Either we are uncharitable to our enemies, or perhaps niggardly with money, or low-minded sexually, or mistrustful of even those whom we love. We may be a little greedy, or a little self-indulgent in putting some extra comfort by for ourself – something, be it ever so little, shows a trace of meanness. But this she did not in any way possess. It was, to me, almost the finest and most outstanding thing about her – next to her unique capacity for love – this complete lack of pettiness or meanness. She never talked about a thing, she always did it. One of her favourite expressions was: 'By the time you finish talking about it you could have it done!'

This does not mean that she was perfect. She wasn't. She was most adorably human. I often wonder if I would call her a saint. In the orthodox sense of the word I don't think she was. That is one who is all goodness, all detachment, all resignation, all sacrifice – she was too vivid, somehow, to be classified that way. But she was the best all-round good person I ever saw. If goodness is active love, an ocean of generosity, a heart full of sympathy, and passionate devotion to God – then she was good to the core of her bones.

She was unspeakably frank – a trait often misunderstood by those who are not by nature themselves frank. If she heard that one of the Bahá'ís, or any friend for that matter, was upset over something . . . which she had actually or supposedly said or done, she would go to the telephone, ring them up and say, 'What's this I hear that you, etc.' She always said it to one's face, whether flattering or otherwise. If it was a compliment, I remember her reply to the conventional protests people make when you flatter them: 'Why should you have to wait till a person is dead before you say good things about them, or have to say it behind their backs?' She was equally direct in giving a person a 'piece of her mind'. One of our young Montreal Bahá'ís – who as it happened was her spiritual child – told me that: 'Mother almost killed me the other day. I telephoned her from a booth down

8

town and she was mad at me for something I had done and she gave me a terrific lecture and the combination of the heat of the lecture and the telephone booth, almost suffocated me!' Needless to say he did not object to her 'lecture' at all!

This was another indication of her character's innate straight-forwardness. She never sulked. She was never cold – that horrible trait so many women have, of showing their displeasure by freezing towards you! – she never nagged . . .

Her generosity was the greatest I have ever personally come in contact with. It was compounded of three things: complete indif-ference to things herself, an immense desire to give and pleasure in giving, and a complete lack of financial sense. It was no use telling her the market was falling, there was a depression, she was using up her capital, etc. She would reply invariably in these terms: 'Abdu'l-Bahá promised me I would never be without money. He said He would always send me some if I needed it,' or 'Shoghi Effendi says we must give like the spring, ever emptying itself and being replen-ished,' or merely 'The secret of having is giving.' These were not words with her; they were her inmost conviction, based, I must say, on a never-failing experience.

She was not the least attached to anything. She did not like owning things. She was against my father's building a home when, after they had been married for about six years, he wished to do so, but 'Abdu'l-Bahá wrote her that as Mr Maxwell desired to build a home with his own money, she had no right to prevent him from doing so. But she always protested against the plan of our having another, summer, home. She had almost no jewellery, a few things left over from her Mother only, and one or two pieces of her own that had been gifts. All these she gave to me, and I think if I had not liked them even as a child, she would have given them to others long before I grew up!

As I look back on her life at home I see so clearly how distinct this detachment from possessions was. I did not at the time realize it because it was my environment and I had no perspective on it. Her furniture was, of course, bought by my father and in excellent taste; but her furnishings were her own. Over her mantelpiece was a large picture of 'Abdu'l-Bahá in his youth. On the right wall beside her bed was a big portrait photo of Juliet Thompson's painting of

Lua Getsinger – her beloved spiritual mother, above her bureau was the Greatest Name drawn by Mi<u>sh</u>kín-Qalam, I believe. She had two small landscapes painted by my father, one of a scene in 'Akká, and a painting of mine of a bowl of roses. These three because she loved and encouraged us in all we did! The only pictures of any value were two framed embroideries my father had hung in her room – one with the head of a saint in its center. Her dressing table was devoid of silver, any small things on it being usually gifts from me. I remember in its drawers were old letters and locks of my hair as a baby and child. On her bureau was a box of black lacquer in which she kept some rock candy the Master gave her, and other souvenirs of sacred memory. She never had very many clothes but always dressed with extreme good taste and refinement. Noble, upright, fine – the breath of life in her nostrils was the Cause of Bahá'u'lláh.

* * *

Many people live in a place they call 'home' but I don't think very many people really have homes at all. We had a home in all the best sense that word can mean. I won't say Mother created it solely by herself because that would be untrue and unfair to my father – but 75 per cent of it she did. She filled it with love and harmony, just as my father filled it with beauty and good taste. Outwardly it was a house that many people would seek invitations through mutual acquaintances in order to visit, as it really was singularly harmoniously and pleasingly arranged and filled with many *objets d'art*, which, though not in the class of millionaire collectors, yet bespoke both knowledge of and love for the beautiful, and were not commonplace in the least. Within this harmonious shell – for surely all such possessions come under the heading of the mere shell in which the true thing itself may or may not be found – reigned an extraordinary atmosphere. I have never found its like anywhere and I know a great many people who felt the same way about it, even though it did not happen to be their home.

That atmosphere I think can best be described as the spirit of love in deed and thought. It filled our house with a strange peace. Not only the Bahá'ís – who were bound to it by many religious ties – sensed this, but people who made no claim to be religious in any way. I remember a young doctor friend of ours saying that when he was tired (he was a scholarship student at McGill University) he would like to be allowed just to come and sit in our drawing room and rest – he would not disturb us, we need not even see him, if we were busy or out. He was not the only one that felt that way.

This very tangible 'ether' was due to a number of factors: first, I believe, to the fact that when 'Abdu'l-Bahá visited Montreal He stayed three days in our home . . .

. . . Mother always kept this before her, that He had said: 'This is my home,' and she acted accordingly. No one went empty-handed from our door; we always held open house for the Bahá'ís; we entertained more than any people – except those in official positions who are obliged to – I have ever met! Every race and class circulated in and out our doors. They were all met by the same fragrance, the fragrance of a radiant nature that in truth loved its fellow-men and was ever ready and eager to help them.

That was one reason – the major one undoubtedly – that our home was blessed with such an atmosphere. The other was our private family life. I believe the major part of home building – the inner home within the shell which usually the man's labour provides – rests with the woman. It has to be a very hard, obstinate and bad character indeed who cannot be moulded and softened by a true woman's goodness and love. The tender sympathy, consideration, and patience of the mother is the foundation stone of the home. Her welcome to those who go out and work and return at night, tired and sometimes irritable; her care to see that the wheels run smoothly – the dinner tastes good and is on time, the place neat and clean and friendly; her readiness to listen to the problems, or the exploits of her husband – regardless of whether they interest her or not! Mother had all these ultra feminine qualities well developed. She had the love, so essential to everything in life, in abundance. She always greeted my father with a kiss, just as she sent him off in the morning with one. She not only never missed this small sign of affection herself but never allowed me to, even though I sometimes was not in the mood for it at all! She would say: 'Mary, go and kiss your father, it's most unkind of you not to, he needs your love.' And so an obstinate and recalcitrant little Mary formed the habit of affection – a very good habit in a woman. She knew that there is more truth than poetry to the saying: 'The way to a man's heart is through his stomach,' and ensured that her husband had a dinner he enjoyed when he came home at night. I have often seen her, when she was feeling ill and remaining in bed, get up and go down two flights of stairs to make sure the dinner would be just right, even though she would go back to bed to eat her own. And best of all – she never talked about these things. She was not one of those typical wives that, when indignant, hurls a barrage at her husband, listing all her virtues and all his faults, such as: 'I go down and cook the dinner for you and slave for you and so on, and what do I get?', and then sums him up in a series of biting epithets! In other words she was not petty. We never fought because we always aired our grievances. We could not go to bed disunited even though we could and did have our differences, explode and feel hurt, just like any other family. But it never remained. This was entirely due to Mother. She could not tolerate the absence of love and harmony; it simply killed her. The moment it was gone she set about re-establishing it. We all felt unspeakably miserable if one was upset with the other. The centripetal feeling was so infinitely stronger than the centrifugal.

* * *

Mother had no reserve at all. She was as friendly as sunshine. She took the most profound interest in her fellow beings of anyone I have ever seen. She could get acquainted with a stone, so to speak, and she did not feel the least bit shy about mixing herself in the lives of others. On the contrary, she seemed to feel that every human being that crossed her path was a special obligation to her. She had a right – and a duty – towards seeing if she could not do something for them or to them! This should not be confused with the 'know-all' people who preach at others. It was utterly devoid of self-righteousness or any flavour of preaching. The first thing, of course, that was always uppermost in her life after she had become a Bahá'í was to share this glorious knowledge with everyone. But she knew not all are ready, not all can grasp the Shining Cord held out to them – but that, to her, was no excuse for ignoring the person. She was a born teacher, an innate psychologist – if one can put it that way. I remember once a very amusing incident in Atlantic City. She was 'getting the air', a thing she had a passion for and which she could not get normally like most people by walking, but had to go stand outside and sniff it in when she had gotten up and out for a little while, and she encountered a mother with a baby in a pram. The baby was howling obstinately, the mother scolding indignantly. She of course immediately took an interest and began to talk to the very ordinary mother of the child, who, as I remember, had begun to shake it. Anyway, inquiring as to the trouble with poor baby revealed that he had 'a very bad temper'; 'which', said Mother promptly, 'he seems to have inherited from his Mother!' After this passage of arms, she withdrew like a ruffled hen to report the incident to me later! This is the only recollection of this nature I have, as Mother was neither rude nor unkind, but she said she thought the woman should have it pointed out to her that it was her own character manifest in the child and not something the child did deliberately! Perhaps that unpleasant truth gave the woman pause for thought next time she lost her temper with her babe in arms. Anyway, the one thing Mother could not stand and which she always immediately mixed herself up in was anything to do with children suffering. It made her simply beside herself. It was a very marked characteristic. I must have climbed hundreds of fences in my childhood, both in Montreal and any place we happened to be summering, in order to locate the place where some child was crying its head off and report it to Mother! Then she would see if it let up, or she would telephone and squirm politely in an effort to find out why the child was crying so! Was it ill? She had a child herself and it broke her heart to hear one crying, etc., etc.! It was something she could not control at all – her reaction to the suffering of children. She was an instinctive Mother.

Her nature was largely composed of a tremendous maternal instinct. God alone knows how many hundreds of children and young people she benefited in her life.

After my birth, as a sign of gratitude to God, she (with my father's help) opened the first milk station in Montreal in the slums. She also sat for a long time on the bench with the Judge at Juvenile Court hearings, as an adviser.

Four different times she took young people into our home for a period of a year or so and helped them on – and these were only the more conspicuous cases of her aid. I remember the first was a baby of a cook of ours, a French-Canadian girl. I was about seven or eight, I think. Our cook asked Mother for permission to go for a few days and see what she described as the 'baby of a friend of hers' in a convent home somewhere in Quebec. When she returned she seemed very upset and upon being pried by Mother she confessed she was very anxious about the child, who seemed to be in a terribly weak condition. Mother, having some experience of these Catholic institutions in Quebec, sent her immediately to bring the child to us. I will never forget that baby! He was two years old but so weak he could not even sit up. He had a huge head, a bloated belly, emaciated limbs and was a bluish colour – in other words he was starving to death. Mother brought my baby specialist to take care of him. We kept him at least a year, as I remember, and he got fat and strong – but he will bear all his life the marks of his babyhood in a frail body, slight stature and slightly wizened look. The girl gave him to her parents, who were devoted to him, to bring up. He often came to visit us when he was older. He spent one winter with us in Montreal [and] one summer in Green Acre, when he was nine . . . There is no doubt he owes his life to her.

Her desire to create love, harmony and unity amongst those she came in contact with led her often to be instrumental in bringing about marriages; in fact, her enthusiasm in this direction was so great that the Master warned her not to interfere in these matters! One very happy outcome, however, of a not *too* energetic interference on her part was the marriage of a girl who had been a sort of nurse–companion to her during her most desperate illness in 1922, after the death of 'Abdu'l-Bahá. Weak though she was when she at last began to recover, she took a keen interest in the love affair of the dark, pretty Nova Scotian girl who had grown dear to her. The young man who was causing her so much grief was delaying marrying her because of the strong opposition of his father who, perhaps for financial reasons or out of unnecessary pride, opposed the girl of his son's choice. When the youth came to Montreal and met my Mother in the course of calling on his sweetheart, he was given a good scolding for tampering with her love, allowing her to get so run down and be so unhappy just because he had not the courage to face his father and marry the girl he loved. The talk bucked him up so much – together, no doubt, with seeing his fiancée again – that without telling 'father' anything they were married in our home! The old man after his first burst of wrath gradually recovered and ended up by becoming devoted to his daughter-in-law and most grateful that his son had married such a woman – a marriage which would never have taken place, I think, if Mother had not called the young man to his senses as the father's policy of discouragement, together with the fact they were so widely separated, was leading to estrangement.

She helped people upward. Her influence was intensely benign and I cannot but believe that the love in her heart – a love of which the Master once said: 'When you love people it is 'Abdu'l-Bahá's love in your heart' – was the lodestone that brought out the best in others. Often she changed people's thoughts and beliefs – but more often she changed their lives and characters.

A Bahá'í whose daughter had gone through a most crushing tragedy – a mere girl of 17 – in despair came to Mother at last and asked her help. The girl, as pure and sweet as a girl can be, had been seduced by a boy she loved, trusted and expected to marry. Her baby had been born, the boy's parents, of a different faith, cruelly forbidding marriage, the girl's parents, with true nobility and vision, faced the situation with their daughter and upheld her in her hour of need. The whole family adored the baby – then it died. This blow, on top of all her shame, the betrayal of her love and trust, was too much for the girl. She was absolutely dazed, like a living dead person. As only the Mother was a Bahá'í, she turned to my Mother for guidance. Mother, I remember, brought the girl to our home for a few days. Realizing how much she was suffering, I kept mostly out of her way. What passed between her and Mother I don't know, but the life came back into the girl a little before she left, then she became a Bahá'í, a Bahá'í mouse I would call her, she was still so quiet, so unobtrusive and shut into herself. As time went by she began to blossom and grow until she ended up by being a poised, radiant, much-beloved Bahá'í capable of taking public meetings, working on Committees and teaching the Faith which had given her new life, new life through Mother. Their bond was very profound, much like a Mother and daughter's love. The man she later married also became a Bahá'í through Mother.

One day some poor French-Canadian children came to the house begging. They told such a pitiful tale, in the dead of winter, of a bold bare home and no fuel or food or money, that Mother decided to investigate. We took the children in the car and went to see the house. A homely, very ordinary woman was cooking some flour and water into a gruel over the fire in a kitchen that had little more than the stove and frying pan in it and a lamp. The other rooms were bare of all furniture except a few packing cases with planks laid on them and filthy bedding for beds. About five or seven children were in the family. The father, pursuant to his usual habits, had gone off with the proceeds of his wages and another woman. For ten years or more Mother took an interest in the eldest girl who had first come to us. She helped the Mother and the children often, but over a period of years became so exasperated with her that she threatened to – and eventually did – stop helping her if she continually went on taking her worthless husband back every time he returned broke to the home and continued with his propagation of the family. The girl had neither the capacity nor the desire to become a Bahá'í, but her admiration for and confidence in my Mother and the influence she exerted, steered her at last through the perilous evils that beset a pretty and attractive slum-born child and saw her safely married to a young man who was devoted to her.

Another child of the slums, though of much better birth on her father's side, the daughter of an Irish charwoman, was often in our home, at first as a guest, and when she grew older as a minor servant. All the girl's aspirations for a better milieu and her innate repugnance for the environment of her home were given expression through Mother's loving aid and guidance, until she married a good man and had a home of her own. The bond always remained of affection and interest through the years and the instinctive turning to Mother for advice in moments of trial in her private life.

It would be hard to count the people who, as servants, stenographers, or people contacted through charity, were permanently benefited through May Maxwell's quick human sympathy and equally generous purse and understanding. So many times, on arriving in a hotel where Mother was staying, I would hear about 'Annie' or some other named chambermaid, how many children she had, what her problems were, what Mother had given her and said to her, etc. She would often buy gifts for such people's children, or if they were young, something for themselves.

Once I left Mother waiting in a taxi in the Bowery in New York City while I went into a store. It was dusk in the late autumn. There was an elevated [railway] overhead and the district was typical of the poor East Side. When I came out it was dark and she was not in the taxi. I looked up and down the street and saw her standing not far off talking to a man; I went to join her and much to even my surprise found her holding the hand of a very tall, old Jew. He was truly of the ancient, Hebrew type, with bent shoulders, grey beard and aquiline nose. I heard him say, 'What for?', and she said, 'Because you are my brother!' Then she let go of his hand and joined me. It seemed, with her usual interest in people, she had watched him come by and stop in front of a cheap coffee shop where coffee was advertised for 5 cents a cup; he looked in the window, but evidently did not even possess that much, and turned away. Mother then got out of her taxi and went after him, took his hand and pressed a dollar bill into it. He was surprised at this sudden gesture and had asked 'What for?' in broken English. Her answer was her whole belief about life.

There were no barriers between her and her fellow-men. She felt just as friendly towards the Negro pastor as the waiter or the taxi man or towards a social equal or, for that matter, a superior. She could get acquainted faster than anyone I ever saw. In fact, it would not be incorrect to say it was practically impossible for her not to get acquainted! Sitting in a railway station in Stuttgart one evening on our way back from Esslingen, where the Bahá'í Summer School was being held, we were, Mother, Daddy and I, talking to Frau Braun, Dr Forel's daughter. I don't know whether it was our friendliness to each other, or that Mother was weak and ill and had to sit on a bench to rest, or something she over-heard, but a young German girl's attention was attracted to Mother. She kept looking at her – this was not wasted on Mother. She just reached out and snapped her up! I don't remember exactly how, through a smile or an enquiry or something, but on her way out of the city to catch her train she literally grabbed that girl, got her name, made an appointment with her and went on in the days to come to become her devoted friend and teach her the Cause – a Cause which, alas, the girl did not wholly embrace at that time as she detected from 'certain Bahá'ís' criticism of the Jews and her sympathies were all with the suffering Jews, though she was not one herself.

In that same city she also befriended a man she met in a café. It was her wont to dress and go out for a little air in the afternoon opposite the Hotel Marquardt. She could not walk far, and when she got tired from standing she would sometimes go into a café. One afternoon she saw a man who looked starved sitting there drinking his coffee but eating nothing. Somehow she got to know him, found he was, indeed, slowly starving to death as he was out of work and his pension from the Government did not provide enough so that he could lodge, eat and keep clean. As he simply could not be dirty (as he himself explained to her) and had no way of doing his laundry himself, he was just wasting away. Mother often had tea with him after that, he as her guest, and she helped him financially. I always remember his hollow cheeks, his bones and sunken eyes – how many people would have been able to make his acquaintance and help him without making him feel hurt and humbled?

All these are small things, most of us have helped other people from time to time. But no one I ever met made this attitude towards others the pattern of their daily lives rather than the exception to the rule. Surely this is the essence of a religious life!

* * *

I remember a Negro cook we had, a huge woman well over six feet tall and proportionately built. She was usually an excellent servant, but it seemed she took some drug sometimes, which we did not realize until one day when she almost killed Mother. She had brought her little boy to spend Sunday with her and after lunch the housemaid reported she was beating him. This Mother would not tolerate, and although she was sick in bed she got up and called down the tube to her in the kitchen and told her she must not beat Harold. To this Isobel replied she would do what she liked, and began to grumble around the kitchen. After this, the housemaid reported she was coming upstairs like a locomotive with steam up, and Mother took me and the maid in her bedroom and we locked the doors – we forgot, however, the door leading to my father's room through a series of cupboards, and she stormed in that way. At first she went for Eva the housemaid. I was a child of 13 or so – but Mother, now sitting up in bed, said, 'It has nothing to do with Eva,' so then she turned on her, picked up a large jug of water and raising it above her head said, 'I'm going to kill you.' 'Oh no you're not, Isobel,' said Mother, as cool as a cucumber, and looking her calmly in the eyes. Isobel hesitated, lowered her arm, put the jug down and left the room grumbling. The police were invited to remove her that same afternoon, though no charges were made against her.

* * *

It is hard to recapture – and will as time passes, grow increasingly difficult to do so – the unselfconscious and burning enthusiasm and conviction with which many of the first Western Bahá'ís searched out and embraced, at last, the Faith. Many of them, like May Maxwell, searched well-nigh a lifetime, from childhood to maturity, for the truth they felt instinctively was to be and must be found. They passed through one sect after another, from philosophy to philosophy, in a passionately restless state of mind, driven by a thirst few people ever know.

Lua Getsinger described one of her experiences, when after being assured by the Minister of some new church that after baptism by total immersion she would receive the Spirit of God, came up, dripping and impatient, from her submersion and glancing anxiously around cried: 'Where is it! Why don't I get it!' when she failed to be greeted by any soul-touching experience. Such naiveté may seem almost stupid to a more sophisticated generation, but it betokened a spirit which burnt like a single flame upwards, unconscious of everything except that it must have light. When once these rare souls did reach their journey's end and found in the 'World's greatest Prisoner' the epitome of those words of Christ: 'I am the life and the way and the Truth' [sic], they became attached to Him and to the Faith He so perfectly typified with a devotion wholly unshakeable, which no other relationship in life could ever supplant and which filled them with a degree of love for the Message He represented and for Himself that the passage of years left undimmed, and neither death nor grief could still.

The magic word 'Master' would kindle a brightness in May's eyes and bring a faint and infinitely tender smile to her lips up to the last moments of her life. To those who do not remember Him a great wonder comes at the uniform reaction of His 'Apostles' to the mention of His name. Perhaps a day will soon come when the generation who only knew His apostles will be marvelled at for the stories they tell, not of Him but of those who in the West first loved Him!

* * *

Mother was a remarkably highly organized, sensitive being. She came from one of those families – particularly, I suspect, on the Bolles side – which one finds in New England and which are not uncommon; they are old stock, inbred, refined in the ways that spelt refinement in this part of the world, but often the blood worn a little thin, the members delicate of health, intellectual, a little inclined to be static and contemplative. Although her whole character was intensely dynamic and her every impulse was to create, to give out, to investigate, to enjoy with a wonderful, vibrant capacity for joyousness, yet her nerves were weak, her body frail, her physical susceptibilities over-sensitive. Her brother was also inclined to be this way, though his health was much better. He, however, showed more of that quality of immobility than she did; he was inclined to be contemplative, in the sense that he approached life less adventurously, more conservatively, could not cast himself into the great tides of human thought stirring in the world and be moved by them as she was.

Mother's sensitiveness went farther than that of the average person and caused her, or enabled her, to be what people choose to call psychic. Whether this was partly inherited from her mother, who possessed definite mediumistic qualifications, I don't know but during her girlhood she often amused herself and others by demonstrations of this power. She used to open the Bible, while blindfolded, at any passage that her mother either read to her or concentrated on; she used a ouija board with success, and used to, by placing her hands on a table with others, be able to get it to move. Later, at the earnest solicitation of a friend of theirs, who warned her that he believed the dabbling in these powers very injurious to her health, she gave up these practices entirely. This was some years before she became a Bahá'í. But aside from these marked psychical qualities, she was a highly sensitized being and I remember a few experiences we had together, due partially, no doubt, to our great love for each other, which were very unusual. One night in a Hotel in New York, I was sleeping in a room on the opposite side of the building from her – as the Hotel occupied almost a whole block and she was on the corner of one side and I not only on the opposite side but at the end of the corridor on that side, we were separated by a long L-shaped corridor. Even if she had called me at the top of her lungs I could not have heard her at all. Yet in the middle of the night I woke up suddenly by hearing her call: 'Mary'. I even got out of bed and opened my bedroom door as I supposed she was calling me outside it. As no one was in the corridor I went back to bed feeling uneasy and puzzled as I thought she might be ill and not able or willing to telephone me to come to her room. The next morning she told me that in the night a drunken man had tried to get into her room, perhaps mistaking it for his own, and frightened her and she had called me, either aloud or in her thoughts.

* * *

It has often been borne in upon me that there is a profound symbolism in life. I do not mean omens; I mean that in some strange way little external things are symbols of great spiritual things or events. For instance: In my prayer book I have a number of photographs of my Mother and Father . . . Mother is shown with two pillars rising up behind her and a lion by her side. I know this was taken on the steps of the Hotel Rockingham in Portsmouth . . . But if one looked the world over one would not find anything to better epitomize Mother's character and her faith and her service to the Cause, than these two symbols – the lion and the pillar, for she was lion-like in her courage and a true pillar of the Faith in every way.

The picture of my Father shows him leaning against the bole of a mighty tree; this is like his own life and nature: he is calm, strong, deeply rooted in his traditions, good and peaceful; nothing could be a better symbol of him than that great tree . . .

Amatu'l-Bahá's biographical account of her mother, written soon after May's passing in 1940, ends here. There is, in addition, the following vivid portrayal, written by her some four years earlier, of both her mother and father:

. . . The extremes represented by my parents I am profoundly grateful for: my father, a born scholar and recluse, who lives every instant of his life through his eyes, who is a connoisseur of innumerable fields outside of direct architecture, who has designed hotels, parliament buildings, churches, chairs, lamps, menu cards and gravestones, who can never absorb enough to suit him and lives almost exclusively in the realm of art, who can paint and draw and sculpture with ease and charm, and is somewhat inventive to boot; and my mother, who has no other artistic ability aside from unfaltering good taste and love of beauty, who speaks and writes, who has been a passionate lover of humanity, has a profound knowledge of its problems, its foibles and miseries, is intensely interested in everything pertaining to life and to knowledge. For instance she adores nature – it bores my father and I have even heard him say he had seen some terrible combinations in sunsets! She loves entertaining and being with people; he is a shy hermit crab, generally speaking. She is foolishly generous; he is the old 'penny-wise, pound foolish' Scotsman. He has a sense of thrift and none of finance – (my mother has no sense for either!). But taken together they were a wonderful combination for helping each other. She has made his life wider and deeper, prevented him from being selfishly shut in to himself, brought out the side in him another type of woman, less free in spirit, less strong in character, would have never developed. He has been her strength, her support and adviser, a balance wheel for her capacity to lose herself too completely in others . . .

There is no doubt that the complementary natures of May Bolles and William Sutherland Maxwell were perfectly united in Amatu'l-Bahá Rúhíyyih Khánum herself.

In 1985, some forty-five years after her initial account, Amatu'l-Bahá began once again the task of writing her parents' biography. By this time, both May and William Sutherland had already passed away.

INTRODUCTION

How does one write a biography? What does one remember of a full lifetime? Standing on a high mountain, looking on all sides, away to the horizons, what does one really see – panorama, outlines, salient features; here and there an outstanding thing leaps to the eye, a rock, a grove of trees, a little city, an old ruin – but there are millions of details that go to make up the composite picture, some may be important, most are mere trivia, repetitions, unending, fundamentally boring to you and to anyone else. So what does one choose? Long ago, in a bedroom of the Hotel Taft in New York, I think it was a hot day, I sat with my mother who, not unusually, was sitting up in bed; I said to her, 'You know, Mother, when you die I am going to write your biography.' As this must have been about 1927 or 1928 and she died in 1940, there was no emergency involved at all. I remember how her very expressive blue eyes lighted up and she said, 'Really, are you?' Then I knew the idea pleased her. Between then and now a whole lifetime – more like many lifetimes – have flown away, but I always considered this in the nature of a promise and it has been there, in the back of my mind, for over 50 years. I like to fulfil my promises.

How to do it, that was the question? I visualized, rather vaguely, all the weighty tomes packed with chronological facts, as well as presumptuous assumptions, of famous biographies and was appalled. Where would I get all those facts; who would ever fill in the gaps? It loomed up, a vast, tiered undertaking, a kind of intellectual skyscraper, for which I could neither hope to assemble the requisite material in its perfection or find the time and ability to erect it. Then I read Agatha Christie's autobiography and a door opened; after all, it was *her* life she had written about, *her* biography; she did and wrote what she wanted about it, with no apology, no sense of inferiority. I was emancipated from the shackles of form; who would know your life better than yourself? Someone trying to capitalize on it for their own benefits, someone trying to think themselves into <u>your</u> mind and disentangle your motives and emotions? So I thanked Agatha Christie mentally (who has seen me through many a hard time in my life with her diverting, intelligent books) and decided it was *my* book and I would do it *my* way. At least those future biographers, who will try to do an autopsy on my family, will have a coherent corpse to dissect – there will be some limitation on how much they can interpret into our minds and deduce from our acts!

What at first was conceived of as the biography of my mother I have come to realize could never be anything but the biography of three people, the Maxwells, mother, father and only child. We were a united and happy family; impossible to deal with one, even the major element, and relegate the other two to shadowy background parts; our family formed an inextricable whole. So they became 'the Maxwells', and the stage was mainly set in Montreal; naturally it became 'The Maxwells of Montreal'.

The question was where to cut it off? My mother died in 1940, my father in 1952. But what about me? After all, I am still alive in 1985 and writing this biography so it seemed only logical the third element should go up to date. Into this framework, however, came a paramount element, my husband, Shoghi Effendi, the Guardian of the Bahá'í Faith. Like one of those armed nebulae revolving in its own orbit, the very motion of this Maxwell family was inextricably linked to not only Shoghi Effendi but, beyond him, to his grandfather, 'Abdu'l-Bahá, whom he had succeeded, who also had been the Head of the Bahá'í Faith in His capacity as the eldest son and chosen successor of His Father, Bahá'u'lláh, its founder. It is impossible to pull any element out of this web of the Maxwells' lives without immediately becoming involved with the personalities of both 'Abdu'l-Bahá and Shoghi Effendi, and, to some extent, the history of this dynamic Movement which commenced during the last century, only 26 years before my mother was born.

So, realizing my biography as a great swirling mass of rather sparkling facts, I wondered where to begin? At the beginning, 1870, with the birth of May Ellis Bolles? That would be the chronological starting point but surely not the hub. What then was the hub? Paris. Quite naturally Paris, for it was there my mother lived, my father studied, my mother heard about the Bahá'í Movement, became the first Bahá'í in Europe; they fell in love; that union was my beginning, and marked the introduction of the Bahá'í Faith into Montreal, the Province of Quebec, Canada when W. S. Maxwell took his bride home. That bride, being one of the earliest Disciples of 'Abdu'l-Bahá in the western world, much loved by Him, eventually was the cause of the marriage of her daughter to His grandson and successor – always the movement within the nebulae, no way of separating the pivotal force from its manifestations. So we will begin in Paris, the hub.

It all began in Paris; like the two arms of a swirling nebulae, May Bolles' and Sutherland Maxwell's life, individually and linked together – and thus my life too – breaks out from this central point.
. . .

We will never know what a superb story The Maxwells of Montreal *might have become had Amatu'l-Bahá been able to continue and complete that starry dance between two lovers in Paris. But we can catch a glimpse of the beauty that was born within the arms of this 'swirling nebulae' in these descriptions she has left us of her parents.*

Mary Maxwell, who was the sum total of their 'wonderful combination', was destined to survive her parents for almost half a century, but since she was known as Rúḥíyyih Khánum by then, their family unit had already come to an end. The story of the Maxwells of Montreal, however, was to prove immortal.

EARLY YEARS

1870–1922

1870–1898

May was called 'May' from childhood, in order to distinguish her from her mother, Mary Ellis Bolles, who had exactly the same name. Her mother was called 'Mamie', presumably to distinguish her from her mother, Mrs Mary Martin, who was known as 'Muddie' in the family from the time that May gave her the nickname in childhood. When May's own daughter was born, she became the fourth 'Mary' in as many generations. But she retained the name just as it was and loved it all her life, although she was given another far more formal appellation by which she was better known by the Bahá'ís of the world.

Mamie Martin evidently loved the good things of this life and knew how to enjoy them to the full. She was broad-minded and liberal in her attitudes, compared with others of her social class and generation, and was anything but a puritan. She had a fun-loving disposition and a worldly character in some respects; she lived with flair, took pleasure in her life, and introduced her children to travel from an early age. Their father, on the other hand, had the temperament of a poet. John Harris Bolles was a New Yorker like his wife, but unlike her, was rather shy by nature and retiring. His 'Promised Land' lay in the idealism of the Psalms and in culture.[1] He yearned for goodness and mercy to follow him all the days of his life, for music and poetry to lighten his solitary hours; he dreamed of friends with scientific and literary tastes, and the simple pleasures of a home, a wife and children. Despite these ideals, he became a mining engineer and worked for a time in finance. Although he achieved proficiency in each profession he may have been ill-suited to both, for while he was endowed with wit and with refinement it is possible that he was not ruthless enough in a materialistic sense nor sufficiently ambitious to satisfy his wife's expectations.

---

[1] This he confessed in a letter written to his daughter some time after his wife's passing, on 1 December 1905.

The couple had a love marriage that would have been unusual in their times. In 1868, when their wedding was officiated by the free-thinking transcendalist, Reverend O. B. Frothingham, it may have seemed to their contemporaries that these two young people not only had the benefit of enlightened ideas and personal attraction to ensure their future happiness, but every advantage of beauty, wealth, and family connections too. May, who was born in 1870, was their first child, and Randolph, nineteen months her junior, their second and last. But despite the romantic ideals that had brought them together and the conventions of the period that did not allow them to divorce, Mary Ellis Martin and John Harris Bolles separated shortly after Randolph's birth. Barely five years after their wedding, they parted company and never lived together again. Such unconventional behaviour would not have been approved by the society to which they belonged nor been acceptable in the homes in which they had grown up. The Martins and the Bolles were both old-established New England families and had a reputation to consider, a tradition to maintain. But though the Martins boasted an impeccably Anglo-Saxon genealogy, the Ellises, according to Rúḥíyyih Khánum, did have an obscure Greek ancestor. No verification has been found for this tantalizing detail except the jokes she often shared with friends and an allusion made by May herself to her 'probable Greek ancestry' in a letter to Sutherland.[2] He was sufficiently in love at the time to wax lyrical about the 'ideals and temperament' of his betrothed which he thought reflected 'the beautiful times of old Greece when men lived, and lived so truly and completely'.[3] But their daughter used to say that whenever she expressed a liking for fatty foods in later years, Shoghi Effendi would look at her with a twinkle in his eye and remark that perhaps her appetite had been inherited from the Greek too.

Amatu'l-Bahá used to sum up the subject of her ancestors by

---

2   18 January 1901: 'You know that we are supposed (my family I mean) to be of Greek origin, & some enthusiast in our family, having cast a searching eye over the past declares that we come, name & all, from the old Greek Province of Elice. It is interesting but a trifle fanciful to my mind, and of course has not the slightest importance anyway, as the material world, physical evolution & body birth & inheritance are all nothing to me. . .' It appears that Elice may have been a village in the province of Teramo, rather than a province itself. But it is also the name of a commune in the province of Pescara in Italy today, which leaves the origins of 'Ellis' even more ambiguous. In addition, the Greek word for 'Greece' is 'Hellas'.

3   W. S. Maxwell to May Ellis Bolles, 12 February 1901.

repeating the story her father told about them, when she was little. One day, when she had asked him, very solemnly, to tell her about her family roots, Mr Maxwell had answered, somewhat laconically: 'All your ancestors on my side were Scottish horse thieves. And all those on your mother's side were Greek fruit sellers!' Rúḥíyyih Khánum invariably concluded the story by adding that this reply, delivered with her father's characteristic dry wit, freed her forever from concerns with family pride.

May's paternal ancestors had migrated to the United States in the early seventeenth century. The Bolles were of Anglo-Saxon and Roman background, with roots in both England and France that have been recorded as far back as the twelfth century. John Bolles was the grandson of Major Harris of Washington Square Artillery and the son of Dr Richard Moore Bolles, a prosperous physician who later became a homeopathic doctor. May's maternal grandparents were David Randolph Martin and Mary Tweed Ellis who belonged to a well-established and wealthy New York family. The Martins were in business, and at one time owned the Ocean City Bank in New York. But one night in 1869, less than a year after the marriage of Mary Martin and John Bolles, this bank was robbed by a gang of ingenious thieves who dug a tunnel into the building from the one next door. The scoundrels managed to get away with everything: securities, money and all the documents in the vault. The disaster was compounded by the fact that the receiver appointed by the government to oversee the liquidation of the bank proved to be dishonest too[4] and since there was no insurance in those days, David Randolph Martin had to sell his entire personal fortune to reimburse his clients. As a result, their ruin was achieved in a single night.

When the family became bankrupt they moved out of New York, across the river to the village of Englewood, New Jersey, and here they had to accustom themselves to much reduced circumstances. The blow to their social standing as well as to their family pride must have been deeply felt and certainly had an impact on the lives of the young Bolles couple, who took up residence next door to the Martins. The stress did not diminish with the scandal, for David Randolph Martin was summoned to testify in lawsuits that continued for the next decade. There was even a Congressional investigation of the bankruptcy that

---

4   Hogenson, *Lighting the Western Sky*, p. 59.

must have taken its toll in more ways than one,[5] for the social disaster experienced by the family was followed a year later by a domestic crisis. By 1872, the marriage which had been embarked on so promisingly in 1868 was to all intents and purposes over, and although it was never legally annulled, Mamie moved out of her own home at this time and went to live with her parents. May, who must have been no more than three, doubtless registered the strain in the family.

In her search for a beginning to her mother's biography, Amatu'l-Bahá Rúḥíyyih Khánum may have looked for it, at first, along the banks of the Hudson. She may have tried, through the glimpses that she found in May's fragmented notes, through her own early memories and those of her mother's cousin Frank Irwin,[6] to piece together the story of this child of acute sensibility and lively imagination, who lived in a modest residence in Englewood, wore the cast-off clothing of her society cousins, and played on the banks of the Hudson, north of New York.

Frank, who was the nephew of Mamie Bolles and spent much of his youth in the company of his cousins May and Randolph, had vivid recollections of those early years in Englewood, when the Bolles and Irwins lived close to the Martins, on the Hudson:

I'll begin with Englewood itself. Do you know it at all? Start with the Palisades, the fine cliffs on the West bank of the Hudson, across from the upper end of Manhattan Island. Plateau stretching west from this top . . . wooded. Then descent . . . into Englewood. (Fine bob sledding on this hill, Palisades Avenue.) Shops in the flat country at the bottom; residences too, and also on the slope of this hill. About ten minutes up the hill, the Martin place. Plenty of grounds round the house. A fine grove of chestnuts, the kind that bear the small nuts. House built of 'fieldstone' a sandstone with yellowish and pinkish shades; two storeys and an attic and cellar. Drinking-water from a well that got to have a good deal of – not unpleasant – taste, and seems to have been salubrious. Other water from the rain that fell on the roof and was stored in a cistern; this had to be pumped up for distribution, to a tank in the attic. (I used to pump sometime on visits.) No delivery of mail in Englewood;

---

5   ibid.

6   He wrote to her soon after her mother's passing on 2 August 1940, presumably at her request.

had to be fetched from the post-office, down below. (Randolph and I didn't always feel like going for it.) One of the drawbacks to Englewood at certain seasons was quantities of mosquitoes; everyone had to sleep under a mosquito net. Englewood now has a number of wealthy people and a country club; but not in those days, though there were a number of pleasant 'Places' like the Martins'. Railroad to Jersey City: Northern Railroad of New Jersey; then the pleasant trip by the 23rd St. ferry to New York . . . Here lived grandfather and grandmother. My father built a small plain wooden house on the adjoining land where I lived the first year of my life; and the Bolles' house was not far away. May christened the two old people 'Fader' and 'Muddie', and Randolph adopted the names when he came along.

In the early pages of her 1940 notebook, Amatu'l-Baha echoes something of these same scenes, which she may have intended to incorporate into the Maxwell story:

> Metal-grey the Hudson flowed between its banks; down to the sea it swept, around New York, the budding great city, still nothing but a prominent New England town rising to heights of importance on the product of its port and its old and well-established prosperous community life. On many a summer day the black clouds lowered over its banks and then indeed, it seemed to May and her brother, Rip van Winkle played bowls again with his men up in the mountain valleys of the Catskills.
>
> The wooded crest of the palisades, where the autumn winds blew brisk and strong and swept the last dying leaves from the trees, where the autumn sunlight lay rich and still faintly warm, seemed still peopled with red men to the imaginative little girl who played the long mornings through, high on the cliffs above the river.

Rúḥíyyih Khánum often spoke of her own close bond with New York. It had not only been called the 'city of the Covenant' by 'Abdu'l-Bahá, but was the city where she had been born and which her mother always considered 'home'. But New York was also the city that May lost in her childhood and therefore may have always wanted to return to. In October 1875 Mamie Bolles and her two children, aged three and five respectively, left America for France. Their trip was intended to be short-term, lasting some six months, but as John Bolles guessed with some foreboding, the separation extended to a lifetime. Writing to his daughter May, many years later, he confided:

> Just before your Mother left me to make a visit, (from Oct. 1875 'until Spring') in Europe, the spirit of prophesy, and almost of despair, fell upon me, and even with the natural over-confidence of youth, in that hour I said to her: 'Like Moses, from some height I shall see the "Promised Land", but "I shall never reach it."'

His wife must have felt that she had every justification in leaving. At about that time, John decided to go west to join his brother Richard Bolles, who was prospecting in Colorado, and the life of a miner's wife was hardly suited to Mamie Bolles. Besides, it was the custom during the second half of the 19th century for many a refined New England family of restricted means to live 'abroad'. Life was considerably cheaper in Paris for visiting Americans than in their own homeland, and the literature of the period is replete with examples of women such as Mrs Bolles, who wished to give the best advantages to their children despite an inadequate fortune. For May, the memories of those days were replete with sweetness. Her recollections merely reflect the delights of her childhood in Paris. An undated note among her private papers, perhaps in response to questions asked by her own daughter, contains some of her most treasured reminiscences:

> Why did you go to see your old janitors in Paris? Because I love them, because they are connected with associations sweeter than honey – because I humbly trust that the memories of my enchanted childhood may never fade away . . . Is it not a deep experience when thro' the mystery of association, some odor, some sound evokes the past, and in a flood of light and beauty it returns upon the soul. When as a free & happy child I walked the Champs-Élysées all the essence of my small human experience was summed up in that perfect joy – the flow of gay & glittering carriages in the bright warm sunshine, the rosy *nounous* with their streaming ribbons, the wilderness of baby faces and scampering children . . . in the cool shade of the luxuriant trees. Amidst these delicious sights and sounds my

little brother and I walked hand in hand, and stood before the tiny
boutiques laden with enchantment – hoops and pails and net bags
filled with colored tops – tall glass jars with sticks of *sucre d'orge*,
alongside of piles of fragrant *pain d'épice*. There we purchased, for a
penny, a sweeter bliss than the world's wealth could buy. Oh what
a wondrous thing, the joy, the glamour, the intoxication of childhood, the fresh young soul equipped only for joy . . . the happy
loving responsive tender little heart, the desires . . .

Rúḥíyyih <u>Kh</u>ánum's own notes reiterate these recollections amplified by
her personal suppositions. Like many children who hear tales of their
parents' past, her imagination must have taken root in the Paris of her
mother's childhood:

Mother used to watch Punch & Judy shows on the Champs-Élysées
in Paris as a child; she ate *sucre d'orge* candies & bowled her hoop,
she told me. Did she also sail a boat on the pond in the Jardins de
Luxembourg on the Rive Gauche?

It seems that the early schooling of May and her brother, from the ages
of six and four, was in the French language. They both knew it like
their mother tongue, and consequently spoke, read and wrote French
perfectly throughout their lives. Rúḥíyyih <u>Kh</u>ánum often mentioned
this whenever she referred to her mother's Parisian accent. It was not
true in the case of Mrs Bolles and Mrs Martin, however. Frank Irwin
wrote to Amatu'l-Bahá that his cousin Randolph even used to make fun
of his mother's accent at times and mocked poor Muddie's frustration
with French:

Aunt Maimie spoke French volubly, but not with her children's
beautiful accent. I remember Randolph asking once: 'Mother, what
did you mean when you told Aline[7] . . . we have the gigot 'this silk'
(*ce soie* for *ce soir*). She used to get her tongue twisted. She regularly
called the *bonne* Emile and the man Rosalie . . . so that once when
she addressed one by the right name the other responded. I remember a tale of a delinquent French dressmaker who had worn out
the patience with promises repeatedly broken. Finally one day my

---

7 Alexandrine Zepherine was the *bonne* or maid.

grandmother let loose on her in English. The woman turned to my aunt: '*Madame dit que je suis insupportable?*'[8]

Frank Irwin also confirmed that 'From their first stay in Paris, when the two little children learned their French, in the Avenue Marceau one of the . . . avenues that radiate from the Etoile, Aunt Maimie always – and rightly – chose her apartment on the top floor, the quatrième.' From such a high vantage point they had a magnificent view across the roof tops of Paris, with the Eiffel Tower on one side and Notre Dame on the other. But the call of the street sellers from below, the smell of the pastries at the corner shop, the clatter of bowling hoops in the chilly Luxembourg gardens and the taste of sugared candies under the tongue soon faded. All things come to an end, and even though they retained the French language, the delights of this Parisian dream were over before they knew it. The exact date of their return is not known, but Mrs Bolles brought her children back to America within three years.

A letter she wrote to her sister-in-law Ella in 1878 seems to indicate that their financial difficulties were still pressing when she returned to Englewood. Mrs Bolles must have felt the pinch badly despite her best efforts to keep up her spirits. Accustomed to past luxuries and inclined to present indulgences, she must have bridled at her relative impecuniousness as well as the strain in meeting her husband:

Jany. 23rd 1878

My dear Ella,

I was in the city yesterday, and John gave me those very pretty collars for the children. They are lovely and so beautifully made, but as Brother is too big a boy now, to wear anything of that sort, May will keep them both. He is in trousers and wears linen collars with cravats! Can you let me know how much I would have to pay for some lace of that same kind, just as fine and well made? I think it would be so very pretty, on a dress I want to make for May and if not too expensive, I will get it. I would want about four yards. I hear that you are all pretty well, and I'm sure I hope you like living over in Brooklyn better than I do. Still it is hardly worth while for us to complain of anything now-a-days, but to take what we can get, and be thankful for it.

---

8 'Is Madame saying that I am unbearable?'

May was old enough by then to feel the gap between her lifestyle and that of her cousins in the glittering city. She became keenly conscious from that time of the contrast between wealth and poverty and years later, when she and her brother Randolph inherited money from their paternal uncle, she did not forget the circumstances in which she had been raised. Her uncle Richard J. Bolles was a very successful business-man and entrepreneur and had become one of the wealthiest engineers of the early 20th century[9] through his investment in mines which his brother John had helped him to identify and evaluate in his peregrina-tions in the far West, particularly the Molly Gibson Silver Mine, and later through his development of the Everglades in Florida. Since he had no children of his own, he generously left almost half his fortune to his niece and nephew at his death. But May never forgot her responsi-bilities towards those less fortunate than herself.

She never forgot her early years in Paris either. She may even have experienced some homesickness for Europe, but the next time she returned, it was not to revive memories of children's hoops and candies. A tragedy occurred in the Martin family in early 1884. May's aunt Charlotte died and although Mamie had visited her sister the previous autumn, she had no idea of the seriousness of her condition. Stoicism under a demeanour of bright gaiety seems to have been a trait of the Martins, and the virulence of the disease and Charlotte's rapid demise came as a shock. Richard Irwin, the grieving widower, explained the situation to his sister-in-law:

> If you think, as you not unnaturally may, that we ought to have told you . . . in October and not let you go home, the answer is plain and conclusive. There was still hope . . . From me *every* sacrifice would have been made for the mere chance of securing it. Now to have kept you here would not only have been contrary to our informa-tion and belief at that time but, however disguised, must at once have told her all and so dashed down the cup we were holding to her lips with so much anxiety . . . It was only about Christmas (1883) that it became clear that the end was near. Even then we all thought

9   Richard Bolles developed the largest producing silver mine in the world between 1885 and 1890, the 'Molly Gibson' in Aspen, Colorado, and was later, around 1908, involved in the building of the Everglades waterways in Florida. After his death, the management of his estate by its Trustees led to the establishment in 1933 of the Richard J. Bolles School in Jacksonville, Florida, a private college preparatory school with an international reputation.

it might be months . . . I should have been glad if the children could have been spared, but could deny her nothing: so they suffered with her and she with them, nerving herself for a daily meeting of, at least, a few seconds and exerting all her tremendous energy of character to appear to them bright and well.

Colonel Richard Irwin was a military man with interests in literature and journalism. He had served in the Civil War until his health broke down in 1864 and was managing the rice trade for the Japanese government from headquarters in London at the time of his wife's death. But for all his commitments to 'duty', he was obliged on 12 February to write to Mamie Bolles and appeal for help. He confessed that 'never was a man so little fitted to lose such a wife', but he knew his children were suffering even more. Frank, the older boy, he told her, had 'never rallied from the shock, wakes every morning with a head-ache . . . I should have sent him back to school long ago, but he has never been able to go.' Agnes, his younger daughter, was especially bereft after her mother's passing and in even greater need of feminine companionship. Although their father had already asked his sister to come and take charge of the household later that summer, he wrote to Mamie asking if her daughter would come to the children's rescue too:

> If you could spare May, we should all be delighted to have her and I would take as good care of her as I know how. I suggested this to (my) Agnes[10] before your letter came and she was delighted. You might either send her with some friend or with my sister Agnes when she comes. This would really be a great favor to me. I would cheerfully pay all her expenses from New York to New York again, and send her to school with Agnes and so on, and care for her, in every way, like one of my own. Would you let her stay a year? . . .
> . . . My best love to your Father and Mother: a kiss apiece from each of the children and one all round for May.

It seemed that Colonel Irwin had an especially soft spot for May. He must have sensed that her compassionate heart would provide the best comfort for his children at this time. And so she went to England at the

---

10 Richard Irwin, as his letter indicates, also had a sister called Agnes who probably travelled with May to London.

age of fourteen in the wake of a funeral. She must have confirmed her uncle's best opinion of her, for when she left it was with all his gratitude. He sent her back to America with a set of books by Jane Austen, each one of which he dedicated to her. One of his inscriptions, repeated in both *Northanger Abbey* and *Persuasion*, shows to what a degree he had adopted her:

> 'The father was . . . a very respectable man though his name was Richard.'

A letter from Frank Irwin to Amatu'l-Bahá, dated May 1944 from his home in California, reflects briefly on the outward events of her mother's sojourn in England during her mid-teens, and her impact, even as a young girl, on her relatives there.

> May came to live with us from autumn of 1884 until the following autumn of 1885. We were living for four years in London in Kensington . . . I was away in Harrow during the school year. Agnes and May went to a day school in Kensington. I remember May for a time insisted on changing her name to Dulcie Bolles. This rather shocked our conservatism!

But the bond which she forged with her cousins in England that year went far deeper than any name. After his closest relatives died,[11] Frank's only family, to all intents and purposes, were Randolph, May and his aunt Mamie, and their love and loyalty towards him lasted a lifetime. It is clear from his 1940 letter to Rúḥíyyih <u>Kh</u>ánum that the early links he forged with his grandparents, the Martins of Englewood, when he and Agnes came back to the States in the mid-1880s, had also been very strong:

> Grandfather was the dearest, kindest man. He didn't, I think, have much of a life of it after he'd retired from the banking business, and didn't have very much to do as my grandmother managed the family property. He worked a lot in the garden to the very end. He grew piles of delicious strawberries, the only ones, almost, I've ever tasted

---

11 Frank was 'orphaned' in his twenties. Following his mother's death in 1884, his father died in 1892, and his sister Agnes in 1897.

in America that could compare at all with English strawberries. He loved a joke; he loved a game of euchre with individual variations (and you had to pay attention if you didn't want to get cheated occasionally); he liked his cigar. My grandmother, who had a somewhat strong Puritan streak, disapproved of the euchre and smoking. This is not intended to be a reflection on her . . . we all loved her.

Frank also recalled a treasured week he spent with the Martins and the Bolles when he was a student:

> In the winter of my sophomore year at Harvard, to my great joy, the family paid a visit to Boston (boarded in a house on Ashburton Place on Beacon Hill). At last the day came for their departure. But the night before there began the Great Blizzard of March, 1888, and Boston was cut off from the rest of the world; that gave me a whole extra week of them. They also came down for my class day two years later. And I remember how proud I was to be seen about the Yard with my pretty cousin.

From the records at hand, it would seem that May's last exposure to any formal education was during her year in England with the Irwins. After that, she refused to go back to school and took charge of her own education. During this period, she and her friends and cousins organized the 'Bright Eyes Easter Club Bee'; among the items recorded in her notebook for the first meeting, on 13 April 1885, is the following delightful agenda for the day:

> Exercises for Manners and Mind and Taste
> To begin at the commencement of Morris' 'English Grammar'.
> To learn from the beginning of the Old English Period in 'A Brief History of England' to the end of the questions.
> To read together at the next meeting 'The World's Foundations' from the beginning down to 'King of Eternity'.
> To learn together what they can of the 'Quarrel Between Brutus and Cassius' in Shakespeare's 'Julius Caesar'.
> To have embroidered three inches on their fancy-work, which is to be brought to the meeting.
> To invent and tell at the next meeting a short interesting story.

It seems that May, like her own daughter after her, was a born icon-oclast. She refused to study subjects in a traditional and disciplined manner, and although in the absence of such formal education she was expected to occupy herself with those feminine refinements that would enable her to find her proper place in society, her pretty young head was evidently less interested in 'fancy-work' than in a passionate love of mankind and a keen apprehension of the mystic oneness which she shared with all things. These were the growing interests of young May; these were the traits that distinguished her character from her earliest days. This year in England witnessed a great change in her and served as the benchmark for the growth of her spiritual life.

* * *

> Once there was a little girl whose heart reached out for higher things. What exactly these were the child did not know for her parents were not orthodox, just good, decent people who, if asked, might have characterized themselves as Christians tho' they seldom went to church. The little girl's heart seemed to impel her to want to worship, to reach out to what she vaguely felt as the Great Being, to praise Him on High. She would gather, in the pleasant semi-wild woods near her home, sticks, leaves, flowers & make herself a crude altar at which she could pour out these vague feelings, these compelling impulses to praise, to pay homage, to raise her face & heart upwards to that benign unknown she craved & felt was there. That child was May Bolles.

Another of Rúḥíyyih Khánum's several attempts to write about her mother's life began with this paragraph. It is undated, and otherwise unidentified among her papers except for its title 'The Little Girl' and the words 'Chapter 2' written on the left-hand side of the page. She had explored a similar thought in her 1940 notebook:

> A deep and passionate adoration for God filled the child's heart. Alone in the woods she would build or find some natural altar where she would worship – scarcely pausing to ask herself why – a creator whom she felt near her, wonderful, and deeply to be loved.[12]

---

12 Amatu'l-Bahá Rúḥíyyih Khánum's Notebook no. 13, pages unnumbered.

It would seem, from this attempted beginning, that Amatu'l-Bahá felt her mother's story was primarily a spiritual one and required a different foundation from the usual life narrative, which begins with a person's birth. No biography of May Maxwell could be written that did not also highlight the efflorescence of her faith and no book on the Maxwells could be written that was not rooted in the growth of the spirit.

Amatu'l-Bahá Rúḥíyyih Khánum often spoke of her mother's spiritual qualities. It is interesting to consider how much of this susceptibility of soul had been inherited from her own father, for in writing to May, years later,[13] John Harris Bolles confessed that 'When a child I carried with me for several years in my pocket Pope's Essay on Man and its great depth and vast reach still delights and stimulates my reflective faculties.' May did not ponder Pope, but her reflective faculties were greatly stimulated in her youth. While staying with her cousins in England, at the age of about fifteen, she had a deep emotional experience which revealed these mystical inclinations. She herself recorded the experience for posterity in her notes:

When I was a child of fifteen – I was at Tunbridge Wells in England, one evening I was coming home from a walk in the country lanes and across the meadows, and in the quiet of evening I stood on a small rustic bridge spanning a narrow stream. The stream flowed winding thro' fields of grasses and along its banks green primroses and forget-me-nots. The beautiful fresh coloring of an English Spring was softened in the twilight to a tender and ineffable mildness – the flush of rose in the western sky – the drowsy hum of insects in the grass, the silent flow of the water, all breathed a poetry at once gentle and penetrating, like the quality in Grey's Elegy – sweet and pastoral, yet lofty tender and aspiring. In the pale blue sky hung the evening star, palpitating in an aureole of its own golden light; and that, mingling with the blue, shed a strange green color that seemed to recall the moonlight glow of some past life.

Suddenly, out of the grass, at a little distance, sprang a bird into the air, with one swift measure of joyous notes. Only a few feet up he darted, then sank a little towards the ground, pouring his music back into his nest. Then up, twice the height, he sprang, as tho' the wild love in his heart for his nest and its treasure held him – spellbound

---

13 1 December 1905.

– while he sang. Yet even higher he rose, his fire-born spirit bearing him towards his home – in the sky – while he scattered out his fresh sweet notes like dew upon the meadow. At last high, high above his nest he sang with such wild joy and freedom that as I listened to the soft rippling gladness, the air became a mist of music – and he the fountain from which poetry and beauty streamed. I stood, a child with a pure heart, lifted up to be filled – and the poignant and triumphant song overflowed me, and the world – when with a final burst of piercing rising sweetness, he sank, with sudden silence, into his nest.

Then from the luminous sky above me – from the meadow below – thro' the air vibrating with the undying music – the spirit came forth to me. Mystery breathed on me and touched my soul – & it opened and expanded like a flower to the inflowing light. Slowly it grew in transcendent power, until it overflowed into the invisible, grown – visible, and I beheld as in a crystal – the sky, the earth, the air were my own – pregnant with an immortal affinity, and existed as palpable emanations of my own creative radiance. The secret was mine, I knew, I knew . . . A moment later I was standing on the bridge alone. Yet never alone again, nevermore alone. The stars were blooming out above me, one by one – the twilight was deepening over the quiet meadows, the faint flush fading from the sky – what was it, what? the secret? I had – forgotten!! God knew – and He had taken me – forever.

In 1990, at the Conference in Buenos Aires for the 50th anniversary of Mrs Maxwell's passing in 1940, Rúḥíyyih <u>Kh</u>ánum spoke about her mother's character and the extreme spiritual awareness with which she had been endowed, a quality that often manifested itself as an extraordinary sensitivity towards others and to nature, and which rendered her so vulnerable at times that it often led to physical as well as nervous disorders:

Mother always seems to have been, from her childhood, very spiritual minded. I suppose that at least when she was a grown-up woman you could describe her as a heavenly soul . . . during her childhood, she used to tell me that she would go out into the woods and pray, which is very unusual; they weren't a religious family. I never heard that they belonged to any denomination, which was very unusual in those days. If they were anything I think they were Unitarians. My mother was very beautiful. She was very petite and a very beautiful woman. Until she was about 21 she was a very active person. She used to play tennis, she used to dance all night. And then, I don't know why . . . my mother developed some kind of a weakness in her body. 'Abdu'l-Bahá said that my mother had been born with an unusual nervous ailment which the doctors have not been able to analyse. So there was nothing the matter with her; she had a very beautiful body, had a very keen mind, but I never walked two blocks with my mother in my whole life. She just couldn't do it. And this increased after she grew older. I tell you these things because I think that it gives us an idea of how much you can serve Bahá'u'lláh [and] with what handicaps.

It is evident from Amatu'l-Bahá's remarks as well as from historical records that even as a young woman May Bolles was in love with the truth. She was a dreamer of dreams, a seer of unusual visions. These susceptibilities made her aware of a force in the world, a magnetic power in the universe towards which her soul was irresistibly drawn. She was a born seeker. At around the age of eight or nine, she dreamed that a vivid light was streaming into her bedroom and enveloping her from head to foot. In the morning, when her mother came in to draw aside the curtains, she cried out with pain and could not open her eyes. Whatever the medical reasons for her temporary blindness that day, she always associated it with the piercing light of her dream.

In another dream which she had in youth, she found herself being carried high in the heavens by angels from where she looked down and saw the earth, chained and covered with waxen seals. To her amazement, these started to crack and break open before her eyes, and as she gazed down, she saw with wonder that a word was written on the surface of the earth beneath them. On waking from her dream, all she remembered of that word were the letters B and H.

Later, when she was in her twenties, she had the strangest experience of all. It happened while the family were on vacation in the northern seaside town of Dinard, in France. She found herself standing by the sea and thought she saw the figure of a man across the water. He was dressed in oriental garb and was beckoning her towards Him. She imagined that He must be Jesus Christ and was deeply moved by her vision.

Left to right, seated: David Randolph Martin and his wife, Mary T. Martin, the maternal grandparents of May Bolles; standing: their daughters Charlotte Martin (later Mrs Richard Irwin) and Mary Ellis Martin (later Mrs. John H. Bolles)

David Randolph Martin

Mary Tweed Ellis Martin

John Harris Bolles

Mary Ellis Martin Bolles

On the lawn of the home of May Bolles's grandfather, David Randolph Martin, Englewood, New Jersey: right, her mother, Mary Martin Bolles; centre, Grandfather Martin; left, May Bolles; on the grass, her brother, Randolph Bolles

Richard J. Bolles, uncle of May Ellis Bolles; his financial legacy to her contributed considerably to the Bahá'í activities she was able to pursue

May Ellis Bolles and her brother Randolph

May Bolles, 14 years old, July 1884

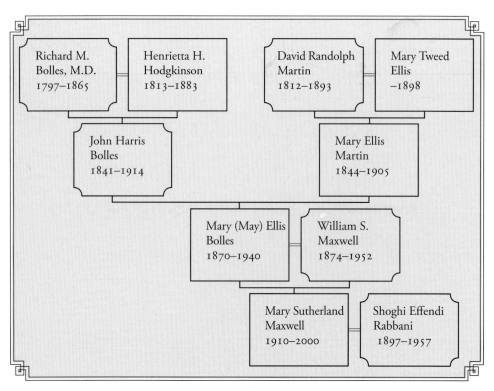

Four-generation genealogy of May Ellis Bolles Maxwell

June 1885: left, May [Mary] Ellis Bolles; centre, Mary Ellis Martin Bolles; right, Mary Ellis Tweed 'Muddie' Martin. On the back of the photograph May has written to her daughter Mary Sutherland Maxwell: 'Your Mother, your Grandmother, your Great-grandmother. You are the fourth Mary.'

May Bolles playing the violin, age 15, in England, 1885

May Ellis Bolles (Photographer: Hargrave & Gubelman, West 23rd Street, New York)

✢ THEATRICALS! ✢

UNDER THE AUSPICES OF THE

ENGLEWOOD LYCEUM CO.,

Thursday, February 18th, 1892,

At Eight O'Clock, P. M.

OUR ✶ BOYS,

THE MOST SUCCESSFUL COMEDY EVER PRODUCED.

✦ CHARACTERS. ✦

SIR GEOFFRY CHAMPNEYS, (A County Magnate),	Mr. Peter Stanford Duryea
TALBOT CHAMPNEYS, (his son)	Mr. Augustus Duryea
PERKYN MIDDLEWICK OF DEVONSHIRE HOUSE, (A Retired Butterman),	Mr. Randolph Bolles
CHARLES MIDDLEWICK, (his son)	Mr. Chester C. Munroe
KEMPSTER, (Sir Geoffry's Man Servant),	Mr. Geo. S. Coe, Jr
PODDLES, (Middlewick's Butler)	Mr. E. Seward Prosse
VIOLET MELROSE, (an Heiress),	Miss May Bolles
MARY MELROSE, (her poor Cousin),	Miss Carrie Coe
CLARISSA CHAMPNEYS, (Sir Geoffry's Sister),	Miss Amy Foster
BELINDA, (a Lodging House Slave,)	Miss Fellows

ACT I. .... AT THE BUTTERMAN'S
Scene .... PARKYN MIDDLEWICK'S COUNTRY HOUSE.

ACT II. .... AT THE BARONET'S
Scene—DRAWING ROOM IN SIR GEOFFRY'S.

SEVEN MONTHS ARE SUPPOSED TO HAVE ELAPSED.

ACT III. .... MRS. PATCHEM'S THREE-PAIR BACK.
Scene—THIRD FLOOR AT A LONDON LODGING-HOUSE.

Scene—IN ACTS I. AND II. .... HERTFORDSHIRE
IN ACT III. .... LONDON

Time—THE PRESENT.

TICKETS FOR SALE AT ROCKEFELLER'S DRUG STORE.

RESERVED SEATS, ORCHESTRA AND DRESS CIRCLE, 75 CTS.

RESERVED SEATS, BALCONY, - 50 CTS.

*Playbill for the theatrical production **Our Boys**, Thursday, 18 February 1892, under the auspices of the Englewood Lyceum Co., with May and Randolph Bolles in the cast. Reviews stated: 'Miss May Bolles won much applause by her strong rendering of "Violet Melrose", the heiress; the part of Charles Middlewick was taken by Mr Randolph Bolles, with great credit to himself.'*

When she was shown the picture of 'Abdu'l-Bahá some years later, she recognized the face of the man of her vision. She realized He was her beloved Lord and Master.

Her longing to find her God led her to investigate many religions. She inquired into the teachings of Islam and Buddhism, as well as the different creeds of Christianity. She even thought of entering a convent at one time, but found, after a while, that her soul was still not satisfied. Before she left England to return to the United States in December of 1885, the year she attained the age of spiritual maturity, she was given the gift of a Bible, which she kept by her all her life. It contains two inscriptions of great significance. The date of the first is 9 November 1885, which was probably the day she was given the book as a parting gift:

Dulcie Bolles, from her affectionate friends, Margaret & Isabel Stewart, Fitzalan House, Kensington

The second inscription is in Persian. It is a prayer written for May Maxwell some eighteen years later, by the brilliant Bahá'í scholar Mírzá Abu'l-Faḍl when he visited Green Acre.[14] The English translation of the prayer reads:

He is the All-Glorious

O my God, my Hope, my Light and my Glory! I beseech Thee by Thy glorious beauty, by the light of Thy countenance, which hath illumined the horizons of earth and heaven, and by the Centre of Thy Covenant, the Dawning-place of the splendours of Thy Testament, Haḍrat-i-'Abdu'l-Bahá, to ordain for this Thy handmaid, Mrs. Maxwell, the good of this world and the next, and to confirm her through the potency of Thy glorious Kingdom. Thou art the Generous, and Thou art the All-Merciful, the All-Compassionate.

Abu'l-Faḍl

30 August 1903 at Green Acre

---

14 Sarah Farmer established this resort on the banks of the Piscataqua River in Maine in the late 19th century. After her participation in the Parliament of World Religions, this daughter of a transcendentalist father and philanthropist mother dedicated the building to inter-religious dialogue and the cause of peace. Her subsequent meeting with 'Abdu'l-Bahá in 'Akká in 1901 inspired her to turn 'Green Acre' into a Bahá'í school. Many inspiring teachers, including Mírzá Abu'l-Faḍl, taught courses there in later years.

Perhaps May wanted the gift she had received in her youth to be blessed by the confirmation she attained in her maturity, for she treasured this Bible throughout her life; she read it many times and pored over these pages over and over again. Indeed she was so well-versed in Christian parables and Biblical prophecies that Rúḥíyyih Khánum was wont to say her mother 'knew the Bible inside out'. It must have been like a final consummation of her prayers for this precious book, which had borne witness to her search for truth, to testify with this prayer to her having found it. Perhaps she wanted her Bible, which had witnessed her thirst for spirituality since girlhood, to confirm that this thirst had been quenched at last, at its almighty Source.

* * *

During May's late teens and early twenties, the expectations that surrounded her in the United States were anything but spiritual. She was just at an age when a young woman of her class and culture was supposed to 'come out' in society and she had been groomed, by her middle-class upbringing, specifically for that purpose. Like most of her female contemporaries, she had been raised primarily to be a wife and a mother and was expected to bring credit to her family by becoming an admired ornament on the mantelpiece of marriage. Given this social background as well as the financial circumstances of the family, it was hoped that she would make an advantageous alliance that would bring credit to her relations. And she had everything to recommend her, after all. She had the arts and refinements of high French culture. She was exquisitely beautiful and endowed with a physical delicacy that bordered on the ethereal. And she was probably the talk of the town.

Rúḥíyyih Khánum's own words, from her memoirs, describe her best:

She was, as easily discerned by her photographs, a beautiful girl, in the words of Juliet Thompson, the painter, 'flower-like and star-like'. Her hair was long, abundant and more auburn than chestnut brown in colour. Her eyes were set large in her head, full of an intense interest in life, a lively humour and deep human sympathy. They were a rich and rather violet blue. She had a true milkwhite skin which lasted in softness, firmness and beauty till the very end of her life. She was tiny compared to the tall girls of my generation, had a natural wasp waist and wore size 2 shoes . . .'[15]

But the years between girlhood and marriage are not easy and the 'awkward age' proved to be a particularly difficult one for May. She shrank away from the solicitudes of her family even though she was dependent on their support. She yearned to escape from the expectations surrounding a young woman of her times and yet feared the full implications of such freedom. So she was prone to extremes. One minute she wanted to withdraw from society and be a nun; the next she was transformed into a lover of life and characterized by what Rúḥíyyih Khánum notes in her memoirs as 'rare buoyancy of spirit'.

Rúḥíyyih Khánum often referred to May's high spirits and spoke about how she adored dancing and going to balls. When she was full of *joie de vivre* she was capable of an immense expenditure of energy and could stay up all night. She was also evidently much enamoured of amateur theatricals. In February 1892, for example, she and her brother Randolph appeared in a play, *Our Boys*, a comedy presented under the auspices of the Englewood, New Jersey Lyceum Company. May performed the role of 'Violet Melrose (an Heiress)' and one can well imagine how the heroine of the piece might have attracted all kinds of attention at the time. Several young men must have fallen in love with her that summer. There were certainly several young men hovering around the Martin house in Englewood, according to Frank Irwin's recollections, like bees buzzing round a honeypot:

One of the grandest times we four cousins had together was on a visit Agnes and I made to Englewood (for a month or so) in the summer of 1886, when I was a sub-freshman. We gathered quite a number of gay people around us. I remember Muddie coming in one day and ejaculating with some disgust: 'There's a whole *raft* of young people on the verandah.' Good and hot it was, too, but that didn't prevent our playing tennis hours a day. Seward Prosser was one of the gang, later head of the New York Bankers' Trust Co., but at that time the younger boy in a family living in quite restricted circumstances; with a face of a quite peculiar homeliness, it wouldn't be too much to say, but always welcome to everybody, always so

---

15 Memoirs of Amatu'l-Bahá Rúḥíyyih Khánum, p. 12 of the transcription.

jolly, and with sterling qualities. Other associates, less frequent, were the Homans boys; Shep was afterwards a Princeton halfback, fairly well known; and later, for a time, joined Seward in an insurance agency on New York's downtown Broadway . . . Randolph and I had buckewheat [sic] cake contests; I got up to 21 once (or was it 18?): I blush to say that this was after a hearty lunch and that we had spent ½ hour shortly before among a neighbor's raspberry bushes. Another terrible contest was to see how long you could keep your mouth attached to a garden hose, swallowing the water! Seward was the champion here.

That May was courted by more than one admirer from among this crowd of dashing young men eager to attract her attention is most possible, given her beauty. That she turned down several proposals is most probable, given her high standards. And that she had different definitions of love from her mother can only be inferred by the consequences. Because nothing happened, despite two 'coming out' balls.

Her first introduction into society took place in Washington, under the auspices of Mrs Phoebe Hearst. According to Rúḥíyyih Khánum's memoirs, the wife of the wealthy Senator and industrialist had been a close friend of Mrs Bolles since childhood, and she was generous enough to invite May to her home for a whole month for the specific purpose of launching her career in the capital's 'high society'. Amatu'l-Bahá always talked about Mrs Hearst's particular fondness for young May. Her memoirs best sum up her mother's relationship to the Hearst family:

Mrs. Phoebe Hearst was a dear friend of her mother, Mrs. Mary Martin Bolles;[16] indeed, at one time she greatly desired to take Mother and bring her up as her own child, a wish that of course my grandmother would hear nothing of. When Mother reached debutante age Mrs. Hearst invited her to her Washington home and launched her amidst the society of the capital. Mother, marvelling at the number of clothes her own daughter – and most modern girls – had, would often recall the three wonderful dresses Mrs. Hearst

---

16 According to recent research, the friendship between Mrs Hearst and Mrs Bolles and her family is referred to in several instances in the Hearst family papers, but how the friendship originated has not yet come to light. These papers were inaccessible to researchers at the time of printing. For further information about Phoebe Apperson Hearst, see Hogenson, *Lighting the Western Sky*.

had especially made for her by a fashionable dressmaker: a morning, an afternoon and an evening gown! . . . She was duly impressed by Mrs. Hearst's dressing-room which contained so many gowns that some had never been worn at all, and Mrs. Hearst could never remember what was available but would have to consult her maid. . . . (O)ne can well imagine how much she enjoyed Washington, and Washington enjoyed her. A number of anecdotes connected with that visit stand out in my mind, the most vivid one being that of how she ran herself a bath in the beautiful and luxurious sunken tub of the dimensions of a small pool, in Mrs. Hearst's best bathroom and forgot all about it. When she went in, the place was flooded and the steam was peeling the lovely paint off the walls. Mrs. Hearst laughed till she almost cried over this typical example of May's absent-mindedness.

Phoebe Hearst was born Phoebe Elizabeth Apperson in Franklin County, in a small Missouri town where she became a schoolteacher. She married George Randolph Hearst, a man more than twenty years her senior who made his fortune in the Californian gold rush. Amatu'l-Bahá's memoirs recount the delightful story of how George Hearst apprised his new wife of his wealth. After their wedding in June 1862,

they went down to the train for their honeymoon. They boarded a private car: 'Ah,' said the new Mrs. Hearst, 'we can't travel on this private car, George!' But he calmed her fears by assuring her it was quite all right as he knew the owner and had his permission to do so. It was only in the course of the trip that he informed her he was the owner!

After he became Senator Hearst and they rose to such prominence in the society of the capital, they possessed a very beautiful and expensive home where Mrs. Hearst was wont to entertain lavishly. But George Hearst remained the same diamond-in-the-rough he always had been, and Mother recalled as one of the greatest evidences of Mrs. Hearst's truly noble character the fact that she never scolded or tried to reform her husband. She left him as he was and accepted with true heart-breeding [sic] his certain unpolished social characteristics, such as leaning over his beautifully-laid dinner table gathered about by a host of distinguished guests, grabbing, during the soup course, a bunch of grapes that garnished its centerpieces, crossing his legs, eating the grapes and spitting out the pits lustily into his plate where they snapped against the china loudly. Mother said she felt she would have died if he had been her husband but Mrs. Hearst ignored the performance and continued serenely, a perfect hostess.

The music room was as large as a small ballroom, expensively decorated and with a grand piano covered with 18-carat gold at one end of it and a Japanese rickshaw at the other end. One day Mr. Hearst and Mother were alone in this room – with its two master-pieces and its wealth of knick-knacks and curios. Mr. Hearst asked her: 'What do you think of this room, May?' Mother, rather taken aback at such a question and not wishing to hurt his feelings, has-tened to answer: 'Why – I think it's beautiful, Mr. Hearst.' 'Do you,' said he, 'Well, I think it's a damn junk shop!'

The girl from the country who had for many years of her child-hood and girlhood accepted the clothes of her wealthy cousins and had made them over to fit her now found herself in the full swing of the radiant and gay society life of the capital. Admirers were not lacking and proposals could easily have been encouraged but the strange independence and unworldliness that always characterized her, worldling though she was by birth and experience, kept her aloof from any such thoughts. She enjoyed herself to the full and was, when her visit terminated, quite content to return to her home with all its country simplicity and small town society.

Whatever the hopes of Mrs Hearst for her god-daughter, nothing came of her first exposure to the world. To everyone's surprise, the entrance of lovely Miss Bolles into Washington society led to an abrupt exit shortly afterwards. And so a second attempt had to be made to launch her mat-rimonial career, as Rúḥíyyih Khánum records:

She was also brought out in Newport society by Mrs. Helen Ellis Cole, her cousin and a well-known society leader. She was (she often told me) under the impression that her cousin considered this her God-given opportunity to make a good marriage and when, at the end of her visit, the charming Miss Bolles was still unengaged in spite of the admirers she had acquired, she was given up as quite hopeless by her prominent relatives!

What was the matter with the charming Miss Bolles? To be still unengaged after two coming-out balls was no joke. There were probably serious
talks, heated discussions, and floods of tears in the Bolles household after
May returned from Newport. Had she given her heart to someone who
did not reciprocate her feelings? Had she been foolish enough to fall in
love with a penniless nobody? Or was she simply unable to make up her
mind? She was doubtless reprimanded for folly. Her 'unworldliness', as
May herself later admitted, became the despair of the family.

It is rare, even in the best of circumstances, to reconcile one's spiritual longings with one's physical desires. For a young woman to achieve
this equilibrium was almost impossible in the 19th century, in the
West as much as in the East. Society forced girls to choose between
one extreme or another, and then condemned them for both. May was
caught between family expectations and her heart's desires, between
social responsibilities and the need to remain true to herself. Whether
precipitated by 'an affair of the heart', as it was referred to in those days,
or by an accidie of the soul, she reached a point of genuine distress after
her aborted 'coming-out' balls.

In his letter to Rúḥíyyih Khánum,[17] Frank Irwin drew a vivid portrait of May as a lovely young *débutante*:

> May was very attractive as a girl. Fine blond hair, slight. She had the
> most fascinating freckles, very light in color and not too many of
> them. They are, I understand, the sign of a very delicate skin. She had
> a delightful sense of humor, as you no doubt know; and had, when
> aroused, a charming way of wrinkling up her pretty lightly freckled
> nose. Of course, one of the things that bulk large in the recollec-
> tions of anyone who knew her during her young womanhood was
> her delicate health. This began, or began to be a really serious matter
> . . . in an attachment she formed for a young man who courted her;
> when this had to be broken off, her health broke down completely. I
> saw her when she was supposed to be getting better, and have never
> set eyes on anyone who looked so near death and lived. I never saw
> him. May told me much about the engagement.

May had always had a sensitive nature and a broken engagement was
all she needed to become a prey to emotional extremes and depression.

---

17 2 August 1940.

Frank Irwin, who had endured the loss of both his parents by then, was keenly sympathetic to his cousin's anguish:

> Her mother told me a pathetic story of an incident in her sickness . . . Do you know at all the feeling that overwhelms the nervous sufferer at times, that makes escape – in any direction, only it be escape – the thing that must be sought? Well, May decided she must escape from it all and formed not a practical plan, of course, but this is what she did. She saved up provisions for her escape from the trays that were brought her, and one day disappeared. It was only after a good deal of a hunt that they found her, hidden away as thoroughly as she could manage, in a closet in the house.

So although Randolph's decision to study architecture in the École des Beaux-Arts in Paris was the ostensible reason for Mrs Bolles to set sail for Europe again, in October of 1894, those in her circle must have suspected that this second sojourn in France was as much due to her daughter's broken health as to the education of her son.

When a girl could not be married off to someone of her own class in the New World at the turn of the 19th century, there was often nothing for it but to hope that she might find a suitor in the Old. But the dilemmas facing a girl without money in the European marriage market were not much easier. For someone of May's susceptibilities, they were hardly to be borne. Her predicament was painful. Whenever she sat in her mother's 'circle' of expatriate Americans in Paris, the only talk was of eligible young bachelors in town. Whenever Randolph brought fellow students over from the Beaux-Arts for a visit, they were importunate in their attentions. It is clear from her private journals and papers during this period that May suffered acutely from what she called the 'shallow conventions, heartless insincerities, frivolous occupations and pleasures' of her days. There are notes which she wrote to herself in early January 1895, a few months after their arrival in Paris, which bear witness to her anguish:

> January 1st, 1895 – 5 a.m.
> One never writes at such an hour – one 'jots down' a thought or impression – I have none. I no longer pray to be led into safe paths – among His Holy Ways. I simply <u>cling</u> without hope – without

fear – He is God. He is near. He is sufficient for us – He only can keep dark despair away from us. If I have waited and clung in Faith <u>so long</u>, surely the Light will come.

January 3rd and 4th
The living inspiration has died out of my life – or grown faint and dim perhaps, I dare not trust so much to anyone. And so I must seek the Light in a life apart from others – the old idea of joining some earnest sisterhood comes to me again . . . I find all things so empty, meaningless, fleeting . . . A bitter cry rises in my soul again and again. A cry for a deeper, truer life . . .

No one is noble enough – no one is <u>true,</u> humble, good – they are all a mockery – or else commonplace, vulgar, poor! I will leave it then – this world where I can find no one to help me. I will lead a life of humble devotion, at least, and try to give the help which I so sorely need myself.

In December of 1897 May fell seriously ill again. Her cousin Agnes' untimely death might have been the reason for it. She succumbed to severe melancholy once again, was plagued by insomnia and laid low with her debilitating physical condition. Instead of circulating in society, she took to her bed and consequently grew so weak that her mother found it necessary to take her to the country, to the Hotel des Voyageurs in Moret-sur-Loing,[18] to recuperate her strength. In fact, this illness was far more serious than any she had had before, in America. She was practically bedridden from the end of 1897 until the following November, by which time her cousin Frank had joined the family at 13 Quai d'Orsay in Paris. This was probably when she struck him as looking like a living corpse.

May's distress was profound. A letter written to her from her cousin, Emily Key Hoffman, reveals how much she must have longed for spiritual companionship at this time, and how high her expectations were of those she befriended. Few among them, men or women, could reach her absolute standards, as Emily confessed:

---

18 Writing to Sutherland in early October 1900, she anticipated their reunion in this same spot: 'We can get rooms at the Hotel des Voyageurs – altho' I do not like it at all because I suffered so terribly there . . .'

. . . How can I ever hope to live up to the beautiful ideals your own sweet soul has placed before me? You have inspired me truly to show my own unworthiness! But rest assured, as far as my strength will let me I shall be ever as true as I can for your sweet sake as well as for the sake of truth itself for to shine in your sweet favor has ever been one of my noblest ambitions. Give my love to your mother & Randolph, & with a heart full of tenderness for yourself, now & forever . . .

May's grandmother also died in Paris that year. Mary Tweed Ellis Martin had travelled with the family to France four years before and her passing gave May another reason to mourn. She had greatly loved 'Muddie', despite her somewhat severe character and habits of condescension.[19] She expressed her feelings in a poem which portrays something of her own state of mind at the time. She inscribed the poem in a small booklet decorated with a tracery of lavender wisteria, below which a little winged seraph holds a ribbon on which she wrote: 'In Memory 1 a.m. 1898':

All these are fled, as she is gone!
We cannot see the Perfect Whole,
But out of each death a hope is born,
And we hold fast
The living past!
Yes gone! but we have them in our soul!

May was twenty-seven by the time her cousin Agnes and her grand-mother passed away. She was obsessed by mortality, in physical distress as a result of protracted invalidism, and in spiritual despair of ever finding 'the Perfect Whole'. Years later, 'Abdu'l-Bahá is reported to have said:

*Had she not found Bahá'u'lláh and His healing message,
she would have died.*

* * *

As the old century drew towards its end, May had no idea of what

---

19 Rúḥíyyih Khánum used to tell the story of how Muddie travelled from the market on a public trolleybus one day, grumbling bitterly about the insalubrious French, only to discover on arrival in her own apartment that the smell she had been complaining about came from the cheese she had been carrying with her all the way!

Millie was a gifted pianist and composed many distinctly charming songs and the family would have musical evenings in which my grandfather 'fiddled' (and none too well), Millie played the piano and daddy the mandolin, whilst my grandmother in all likelihood knitted yards of dainty lace.

William Sutherland needed no incentive to study, even as a young boy. He was conscientious by instinct. On 3 February 1888, when he was just thirteen years old, he was presented with a prize 'for Regular Attendance during the year 1887' at the Knox Church Sabbath School. The prize book was a rousing piece of Christian sentiment and high morality by the prolific children's author Charlotte Maria Tucker who wrote under the pseudonym of A.L.O.E.; it was entitled Little Bullets from BATALA.[23] But one has the impression that young William did not need anyone else's bullets to exhort him to strive for excellence. Later he went to the High School of Montreal, in Edward's footsteps, played sports like him and enjoyed a happy childhood. He was a born perfectionist and meticulous in all that he set his mind to; his aesthetic sense too was highly developed from an early age, as was his innate modesty. His parents who had 'emphasized the importance of family life, diligent work and integrity'[24] had instilled in him a natural scepticism. He thought it presumptuous to trust in anything but the sweat of his own brow.

In late 1888 he was writing letters to his greatly admired elder brother Edward, who had left home three years before and was learning to be a draughtsman in the Boston offices of H. H. Richardson. Edward was clearly an inspiration for William; the boy writes to his brother with touching enthusiasm and a transparent desire for approbation. He shares his triumphs in class with him as well as his fascination with railway bridges:

Dear Eddie . . . The C.P.R. is nearing completion and they have the bridge at Green Av. finished . . .

I guess I will get up a little this month in class, last month I did pretty well, better than any month last year. We have not got our

---

23 Published by Gall & Ingles in London and Edinburgh.
24 Courtesy of Henry Yates.

places yet but I will get up a few places . . .

. . . the CPR Station will be opened some time in December they say . . .

I played billiards the other day. . . I hope you are getting on all right and wont get the sack.

I am your affec. Brother,
WS Maxwell

Curiously enough, the Canadian Pacific Railway to which William referred with such excitement in this letter was destined to become one of the main financial backers of the Maxwell brothers' architectural firm in later years, along with its shareholder, the Bank of Montreal. William would find himself responsible for designing bridges and railway stations, hotels and public buildings all along its route from St John's, Newfoundland to Vancouver in British Columbia. Unaware of the ironies of history however, and unburdened by the future, he wrote another letter to his brother when he was just sixteen years old. It reveals how inventive William already was, and how evident his artistic inclinations. It also betrays, once more, how eager he was for his older brother's approval and how anxious to secure his good opinion:

Dear Eddie,

I have forgotten to send on the other letter but will stick this in with it. I tried my ice boat last Saturday but the sail was too small and the wind not strong enough, but I made another sail last week and tried her on Saturday; she went splendid . . . considering the small space she was sailed in, it being only about 100 yards long and the ice very rough, she went as well as an average horse if not faster. I made a pretty good job of the boat and she is very strong for her size, there is not a nail in her only screws and bolts. I was the first to get up the idea – and two or three have followed suit but they have not succeeded in making one to carry them . . .

This afternoon I collected together some architectural books etc. and have made a catalogue . . .

On the reverse side of the page William drew three sketches of his ice boat, adding:

Here is a sort of a plan of it: the rudder is like this: a = tiller or upside down.

At the end of his high school years, William fell ill with chicken pox and although everyone else matriculated, he missed his final examination and did not do so. After his recovery, Edward urged him to sit the exam again, but William thought it a pointless academic exercise. Despite his usual subservience towards his older brother, he flatly refused to follow his counsel in this instance. There was an odd quirk of character in this gentle and peace-loving man, whose natural predisposition inclined him towards outward conformity and compliance. On rare occasion he took a stand and whenever he did so, it was always on principle. This was the first but not the last time in his life that it occurred.

In fact, William preferred to follow his older brother's example rather than his advice. He wanted to be free from the formal constraints of education and plunge directly into the real world of work. Above all he wanted to travel to Europe. But before doing that, he first had to become an apprentice, like Edward. And so at the tender age of eighteen he found his first job as a draughtsman and began working at his brother's office, in the Sun Life Building on Notre Dame Street. He wanted to start learning his craft without further delay. Although there is some discrepancy regarding the exact date of his departure, he apparently left Montreal for Boston, and was in training in an architectural firm there by early 1895 at the latest.

He joined the Atelier run by the Society of Architects in Boston, instead of applying to study at the School of Technology. The latter would have required credentials that he did not have. He also attended free lectures at the Technology Institute and joined the Boston Architectural Club, where he learned about the latest developments in American architecture. It was a pattern he would repeat when he went to study in Paris. In this Club, William came under the powerful influence of Constant-Désiré Despradelles, a Frenchman who had studied at the École des Beaux-Arts, won the Grand Prix de Rome, and emigrated to America to become a professor at the Massachusetts Institute of Technology. It was here, too, that he may have sharpened his appetite for Paris and his longing to become a special student at the Beaux-Arts. He wanted to perfect his craft. The Arts Club of Montreal which he set up on his return to Canada and his own atelier, created in later years in conjunction with the Beaux-Arts Institute of Design in New York, both encouraged this method of apprenticeship rather than formal study which he learned in the Atelier Pascal.

Years later, Rúḥíyyih <u>Kh</u>ánum recalled how unimpressed her father was by those who placed more emphasis on theory than on practice, and who laid stress more on diplomas than on an artist's actual experience. She said her father did not need a diploma to be an architect. He knew instinctively that the way to hone and perfect raw talent was through scrupulous and meticulous practice. An artist, in his mind, was one who had been born with a spiritual gift, which he had to work night and day to deserve. Although William Sutherland Maxwell finally earned his place in his profession and was rewarded with public accolades for his achievements, she always said that this was due to his own merits rather than to any meretricious influence.

To appreciate his achievements, one has to recognize two factors in the nature of this man that must have been distinctive even from his earliest years. One was his goodness; the other his innate artistry. And their combination made him unique.

As far as the first is concerned, no less an authority than Shoghi Effendi himself attested to his 'saintly life' in the obituary cable he sent to the Bahá'í world after the passing of William Sutherland Maxwell in 1952. This goodness in him was what had initially attracted May to him in his youth. This innate nobility was what distinguished him throughout his life until his very last days. He was an upright man, a truthful man, a Scotsman of the highest order, who never approached another human being except in a spirit of courtesy, of friendliness, and of that quality of graciousness that is the essence of the democratic spirit. He had a trusting nature but a sound judgement, too, in human relations.

His creativity was Sutherland Maxwell's second distinctive characteristic. As his daughter always put it, he was an artist through and through. An architect rarely has the freedom to express his personal ideas; he is always reined in by his clients' expectations and desires. But the creative genius of this architect was distinguished by an encyclopaedic knowledge of the arts and a remarkable capacity for unique ideas. He was a fund of new ways of seeing the world, of fresh and startling forms of expressing it. His wife, who knew him better and appreciated him more than anyone, attested in her letters to him that, 'You have the

*William Sutherland Maxwell's parents: left, Johan MacBean Maxwell;
right, Edward John Maxwell, December 1905*

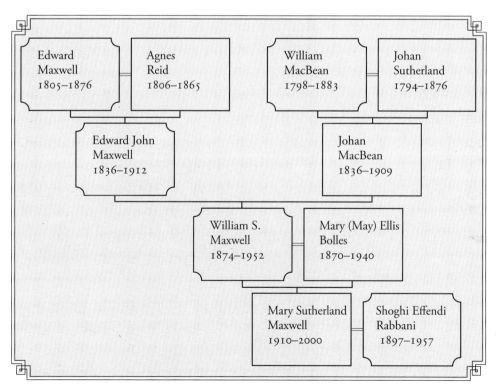

*Four-generation genealogy of William Sutherland Maxwell from the time his family migrated
from Scotland to Montreal, Canada*

William Sutherland Maxwell, circa 1877, about 3 years old, in Montreal

Mother and son: Johan MacBean Maxwell and William Sutherland Maxwell, Montreal, late 1870s (Photographer: Notman & Son)

The Maxwell family: left to right, standing: Edward Maxwell, Jessie Maxwell; seated: William Sutherland Maxwell, Johan 'Nana' Maxwell, Amelia Maxwell, Edward John 'Papa Johnny' Maxwell

Original site of the E. J. Maxwell Lumber Company, Montreal, on the corner of Craig and St Alexander Streets

*William Sutherland Maxwell at age 10, 1884. Rúḥíyyih Khánum writes in her memoirs:
'This picture of my Father shows him leaning against the bole of a mighty tree; this is like his
own life and nature: he is calm, strong, deeply rooted in his traditions, good and peaceful;
nothing could be a better symbol of him than that great tree.'*

charm of originality.' It was a quality that must have greatly endeared him to her. In a letter to her daughter written many years later, in 1934 about another artist who was a Bahá'í, she confided:

> Having lived with this fascinating artist temperament all my married life I find it precious, simple & trusting . . .

These twin capacities – of saintliness on the one hand, and creativity on the other – are not often found together. But they were conspicuously combined in the nature of William Sutherland Maxwell. He exercised them with a rigour and commitment that earned him the three greatest rewards in his life. The first of these was his happiness in marriage. The second was his success in his work. And the third, and possibly greatest, was a bond of intimacy and respect which he developed with the Guardian of the Bahá'í Faith in the last decade of his life. It was a bond that gave rise to his *chef-d'oeuvre*, the superstructure of the Shrine of the Báb.

In his early twenties, however, standing on the slopes of Mount Royal perhaps or gazing out over the frozen St Lawrence, his future was still hidden from his eyes. He may have sensed its brightness on the far horizon like a hazy sun in a Turner painting. He may have felt its first rays, instinctively, like the certitude of the spring thaw, penetrating the western world in folds of light. But all he knew consciously at the time was that he would attain his heart's desire if he could only go to Paris.

The first thing to do was to complete his apprenticeship in Boston.

* * *

When William Sutherland Maxwell entered the firm of Winslow and Wetherell in Boston as an apprentice in the early 1890s, he earned barely enough to make ends meet. But he soon made his mark. He was a young draughtsman at the time, and was paid very little accordingly, but his remarkable flair for design and drawing was immediately noticed, and exploited. There was nothing his hands could not do to construct the images conceived by his mind and he was rapidly given assignments, relating to the ornate detail on the exterior and interior of buildings, which it was clear he had both skill and imagination to create. Writing to his brother on Winslow and Wetherell letterhead, some time after he began work in Boston, he described a fellow architect who would later become a partner in the firm and who may have played an important role in influencing his own interest and talent in interior design:

> I have been working a good deal with Henry Forbes Bigelow lately and am now carrying out a large country house for him, he seems very satisfied with my work . . . he is a very clever young fellow (29 or 30) and knows more about planning, designing etc. than anyone else in the office.

From 1893 onwards, through to 1900 when he was in France, William Sutherland began the practice of keeping sketchbooks to enrich his architectural vocabulary. It was a habit he would maintain throughout his life. He also began to travel during his time in Boston, visiting nearby towns such as Marblehead, Massachusetts, and Portsmouth, New Hampshire, to make drawings of noteworthy buildings. This too became the habit of a lifetime. He was also a keen amateur photographer, and must have started this hobby well before leaving Montreal. The following letter written to his mother on 13 January 1895, soon after his arrival in Boston, illustrates his attachment to this art. He was an avid collector as well as taker of photographs throughout his life:

Dear Ma,

   I am sending you this note to ask you to give Miss Rowe my flash lamp and also my printing frame with the camera. I propose to take pictures and get them developed at a photographer's and to make my own blue prints. This will not injure my nails at all (my nails are very much better than they used to be and are improving in appearance).

   Yesterday I had a walk on Commonwealth Avenue and saw more sleighs than I ever had seen before in my life. The weather down here has not been as severe as you have been having. Some weeks or so ago, I would sit in my room with the window wide open, then we had a few days ten below zero, and then the snow, this brought every sleigh in the country out.

   I start my classes at the Atelier tonight. Every Wednesday evening I attend a free lecture at the Technology Institute on the modern architecture of France and I enjoy them very much.

Also give my flash powder to Miss Rowe.
With love,
W. S. Maxwell

A letter written to his father on 26 November 1895 reveals a little of young William's indigence at that time, as well as his characteristic dry wit.

Dear Pa,

Last week I received the box of beautiful apples that you and Ma sent me. They arrived in excellent order and I wish to thank you both, very much indeed, for sending them . . .

I have not got your letter with me so that I shall have to reply to your queries in my next. I do not intend joining the Architectural Club, for reasons that you no doubt know by now, but, I have made application to join the Architectural Atelier, which the Society of Architects are going to carry on this winter. In the Atelier one learns much the same matter as is taught in the School of Technology. It will take up at least three or four nights a week. I am enclosing a circular if I can find it.

I heard the Symphony Orchestra on last Saturday night and enjoyed it immensely; they played the Mendelssohn's Scotch Symphony . . . Madame Braema was to have sung but was delayed by the steamer not arriving in time, a Miss Clark, who weighs about two hundred and fifty pounds took her place, and sang beautifully. She received quite an ovation . . .

A very great deal of my time is spent in the Public Library, one unconsciously gets to feel an ownership in it specially if one goes there often. At the office I am still doing practical details and am learning a great deal in this manner.

Your Affectionate Son
W. S. M.

William made notes on the Boston Public Library too, which had been opened in 1895. He also saved, among his personal papers, a newspaper clipping about the Touraine, a hotel that was commissioned by the firm and completed in 1897, which seems to suggest that he may have been involved in its design. His sketchbooks recorded in a meticulous manner the subject matter as well as the date of each of his drawings. Among his sketches from this period are 'The Village Gossips', the 'Gateway of the Torre de las Infantas – in Spain', the 'Old Barge at Allan Wharf', and several portraits including a woman in an evening gown, a soldier in uniform and the drawing of an unnamed but presumably admired 'Miss Puff Sleeves'!

In March of that same year, he wrote two other letters to his parents about his life in Boston. Despite the hard work and relatively low pay, he was still finding time to enjoy himself. Evening concerts were free those days and his love of music, like his love of photography, was to sustain his soul throughout his life. But the letter to his father also reveals a competitive edge that was all the more remarkable in light of his humility. William was a modest young man but it did not stop him from striving to be the best in his field. It also shows the lengths to which he went to find ways of earning extra money, in addition to his daytime work as a draughtsman, in order to become self-supporting:

Dear Pa,

Replying to your welcome letter of March second – my correspondence has been rather irregular this winter I admit, but then my time has been taken up a good deal as you know working at night and studying.

I attended an amateur performance last week at Somerville – one of my friends in the office took the leading part very successfully – I enjoyed myself . . . How did the 'Musical' come off, were you there?

I rendered a drawing in colour for Dave Brown last week. He got third place in the competition for the Yacht Club as you probably know.

The referee mentioned my perspective as being very nice – but did not like Dave's plan . . .

That same day he wrote his mother, for whom he cherished a deep affection:

Dear Ma,

Being at home for the evening, I can think of nothing better than writing a line or so home! . . .

My work of the last eight or nine months is beginning to show up. Mr. Wetherell is very much pleased with everything so far and says that the Hotel interiors are going to contain about the best ornaments in Boston . . .

I rendered a perspective in water colour last week for Brown MacVicar & Heriot of Montreal; it was the second one that I have done for them. They seemed to like it quite well . . .

I have sold to my agent over eight hundred of my photographs and to the boys in the office several hundred. This coming season I intend taking a great many at Newport and other places.

Hoping all are well I remain with love, Your affect. Son,

W. S. Maxwell

Although his communications with his parents were restrained and decorous at best, bordering on dryness at times, he had an affectionate and sensitive nature. Amongst the many books in his library which he kept to the end of his life is one entitled *Coaching Days* dedicated to 'Willie' by his mother at Christmas 1894. His love for his family was deep rather than frank; he preferred silence to hurt feelings. His letters to his sister and his brother, too, testify to much that is unspoken. It is only in comparison with the flood of letters that he wrote to May in later months and years, that we can see how much this young man had been restraining himself.

An early letter written to his brother, who had just returned from his European tour in March of 1895, is a classic example of all that was not said between the Maxwells. It must have been evident to Edward that William was not writing just to tell him about the postcards he had bought in Boston, very inexpensively, depicting famous buildings in Rome, Paris and Florence. Nor merely to inform him of his latest finds in antiquarian bookstores, which Edward had asked him to hunt down. It was important to become acquainted with the illustrations of old buildings in history books, of course, which is why he and his brother both avidly collected them.[25] But the best way to learn about architecture was to see the buildings themselves, in the flesh, as it were, of mortar and stone. The real subject on William's mind when he wrote

---

25 In a letter to Edward from Boston on 16 March 1895, he wrote: 'I can confidently recommend the following: 1st A bargain. Nash's Elizabethan houses, 5 vols, original Edition (same as those Mr. Learmont lent you) at Estes and Lauriats. These vols. are very scarce. Cost $16 or $17 I don't know which. There is one set only, if you want them let me know immediately.'

this letter to Edward was his own longing to go to Europe. And his brother knew it: ·

> Dear Ed, I guess by this time you are home. You must have had a grand trip. Did you do any sketching or did you confine yourself to sight seeing and buying photographs? I have been getting on very fairly down here, have attended classes (2) at the Atelier and have learned considerably thereby. I have caught my old craze of buying books etc. Have subscribed to 'Concours Publics' it being a magazine (monthly) giving plans, elevations etc. of the prize winning plans in the competitions held by the French Government etc. I was the first one to subscribe to it in our office, 5 others subscribed immediately after me. It is a splendid publication and costs $9.40 a year.

The reason why William began to subscribe to *Concours Publics* must have been fairly evident to his brother in 1896. Perhaps Edward had even encouraged him to do this. His enthusiasm for the French style was already evident by then, as Rosalind M. Pepall has noted.[26] The École des Beaux-Arts in Paris was a major influence on American architecture at the time and the Atelier Pascal, associated with the École, was the place where many of the leading architects in the United States had been trained. Jean-Louis Pascal had influenced several American architects who were working at the Boston firm of Winslow and Wetherell where William Sutherland Maxwell himself had been apprenticed. He was obviously preparing to go to France years before he finally boarded the steamer in New York.

He had been encouraged to apply to study under Jean-Louis Pascal by Edward himself, who was acquainted with some of the top American architects who had been trained there.He was promised his support too, during his stay in France, because Edward had recognized his originality and was keen to develop his talent as well as encourage his further studies. William was determined to spend as little money and acquire as much knowledge as possible while he was in France, because although he had been granted a scholarship by the Canadian Government he was still tied to his older brother's purse strings for his living expenses. He no doubt vowed to himself to learn all he could and return as soon as

---

26 Pepall, 'The Architecture of Edward & W.S. Maxwell'.

he was able in order to repay his brother's trust. He was going to go into partnership with Edward on his return.

It was a promise he had made not only to himself and to his brother, but to the entire Maxwell family. Everyone – mother, father and even his sister Amelia – expected prudence from him, diligence and lifelong gratitude for this great chance that he had been given. To study art in the capital of culture was not something a man of his background could do lightly or without due sense of obligation. And it was primarily about this expectation that they wrote to him when he finally left for Paris. They wrote about his studies too, of course; about the money he requested; about the friends and family he should meet on their behalf; and the little purchases he should make for them. But above all, about his return to life and work in Montreal.

He was expected to tour the major capitals of Europe when he was not studying at the Atelier. He was expected to return in a year. But the last thing anyone expected was that he should fall in love.

* * *

Love was certainly the last thing on May's mind when she returned to Paris in 1898. Her vital spirits were depleted despite the prospect of living in luxury on 13 Quai d'Orsay. Unlike other occasions when the Bolles rented modest accommodations on their return from Brittany, they had been invited to 'house-sit' that year and had taken up residence in what was probably the guest wing of Phoebe Hearst's grand apartment overlooking the Seine. That autumn, Mrs Bolles was no doubt planning a grand Thanksgiving. She probably wanted to invite the best of the Americans in Paris to Phoebe's elegant drawing rooms. But when news came that Phoebe herself was going to descend upon them in a few days, May begged to be left out of the celebrations. She was in no mood for company and retired to her bed with implacable headaches. She began to decline, not only invitations but in every sense.

Her mother must have been at her wit's end. Her dear friend and benefactress had set sail on 22 September, and even as May sank deeper into her pillows news came that Phoebe had already docked at Cherbourg and was expected to arrive from one day to the next. The main drawing rooms along the length of the piano nobile, overlooking the banks of the river, had been shuttered all summer and had to be opened and aired without delay. Fires had to be lit in all the grates to remove the chill of the autumn air. Enormous bouquets of lilies had to be ordered to fill the bedrooms with fragrance. Butchers and traiteurs, bakers and chocolatiers of the highest excellence were delivering crenellated aspics and towering confectioneries in anticipation of Phoebe's style of entertainment. A flock of extra *bonnes* had to be vetted and hired to remove the white sheets that covered the antique furnishings and dust the art works. Mrs Bolles would doubtless have been much relieved if Robert Turner, Phoebe's impeccable butler, had arrived ahead to help oversee the preparations, for she had probably heard by then that his mistress was not coming to Paris alone.

Mrs Hearst rarely travelled alone. She usually moved from place to place in considerable luxury, and with a train of dependents who served as her companions and her helpers on her journeys. This time she was on her way to Marseilles accompanied by a large entourage which was eclectic, to say the least. The group consisted of her niece, Anne Apperson and her cousin, Agnes Lane; a tutor for Agnes, Julia Pearson, hired especially for the journey; her homeopathic doctor Edward C. Getsinger and his wife Lua; her old friend Harriet Thornburgh, accompanied by her daughter Virginia (usually called Minnie); her butler, Robert Turner and Amalie M. Bachrodt, her maid. In addition, she was attended by a Lebanese physician, Dr Ibrahim Kheiralla and his English wife, Marian.

From the moment they arrived in Paris, the Hearst party became the talk of the town. They were thought to be heading for the Nile. It sounded so exotic! They were said to be going on a sightseeing tour to Constantinople and the Aegean isles. Or was it Armenia? Perhaps this was an archaeological trip, an expedition for artefacts to add to Phoebe's private museums; perhaps it was a spiritual quest, for everyone knew that the wealthy widow, who according to her dead husband's will could not remarry without the loss of all her money, had been much shaken by the recent death of her close friend, Dr Pepper. He had nursed her through a heart attack some years before and now she had nobody she could turn to as a confidant. There must have been quite a few raised eyebrows in the drawing-rooms of St Germain when mention was made of the other so-called doctor and his strange cult which Dr Getsinger and his wife Lua seemed to have espoused. It was the latter, apparently, who had rouséd Mrs Hearst's interest in the Orient. It was through the Getsingers that she had extended an invitation to Dr Kheiralla to join her. But could Phoebe be seriously interested in religion? Everyone wanted to know what was going on, for everyone was aware that her son, William Randolph, had his eye on the White House and was angling for a political career. The gossip must have been greatly entertaining.

Despite all the talk, however, no one guessed the truth. The fact was that the Hearst party was on its way to visit the holy tomb of Bahá'u'lláh outside 'Akká, Palestine. These men and women were the first group of pilgrims and seekers from the West who were going to meet 'Abdu'l-Bahá face to face. But the Americans in Paris had no inkling that their compatriots were about to be introduced to the Centre of the Covenant of the Bahá'í Dispensation. None of them had any idea how historic this journey would prove to be. All they heard at the time was that the Hearst party was heading for the penal colony of the Ottoman Empire in Palestine.

As soon as Phoebe Hearst arrived in Paris, she became privy to a different kind of gossip, however. She heard even more disturbing news: not only about the recent Spanish–American War, which she feared her own son might have been responsible for inciting through his newspaper; nor just about how her spiritual interests might affect William's political career; but also about the fragile condition of her god-daughter. When Mrs Hearst entered May's bedroom in her guest apartments at 13 Quai d'Orsay she found Miss Bolles sunk into her pillows with dark circles round her eyes. She was shocked. Was this the pretty girl who had performed on the Englewood stage with such gaiety and aplomb just a few years ago? Was this the lovely creature who had danced past midnight at her 'coming out' ball? Why, she looked positively at death's door! Mrs Bolles must have confessed to her friend Phoebe in broken whispers that she had stopped worrying about whether May would get married any more and was wondering whether she would survive. Something had to be done. So Mrs Hearst naturally sent for Dr Getsinger immediately.

He came. He checked the patient's condition, briefly. And then he conferred with Mrs Hearst outside the door. Miss Bolles, the doctor recommended, might be better off seeing his wife rather than himself. It was evident to him that May was suffering from more than a mere physical ailment. Lua, he told Mrs Hearst, could help the young lady better than he could. This one needed spiritual guidance.

Thus it was that May learned of the true goal of the Hearst party's trip. Lua Getsinger told her of the Faith and she heard the name of 'Abdu'l-Bahá first uttered like a prayer in the privacy of her chamber as she lay hollowed out on her sick bed. Some months later, when she was passing through Egypt and saw a portrait of the Master in His youth, she recognized Him instantly as the luminous figure she had seen in her dream, beckoning her across the water, so long ago. But according to her own records, all she registered at that first moment were the words on Lua's lips:

There is a Prisoner in 'Akká who holds the key to Peace.

That was enough for May. Her parched soul responded instantly. As Rúḥíyyih Khánum often said, whenever she repeated this well-known story about her mother's recognition of the Faith, the minute May heard Lua's words she half-rose from her pillows, exclaiming: 'I believe, I believe.' And then instantly fainted.

* * *

Lua Getsinger became May's spiritual mother from that moment and taught her all that she knew about the Bahá'í Faith. It was not much, but it was enough to set her heart on fire. Even though the teachings were somewhat distorted at this time by a combination of linguistic incompetence, wishful thinking, and ambition on the part of Dr Ibrahim Kheiralla, this first teacher of the Faith in America had nevertheless managed, in spite of himself, to convey enough of its truth to attract the hearts of the early western believers to the Cause. It was because he raised the banner of Bahá'u'lláh in this way that he was given the title 'Bahá's Peter' by 'Abdu'l-Bahá.

Lua had met Ibrahim Kheiralla in Chicago, where she had gone to train to be an actress in the mid-nineties. She had learned of the Bahá'í teachings through him around the same time that she had met Edward Getsinger, whom she married in 1897. Lua had become an ardent teacher of the Cause in the course of the previous year and had attracted many people to Kheiralla's classes. Having passed through the classes, the 'pupils' were then expected to write a letter to 'Abdu'l-Bahá, confirming their belief in 'El Baha'. This May did too. Once she heard of the Faith, she wrote to the Master immediately, sending streams of supplications to Him, pouring out her yearning and her devotion to Him, telling Him of her ardent faith; her love for 'Abdu'l-Bahá was instantaneous and intense. Her letter of belief written to the Master has not been found, but certain undated fragmented notes she wrote have survived among her papers:

O my Lord, my Lord – whom I have loved and sought as Jesus Christ, whom I have now found and adore as Abbas Effendi, I do beseech Thee to hear the voice of this lost child . . . [With a] mind distraught and clouded, [with] the love of my soul sapped, and the light dimmed, I went wandering alone. Yet so sure was I that if I had but missed the Way there still was a Way. So fast my soul clung to my God, that He sent to me a friend whose tender love and pity shot a ray into the darkness to me – a ray so pure and radiant, that by its light my soul was born again to love and hope and peace . . . and I gave my life to God . . . my hands were stretched forth in unspeakable prayers to God, beseeching Him to let me but come near enough – near enough to His beloved son to touch His healing garments' hem. And He heard – as before – and He answered as before, and He sent His messenger to me, who laid his hands on me – and I walked – I lived. And I live – for he that believes on Thee tho' he were dead yet shall he live.

Oh! Abbas Effendi in the past days as the Truth has been entering my soul, I have dared to breathe Thy name, and I will try to have the courage now to beseech Thee to look for one moment into my heart and behold that my sins, my sins – Oh! My Lord make me afraid . . .

Oh! Thou whom I love, I beseech Thee and beg of Thee, in the name of God, Who sent me forth long since to find Him, whom I sought unceasingly, and on the threshold of whose Kingdom I am standing knocking – wilt Thou open unto me – wilt Thou – if it be the Will of God – grant me the grace of Thy permission to come and lay down my life at Thy feet . . . I do most humbly implore Thy help, to be more worthy to approach that Holy place, for which my soul is hungering and thirsting, and Abbas Effendi – Prince of the World, my love and my life I lay at Thy feet – for God – that Thou His Shepherd may gather into His Fold – one more lost lamb.

Then Thou camest to me in a dream, standing beside the deep

blue waters, and I was on the opposite bank, in a multitude of people all hurrying to and fro like ants, save one or perhaps a few who stood beside me and gazed at my face where they saw the light reflected from the glory of Thy countenance. And my eyes were steadfastly upon Thee, and I said – Jesus, I am coming. And if it be Thy will I ask Thee to permit that the work of healing begun by Thy servant, may soon be completed, and if Thou seest me to be worthy that thou wilt allow me to be touched by the Holy Leaves of God, that health may be mine, that I may be made whole, so that, as my soul drinks of the water of Life, those endowments for which I may be best fitted, may grow, and Thou mayest send me forth to work in God's vineyard, and to bear the tidings of His glorious Truth to as many as He will enable me . . . Oh! My Lord – I look back upon the long wasted years nameless in shame and sorrow – and I humbly beseech Thee to hear the voice of my prayer, that my waiting may be ended, that I may rise up and live to the glory of my God, Him whose Greatest Name I am not yet found worthy to know.

In later years, Agnes Alexander summarized May's 'conversion' beautifully. Recalling the impact on her of the Revelation of Bahá'u'lláh,[27] she wrote:

When she heard the Message from Lua in Paris in 1898, her whole being became alive with the love of her Lord and service to Him, never relaxing until her last earthly moment was spent.

May burned like a candle in her yearning to see 'Abdu'l-Bahá. But her spirits were in a turmoil. She longed to travel to the remote fortress of St Jean d'Acre in Palestine and meet the mysterious 'Prisoner of 'Akká'. But she did not have the means to pay her way and could not depend on her mother for the ticket. The family finances, she knew, were unequal to it, especially since her grandmother's passing.[28] According to Rúḥíyyih Khánum, when Mrs Hearst heard that May was arranging to sell her few pieces of jewellery in order to pay for her passage and join them, she immediately intervened. She took the young woman under

---

27 Agnes Alexander, in her account 'May Maxwell – A Tribute'.
28 The mortgaged house in Englewood may have only been restored to Mrs Bolles after her mother's death through Phoebe's magnanimity. She was indeed not only May's 'good fairy', but 'the good angel of all the family', as May wrote in a letter of gratitude to her.

her wing, treating her with a magnanimity that May never forgot and would always emulate towards others in later years. She welcomed her dear god-daughter to travel with them.

Mrs Hearst no doubt imagined that a change of air would help the young woman overcome her health problems, that the journey down the Nile would give her a broader perspective on life. Perhaps she also hoped that she might interest May in Egyptian culture, in ancient art, in intellectual improvement, for Phoebe, whose first love had been teaching, never forgot the importance of education for a woman and was eager to improve her god-daughter's mind. She must have thought it a shame that May's schooling had stopped so abruptly at the age of fourteen and may have attributed her malaise to mental boredom as well as spiritual thirst. It is evident from May's promises in letters written at this time that Phoebe must have been encouraging her to study. The only studies she applied herself to, however, were Dr Kheiralla's.

Unlike her friend and benefactress, Mrs Bolles was not so keen on archaeology. She was not too excited by the prospect of dusty artefacts and trophies from the times of the pharaohs either, but she did believe that travel broadened the mind. And perhaps Phoebe would encourage May to befriend some of the more prosperous young Americans in Paris when she came back. Education was hardly a guarantee of marital happiness, but she was very grateful to Phoebe for taking May along to Egypt.

There was doubtless great excitement at 13 Quai d'Orsay as they prepared for the journey. There was also great secrecy, both to protect Mrs Hearst, a well-known figure in society, from undesirable publicity and also because any attempt to meet a prisoner of the Sublime Porte might prove dangerous for the Prisoner as well as His visitors. References to the object of their quest could only be in code. Names were at all costs to be avoided. Writing to May on 22 December 1898, for example, Helen Hillyer shared news of the arrangements she was making for her journey from New York to Naples in the following terms:

My dear Miss Bolles,
In a letter from Mrs. Hearst this morning she has told me the good news that we are both to go to Headquarters in February . . .

Despite the coded mystery surrounding their travel plans, Mrs Hearst embarked on the journey in her usual grand style. Before leaving for

Cairo two months ahead of them, she bought May, and her niece and cousin, all kinds of comforts and all manner of luxuries, including beautiful Parisian gowns to wear when they were presented to the Master. She even purchased several ornaments and expensive jewels as presents for the ladies of His household. She was the essence of generosity.

There is a sale recorded, in the day journal of the famous French jeweller Vevey, for a costly brooch that was bought by a certain 'Mrs Hurst' on 29 December 1898. Was this ornament for Phoebe? For her niece, or May perhaps? Or was it among the gifts she offered the Persian exiles in accordance with the instructions of Dr Kheiralla, who had apparently advised his 'flock' to prepare themselves as if for a presentation at the court of the Sultan? Phoebe Hearst could not have bought it personally, although it may have been purchased for her by her agent, because by 29 December 1898 she herself was in Cairo. She had already passed her brief two-day pilgrimage by then, in the company of Minnie Thornburgh-Cropper and her maid, Amalie, and had returned to Egypt from 'Akká on 22 December. They celebrated Christmas with other members of her party in the luxurious surroundings of the Gezirah Palace Hotel, from where she planned to set sail, on 2 January 1899, on her six-week archaeological expedition down the Nile. But before leaving Paris perhaps she had arranged for the Vevey jewel to be brought to 'Akká by May.

In later years, when writing to a friend[29] about the arrival of the Hearst party in 'Akká, May included the following interesting description of 'Abdu'l-Bahá's reaction to their presents. When they offered their jewels, she said that He

> . . . looked with wonder upon these objects, then turned to us and with the utmost love and kindness said, or words to this effect, all these I accept because they come from your love but 'Abdu'l-Bahá has no need of material gifts. He wants your hearts for God alone, purified from all else save God. A few days later we learned all these baubles of the West were sold in the market place of 'Akká and the money distributed among the many poor.

May had only one gift to offer. She took her heart to 'Abdu'l-Bahá on that journey, 'purified from all else save God'. But she was amply recompensed. Her historic journey to the Holy Land marked the beginning

---

29 Letter from May Maxwell to Mrs Katherine Page, 9 September 1930.

of a new chapter in the destiny of Europe and signalled the springtime of her own emotional and spiritual life.

* * *

As conditions were uncongenial for the prisoners in the Holy Land and 'Abdu'l-Bahá was under strict surveillance and could not easily receive visitors, the Hearst party had been advised to arrive in 'Akká in small groups, discreetly and apart over several weeks. Dr Kheiralla had hurried ahead but Lua and Edward Getsinger, who left Paris soon after celebrating Thanksgiving with Mrs Thornburgh, were the first Westerners to reach the presence of the Master, on 10 December. Phoebe Hearst and her two companions, arriving ten days later, were in the second group, the only one to travel to 'Akká incognito and under cover of darkness, the only one to stay no more than one brief night and day in the presence of 'Abdu'l-Bahá. These precautions were presumably taken to protect Mrs Hearst's own reputation and her son's, as well as to avoid bringing undue attention to the Master. As it was, there is reason to believe that the knowledge of their visit to 'Headquarters' may have been partly responsible for the increase of strictures placed on 'Abdu'l-Bahá in the following years. The arrival of Westerners of such fame and political power in the vicinity of the penal colony of the Ottoman Empire could hardly pass unnoticed, especially with so many enemies posted at the gates of 'Akká, watching all activities.

Marian Miller, the English wife of Dr Ibrahim Kheiralla, was the third visitor to arrive in Palestine, via Milan, in late December 1898, and May herself, in the company of the elderly Mrs Harriet Thornburgh, came in the fourth group. After travelling from Marseilles to Naples, they boarded a ship on 9 February 1899 bound for Port Said, Jaffa, and finally Haifa, a small fishing port at the foot of Mt Carmel where they arrived on 16 February. Their first meeting with the Master took place in a house especially rented for that purpose in Haifa, where they were joined soon afterwards, on 20 February, by the fifth group comprised of Anne Apperson, Julia Pearson and Robert Turner. May's record of this visit is a witness of these unforgettable days:

> We sailed from Marseilles on February 9th, 1899, on board the S.S. Carthage bound for Bombay and arrived in Port Said on February

13th ... We were obliged to wait two days for the little boat running along the coast of Beirut, and we went on board about seven o'clock on the evening of the 15th ... we stopped at Jaffa the next day and ... continued on our journey, sitting quietly on deck until the twilight fell about us ... we all stood in prayer and worship as the ship slowly entered the bay of Haifa and cast anchor ... we were rowed ashore and saw the faces of our American brothers beaming upon us. They greeted us cordially as they helped us out, and said, 'Our Master is in Haifa.' We were driven to the house which the Master had taken for the American pilgrims ...

On the following morning, Friday the 17th, at about seven o'clock, sister Maryam hurried into our room and announced that 'Abdu'l-Bahá would arrive in a few moments. We had barely time to dress when a sudden stir without set all our beings in commotion. We went out into a large central hall from which opened all the rooms in the house and opposite the door of one of these we saw the shoes of the believers; thus we knew that the Blessed Master was within.

The others preceded me. In a moment I stood on the threshold and dimly saw a room full of people sitting quietly about the walls, and then I beheld my Beloved. I found myself at His feet, and He gently raised me and seated me beside Him, all the while saying some loving words in Persian in a voice that shook my heart. Of that first meeting I can remember neither joy nor pain nor anything that I can name. I had been carried suddenly to too great a height; my soul had come in contact with the Divine Spirit; and this force so pure, so holy, so mighty, had overwhelmed me. He spoke to each one of us in turn of ourselves and our lives and those whom we loved, and although His Words were so few and so simple they breathed the Spirit of Life to our souls. To me He said among other things:

You are like the rain which is poured upon the earth making it bud and blossom and become fruitful; so shall the Spirit of God descend upon you, filling you with fruitfulness and you shall go forth and water His vineyard ...

The Spirit of God is shining in your face. You shall have every blessing. Be not anxious for with a little time and patience your mother and brother and all of your family will believe. Every blessing is coming to you for yourself and all whom you love. Your breast shall be widened (in answer to my dream) *and your heart filled with the fire of the love of God.*

You shall attain great spiritual gifts and be confirmed by the Holy Spirit (in answer to my dream: a symbolic dream of fish on a silver plate; after I had performed many tasks and been approved by Molana, He took me to the top of a mountain and gave me the fish to eat and a great light fell upon me, and I was blessed).

You will become a great teacher both in America and France. You will translate the teachings into French and become a great light to the French people, and do a great work, and lead them. You are the child of God and of the Kingdom, and the ties of the flesh are nothing, but the ties of the Spirit are all. We are your brothers and your sisters, and you must be glad and rejoice for I love you exceedingly.

It has rejoiced us to see you and made our hearts glad, and the blessedness of having come here among the first, you cannot yet know.

Now your troubles are ended and you must wipe away your tears, for you know the parable that Christ spoke of the sower and the seed; and so as in nature the good ground is made ready by rain and storm and ploughing and sunshine for the good seed to be sown, so is it in life, and the heart is made ready by all experience for the seed of life.[30]

Rúḥíyyih Khánum shares another priceless memory of that first pilgrimage in her notes for her mother's biography. She gives us a more private glimpse of May who had 'barely time to dress' before her first meeting with 'Abdu'l-Bahá:

Mother was in her room getting dressed to see Him. Mrs Hearst had bought her a beautiful gown in Paris as a present in which she was to 'be received' by 'Abdu'l-Bahá. But at the moment she wore a very

---

30 Maxwell, *An Early Pilgrimage*, pp. 9–13 passim; the first and last paragraphs of 'Abdu'l-Bahá's words to her were published in that account, but paragraphs 2–5 were not included; they are sections of her handwritten account from which *An Early Pilgrimage* was taken.

old padded pink dressing gown and was brushing her long thick hair preparatory to dressing. Suddenly she heard Anne Apperson [sic][31] calling: 'May, He's coming, quick!' At these words Mother, oblivious of everything in the world except the fact that now, at last, she was going to see 'Him', the one who might prove the answer to the quest of all her life, the one for whose Message she was literally dying, rushed from the room, down a corridor and stopped at the entrance of a room. She beheld the face of her Lord, who was seated on the opposite side from where she stood. The next thing she remembered was being raised up from His feet, upon which she seemed to have fallen and over which her hair had streamed. She was then bidden by Him to be seated at His side. She related that as she looked on His face she felt as if all her life, her very being, was ebbing out towards Him as if by an irresistible attraction. She felt very weak. Suddenly He turned and looked at her and spoke quickly to someone in Persian who came and led her to a seat on the other side of the room farther from Him, where she gradually began to recover herself.

Five of the pilgrims – May Bolles, Harriet Thornburgh, Anne Apperson, Julia Pearson and Robert Turner – all had the blessing of staying in the House of 'Abdu'lláh Páshá for three days. Soon after they left 'Akká another group arrived, on 5 March, consisting of Helen Hillyer and Ella Cooper. After visiting the Riḍván Gardens and paying their respects at the Shrine in Bahjí, after being blessed with a sight of the portraits of the Báb and Bahá'u'lláh in the room of the Greatest Holy Leaf,[32] these pilgrims all bade farewell to the land of their hearts' desire and turned their faces, one by one, back towards the West. Finally, a solitary and unexpected visit from Margaret Barton Peeke[33] concluded that first historic pilgrimage.

May's group left 'Akká on the morning of 25 February, their eyes streaming, their hearts aching. They sat speechless as their carriage rounded the sandy bay, and once in Haifa they boarded, still in silence,

---

31 Anne Apperson did not arrive until 20 February; this was more likely Marian Kheiralla. See Hogenson, *Lighting the Western Sky*, p. 103.

32 It was in this room and at this very time that unbeknownst to the pilgrims, the remains of the Báb Himself and his companion Anis, so long hidden and so long preserved, had been carefully secreted after fifty years of troubled concealment; it was here that the sacred casket was kept, awaiting final interment on Mt Carmel.

33 Hogenson, *Lighting the Western Sky*, pp. 152–8.

the steamer that took them down to the port of Jaffa. The Hearst party was waiting for them there. Once on board the *S.S. Augusta Victoria* with the rest of their friends, they continued the cruise through the Bosphorus to Istanbul, and finally back to Marseilles through the Greek islands. But in Istanbul, according to Rúḥíyyih Khánum, May awoke from the dream of pilgrimage with the taste of rose-petal jam on her tongue. There was nothing else of that Mediterranean journey that she recorded.

But the sweet taste of her first meeting with the Master lingered far longer in her memory. May was transformed on her return to Paris, but not in the manner that Mrs Hearst may have supposed or even her mother might have hoped. Change by definition cannot always be anticipated. Mrs Hearst's own experience, as she wrote to May on 10 January 1899, was 'different in some respect from any idea I had before reaching Haifa'. But in May's case, the difference proved immeasurable in all respects. Writing to her benefactress some time later, possibly when Phoebe was returning to America, May offered her a little memento and her abiding thanks:

My dear Mrs. Hearst,

If it gives you half the pleasure to use this little cushion as it has given me to make it for you, I shall be very glad. I have tried to make something that 'looks like you'. I trust I have somewhat succeeded. Every moment that I gave to it my thoughts were with you, and much true love and warm admiration have been stitched and pinned into its fragile pink bosom! I can seldom express to you any of all that I feel – but <u>you</u> <u>know</u> that our gratitude and our affection follow you across the sea and wherever you are we wish for your happiness and your peace, <u>always</u>. You have been <u>my</u> 'good fairy' for many years and now you seem to be – 'good angel' of all the family! I will not say 'good-bye' – but au revoir et bon voyage, dear Mrs. Hearst. I am your loving friend, May Ellis Bolles.

This 'good angel', her godmother, had been instrumental in May's rebirth; she had helped to transform her world entirely and had given the opportunity to the first pilgrims from the West to meet their Lord. As May wrote in one of her initial preambles to the booklet she called *An Early Pilgrimage*, 'within the spacious walls, stone floors and raft-clad ceilings of this great Turkish Prison these children of the world first learned the mystery of divine love'. Thanks to Mrs Hearst, she found her Beloved at last after so many years of searching; she was restored and made anew by the Source of her creation. She now gave her heart and soul to 'Abdu'l-Bahá, and from this moment to the end of her days, the Bahá'í Cause was her priority.

As 'Abdu'l-Bahá had promised, May seemed to have been 'filled with the spirit of God' after her pilgrimage. When she left Him, these parting words of the Master became May's blueprint for life. She shaped her future on this pattern He had set for her:

> *You have come here among the first and your reward is great . . . and I say unto you that anyone who will rise up in the Cause of God at this time shall be filled with the spirit of God, and that He will send His hosts from heaven to help you, and that nothing shall be impossible to you if you have faith. And now I give you a commandment which shall be for a covenant between you and Me – that ye have faith; that your faith be steadfast as a rock that no storms can move, that nothing can disturb, and that it endure through all things even to the end; even should ye hear that your Lord has been crucified, be not shaken in your faith; for I am with you always, whether living or dead, I am with you to the end. As ye have faith so shall your powers and blessings be. This is the balance – this is the balance – this is the balance.*
>
> *. . . look at Me, follow Me, be as I am . . . ye must die to yourselves and to the world, so shall ye be born again and enter the Kingdom of Heaven. Behold a candle how it gives its light. It weeps its life away drop by drop in order to give forth its flame of light.*[34]

One of the earliest Tablets addressed to May Bolles by 'Abdu'l-Bahá reached her hands shortly after her return from her historic first pilgrimage. The date of its translation is 7 July 1899:

> *O thou beloved gem, who hast fixed thy gaze upon the Horizon of the Shining Light!*
>
> *Take heed, and turn thine eyes from all save God! Let thine heart be enkindled with the fire of the love of God. Rejoice at the sweet savours of God, and baptize thyself with the Divine Spirit, overflowing abundantly from the Kingdom of God! Then shalt thou have whatsoever thou*

---

34 Maxwell, *An Early Pilgrimage*, pp. 39–42.

dost wish and desire from the gifts of God, O thou the maidservant of God.

From this time on their correspondence is almost unbroken. On 13 April 1900, less than a year later, May wrote the following supplication to 'Abdu'l-Bahá:

> O my Lord & Beloved Master!
> . . . I humbly entreat that Thou wilt enable me to be emptied of self, & cut from all things here below, and grant me the confirmation of the Holy spirit. And if it be Thy good pleasure, may I receive from Thy Precious Pen instruction regarding my Teaching & the way to deliver the Truth with power. Thus I shall attain to that for which my soul longs: to be emptied of everything and be Thy servant and in Thy Hands, to glorify the Sublime Cause of God, & witness before long in this country the wide-spread diffusion of the Light promised in Thy Blessed Tablet to this servant.
> O my Lord! I earnestly beg and supplicate for Thy Mercy upon my Mother! That my heart may burn with such love for her that I may lead her to the Path of Salvation! . . .

Even when she did not receive actual Tablets from the hand of the Master, she was given His verbal messages through the other pilgrims who had returned from or were writing to her from the Holy Land. They asked questions on her behalf and brought her answers. When Lua was on her second pilgrimage, for example, she wrote to May on 8 October 1900, conveying 'Abdu'l-Bahá's love to her, repeating His words:

> I have rec'd your dear letters and have fulfilled all you asked of me. And I must tell you dear how much our Beloved Lord and Master loves you for He always mentions you and tells about your work. He just said to us – 'Tell Miss Bolles I know all of her troubles and she must not be sad at all but must always be happy – if she has not a single penny tell her not to be troubled – I pray for her that she may receive spiritual riches and that the blessings will descend upon her in great abundance.'

And when there were no messages, there were memories, for the presence of 'Abdu'l-Bahá had been shared with other souls who had returned to Paris. The spirit of the Master literally reigned over that little group. One year after her pilgrimage, May received a letter from Edith MacKay who had visited 'Akká shortly after her:

> Oh my dearest! When I think how near heaven I was a year ago tonight! Our boat was balancing itself on the calm blue waters, and the silvery moonlight was radiating on Mount Carmel – We could see the lights glimmering from every little white house and were wondering which one was the Blessed Household! and we were faint with joy when we thought of the morrow – of the dawn that would rise on the day we were to see Our Beloved! Oh that night on the still sea, with those millions of stars! It comes back so vividly tonight, that I can almost feel the warm air on my face, and smell the roses which sent their fragrance as a welcome – Oh! to be for one second at His Feet and feel submerged in His Love and Peace –! How happy was that Believer who died in His Arms, May – and whose last look met with His Beloved Eyes!

But while memories like these were precious, and messages received through others were gifts beyond compare, there was nothing for May like receiving Tablets from 'Abdu'l-Bahá Himself. Even if transcriptions were poor, even if translations were approximate and dates uncertain, the words of the Master were the foundation of her very faith. When May read such words as these, she was energized:

> *To the one who hath hearkened to God's good tidings and hath pro-claimed His bountiful favours!*
> *I assure thee that all the heavenly souls are praying for thee, for thou hast spread abroad the sweet savours of the wondrous garden of the Kingdom of God, and thy face hath shone forth with the effulgent light rising above the horizon of the all-powerful Lord. Thine ears were thrilled as they hearkened to the call from heaven, and thy heart hath been quickened by the new-born spirit of the glorious Cause of God!*
> *Erelong thou shalt behold the celestial blessing of this prayer, and the radiance of the light of God's mighty Cause. Thou shalt witness the widespread diffusion of this light to the highest heaven, and thou shalt*

see how from this new spirit a mighty power is released over the entire creation.[35]

The Master's Tablets charged May with strength and vigour. She evinced such a vitality on her return from 'Akká that not only her family but all who knew her were amazed. She seemed to have been recreated, made anew.

---

35 No copy of the Tablet upon which this approved provisional translation is based has been located at the Bahá'í World Centre; it was rendered from material found among the papers of Amatu'l-Bahá Rúḥíyyih Khánum.

1899–1902

One autumn evening in October 1899, at a time when his sister was totally preoccupied with her Bahá'í work, teaching her 'pupils' according to Kheiralla's system and conducting them step by step towards the knowledge of the 'Greatest Name', Randoph Bolles invited a new friend to dinner at 100 rue du Bac. They had vacated Mrs Hearst's grand apartment at the beginning of the summer, when they left for Brittany as was their wont, and the new place they had rented in Paris had been taken over by May's activities since they returned from St Enogat. But Mrs Bolles may have insisted on a family dinner that evening. While she was doubtless relieved to see that her daughter's spirits had revived since her trip to Palestine and was broad-minded enough not to interfere with her new-found zeal, she could not forget that May was twenty-nine years old and still unmarried. She was curious to meet this young man whom her son considered such a capital fellow.

Their guest that night did not initially seem to be much of a 'catch' as far as Mrs Bolles was concerned. She must have quickly realized that Mr Maxwell had no 'connections', living as he did with a bunch of students at 83 Boulevard Montparnasse. You could hardly blame the poor boy for being Scots-Canadian, but he had neither family nor fortune to recommend him. Now if he had been the son of an Admiral, for example, she might have been more inclined to take him seriously. But despite his lack of pedigree, she guessed that he had prospects. He was well-bred, he was hard-working, and he was evidently very talented. He also seemed like a decent fellow, and might even be a good influence on her son. After he left, she may have been attempting to say that Mr Maxwell seemed rather nice when May, turning sharply to her brother, interrupted:

'Don't ever bring that big Canadian here again!'[1]

---

1 Rúḥíyyih Khánum often told different versions of this story and changed it according to her different audiences. In one version, May apparently told her brother, 'Don't ever bring

The silence following that remark reverberates with irony across the years. Mrs Bolles probably rolled her eyes. Randolph doubtless shrugged his sloping shoulders. He was accustomed to his sister's exaggerated reactions. She had such an odd way of assessing people. Her extra-sensory perceptions were either uncannily right or else entirely wrong. But whichever was the case on this occasion, he must have thought it rather extreme. When he asked her, in astonishment, to explain the reason, dash it all, why he was required to cut off relations with possibly one of the best chaps he had had the good fortune to meet since coming to Paris, May replied:

'He stared at me all the time!'

But Randolph kept inviting the young man over, in spite of his sister's protestations. He kept showing up with good old 'Max' at 100 rue du Bac, even when she was holding her Bahá'í classes in the salon. It was very awkward. At first she assumed that he was coming to help Randolph with his work, except that he spent so much time listening to her. Then she began to wonder whether he too might not also be a seeker after the truth. Was the big Canadian attracted to the Bahá'í Faith? Was he interested in hearing about the Cause? But although he was perfectly polite, her brother's friend never asked a single question on the subject. He just stared.

Mr Maxwell's explanation of his seeming rudeness in later years was that he had fallen in love with Miss Bolles. He was frankly smitten at first sight. She had eyes like violets,[2] and a smile that plucked at the strings of his heart. He thought her utterly beautiful. In an article he later wrote, in 1903, on 'Architectural Education', he described with vivid precision the 'powerful influence' of the exhibitions he participated in during his time in Paris, which 'get a man out of a rut, stimulate his imagination and broaden his point of view'. In retrospect, this describes May's impact on him too. The impression she made was certainly powerful, and she stimulated his imagination more than he cared to admit at the time.

From then on, young Mr Maxwell's attentions were totally absorbed

---

that young man here again!' The version printed here, referring to 'that big Canadian', has been published in Janet Ruhe-Schoen's book, *A Love Which Does Not Wait*, p. 49, transcribed from a taped talk by Amatu'l-Bahá on 'The Life of May Maxwell'.

2   The notion of 'violet eyes' was a very Victorian one. Violet, as a colour as well as a flower, was thought to be romantically feminine during the 19th century. Phoebe Hearst was also called 'the Violet Lady' by Ella Goodall.

by Miss Bolles and his studies. Nothing else mattered. When he was not working at the Atelier of Jean-Louis Pascal, drawing models and sketching buildings, he was hovering at the door of 100 rue du Bac. And when he was not looking for excuses to borrow a book from Randolph or do his homework for him, so that he could see May one more time, he was thinking about her as he worked on his architectural drawings and walked through the streets of Paris. Although he later told his daughter that he had made up his mind, from that very first night in October 1899, that he was going to marry her mother, it took him almost six months to establish more than merely cordial relations with Miss Bolles. Their courtship did not really begin until late March 1900. In his 'Outline' of her life dated 8 March 1940, he sums up his love affair with May:

> I left Montreal for Paris in September 1899 to study Architecture in the École des Beaux-Arts, Atelier Pascal, and met Randolph Bolles; there we became great friends and later I met his sister in their home, 100 Rue du Bac. After seventeen months[3] I returned to Montreal, a happy young man, as I was engaged to May Bolles.
>
> I returned to Paris in the Spring of 1902 and we were married in London on May 8th, 1902, and for thirty-eight years we were blessed in being together. Happiness was ours with never a cloud on the horizon. What the coming of our blessed daughter meant to us cannot be adequately expressed in words.

Whenever she spoke of her parents in her later reminiscences, Rúḥíyyih Khánum often emphasized the fact that their courtship synchronized almost exactly with the growth of the first Bahá'í community in Europe. Its evolution coincided closely with the early stirrings of the Faith in France. May was engaged in nurturing the little group in Paris when Sutherland first met her in October 1899. She was in love, first and foremost, with the Cause. But her heart was stirred with human love after she began to know him; her spiritual awareness acquired a vivid intensity, a personal immediacy because of him, which lent a special poignancy to her efforts to teach the Faith. In fact, the two love stories are so closely intertwined that it is impossible to do justice to the one while ignoring the other.

---

3   It was more like fifteen months.

William Sutherland Maxwell was not the only person who frequented 100 rue du Bac. The Bolles were generous and open-hearted and their home was always filled with visitors as well as family members. Frank Irwin, who stayed with his aunt and cousins in France after his sister Agnes died, fondly recalled his time with them:

> Twice in Paris I made my home with the Bolles (and my grandmother while she was still alive) except that there wasn't a place for me to sleep in either apartment . . . From the summer of '97 to the next spring at 13 quai d'Orsay; and again for a year from the summer of '00 at 100 rue du Bac. (The two visits to Brittany came ... at this time.) This was a great boon to me. After my sister's death in '97, I was very much alone in the world and very lonely. I was sick so that my loneliness wasn't mitigated by an occupation. Both the Irwins and the Martin-Bolleses, including my Uncle Ellis, were very good to me, but I always felt much more at home with my mother's people; my temperament was more like theirs.

Sutherland found that the Bolles' temperament was much to his liking too. He found a liberality of spirit and a freedom of expression among them that drew him back to 100 rue du Bac again and again. But while he was falling head over heels in love with the daughter, many of his friends were also fascinated by her mother. Mamie Martin loved the company of young people, just as her own granddaughter would do years later. Her bohemianism in those years may have been equal to that of all the artists put together whom her son frequented. On one occasion, she may have even frightened one of them away, as she jokingly confessed to Sutherland afterwards:

> I was not the dignified Lady Randolph, I can assure you . . . but just the natural, gay and happy woman you know and at times even at my age, I am made frivolous by my health and overflowing spirits.[4]

---

4   Writing to Sutherland on 4 January 1901, May confided that 'Mr. Hutchison called again, & Mama was in one of her gay moods, & she "carried on" so (as my grand Mother used to say,) that she was afraid she had shocked him.' Mrs Bolles confessed as much herself on 3 March 1901: 'Your friend Hutch, I am sure is quite convinced that your belle-Maman is a very giddy person, and you must some day tell him I am a most sedate old lady. I did behave like "time let loose" one evening when he was here and he never appeared again for weeks!'

Mamie Martin was unconventional in many respects, and her nephew Frank Irwin, writing to Rúḥíyyih <u>Kh</u>ánum on 2 August 1940, told her just how liberal she could be:

> You will have heard much about the French period from your father. But I might make a jotting or two. Randolph's dog, Puck, a delight-ful black caniche, worshipped his master as a sort of god. Randolph and I had many ping-pong contests on the dining-room table (rue du Bac). Aunt Maimie finally allowed us to keep the net up even at meals, so we ate off ½ the table, and Puck lay in the vacant court and would hang his long ears over the net, for company not for food. Sometimes the ping-pong balls went out of the open window, and down four stories to the court below . . . Another anecdote, char-acteristic in its way of my aunt, was of a time when they set their rooms in Paris on fire and summoned the 'sapeur-pompiers'. But they managed to put out the blaze before the fire-apparatus arrived – it's slower in Europe! Aunt Maimie, who knew of a fine inflicted in the circumstances, stoutly held the door against the firemen and refused admittance.

When there were no ping-pong matches taking place at the dining-room table, or giddy conversations between Mrs Bolles and her son's entourage of friends, there were frequently meetings in the salon of 100 rue du Bac of people who were interested in Miss Bolles' new reli-gion. William Sutherland Maxwell found himself competing for May's attentions with many admirers. There was a fire kindled in her after her return from the Holy Land that no '*sapeurs-pompiers*' could have put out, and an incandescence in her smile that drew the moths from all around. May had often been the object of such attentions in the past. She knew very well that most men wanted a God with a face, preferably beautiful, and had suffered enough from being the object of physical attention when what she wanted was to have spiritual communion. But for the first time in her life, she had something important to say to these seekers. She wanted to help them distinguish clearly between the Truth and herself. She wanted to teach them the Bahá'í Faith.

Although she did not guess that this particular young man was destined to become her closest companion in life, May must have won-dered what young Mr Maxwell thought about her religion. What was his opinion of the Bahá'í Faith? Her capacity for passion must have thrilled him but perhaps it confused him to see where she was directing it. But in the last analysis, perhaps it was because she was so different from others that young Mr Maxwell was fascinated by Miss Bolles; perhaps it was her intense spirituality which had attracted him from the start. While he was undoubtedly drawn to her slender loveliness, her dark blue eyes, her tender smile, his love must also have been kindled by May's vision.

She was so idealistic and high-minded. She was so ethereal in appearance and yet her gestures were human, her kindness real. Nothing in his upbringing or culture had prepared him for such a girl. She was a bundle of paradoxes. There was an ardour in her that he wanted to understand. And there was a restlessness, too, that he wished to resolve. Not only his heart, but all his aesthetic sensitivities were quite stirred up by her. She was loveliness incarnate. 'I compare you', he wrote to her in one of his early letters, 'to the purest Gothic.'

However 'gothic' May still looked, with her pale translucent skin, her huge eyes and her wasp-like waist, Mrs Bolles must have been greatly relieved to see the improvement in her daughter's health in the course of that year. She was beginning to sleep more regularly and eat with better appetite. She was more animated too, like her old self, and full of enthusiasm. In fact, she seemed to be positively glowing. She was laughing more as well, particularly at young Mr Maxwell, who had become a frequent visitor. For after he overcame his initial shyness, Randolph's new friend proved to be a lively *raconteur*. He amused them with his daring descriptions of being stripped to the skin and covered in paint during initiation rites at the École des Beaux-Arts. He entertained them with his escapades in the upper storey of the boarding-house he shared with other students.[5] Mrs Bolles thoroughly enjoyed his wry sense of humour, his dry, understated wit.

Rúḥíyyih Khánum many times recalled the funny tale her father told about his French landlady's tortoise. The pet was very small and one day

---

5   Maurice Cullen was a fellow artist who was to make a name for himself as the first Canadian impressionist in the early decades of the 20th century. He also passed through the Beaux-Arts experience in Paris, like many of Sutherland's friends, such as the painter Frederick W. Hutchison, but unlike the latter, Cullen probably did not coincide with Sutherland during his stay in Paris, although he visited Europe briefly in 1901. He was closely associated with the Maxwell brothers in Canada, however, and was commissioned to paint murals in the private homes designed by them in later years. See Appendix II.

her over-exuberant lodgers stole it from under her nose and replaced it with a slightly larger one. After a second and then third exchange, the landlady became convinced that her pet was growing. She was beside herself with excitement and told her neighbours all about it. But at that point the students reversed course and after a few days she discovered, to her considerable dismay, that her tortoise appeared to be shrinking. No matter how much she fed it, it grew smaller every day. By the time the young men had slipped the original creature back into the garden, the poor lady had become hysterical. Their experiment in the psychology of scale caused an uproar in the neighbourhood.

Yes, young Mr Maxwell was certainly very droll. He described the cafés he sat in, the people he watched with a vivid eye for detail and a charming sense of irony; he beguiled them with descriptions of his student friends who shared his apartment at 83 Boulevard Montparnasse and their jolly games of billiards. May began to see why Randolph liked him so much. She may even have worried that her brother was taking advantage of his talents. He was evidently the most amenable fellow.

Her mother liked him too. Mrs Bolles asked 'Max' to take her to galleries; she invited him to join them at the Opera. She even thought him handsome enough to be her escort at the Paris Exposition. Indeed, the 'big Canadian' had distinguished himself in her eyes, because unlike all the others who flocked through the doors of 100 rue du Bac through the winter of 1899 and spring of 1900 he was clearly not coming there to sit at her daughter's feet and imbibe the wisdom of the East. Mrs Bolles noted with satisfaction that 'Max' seemed to have a sensible head on his shoulders. He was evidently more interested in May than in the Bahá'í Faith.

Although no one could have been more susceptible to her charms and no one could have been more attentive to her words, no one could have been more impervious, either, to the subject of religion. When May talked earnestly about the message of Bahá'u'lláh, Mr Maxwell never sighed piously or pressed his hand to his breast, like Monsieur Henri. Unfortunately May lavished Monsieur Henri with all her attentions. And when that gentleman finally became a Bahá'í, Mrs Bolles was not amused.

* * *

May's records of her time in France after her first pilgrimage are reminiscent of the pages of *The Dawn-Breakers*. They recall the age of heroism in the Cradle of the Faith and are unique in the history of the Cause in the West. Each of her encounters during this period seemed destined; each experience conveyed a meaning and a vital message to herself and to others. As a result of the charged atmosphere which she seemed to carry around with her and which she was able to communicate to all who met her, the Bahá'í community of Paris rose from one Bahá'í to over twenty-five within a short span of time. In barely two years, between 1899 and 1902, many distinguished people heard about and accepted the Faith through her efforts.

Some among them were to become household names in the Bahá'í community of the West. Many were destined to champion the Cause of Bahá'u'lláh in different continents and countries around the globe, and most of them were Americans. Whoever met May during those early years remembered her forever, but whoever responded to the Faith she taught was never forgotten. Although it is impossible to include a detailed list of all who were touched by her charisma or describe how each of them became a Bahá'í and served the Cause, a few of the most noteworthy among them deserve mention here. Their stories, even when not illustrious, are sometimes deeply moving and in a few cases salutary.

The first soul who accepted the Faith in Paris at this time was an artist, Brenetta Herrman, whom May had met some years before in France and had befriended. Brenetta had been born in Toledo, Ohio, and was studying at the Academie Carmen under the direction of James McNeill Whistler; she was well known in later years for her impressionist landscapes and pointillist portrait miniatures. She married the American painter/etcher Earl Stetson Crawford on her return to the United States, but there are no records regarding her allegiance to the Faith in later years. It may have been that, like several other young women of her time, she was unable to maintain contacts with the Bahá'ís after her marriage, and was obliged to place her family obligations before her faith. Brenetta developed an intense love for May, whom she called 'Ellice', from her early twenties. May symbolized the highest sort of idealism to her, the loftiest standards – of truth, of morality, of beauty – to which an artist could aspire. Writing to her on 10 February 1898, Brenetta confessed: 'Oh if I only could do something worthy of you my little Ellice. It is so hard to wait until my poor stupid hands can put on canvas what I feel. Will the day ever come do you think dear?'

Shortly after she heard of the Faith from Lua, May found the courage to mention it to Brenetta, but the attempt was abortive at first. It was in December 1898. The Getsingers had just left for 'Akká and Mrs Hearst, who followed in their wake, was already in Cairo. May was alone in Paris. She had gone through her thirteen classes and attained 'the Pith' of the Greatest Name, and was longing to share the news of the Faith with her friends. Brenetta was one of the closest. Writing to Edith Sanderson years later, May described what happened when she told her:

> I remember well the night when, having bade farewell to my beloved teacher Lua and her husband at the Gare St. Lazare, when they were leaving for the Holy Land, I returned alone in a cab through the streets of Paris. The wonder, the awe, the rapture in the new born life through the knowledge of the Blessed Beauty and the actual Presence of 'Abdu'l-Bahá in the Prison of Acca, so dazzled my eyes and drowned my soul in a sea of light, that the great city of Paris seemed to palpitate with a new and wondrous life, and in the darkness of the night the lamps shone like stars. I was aware of being a tiny atom in the vast universe of God, yet a living atom charged with His Sacred Life. My first venture in this new field of consciousness was not very successful! I had begged my dear friend Brenetta Herrman to come with me to Lua to hear a wonderful message, but she refused, yet as soon as Lua left Paris, my friend had a vision of me standing at the foot of her bed while a voice said to her, 'This is your teacher.' I was greatly disturbed when she told me this and was terrified at the responsibility of sharing the wonderful news of the advent of Bahá'u'lláh with any one, and well I might be, for my friend had heart trouble and in my excitement I told her everything at once, and she promptly fainted.

It is evident that Brenetta, like May herself and Thomas Breakwell later, needed to take no more than a single step to recognize the Cause. In fact, she accepted the truth of the teachings before May even left for Palestine, in January 1899; when recording the names of the first believers, May recalled how Brenetta had presented her with a flower and a message of love and spiritual longing to take to 'Abdu'l-Bahá in February 1899, just before she went on pilgrimage. She was only twenty-three years old and the first soul after May to become a Bahá'í in Paris. ' 'Abdu'l-Bahá never forgot her,' May continues, 'and when He was in New York, she brought her child to see Him.'

The second soul to recognize the truth of Bahá'u'lláh was Edith Theodora MacKay,[6] a singer of considerable talent in Paris. When she met May she was already performing in public concerts as well as private homes with some success. Her rendition of 'The Holy City' was to penetrate the heart of Sutherland with its sweetness, and would be remembered by him long after he left France. Writing about her to him on 15 January 1901, May described the impact of her voice:

> My lovely little sister Edith sang last night twice, & it was wonderful & beautiful. I love her as never before, & I sat where she could just turn her dear head and give me one clear look before singing 'The Holy City' and at the end the room full of silent people vibrated with the thrilling power, and our whole hearts & souls overflowed with mighty wonderful love. This love of God is rising all over the world like a supreme tide, that will finally unite every heart in His love, worship and service.

Recalling Edith's acceptance of the Cause years later, May describes a communion between the Bahá'í teacher and the one taught that is surely a model for all times.

> One day shortly after my return from Acca I was seated in my room at 13 Quai d'Orsay when I felt the breeze of the Holy Spirit blowing thru' me. Then suddenly I thought of Theodora MacKaye. She was a beautiful girl whom I had met once or twice – and a few days before I left Paris for Acca she had called to see me. I had noticed then a great unrest; she seemed filled with vague longing and desire which she sought to satisfy by the things of the world. When she bade me good-bye she made me promise to go to see her on my return – although she did not know where I was going or whom I was to see! It was with

---

6 She later married Joseph de Bons, a Swiss dental surgeon, and became the mother of Haenni de Bons who continued, in her parents' footsteps, to serve the Cause in Switzerland for years afterwards.

these thoughts in my mind that I arose and went to the rue Coloni [?] to see Edith – as we then called her – for it was 'Abdu'l-Bahá – the Beloved – who called her by her second name – Theodora.

When I arrived she was singing, and after our first warm greetings she went to the piano and sang for me again. Her voice, which was of divine and penetrating sweetness, seemed to melt my heart & when she finished my face was wet with tears. When the song was ended she came & sat beside me, and took my hands in her ardent girlish way and gazed at me, her lovely face agitated – her dark blue eyes deep and luminous – and she whispered, 'Speak to me.' I said, 'I have come to speak to you – to tell you of the coming of the Kingdom of God,' and with those words a great light enveloped us.

Then I told her all – beginning at the foundation – the Unity of God, of Truth – the Oneness of divine Revelation – the Message of God to mankind thro' all His Prophets – and finally the fulfilment of His Supreme promise in the coming of the Manifestation of God in the last days. While I spoke all her face grew pale – her eyes burned with an inner fire – and she hung on my words – as I had hung on the words of my spiritual Mother when she gave me Life.

Thus the wonderful glad Tidings, the Word of God went into that pure heart – this precious soul was agitated by the Power of the Holy Spirit – & all her being was in commotion. In order to calm her we went out into the beautiful gardens of the Tuileries – and there beneath the leafy trees, she opened her heart to me.

From that hour Edith MacKaye became one of the faithful servants of the Lord – and she grew in spiritual beauty and grace until some two years later she and her mother, to whom Edith had imparted the Truth, made the pilgrimage to Acca, and by the transfiguring Power of the Master Theodora became a luminous star.

From the day that this beautiful spiritual child received the Message we loved one another with a love that surpassed all earthly attachments and lifted us both into the realm of God. When we met it was perfect joy, sweetness, and harmony – and thro' the years this bond has never been clouded or broken. This love became the nucleus of the Cause in Paris – for as each beloved soul entered the light this love enveloped them until all of our little group of believers found shelter, strength, and life in this wonderful all-encompassing love of God.

We were like children in the Truth – we lived in it – thought of it by day – dreamed of it by night, and loved it with an intensity that really belongs to little children.

When we met we were so happy, so joyous – our hearts seemed to rush together – our faces shone – we smiled and laughed – and beneath it all was a deep tremor of such love for the Master – such adoration of Bahá'u'lláh – such profound earnestness & devotion that I thrill and tremble as I write of it. This atmosphere of love was the very breath of our existence and we almost unconsciously guarded it jealously. If one of the believers became disturbed or displeased we exerted our utmost endeavour to dispel the shadow, and as I look back to those most wonderful & blessed years, I realize that we sacrificed everything to this end – no sacrifice of our personal wishes, feelings, habits or opinions was too great to make to enable us to live and to breathe only in that atmosphere of love – and the love was so real, so great, so immense that we acted spontaneously, without hesitation or thought – again like little children! Oh! we had found the priceless treasure – we had tasted the divine intoxicating sweetness of perfect love – that love flowed to us in a pure living stream from the heart of 'Abdu'l-Bahá and the world was forgotten – existence had passed away and we lived! For truly the love of God is Eternal Life. Our egos were laid on the altar of sacrifice in order to maintain this burning fire of love.

Those were the early days of the Cause, and we had so few Utterances and Tablets translated – but we lived on these – they were our food, our life – and at the meetings we read them over, gaining ever deeper insight and understanding of their unfathomable meanings and significances. A Tablet from Acca was like a new Springtime in our midst – quickening and strengthening us with our ever-unfolding spiritual life . . .

Laura Barney also met May during this time, and was attracted to the teachings of Bahá'u'lláh through her. She was a highly intelligent person who was to distinguish herself in later years through her activities in promoting the League of Nations, becoming a *chevalier* and then *officier* of the French Légion d'Honneur for her services to France during World War I. Laura came from a wealthy Washington family. She was high-minded and magnanimous and not only financed the visit of

Mírzá Abu'l-Faḍl to the United States after his sojourn in Paris but also helped, together with Mrs Jackson, in the building of the House of the Master in Haifa.[7] Her mother was a well-known artist and her sister, Natalie, acquired notoriety in Parisian circles, but the reason Laura will always be remembered is for the book *Some Answered Questions*, which consists of the 'table-talks' she had with 'Abdu'l-Bahá over the course of 1904–06. In praising this unique compilation, May later recalled Laura as 'a girl so gifted and brilliant that her name is imperishably recorded in the early annals of the Faith'. She subsequently assisted her husband, the distinguished Orientalist Hippolyte Dreyfus, whose story is summarized in the following pages, in the translation of this work into French, entitled *Les Leçons de Saint Jean d'Acre*.

Another person who became a Bahá'í during this remarkable period in Paris, and who would remain one of May's closest friends for decades to come, was Juliet Thompson. This talented young American painter had been generously invited by Alice Pike Barney, Laura's mother, to come and study art in Paris at the turn of the century. While living in the artists' colony in Montmartre, she met Lua, and then May, and through the latter became a devoted disciple of the Master. She went on pilgrimage on several occasions, once in 1909 and again in 1926, through May's generosity, and she later earned the privilege of painting a portrait of 'Abdu'l-Bahá. Her Diary, one of the few spontaneous records of that time, was to immortalize the days passed in the Master's company during His historic visit to the West.

Marion Jack, who embraced the Faith in 1900, was also one of May's spiritual children and always referred to May as her 'spiritual mother'. Like many who associated with the Bolles at this time and one of the handful of Canadians introduced into their household, she too was an artist, was often in the company of the foreign students at the Beaux-Arts and frequented the artistic community in Paris. She was an imposing woman and was called 'General Jack' by 'Abdu'l-Bahá during her first pilgrimage. After serving the Cause in both Canada and Alaska, she lived up gloriously to the name given to her by the Master by staying at her pioneering post in Bulgaria until her death. She received great accolades from Shoghi Effendi for her courage in remaining staunch and firm, despite poverty and destitution, through the bombardments of World War II.

---

7   This loan was paid back in full by 'Abdu'l-Bahá when the construction work was complete.

There were a few, however, who did not stay so firm. It was during these same heady days in Paris that May was able to teach the Faith to Mason Remey.[8] She herself recorded this event with characteristic verve:

We had just moved to 100 rue du Bac to be nearer to the École des Beaux-Arts where my Brother was completing his studies as an architect; the packing cases were still unopened, some of the necessary furniture had been set in place, when, one afternoon . . . Charles Mason Remey called. My Mother was alone but she received him with her habitual cordial informality & excused the appearance of the apartment. Mason . . . offered to help, and while they straightened things out a bit, he became confidential. In my mother he found a sympathetic listener, as he told of the great change that had taken place in his inner life during the past few years. He was the eldest son of Admiral Remey – of a fine old family in Washington D.C. and his brilliant social and cultured life had produced a man of rare charm and distinction. As the Master once wrote of him: 'no more distinguished person could be imagined'. But of late, he told my mother, society had palled upon him, he felt an inner unrest & longing, a constant search for something just beyond his grasp – a deep stirring of his heart & soul.

My mother suggested that he needed love and companionship, perhaps to marry. 'This is not it,' he replied, 'there is something far deeper that I long for & cannot find.'

With her delightful humanness and humour my mother told him to see her daughter – 'she is just what you need. She has been thro [sic] all that and is like a new being since she found some new strange Religion!'

He came the very next day and I never met a more thirsty soul. He could hardly wait from day to day for me to tell him all the little I know.

According to Mason's memoirs,[9] when he first came round to 100 rue du Bac, Mrs Bolles had told him that she could give him no information,

---

8   Mason Remey, like W. S. Maxwell, was studying architecture at the École des Beaux-Arts and became a Bahá'í on New Year's Eve 1899/1900. Unfortunately, having embraced the Cause in the days of 'Abdu'l-Bahá and having served Shoghi Effendi with diligence all through his life, he failed the test of faith after the Guardian's passing.

9   Remey, *Reminiscences and Letters*, quoted in Hogenson, *Lighting the Western Sky*, p. 180.

'as practically no information had been given her'. If no information had been given to her, it may also have been because she did not ask for it, for May was longing for her mother and her brother to inquire about the Faith. Some months after her Mediterranean cruise, she wrote to Julia Pearson, saying: 'I would be so glad to know how you found your family, if your Brothers find you greatly changed, and if their hearts seem drawn to the Truth or if you must endure the long waiting for your dear ones that is my lot.'[10] She counselled herself to patience and waited, however, for if they did not ask, she knew it was because they were unready for it.

But May was not idle as she waited. There were many other people who were asking her to tell them more about the Bahá'í Faith at this time. One of them was Herbert Hopper, another young architect at the École des Beaux-Arts, who graduated at the same time as her brother Randolph. A second was Sydney Sprague, who later travelled with Herbert to Iran and married an Iranian woman. A third was 'the lovely and gifted Marie Squires' who became a Bahá'í in Paris and later married Herbert in America. Finally there was a member of May's own family:

> It was that year also that my cousin Helen Cole came to Paris, a widow in deep mourning for her husband, and received the same advice from my dear mother as she had given to Mr. Remey, to go to her daughter who, through some new religion she had found, possessed a transforming power in people's lives. Helen Cole was so stirred by the message that she made the pilgrimage to Acca, and on her return she told us that one day the Master had said to her: 'Do you know how you came to me? It is your husband who led you to me.' Astonished, my cousin asked 'Abdu'l-Bahá how this was possible since her husband was dead and had never heard of 'Abdu'l-Bahá. He looked at her wistfully and said: 'In what world do you think 'Abdu'l-Bahá is manifest? Verily He is visible and manifest in all the Worlds of God.'

Not all these souls remained firm in the Covenant. Sydney Sprague, like Mason, was one of those who 'haunted' the home of Mrs Bolles,

---

10 Letter from May Bolles to Julia Pearson, 1 August (1899?), Maxwell papers, United States Bahá'í National Archives. Quoted in Hogenson, *Lighting the Western Sky*, p. 170.

drawn irresistibly like a moth to the light, held captive by the power of love, only to fall away in later years. May never forgot such people. In a handwritten note found among her papers many years later, she averred: 'In the history of the early days of the Faith in France (Paris), we <u>should</u> mention those who, like Sydney Sprague, have rendered service even altho they have later been unfaithful.' During those days, as May herself attested, it was a time when there were no veils, no impediments between such souls and the Cause:

> No need in those wondrous days when the living Presence of the Covenant was on earth, for long laborious teaching, weeks of effort, questions and discussions, for in that wondrous Springtime the like of which the world has never witnessed, the spirit of God was all surrounding, the penetration of the Word in the pure receptive hearts was instantaneous, and the souls passed from the darkness of the world of nature into the world of light, from sleep to awakening, from death to life in one breath, one flash.

The last to deserve mention here among those who passed 'in one breath, one flash' from doubt to faith during the Heroic Age in Paris, was Agnes B. Alexander. She opened Japan and the Pacific to the Faith while 'Abdu'l-Bahá was still living and was later appointed a Hand of the Cause of God by Shoghi Effendi. Years afterwards she herself described how she recognized the truth of the Cause through May:[11]

> In Rome, Italy, the Light of the New Day was revealed to me on November 26th, 1900. After that day I was alone for three months with but one Bahá'í prayer. Turning to God for knowledge, day by day the Bible prophecies of this Day unfolded to me, until at last I felt I must know others who believe. Looking at some addresses which had been given me in Rome, on November 26th, I found the nearest believer was Miss May Ellis Bolles, rue du Bac, Paris. From the depths of my longing heart I wrote, asking if she could tell me more of this wonderful Message. The heavenly letter which came in reply was so permeated with divine love that my heart was filled with assurance. For nearly nineteen years I kept the letter with my most sacred treasures, until in a fire it was consumed. The words

---

11 Alexander, 'May Maxwell – A Tribute', pp. 1–2.

it contained, though, were forever burned in my heart. She wrote me that two years before she had the great bounty of making the pilgrimage to 'Akká with the first group of American pilgrims, she had twice seen the Master in visions, and when she met Him, she recognized her Lord. In the letter she enclosed some prayers and wrote, 'Learn them by heart and say them two or three times daily, then we grow with great power and spiritually for these prayers are from God.' She bid me come to my brothers and sisters in Paris and there receive the full Revelation. With her mother and brother, whose spiritual eyes were not opened to the glorious Message, she was living then in Paris.

In the spring of 1901, I reached Paris. The first meeting there with beloved May is one of the most precious memories of my life. She was then very slender and seemed to me like an angel of light. She gave me some pressed violets which had been given her by the Master in 'Akká, and a photograph of our Lord taken when he was a young man in Adrianople. The feelings which came over me as I gazed on the photograph cannot be described. From that day May became my spiritual mother, and through all the years her tender love has been a guiding star in my life . . . From the purifying fire of tests and temptations she emerged, as 'Abdu'l-Bahá wrote, 'pure in heart and attracted in soul'.

May's own note about Agnes's arrival in Paris adds a spark of humour to the proceedings which does not in the slightest diminish their exquisite spirituality:

On the day that she arrived at our home in Paris I was out, and with an overflowing heart she greeted my Mother as her 'beloved sister'! My Mother, who had a keen sense of humour and was not at that time a Bahai . . . checked Agnes in her affectionate greeting, saying – 'Reserve all this for my daughter, it is she you are seeking!'

Never shall I forget our meeting – this lovely fair girl, with dove-like eyes, her soul burning with love and longing – and the hours and days all thro that Spring that we studied together the divine teachings – so few – so precious – from which we extracted every drop of the elixir of life. Her purity – her faith – her selfless simplicity which only deepened thro the years have been the foundation of her far flung pioneer work in Hawaii & Japan.

Nineteen years to the day after she accepted the Cause, Agnes Alex-ander received a Tablet from 'Abdu'l-Bahá, written on 26 November 1919 when she was in Tokyo. In it the Master explicitly identified May Maxwell as the source of her faith and the well-spring of her continued inspiration. By one of those strange coincidences to which May was so finely attuned throughout her life, she herself was writing a letter to 'the Beloved spiritual children of Agnes' in Japan from her Mon-treal home on that very same day. The Tablet of 'Abdu'l-Bahá sealed the bond between them:

> *Thou hast undoubtedly met the attracted maidservant of God, Mrs. Maxwell, before sailing to Japan, for that maidservant of God is ablaze with the fire of the love of God. Whosoever meets her feels from her association the susceptibilities of the Kingdom. Her company uplifts and develops the soul.*[12]

The seeds that were sown by May in French soil during this period were to take root all over the world. They were to cause the Faith to germinate in the hearts of many and were destined to raise Bahá'í communities all over the planet. Even if the faith of some withered, the ardour of others grew and was to shed lustre on generations. Some stayed in France, like Hippolyte and Laura Dreyfus-Barney, like Edith Sanderson too, in whose home, as in Mrs Jackson's as well as Mrs Bolles', many of those early Bahá'í gatherings were held. Others travelled across the world to settle in far-off countries, like Agnes Alexander and Marion Jack. But whether they died before her like Thomas Breakwell[13] and Lua, or lived long after she had passed away like Juliet Thompson, May remained a mother and sister to them forever, a true friend of the spirit all their lives. She nurtured these early believers and was a guardian and a guide to them, as the Master instructed. She also tried to keep in touch with the seekers who had accompanied her to 'Akká. Writing to Helen Hillyer on 18 July 1899, for example, she asked for her news and gener-ously shared her own. She did all she could to strengthen the bonds of unity and faith between souls:

---

12 *Star of the West*, vol. 10, no. 13 (4 November 1919), p. 247.
13 See pp. 146–9, 162–6 below.

My Dear Helen,

Your letter has just come, and no doubt the precious little box will come today. How happy it makes me, and will make my friend . . . And Mrs. Cropper also writes me that she has a letter for me from Acca, which she is forwarding, so my cup is full! A few days ago, I had a long letter from Anne, and she has begun to teach the Truth, and her heart is bursting with happiness.

Is it not beautiful, dear, and what a joy for dear Mrs. Hearst – she has no doubt written you. You do not say anything about your work, so I suppose you are just going about it in your quiet determined way, and by and by you will surprise us all, and be able to tell us some of those many things that we all long to know. I know that you will not get discouraged, for we know that the way of the Truth is long and difficult, whichever path we choose, but it is so radiant! I find it a hard struggle against all the selfishness that is in me, and the persistent <u>will</u> that wants to go its own way, instead of laying itself down daily at the Feet of Him Who alone has Wisdom and Knowledge, and who is sufficient for <u>everything</u>. I hope you are well and happy my dear sister – and I should be so glad if you would write to me sometimes. I am your loving friend and sister in the Cause of God, in Whose Blessed Name I greet you,

<u>Allahu Abha!</u>

Her spiritual mother, Lua, had first exemplified this art. Writing to her from the Holy Land in March 1901, Lua praised the new Bahá'ís to whom May had taught the Faith:

How happy I am to have met and made this visit with so many of your dear pupils. They are all an honor and glory to their 'Heavenly' Teacher, and she – thank God – is a star in my crown – Oh my own dear, little Violet – I praise God and thank Him that through you so many have been guided into the Kingdom, may your light continue to shine brighter and brighter and each day may your soul become more and [more] illumined by the Beauty of our God and the incomparable Perfection of our dear Lord and Master (rouhi fedah) . . . Oh may God bless all of you dear people in Paris who have turned your faces unto Him – and bestow upon you His greatest and choicest blessings.

But the principal reason why May's work in France was blessed lay in its foundation of unity. The American Bahá'ís who had heard of the Faith through Kheiralla were severely tested when the first group of pilgrims returned to the United States. Instead of being galvanized to spread the Word of God, they found themselves divided into two camps. There were those who supported Kheiralla and those who realized that their trust may have been abused by the ambitions of this man. What was the truth about 'Abdu'l-Bahá? Was He really, as their teacher had told them, the return of Christ? Was this actually an example of reincarnation? Or was He just another guru and wise man from the East? Was Kheiralla the head of the Bahá'í Faith in the West, or not? Who was right and who was wrong? From the middle of 1899 and for the next few years, there was a rift in the American community and considerable muddle about the meaning of the Bahá'í Faith. It was only in early 1900 when one of the Bahá'ís in Egypt, Anton Haddad,[14] was able to publish a little pamphlet entitled *Message from Acca,* recording his conversations with 'Abdu'l-Bahá, that the salient features of the Cause were clarified. A thousand souls had embraced the teachings through Kheiralla by then, but more than half of them fell away in the course of 1901 as a result of disillusionment. Only a handful remained loyal to him in the end but the friction he created and the tension he aroused was writ large across the United States, from Kenosha to Chicago, from California to New York.

This state of affairs was in stark contrast to the atmosphere in the Paris Bahá'í community. May generated a glow of love, a bond of unity, and a deep and sincere harmony around her wherever she was. The early Bahá'ís to whom she taught the Faith in France were characterized by a spirit of oneness which brought great joy to the heart of 'Abdu'l-Bahá. When the Getsingers passed through Europe after their pilgrimage, a photograph was taken of some of those early believers which would later inspire the Master to address a beautiful Tablet to them.[15] They were all young and they were all women and that picture symbolized their spiritual fellowship and true unity. It also exemplified

---

14 Anton Haddad had become a Bahá'í soon after Kheiralla, and had encouraged him to come to the United States, but unlike his friend, Haddad had become a deepened Bahá'í after his meeting with the Master. See Hogenson, *Lighting the Western Sky,* Chapters 12 and 13, for a fuller account.

15 Edward Getsinger may have been the photographer of the portrait of the 'Five Leaves' as there is one version with him included. See p. 177 below for 'Abdu'l-Bahá's Tablet to the Five Leaves.

the difference between the Paris group and the American Bahá'ís who had become so sadly divided in their loyalties at that time.

By refusing to be pulled into the controversy, Lua and Edward Getsinger were able to diffuse much of the poison in the American Bahá'í community. Even before her return to the States, Lua had alerted May to the importance of including Kheiralla in her circle of love when he passed through Paris en route back home:

> We must all show only kindness to Dr. K. and try by constant example to show him the better way in all things. If you see them in Paris please be kind, for the cause's sake and because our Master loves him, and desires that we all should.

And May did everything to comply. She was the essence of love, the distillation of compassion. Her magnetism directed all who met her towards the Cause. A note from one of the early believers[16] bears witness to her impact on others:

> I first heard of the Bahá'í Cause a little before 1900, while I was in school in Paris. There I met a small group of people, a few American students, like myself, who seemed to be involved in a new religion stemming from Persia. I can't say that I was especially impressed by what they said. Rather I was attracted by these people as unusual people – one in particular, a very beautiful girl who seemed to radiate a special magnetic charm. I was completely captivated by her and not understanding what she was saying, I just silently sat in wonder, somehow feeling her special station. Her name was May Bolles . . .

Among the Maxwell papers is a fragile pencilled record of some of these early believers. Although the list is not exhaustive, May apparently noted the names and times when these souls declared their faith to 'Abdu'l-Bahá in those very first months. Years later at Shoghi Effendi's request, she also wrote about the lives of some of the most notable Bahá'ís, a few of whom were not included in her original record:

Brenetta Herrman – Wrote letter of acceptance to Acca, January 1899 (Paris)

---

16 Berthalin Allien, 'The Luminous Hour – Remembrance of an Early Believer'.

Theodora Edith MacKaye – Wrote letter of acceptance to Acca, May
16th, 1899 (Paris)

Henry Badge Pennell – Wrote letter of acceptance to Acca, May
28th, 1899 (Paris)

Edith Cléray – Wrote letter of acceptance to Acca, May . . . 1899
(Paris)

Elfrida Hildegarde Klamroth – Wrote letter of acceptance to Acca,
July 1st, 1899 (Brittany)

Helen Ellis Cole – [Wrote] letter of acceptance to Acca, December
7th, 1899 (Paris)

Charles Mason Remey – Sent letter of acceptance to Acca, January
[1st], 1900 (Paris)

Gustave Henriclundquist – [Sent] letter [of acceptance] to Acca,
May 3rd, 1900 (Paris)

Edith Sanderson – [Sent] letter [of acceptance] to Acca, May 23rd,
1900 (Paris)

Elsa Barney[17] – [Sent] letter [of acceptance] to Acca, May 31st, 1900

Ursula Puthod – [Sent] letter [of acceptance] to Acca, June . . . 1901
(Paris)

Thomas Breakwell – [Sent] letter [of acceptance] to Acca, August
8th, 1901 (Paris)

Eleanor Myler – [Sent] letter [of acceptance] to Acca, August 9th,
1901 (Paris)

* * *

While her services as the Master's chosen disciple in the West are
inscribed on the scrolls of history, the more personal side of the story,
which touches on May's relationship with William Sutherland Maxwell,
is less well known. In her notes about the Paris period, May later
recorded what she called 'the mystic yet definite facts' of this remarkable time[18] which saw such an efflorescence of the Faith in France, but
there were other facts, rather less 'mystic', which also deserve recording.
The spiritual quest she had embarked upon in her youth culminated in
a maiden voyage to the Holy Land in February 1899, and the love story

---

17 Laura Barney's first name was Alice; she called herself 'Elsa' in her youth to distinguish
herself from her mother Alice Pike Barney.

18 This reference was specific to the summer when Thomas Breakwell became a Bahá'í.

between herself and the young man she called Sutherland began early in the following year. It was a love affair destined to last a lifetime.

Although young Mr Maxwell showed no interest in religion, Miss Bolles could not remain impervious to his attentions forever. Soon after the New Year and the start of the new century, there was a turning point in their relationship, because of Randolph. May's brother, who may not have been as rigorous as he ought in keeping up with his assignments at the École des Beaux-Arts, must have asked his Canadian friend to help him meet his deadlines for the mid-term tests that February 1900. If he dubbed him '*nègre*'[19] in later years, it was precisely because Sutherland had done his work for him at this time. Indeed, Randolph might have failed his diploma had his friend not intervened. Perhaps Mrs Bolles was not told of the crisis, which may be why May assumed the responsibility for expressing gratitude when it was averted. Perhaps she had been told, and in lieu of thanks, an invitation was extended to Mr Maxwell to join the Bolles for a visit to the woods of Fontainebleau that spring. Whatever the circumstances, one can only imagine how eagerly Sutherland responded to May's letter to him, on 17 March 1900:

My Dear Miss Bolles

. . . I have just been reading your much appreciated letter and though I am not deserving of all the thanks that you send me, yet believe me your thanks are appreciated as the thanks of very few others are. You say 'You are my brother's friend, perhaps you will be mine.' In as much as I am your brother's friend, I sincerely hope to merit your friendship and keep it for all times. My stay at Fontainebleau I shall always look back upon as the brightest spot that has yet appeared in my existence in France; that other such spots may appear in the future I sincerely hope . . .

I hope to be at the Atelier tomorrow and I shall enquire of Randolph as to your well-being. When you are well I feel cheerful, when you are unwell, I feel sad and in your suffering believe me to be always your sincere and sympathetic friend.

I trust to hear from you soon and I hope to see you soon, in the meantime believe me to be

Yours Sincerely
W. S. Maxwell

19 slave or 'ghost' as in ghostwriter.

May's heart – that most susceptible instrument – was soon in a flutter. It was true that Mr Maxwell had merely offered her his 'regard' on first acquaintance, in the usual manner of polite young men. But over the next few weeks, his conventional expression of respect seemed to be swelling into a 'friendship' which she feared was beginning to acquire a capital F. His 'sympathies', too, were assuming alarming dimensions, and the 'care' he expressed for her during their walk in the woods was now being qualified as the 'fondest'. She began to suspect from his demeanour, that if young Mr Maxwell had been so very diligent in helping Randolph meet his deadlines that winter, it might possibly, at least in part, have been for her sake.

May was determined to put the friendship on a proper footing. Perhaps as a result of past experiences, she could not bear relations that were not founded on spiritual understanding too. After the Fontainebleau visit, she tried to draw young Mr Maxwell out; she tried to go beyond superficialities and know him better.

What May really wanted was for Sutherland to recognize the validity of Bahá'u'lláh's Message and to see 'Abdu'l-Bahá as she did. The few 'courtship letters' which follow are only a sample conveying her ardour in bringing him close to the Cause and Sutherland's influence in having a moderating effect upon May.

* * *

The following note written from 83 Boulevard Montparnasse on a Friday evening may be regarded as Sutherland's first 'love letter' to May:

> My Dear Miss Bolles,
>
> I have just arrived home and I will now start that which I never finished, or showed to you – namely a letter. Now, to settle the above enigma. The other night upon arriving home, I started a letter to you, I had nothing particular to say but I found it such a natural thing to do; for you always leave such pleasant impressions and thoughts with me after having been in your presence for an evening.
>
> Tonight passed so pleasantly and I so thoroughly enjoyed our little talk. That you now know me in a deeper manner after our interesting little cross-examination and that you find me not any the less interesting affords me the keenest pleasure . . .

This may reach you before we deposit your brother's renderings in the 'Charette' and in case it does I bid you cheer up for the worst is yet to come; and in any case Randolph and Sutherland have had much valuable experience in doing the 'Salle de Concert'. Somehow I now think of Fontainebleau and its treasures, and it is a source of satisfaction to me to think that one of them is now in Paris and that I may have the pleasure of seeing that treasure ere the sun sets tomorrow evening.

As ever Your Sincere Friend

W. S. Maxwell

The sincerity with which young Mr Maxwell signed off this note became the hallmark of all the others he exchanged with Miss Bolles over the next two years. There is no precise record in the course of their courtship of when acquaintance turned to friendship or how friendship turned to love, but these progressive stages can be gauged by the manner in which Sutherland addressed May. From the winter of 1899 until the spring of the following year, the two young people appear to have remained on fairly formal terms and were possibly not even corresponding. Indeed, Mr Maxwell was using the appellation 'My Dear Miss Bolles' right up to 17 March 1900. But the transformation was rapid after that. By 17 April 1900, just after Easter Sunday, all formalities had dissolved. Within days Sutherland had graduated from 'Miss Bolles' to the warmer fellowship of 'Dear May', and by the end of the month he was signing off as her 'Sincere Friend' and referring to her as his 'Sweetest Friend'. During his Italian tour in September of that same year, she signed all her letters to him as 'Penelope', but by the time he left for Montreal in December 1900, she had become what she would remain for the rest of her life: his 'Dearest May'. His deployment of 'Dearie', so typical of the use of the diminutive in the Maxwell family and so prevalent in his letters sent to her from Montreal through 1902, she evidently disliked enough for him to expunge from his vocabulary entirely after their marriage.

One of the most touching aspects of these courtship letters is the gratitude evinced by both of them to each other. Sutherland often wrote to May simply to thank her:

Tonight was so beautiful, you were so sweet and kind Dear, each moment seemed a second, each second was a precious jewel, my sole regret was that Time is such a hasty creature.

Once, when she was away in the country, Sutherland thanked her for being alive:

How happy I am that I have been allowed to spend such months – may it be years – of my life, in Paris. What a terrible loss it would have been to me had I been denied the happiness of knowing you Dear. What an unfinished affair my life would have been without your friendship . . .

May frequently thanked Sutherland in the same vein.

* * *

The hour when Sutherland usually came to see May in the Spring of 1900 was 1:30 p.m., when she was sitting for her portrait. Pierre-Emile Cornillier was the artist, who would later make a name for himself as the 'painter of the soul'. She went to these sessions reluctantly at first, until they became a chance to meet her beloved.

Since there were always duties to perform, obligations to fulfil, Sutherland's work at the Atelier and May's Bahá'í activities, these sittings soon became sacrosanct for the young couple; they became a rare opportunity for them to walk together and talk afterwards in a nearby park. In fact during the spring of 1900, Sutherland's day revolved around the time he could hurry over to see May. How eagerly he must have admired her as M. Cornillier daubed the oils on her face![20]

I am coming to see you tomorrow Dear. I will be there at about one thirty – or – a few minutes earlier. I will find you fairly well, and how you will hate to pose. However there's a good time coming and we'll all take part . . . It has been such a pleasure to write you these lines . . .

---

20 Sutherland returned to Montreal with this portrait. During their subsequent separation, by his own admission, he worshipped it like an icon, although he felt that it did not do justice to the original. It appears as the frontispiece to this book.

And how ardently May must have longed to unlock Sutherland's soul in the course of these talks. A note written around this time shows that she anticipated each *rendez-vous* as an opportunity to teach her young man about the Faith.

* * *

One weekend in April 1900, when Mrs Bolles had made all the arrangements to travel up to Compiègne by train with May, with Randolph and his new friend 'Max', her daughter suddenly announced that she could not come. They had been invited to stay with old friends in their beautiful country house before the two young men went off to tour northeastern France, but May had several Bahá'í visitors[21] arriving just at the same time. She had to stay behind, she said, to host these Persian gentlemen who were passing through Paris on their way to the United States. 'Abdu'l-Karím was the first of the teachers sent by 'Abdu'l-Bahá, to help remove the misunderstandings caused by the spurious claims of Dr Kheiralla. The great Bahá'í scholar Mírzá Abu'l-Faḍl, who arrived in Paris one year later, would be the last. As it turned out, both visits occurred at equally awkward times as far as Mrs Bolles was concerned.

She was indignant when she heard May's announcement. It was really very inconvenient of all these Persians to arrive just over the Easter break. Why, their hosts in Pierrefonds were the very best sort of people and had gone out of their way to welcome them over the holiday. And besides, it was the only time that Randolph and 'Max' were free from work at the Atelier. Couldn't this Abdul fellow do what he had to do in Paris without May? She was going to spoil the family outing!

Sutherland, too, heard the news with dismay. He had been so looking forward to May's company in Pierrefonds. The weekend trip was to be the first leg of his bicycle tour with Randolph during their Easter break. The two friends were going to explore Picardie and cycle through Champagne and Lorraine before returning to Paris. If May did not come to Compiègne, he would not see her for more than a week.

Time was a factor of considerable importance to William Sutherland Maxwell in the year 1900. He did not have enough of it. Since his

---

21 'Abdu'l-Karím-i-Ṭihrání, Dr Sadri Raffi and another Persian translator. 'Abdu'l-Karím had taught the Faith to Ibrahim Kheiralla in Egypt and believed that he could heal the rifts that had afflicted the American community as a result of Kheiralla's public defection after his return from 'Akká the previous year.

arrival the previous autumn he had spent much of his time absorbing the Art Nouveau designs in vogue in the French capital. A composition which he made at this time – entitled 'Proposed Salle des Fêtes' – was later described by John Bland, Professor Emeritus of Architecture at McGill University, as 'exquisitely rendered . . . Its opulent sumptuousness is of a character almost unimagined outside France, indicating that it may have been prepared as some sort of qualifying submission'.[22] One of Pascal's students recalled that the style of architecture encouraged at the Atelier Pascal, which was associated with the École des Beaux-Arts in Paris, 'was and looked distinguished',[23] for the architect in this establishment was considered first and foremost an artist. There is no doubt that Sutherland's exquisite plans and his love of drawing made him ideally suited for this method of training.

He had spent some of his time visiting England and Scotland the previous summer and had used some of it to see the Universal Exposition earlier that spring. He was going to spend the rest in the exquisite buildings of the Petit Palais and the Grand Palais when he came back to Paris at the end of the month. Only a few months now remained for him to travel around the Continent before he would be obliged to return to Montreal. He could not forgo the chance of seeing with his own eyes the historic buildings he had only read about in architectural books and could not return to Canada without touring Italy. So he was beginning to anticipate, with certain dread, his last months in France. The trip to Compiègne was the beginning of the end.

He swallowed his disappointment when May explained her reasons. She would try to join the family later in Pierrefonds, but she had responsibilities for this weekend, she told him gravely, and could not come to Compiègne. She had a special mandate from her Master. It was a time of great upheaval among the Bahá'ís of America and there were going to be daily meetings for the little group in Paris too, which would be very important for the unity of the friends. 'Abdu'l-Karím was going to teach the Bahá'ís to distinguish between weeds and the true flowers of faith.

The day before the Bolles party left for the country, May received a

---

22 (1) Maxwell Architectural Archive, McGill University, W. S. Maxwell biography by John Bland; for a reproduction see Pepall, *Construction d'un musée Beaux-Arts*, p. 89; (2) *The Canadian Architect & Builder* (June 1901) and (3) *The Architecture of Edward & W. S. Maxwell*, p. 57.

23 Quoted by Nancy Yates, 'The Artistic Achievements of William Sutherland Maxwell', in Appendix II.

sweet spray of *muguet* from Sutherland, a delicate bouquet to mark the season and his sincere esteem.[24] Lilies of the valley were her favourite. She asked him to buy himself some violets in return, in remembrance of her. It was during their period of spring showers and momentary bursts of sun when he answered on a 'Thursday morning':

> I certainly like the dainty little blossom with its delicate firmness equally as much as you do – and now that I dwell on the subject of flowers I must hie me off and get that bunch of violets which awaits me. Today I expect that the remnant of our party will pay Compiègne a visit! Your presence will be very much missed but I am sure that you will do yourself so much good by seeing Abdul etc. that we will be compensated by the thought that you are happy. That you will take care of yourself goes without saying. I find that I do things best when I am trusted with a responsibility, and I feel that you are somewhat of a similar mind. Your absence will be much felt by all, but as I am a firm believer that you will come back to us filled with the pleasure that your seeing Abdul will give you, and the anticipation of seeing us all, I can only say, 'Au Revoir' and a speedy return to those who care for you so sincerely. Your sincerest of Friends,
>
> Sutherland

Mrs Bolles had begun to fret, as she did every year, about moving to the seaside to escape the excessive heat in the capital. She was in the habit of subletting her Paris apartment to American visitors each summer and hiring a house on the Brittany coast for her family and their friends. Everything depended on how many people she had to cater for. If she only had to worry about the children and herself, maybe they could stay in one of the villas or hotels in the fashionable seaside resort of Dinard. But it had become so frightfully expensive, this 'French Brighton' of the late 19th century, that if more young people were going to join them that summer, maybe she should rent a cheaper place – in Dinan, perhaps, or in St Enogat-Dinard – so they could come and go to the beach. Her plans were all up in the air.

'Your Mother is in the middle of her troubles,' Sutherland wrote to

---

24 Years later when her mother died, Rúḥíyyih Khánum begged that a bouquet of lilies of the valley be placed upon her coffin; it was not possible to find any 'muguet' in Argentina at that time. This flower, associated with 1 May in France, remained the symbol of Sutherland's love from the time he offered May that first spray.

May, 'deciding what to do and where to go this summer.' But May's attentions were still taken up with 'Abdu'l-Karím and she did not want to become involved in her mother's troubles. Randolph may have urged her to invite 'Max' to join them that summer; his cousin Frank was coming over and it would be fun if his friend came too. But May would not commit herself. She was busy with her Bahá'í work.

Sutherland must have felt very low as the Bolles prepared to leave 100 rue du Bac for the seaside. The apartment was in an uproar. The place had to be vacated and made ready to sublet. And although, to the great relief of Mrs Bolles, the Persian visitors finally left, her nephew Frank Irwin arrived from the States at the same time and May, who had a propensity for charity cases, decided it was just the moment to look after a sick friend. She simply had to be alone for a few days, she told her mother. Miss Hysler needed a rest as much as she did and it was imperative to escape from Monsieur Henri's attentions. As her cousin, Frank, later told Rúḥíyyih Khánum,[25] 'it would become absolutely necessary at times for her to get away from people'. And so in the middle of all the packing, in the late spring of 1900, May went off to the countryside for ten days with her ailing friend, Miss Hysler.

But Sutherland had finally been invited to join the family in Brittany that August!

* * *

May took her four years' seniority very seriously. She saw herself as Sutherland's mentor when it came to the spiritual nature of love:

> I thank God always for you dear . . . That is one reason why my heart longs to share The Truth with you, not alone because it is the dearest and highest & best to which man can attain, but because then I shall feel indissolubly united with you, in a bond that no time, space nor any conditions of our lives can alter in the least . . .

Sutherland was more than happy for May to hold his spiritual keys. He also offered her the garden of his heart to pluck and plant in as zealously as she pleased:

---

25 Frank Irwin to Rúḥíyyih Khánum, 2 August 1940.

. . . if you should find a weed in my unpretentious garden I pray you to pluck it. You have already plucked many and I am plucking as I am becoming able to distinguish the weeds from the true flowers of life. Your garden of Love contains so few weeds of selfishness, and so many flowers of life, beauty, and loving kindness to others, you must plant these seeds in mine . . .

Sutherland was inclined to be a believer in Cupid at that time, rather than in any other sort of god; he was a devotee of art rather than religion. But he was ready to forswear all, for May's sake.

Who can blame her for being muddled? It was hard for her to be in love and teach her young man about the Truth, to abide by the will of God and the will of her beloved, particularly since Sutherland insisted on putting her will before the will of God! May drifted about the streets of Paris too, thinking of him everywhere she went.

The petals of that opening flower taught May many things about herself. Although Sutherland did not immediately accept the Bahá'í teachings at that time, she soon found that despite her seniority she was the one who was learning from him. Sutherland was teaching her about the Faith she loved so much:

. . . Sutherland, my love for you has brought me nearer to God than all the books I ever read, all the teachings I ever studied – for His law is love – it is the light of this world and the gateway to His Eternal Kingdom.

He was actually showing her how to put the Bahá'í teachings into practice. She wrote:

How love opens the doors of our souls wide – wide – so that we feel in harmony with all the deep sweet music of life – we feel united with every creature – like so many drops in one great sea!

Their love was drawing them towards the same end by different means.

Dearest, the reason that your love and mine is so wonderful, so beautiful, so blest is because it springs from the love of God. The more we love one another – the more deeply – ardently, unselfishly, tenderly – the more we are drawing near to God – the Beautiful, the Wonderful, the Beloved of my heart, and the goal of the worlds.

* * *

Sutherland had shipped his bicycle to Paris from Montreal, together with his certificate of membership in the Cyclists' Touring Club,[26] and when he first travelled in Randolph's company and then with his student friends that summer, it was on his own wheels. He fired off postcards to his beloved from all over France – first from Soissons, from Laon and from Rheims during the month of April, and later from Tours, from Blois, from Chartres, and from the Valley of the Loire, in June. He wrote letters which were a record of his heart's journey as well as a witness of the scenes he passed. They were like paintings in a gallery, like glowing photographs on a wall. He described not only the architecture and the monuments he saw, but also the people, the village squares and roadside cafés, the children playing in the street, a cascade of flowers tumbling down against a ruined house. The whole of France fell at the feet of May in rich profusion from her lover's pen. The letters he wrote to her during his tours of France and Italy are a living mirror reflecting his artistic nature. In his observations of human lives one can see all that he saw.

From Soissons he wrote:

> Randolph then retired to his room for his usual and this time extremely necessary repose, and I took my little walk . . . [A]s I passed and repassed the cathedral, with its three portals, so grand and exquisite in proportion, with their simple mass as yet una-dorned with sculpture, I thought of some master's hand arrested in its inspired efforts . . . the setting sun caressing these quiet, warm-toned walls, the infinite variety of beautiful colours, Time's gentlest touches . . . emphasized by nature's beautiful sun.

After leaving Soissons, Sutherland passed through Rheims and wrote to May again:

---

26 It is in the form of a 'token' in a small red leather case, with 'No. 60062, W. S. Maxwell, 10 Rue de Rouse, Paris' written on it, signed by 'Ernest R. Shipton, Secretary'. Printed on the back is the trademark emblem and in large letters: 1899.

When we landed opposite to the cathedral I noticed an equestrian statue of Jeanne d'Arc, at a distance. I was not so especially impressed because the lofty grandeur of the cathedral façade seemed to dwarf the figure and horse, both of which were about life size, but upon closer inspection I became aware that I was in the presence of a great work . . . The focus of interest was to me undoubtedly the face of the girl, the expression was so sweet and religiously inspired, the poise so calm and trustful that I shall always remember it; and upon looking I was strangely reminded of you dear, there was something in the form of the face and the expression of her trustful countenance that made me feel that you were not so far away after all.

He could not have dreamed, at that time, that 'Abdu'l-Bahá would one day tell May that she was the reincarnation of the spirit of Joan of Arc for this age.[27] But there was something prophetic in many of his letters written to her on this journey. In another, sent from Blois, on the second lap of his tour, he depicts a classic family portrait:

. . . seated upon a chair is the husband, seated by his side is his better half – upon her knee is a little girl, she is leaning away back and her face is wreathed in smiles, her position looks perilous but she in her unconscious faith does not feel it so, for does not the faithful and loving arm of her mother support her? The husband is playing and mimicking the child; the mother is looking with a look of maternal love at . . . 'her cherished one'. The whole atmosphere is permeated with cheerful happiness – and more than riches has made that happiness . . . If such could only be my lot.

* * *

Their reunion in Brittany that August must have been a happy one. Mrs Bolles had extended her hospitality to several people that summer: to her nephew Frank Irwin, and to May's Bahá'í friends, Emogene Hoagg[28] and her mother. It was, as Emogene later recalled, a very merry gathering. Mrs Bolles was the essence of generosity. She had rented

---

27 Letter from May Maxwell to Lucienne Migette, 11 February 1938.
28 Emogene first heard of the Faith in 1898 at the home of Phoebe Hearst in Pleasanton, California and went on pilgrimage in 1900.

a villa close to the beach, with plenty of rooms and tennis courts for the young people, and under her generous patronage and the summer sun, they basked in each other's company and partook of bathing, of shrimping, of drinking the waters at the local spa and other delights. She herself, together with Mrs Hoagg, performed the role of chaperone, for Mrs Bolles must have guessed by now that something was up between her daughter and the 'big Canadian'. She could hardly ignore the perfect deluge of postcards and letters that had arrived for May over the past weeks! And the correspondence did not stop once they were together. May's notes to Sutherland during their reunion fairly ripple with delight:

> Mama wants me to go down on the beach with her, so we all expect you to join us there as soon as you get here. I shall only wait for your coming, and if you delay I shall make an excuse & come after you!

* * *

The stark contrast between a loved one's presence and the emptiness left by his absence was acutely felt by May after Sutherland's departure for Italy in late August 1900.

If Mrs Bolles still had any doubts as to the sincerity of her daughter's feelings or the seriousness of young 'Max's', the postal service soon put these to rest. For Sutherland wrote to May all through September 1900, sending her notes from Assisi, Rome, Tivoli and Florence, as well as Venice, Pompeii, Pistoia and Perugia. He scored her name across the map of Europe.

The speed with which Sutherland was travelling, however, was becoming a matter of some concern to May. In the beginning he confessed to her that he had gone 'sixty hours without sleeping a wink' in order to reach his destination. She was appalled:

> Sutherland I want to beg of you not to travel too hard and fast – not to overdo, and tire yourself. You did too much at one stretch those first 2 days dear – please do not, any more . . .

Sutherland saw with an artist's eye and captured the essence of every scene. He had scattered Monet's poppies and cornflowers for May across his letters from France. Now he painted Venice for her in the colours of

Turner, evoked Naples for her with the vigour and force of Van Gogh, described the characters he met with the eye of Hogarth, and conjured tavern scenes and market places like a veritable Brueghel. And everywhere he went, in churches and piazzas, in pensions and gondolas, he discovered representatives of her countrymen whom he gleefully depicted:

Last night another American (no flags attached) heard another American (your loving S.) was in the same hotel so he immediately opened up communications, the head waiter being the intermediary – Result was – he wanted to go to Paris – I did not. He wanted to go with me – I did not object. Result here we are – He is a Baltimore man age say twenty-eight – moustache only – also some intelligence – He is an amateur student of architecture and is able to tell a gothic cap from a bottle of beer – How delighted he would be if he could look over my shoulder and read this gentle analysis – and – he sits opposite to me – We go as far as Venice together.

With a swift stroke of his pen, he rendered one caricature after another:

I am going to describe a literary man who sits next to me at the table – name – Ryan – business – newspaper work – not of an editorial kind – simply the managing of a paper. He comes from the next town to Osh-Kosh, way out in Wisconsin – He is, say thirty-seven years old – head not yet bald – He wears glasses and has a moustache of a black twist sprinkled with iron grey hairs. His chin is covered with bristles about one quarter of an inch long – and of a good old dusty colour – His eyes are grey but they are not dark, nor do they sparkle – You take a lean yellow chicken with dark feathers, pluck the bird, but do not singe it – and you have Ryan's chin . . .

In fact, chins were a recurring theme. Some days later, he met another one:

I had as a travelling companion, as far as Ferrara, a lady from California who was staying at the pension. Her presence, and it was of a kindly nature, did not permit of a continued contemplation of the superb picture I had enjoyed. Her conversational powers were of a staying character, if not of brilliant calibre – She had a kindly face and was good-hearted – Her lower teeth overlapped the upper row, thus causing the chin to vie in prominence with her happy nose. Her costume matched the face very harmoniously – She had a habit of pausing after every six words and saying, 'And, oh' etc. – then would follow details of a nature quite foreign to the subject matter. I had a pleasant journey with her, but I must confess that had I journeyed much further in her company – my nerves would certainly have suffered.

In addition to the caricatures in these wonderful letters, there is a cinematographic quality about Sutherland's descriptions. He not only sent May still photographs, but captured every living, breathing moment that he was experiencing so that she could participate in them with him. His scenes literally pulsed before her eyes. These Neapolitans he depicted – and their animals – were and still are vividly alive:

A blacksmith takes his red hot shoe out on to the pavement and then does his shoeing. Venders of fruit, lemonade, pastry, all have their little stands out in the open air . . .

The dwellings have clothes lines covered with all manner of gay garments. Donkeys as light as Puck pull loads that a large horse ought to handle. The harness on the animals is gaily bedecked with all manner of fantastic brass work – fur, tassels, etc.

Flocks of turkeys, stray hens, herds of goats, cows, and even stray pigs, are seen mixed up with the louder torrid human beings – and when the Neapolitan is enjoying himself you can hear him . . .

Side streets, that one could hardly walk down, tables, goods, animals, and a mass of human beings form a difficult barricade to pass. A stable, a junk shop, another stall, then a restaurant; tables in the street and loud-voiced people taking their humble repast of bread and wine.

A 'kid' stuck his head into the restaurant where I was eating – he may have been about six years old; he looked hungry, I gave him some bread, he hurried out for fear the waiter would accelerate his movements, the bread was half eaten ere he passed out of my sight. A minute later the same 'kid' sticks his head around the corner – I beckon to him and he comes. I give him a piece of my cheese, and his eyes sparkle – this certainly is a feast day for him.

The costumes of the people are gay in colour. Yet dirt considerably softens the effect. The men and most of the women are barefooted. Occasionally a man or boy passes, he has but a pair of bathing trunks and a ragged cotton shirt. One poor chicken is having a tough time of it scratching among the rocks; he is all alone, yet quite unconcerned. The many piles of filth serve to satisfy his pangs of hunger. A little grey donkey is hitched up to a wall, he looks for all the world like a bas relief; his motionless form seems carved out of the grey stones . . . This time the dirt, squalor and poverty are the things that we cannot avoid seeing, and when after four hours going and three returning, we find ourselves pretty tired, it is not to be wondered at.

Finally one night, as he scribbled in an open-air café, a brass band started up:

They are playing, and playing well, a selection from Verdi's 'Aida' and how stirring is the theme of the march. It makes my blood jump for it is one of my favorite pieces. The grandeur of the scene and the fascination of the colour bring to my mind visions of what I will do in the future. I feel a great force within me and I listen with wrapt [sic] attention. Presently I feel that I cannot stay there until this ends; I must leave immediately, lest my grand thoughts and inspirations do end with the music. I hasten to my little home and I cling to the music that is inspiring me – and may it never come to an end. I arrive and grab a lamp, some paper, and I start to tell you all of what has taken place; surely this was not intended for me alone . . .

Some day I hope I will be able to do some works that are worthy of the thoughts that inspire me every day of my trip in Italy – and your presence and companionship will certainly prove a motive force of incalculable strength.

May recognized the value of such letters; she knew her privilege in receiving them:

Day before yesterday I received the letter you wrote in a restaurant in Pistoja – dearest, I never dreamed that you could be able to write like that! . . . your keen and profound observation of human nature

delights me – and I smiled with tears in my eyes over your account
of the father & mother & child on the train – such a loving sympathetic touch running thru' it all – & I laughed when I read about
the young man who was so careful of his neatness – your humor and
cleverness were equal to many of those writers who delight to make
us laugh – and who often do not succeed as well as you did.

She might not be impartial, but she knew she was in the presence of a
great artist:

> . . . you see beauty so differently from most men, dear – but then
> you cannot expect me to think that there is another man on this
> earth – as far as I am concerned!

She copied prayers out for him, like a prescription – 'You will say them
often every day I know' – and when he lost them, she sent them again.[29]
She wrote him letters lyrical with trust, seeking every means to remind
him of the source of their love. She laid down the spiritual foundations
for their future in these letters:

> I want my letters to be such an inspiration to you that when you are
> far away from me they will help and strengthen you in your work –
> and put the light of real joy and gladness into every pleasure of your
> life, & this too will inspire me, and help me . . .

* * *

The time had finally come for Sutherland to pack his bags. He had
delayed the evil hour as long as he could but there was nothing for
it: he had to head off at last for London and then travel up by train
to Liverpool, where the ship was docked to take him home. Already,
ever since September, he had been receiving letters from Montreal that
indicated there was some concern in the Maxwell clan regarding his
late return. Unlike the letters he received from May, which were so
filled with warmth and love, the correspondence between the members

---

29 Sutherland touchingly admitted to the loss and himself asked for the replacement. He
wrote on 29 August from Verona: 'Will you send me another copy of that prayer, I have
mislaid my copy and I remember most imperfectly the words . . .'

of the Maxwell family was wholly understood. Writing to Edward on 10 October from Paris, for example, Sutherland announced his return from Italy in muted terms:

> I found Italy very interesting but all in all France can well hold her own. I will wander around until the financial condition makes a homeward trip necessary. Many, many thanks for your accommodating generosity. I will put it to good use.

Even his mother's affections, which he never doubted, were wholly understated. When she wrote to him during his absence in Europe, she kept tight hold of her emotions. He had to guess that she was pleased with all that he was doing and seeing because it was only after the business matters had been dealt with that she allowed herself to commend him, on 30 September 1900, on his decision to see Italy before returning:

> My Dear Willie,
>
> Just a line to tell you . . . I sent the money. I gave Eddie eighty dollars to send to Paris; he sent it to the address you gave, and Eddie sent one hundred to you to Daniels in London. You need not think I did not want to send you money. I would have sent you more, but Eddie said you had enough . . .
>
> Mrs. McKyes offered to send for a few yards of lace for me; she said if you would call on her brother-in-law he would give you the parcel . . . Mrs. McKyes said he would be pleased to see you, and he would do what he could to show you round the City . . .
>
> I expect Eddie and Libbie and Millie home Tuesday morning also Pa from New York. I am glad you took the trip through Italy. I am sure it will give you new ideas and you will see so much. We are all well, with love to you – Your Affectionate
> Mother J. Maxwell

Yes, he would see them soon enough, and could hear them already. But there was some unfinished business to attend to. He had visited all the great sites; he had seen sights even greater than he expected; he had studied and learned and lived like a prince on a pauper's allowance. Above all he had loved, and better still, found himself loved in return. But he had not had the courage to ask May to marry him.

They had been circling the subject for a while without broaching it directly. It seems that Sutherland wanted to make sure that May loved him enough before he dared to ask for her hand and May wanted to make sure that Sutherland realized the importance of the Bahá'í Faith to her, even if he was not a Bahá'í himself, before she accepted his proposal. They may not have spoken about it until it was almost time for their last farewell. Could it have been Mrs Bolles who popped the question to her daughter? Young 'Max' had been frequenting their home since that spring. They had met him almost daily through the summer. Everyone in Dinan was asking about him. Mrs Bolles was a conventional woman in this regard. Was it not time for the young man who had become such a permanent fixture in the family to make his intentions clear once and for all?

The story of Sutherland's proposal and May's response perfectly depicts the nature of the young couple's relationship. According to Rúḥíyyih Khánum, when Sutherland finally found the courage to raise the subject, he did so with such shy diffidence, such uncertainty and hesitation that after listening to him mumbling for some minutes, May finally accosted him herself.

'Sutherland, are you proposing to me?'

He was so taken aback by the question that he humbly concurred.

'In that case,' May replied, 'I accept.'

They were formally engaged on his birthday, 14 November 1900, but Mrs Bolles was not told of their age difference! May was still keeping her mother in ignorance of this little detail even two years later, as this letter to Sutherland reveals:[30]

Two years ago tomorrow we celebrated your birthday and yours and May's engagement. We were all very happy then – and we are happier now – and we will be still happier as the years go on and we learn to know each other better and love each other more. I am writing this to send you my sincerest love and to wish you many happy returns of your birthday. I don't know how old you are! but it is 32 n'est-ce-pas? Your wife says I can write no more and I am obedient. God bless you my boy and bring you happiness and peace.

Ta Belle-mère dévouée.

---

30 13 November 1902.

100 rue du Bac, Rive Gauche, Paris. May Bolles, her mother and brother, as well as May's grandmother, lived here when May heard of the Bahá'í Faith in 1898

Mary Ellis Martin Bolles in Pierrefond, France, 1900; in the forefront is Randolph's dog, Puck

Lucinda Louisa Aurora Moore Getsinger – 'Lua', the spiritual mother of May Bolles, circa 1897–9

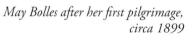

May Bolles after her first pilgrimage, circa 1899

'The Five Holy Leaves', 1899, as 'Abdu'l-Bahá called them: seated, left to right, May Bolles, Anne Apperson; centre, Lua Getsinger; back row, left to right, Julia Pearson, Brenetta Herrman. Standing in the back row, right, is Lua's husband, Edward C. Getsinger

*May Bolles with
Puck, probably 1900
or 1901*

*May Bolles at St Enogat,
France, 1900*

Randolph, Sutherland and May, 1900, in Pierrefonds, France

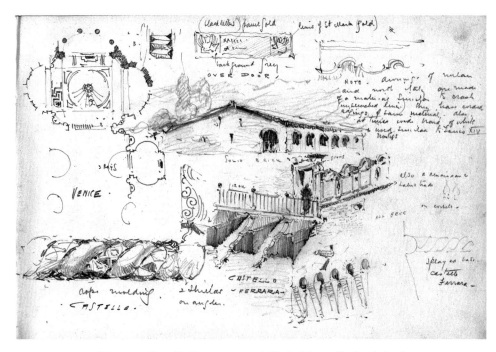

'Venice – Castello Ferrara, 1900', W. S. Maxwell, sketch book

'Versailles – 19 October 1899', W. S. Maxwell, sketch book

'Dinan – Chateau Coninais – 4 August 1900', W. S. Maxwell, sketch book

'St Malo – 6 August 1900', W. S. Maxwell, sketch book

'Milan Cathedral', 1900,
W. S. Maxwell, sketch book

'Caen – St. Sauveur. Stunning odd little
church remarkable for interesting details
here and there. 5 January 1900',
W. S. Maxwell, sketch book

His family were informed of the happy event, of course, not only by Sutherland but by May herself. She wrote a most loving letter to his mother two weeks later, on 1 December 1900, just before his departure. Her words conveyed the essence of candour and testified to the sincerity of her heart, the depth of her feelings:

My dear Mrs. Maxwell,

Your son wrote to you telling you of the great happiness that has come to us, and which we want to share with you. I am sure that there is nothing that I can tell you, his mother, of the strength and beauty and goodness of his character which you do not know, but I want to tell you that I love him deeply and truly, and that I believe that our love and happiness are founded upon those things which are the highest and most enduring.

I believe that you will find Sutherland greatly changed, as this year abroad has been just what he needed and he has developed very fast in the time that I have known him. He is very appreciative of this great opportunity that his brother has so generously given him and he is returning to you full of purpose and hope.

My dear Mrs. Maxwell, I cannot tell you how tenderly I feel towards you, and to all of those who are dear to the one who is the dearest to me in the world.

I hope that someday you will take me to your kind motherly heart, for his sake, and if you can for my own. I send to you my love, and to all of his family my warm regards.

I am very faithfully yours,
May Ellis Bolles

What the Maxwells must have thought of receiving such a letter from someone they had never met is hard to imagine. They must have been full of trepidation at first, about this rather effusive woman from Englewood, New Jersey. They may have been rather worried too about their boy's infatuation with a girl who belonged to some odd Oriental religion. What on earth did he see in her? And how was she, actually? It was all so very unsettling.

Her paternal relatives, as Amatu'l-Bahá used laughingly to relate, continued to refer to her mother for some time after her marriage as 'that peculiar wife of Willie's'. But though they may have been cautious in their acceptance of her at first, they were certainly won over by her once they met her. It was difficult not to love May.

* * *

In February 1900, Sutherland had ruefully admitted to the secretary of the Province of Quebec Association of Architects that 'Paris is delightful and I wish I could prolong my stay for years'. If that is how he felt before telling May he loved her, one can only imagine his feelings ten months later when he had to leave her. He may have been experiencing something like 'culture shock' when he stepped onto the translatlantic liner which he described in his first letter to May as 'a miniature American city' taking him back home. He certainly met some motley souls on board:

> Mr Ratcliff age 19, destination Pittsburg, home England. He is a type of English youth that calls for no special mention . . . Mr Dickson – age 24, clean shaven, heavy chin and large mouth, born in England, lived in Chicago since he was four years old – is in a Steam heating company . . . Mr Platt – clean shaven, age about thirty, profession, lawyer, hobby archeology – specially printings – He is bright and interesting . . . the most interesting thing about him is that he lives in Englewood and knows you all. We have 'chinned' about you all . . .
>
> I have not found a really interesting person on board – a person to whom I can talk as I do to your Mother and Randolph & Frank . . . I, the more I see and know of my fellow passengers, am forced to see the great difference between you and them . . .
>
> We are going to be late – Instead of landing on Wednesday we will not see New York until Thursday night or Friday morning –

The *Majestic* tossed and pitched in gale force winds on the crossing. His first letter to May described a voyage which, according to one of the stewards on board, was 'the wildest the ship had encountered'.

* * *

In the course of 1901, several of Sutherland's letters to May illustrate how he was living in two worlds. On 28 February for example, he wrote:

Dearest I am beginning to like the hand pianos that [are played] on our streets. I was so delighted the other day when the beautiful and suggestive strains of 'Jerusalem' floated over to me. It reminded me of all that is beautiful in dear Brittany, of how you loved to hear Edith sing it,[31] and how well she did so . . . (L)ast night I took up a violin and I played while walking up and down the room, my spirit rose above my limited powers of technique and I produced an odd mixture of the swing and spirit of a piece combined with many shortcomings, stray notes etc – I went to bed singing and humming, softly to you my Love. I used quite often to try to play but not very much lately (no time).

As time passed, Sutherland's comparisons began to assume a new dimension. Although his heart was divided between two continents, he no longer indulged in nostalgia, but rather affirmed the present world. He dwelt in it fully, gratefully and in the expectation that May would one day join him there. Writing on 12 May 1901, he described a walk he had just taken on Mount Royal:

This morning I went for a walk on the mountain. The mountain is but a ten or at most fifteen minute walk from the house – I saw more clearly than I ever have before the real beauty of our little island, of Montreal – I saw with new eyes – for now I see as I did not in times before our love blossomed, how gentle the easy hillsides, how fine the wooded crests and the carpet of fawn-coloured grass, not yet tinted with the freshness of this seasons grass, how much like a gem with its setting of wistful pale violets; it almost made me sad to pull them . . .

Within days of arriving back home, he had settled down at the draughting tables at the office and plunged into the tasks before him. He also threw himself into all kinds of activities, including various clubs and sports. By the beginning of 1901, he had already become a member of the Art Association of Montreal and by the end of March had joined the Art Gallery in anticipation of attending lectures there with May the following winter. He also became a member of the Renaissance Club in Montreal. Telling May about the highlights of the year, which included

31 Edith MacKay.

the death of Queen Victoria and the beginning of the Edwardian age, he wrote on 25 January 1901:

> I joined the Heather curling club – two days ago, and I have curled every night since – I am very fond of the sport and it is splendid exercise for me . . .
>
> Our Queen is dead. The town is draped in black, universal mourning is apparent – dances etc. being postponed. I sent you a paper today telling all about the Queen's life – I think she was a fine true woman, and the story of her love, and of the Queen and Prince Albert is really beautiful. It will be our aim Dearest to live in just such a beautiful way, everything being tempered by love and reason, a combination that ought to keep everyone happy.

But most importantly, within weeks he found himself offered equal partnership in the architectural firm whose offices were situated on Beaver Hall Square in Montreal and which was to make such a name for itself in Canada in the first decades of the 20th century. It would seem that his brother Edward had not forgotten his commitments to him either. Sutherland's promotion as a fully fledged associate, colleague and collaborator in the Maxwell brothers' firm came as a complete surprise, and without fanfare or fuss, as he told May in his letter of 29 January 1901:

> I have news for you – I noticed the painter working on the front door, but I paid no attention to him – when going out at six, I looked and behold, there was painted on the glass panel: E. Maxwell. And below it was 'W. S. Maxwell' and below again – the word 'Architects'. So Dear your Sutherland is now a practising architect and a member of a prominent firm – *que pense tu ma cherie*?
>
> Ed gave me no intimation of what was going to happen. He just had the name put on the door. It was so characteristic of him. He does many good acts but always in that way – no noise, no fuss, it just happens . . . I have not mentioned money matters to him but now that my name is on the door we may be sure that we will have at least the necessities and a little more, if not the luxuries of life . . .

The prospects looked good from the very start. Edward was busy with important commissions and had established a strong network from the early 1890s. His corporate as well as private clients were among the most influential people in Montreal. His business associations were with families and firms, banks and industries that comprised the most powerful elements in the community. Sutherland was deeply impressed by his achievements, and had the highest regard for his brother's skill and business acumen. Writing to May later that year, he affirmed:

Ed's knowledge, ability for hard work and his talent are of a very high order and it is a source of astonishment to me how he has, with the class of draughtsmen that are available in Montreal, carried on such a large and successful practice.

All these factors ensured the stability of the brothers' partnership and provided for a high degree of excellence in their work. Mutual respect played an important role in their collaboration. Soon after Sutherland's return, Edward gave him significant responsibilities in the firm. He had acquired the contracts to build a large number of grand houses and private hotels in the city as well as municipal halls and government offices, and he delegated the responsibility for the conceptual work and construction of all the exterior ornamentation and interior decoration of these buildings to his younger brother. All the carved panelling, the sumptuous mouldings and fine plaster designs were placed under Sutherland's direction. He became a very busy man.

While engaged in work that drew upon his architectural experience in Paris, Sutherland also received a card from the Art Association of Montreal in the month of January notifying him that the Hanging Committee had accepted six of his sketches for the Spring 1901 Exhibition. The date of their presentation was to be Thursday, 7 March of that year. Writing to May shortly before[32] he told her with a mixture of modesty and diffidence which of his paintings he was going to be offering because several of them had too tender associations for them both:

I sent my ship after all. The boys in the office liked it very much and advised me strongly to send it in so I did so. It really looked pretty well when the frame was on. My project looked very well indeed and came out successfully. At the last minute Dame MacFarlane induced

32 28 February 1901.

me to send in that sketch of the leafless trees that I made when we were in beautiful Dinan. I took it over to 'Scotts' the picture dealer and he liked it. He thought [it] had a nice tone and so acting upon his advice I had it framed neatly with a gold mat etc and it came out very well. If they accept all of my pictures I will be lucky . . .

It must have been very gratifying to Sutherland to find his talents recognized on his return to Montreal, but he quickly discovered that it was not easy to have an artistic temperament and meet one's business obligations at the same time. It became obvious to him, over the next few months, that there was a gap between his personal aspirations and the commercial imperatives of the Maxwell firm. He was, in effect, experiencing the tension between practical demands and artistic aspirations, human needs and spiritual goals, pragmatism and idealism which was to characterize the lives of all three of the Maxwells. In a letter to May written on 2 April 1901, he confessed:

Dearie, business is a hustling bustling affair especially when responsibility rests upon one. It means decisions, firmness, health and close attention on the part of the person concerned – the gloss is very apt to be rubbed off if one is not careful, but . . . I try and I pray that the pursuit of a commercial life may not impair any of the ideals that I hold to be above all monetary considerations and to be the essence of a life truly lived. One of my regrets is that my time is so taken up; last week and I expect this week will require my returning to the office, where I worked until a little after ten.
. . . and about our future. Our future will depend greatly upon you Dearest.

That would prove to be true in ways undreamed of by William Sutherland Maxwell.

* * *

In early 1901 plans were being made for a little group of pilgrims to go to 'Akká. They included Mrs Helen Ellis Cole and Laura Barney, as well as Monsieur Henri who had just become a Bahá'í. This pilgrimage, one year after the first one, would result in the return of Mírzá Abu'l-Faḍl to

Paris. May had asked permission to go to 'Akká too and Helen Cole had offered to take her along. Writing to her on 12 February, Sutherland had encouraged her to go, although he reassured her that even if she did not, she could always take such trips with him in the future:

It will be simply splendid for you to take the trip to Acca in company with your dear friends. And it means so much to you and it will make you very happy. It will be such a beautiful thing to remember Europe by and your stay abroad. But Dearie we will go to Europe whenever we can find it possible; Ed thinks an architect should go abroad every few years to brush up against good work and when I go I will have the Senior member of the firm as my travelling companion and the member's name is Penelope.

Even Mrs Bolles had written to 'Max' about this plan, while taking the opportunity once again to ring the marriage bells in anticipation of that June:

May wrote you about her desire to go to Acca, and she also, no doubt, told you about the money Mrs. Cole left for her with a promise for more in case she wanted to go. When I told May about it, I also told her that I was not willing that she should plan to go without consulting you. And naturally she would not want to, but she said that it was all understood between you before you left, and since then you have written her about it. I do not much believe she is going, and it would seem now about too late, as April is about here and by June 1st she should be ready to marry . . .

But the reasons for May's not going had nothing to do with her wedding date. She had received a reply from 'Akká. Despite the glowing praise, despite the encouragement, 'Abdu'l-Bahá had turned down her request to come to Palestine. He had told her that her priority was to stay in Paris at that time:

O thou who art attracted by the magnet of the love of God!
Rejoice at the grace of God and at the favours He hath vouchsafed unto thee, for He hath illumined thy heart through the light of His bestowals in the prime of thy youth, and hath drawn thee away from all

things through His love. Thou hast thus occupied thyself by day and by night in praise of Him and in prayer to Him at morn and at eventide, and hast been enkindled with the fire of His love both in the gloomy hours of the night and in the brilliant light of the day.

O maidservant of God! By God the Eternal Truth, verily the mercy of thy Lord upon thee is great, very great, and He shall soon strengthen thee in that wherein no one hath been strengthened in those regions. Then thou wilt proclaim and cry aloud, saying: 'How blessed am I for this great favour, and how rejoiced am I for this manifest bounty.'

As to thy request to come to this blessed Spot: for the present, it is necessary for thee to be there [Paris] and to remain with the beloved ones [believers]. Until the Cause of God is firmly established in that city, it is not permissible for the believers and the maidservants of the Merciful to disperse. Nay, it is necessary for all of them to assemble together and exert themselves to the utmost to diffuse the fragrances of God. When the opportunity presents itself, thou wilt be permitted to come.

* * *

Edward had already begun to make his own arrangements to go to Europe that March. It was a business trip, to buy furnishings for clients of the Maxwell firm and attend the annual art exhibition, but Sutherland would have known that his brother was going to take the opportunity to meet the prospective member of his family as well. After sharing a cautionary, if brief, description of Edward's character with May on 14 March, Sutherland added, with a certain diffidence:

Bye the bye Ed will be in Paris about the middle of April if not sooner. Some think we look alike, you will see.

One can sense his trepidation, for he was probably as anxious to have Edward approve of May as to have May accept Ed, whom he knew was not easy to know at the first encounter. One can sense the wistful envy too, for Sutherland must have wished with all his heart to be crossing the Atlantic in his brother's stead:

Dearest
I am to be left to myself for the next five weeks. Ed leaves tonight

at seven. I am snatching a few minutes to tell you how I am and to send you my love . . .

Ed goes to Liverpool, then to Edinburgh then say eight days in London and you will see him in beautiful Paris about the middle of April. He will have a glorious time and will see thousands of beautiful silks and tapestries. I love to select such articles for clients . . .

Sutherland had selected a modest ring for his beloved, which Edward was going to deliver for him. He had at first ordered one made to his own specifications, for as he wrote to May on 4 March 1901, 'I know you would love to have one designed by me.' But when he saw the results of the jeweller's efforts, he was dissatisfied:

I received the ring that I designed and I am not pleased with it. The design was all right but the execution simply abominable. I went to the best jeweller in Canada and asked him to make the ring delicate and light. The article I received is heavy – uninteresting and poorly executed. I naturally was very disappointed. I am going to return the ring and select a stock one – the only one that I recollect as being interesting had a little blue stone in it – very small and unobtrusive . . .

When Edward set out for Europe in mid-March, he was carrying this unobtrusive ring with him. Its acquisition was Sutherland's first attempt to make public his personal feelings. 'I felt', he wrote afterwards, 'that the quiet gold and the simple blue stone, both so harmonious in colour, would be to your liking.' He probably hoped it would also be to her liking to wear this outward symbol of their inner commitment. For May had been sending Sutherland contradictory messages on this subject. Only one month after his return, on 4 January 1901, she had cautioned him against a public announcement of their engagement:

I have not yet told . . . anyone of my engagement. I feel that it is best to wait – & so I am guided by this feeling – for I am sure there is a right time for everything.

Perhaps the reason there is so little reference to her engagement in subsequent correspondence with Bahá'ís in the course of 1901–02 is because after several inquiries like this one from Marie Squires, written on 29 January 1901, May might have told her friends that she preferred not to discuss the question:

> When you come to America you will be so happy to see what great work you can do. Do you ever think of coming soon? Has the Master told you to stay longer in Paris? And sweetheart do you mind just telling me are you ever going to marry a certain dear man – I can't help but be interested. I feel sure I can understand you either way you have decided . . .

Everyone in the family was expecting a June wedding.

* * *

In the meanwhile, everyone else in Paris seemed to be getting engaged. May told Sutherland on 7 March that M. Cornillier, her portrait painter, had announced that he would be married to Annie Martin in two weeks. Ten days before she had mentioned that Frank, her cousin, appeared to be infatuated with a certain Mlle Puthod, 'his Ursula', as May called her. And even Monsieur Henri finally found himself a wife.

To crown it all, these people and many more besides were flocking to 100 rue du Bac to hear about the Bahá'í Faith in early 1901. It was a curious medley. Although some were to become shining lights in later years, others would prove less sincere and several had rather strange ideas. There was, to put it bluntly, a considerable amount of 'mumbo-jumbo' in the air at the turn of the 20th century, and much of it was being substituted for the teachings of Bahá'u'lláh. The early believers had a tendency to muddle the Bahá'í Faith with other doctrines such as Christian Science, Rosicrucianism, ideas about reincarnation and communication with spirits. Writing to Sutherland on 9 April, Mrs Bolles said:

> If it were not for June and you I could not keep as patient as I do because I see among certain people such a lack of true sincerity, and an ability to manage matters according to their own desires and selfish aims under the name of religion, and profess that through prayer God tells them what they are to do. I consider such people

harmful in their influence and indeed I am looking forward to their departure with pleasure.

Before 'such people' departed, however, Mrs Bolles had to accommodate herself to others who came. May, she assured Sutherland, was well and 'tugs away at her work with great interest' but some of the new visitors were apparently adding to her work considerably. In her 7 March letter to him, May told Sutherland who they were:

> By the great mercy of God, I have now many pupils – & we hope that when all of our dear teachers & guides come to us – some time this month – that the Truth will be spread with great power in this City.

Her teachers and guides were Mírzá Abu'l-Faḍl[33] who was on his way to the United States, and his interpreter, Anton Haddad. Several other pilgrims had come with him, including Ali-Kuli Khan, Lua Getsinger and Laura Barney. He had been sent in the footsteps of 'Abdu'l-Karím, who had come the year before, to enlighten the friends about the Faith, to counteract the disunity spread by Dr Kheiralla, and to assist May in deepening the new believers who were largely ignorant or misinformed of Baháʼí principles and history. His three-month sojourn in the capital of France was some indication of the importance given by 'Abdu'l-Bahá to the development of the Faith in that country. Marion Hofman, writing about this period,[34] recorded that

> For perhaps a month he taught them almost daily, through the translations of Anton Haddad and ʻAlí-Kuli Khán. Of those memorable hours Agnes Alexander has written: 'An atmosphere of pure light pervaded the Paris meetings, so much so that one was transported, as it were, from the world of man to that of God'; to which Juliet Thompson's testimony is added: 'That Paris group was so deeply united in love and faith; May, Lua, Laura and Khán, these four especially so inspired, so carried away, so intoxicated with love for the

---

33 According to Ahmad Sohrab's diary, cited by Rúḥíyyih Khánum in her notes, the Master said of this great soul: 'The life of Mírzá Abu'l-Faḍl was God-controlled & God-propelled. Not for one second did he set his own will above the Will of God. He effaced self & lived eternally in God.'

34 In Memoriam article on May Maxwell, in *The Baháʼí World*, vol. VIII (1938–1940), p. 634.

beloved Master; our great teacher, Mírzá 'Abu'l-Faḍl, so heavenly wise – that those days were the days of miracle, of all but incredible confirmations.'

The Master had His eyes fixed on that fledgling community. He wanted to protect it from the odour of defection, from the taint of Covenant-breaking, from the confusions bred by ambitious minds which had undermined the unity of the American Baháís. He must have hoped that the wisdom and erudition of this trusted teacher, in conjunction with the enthusiasm and spiritual receptivity of May Bolles, would not only attract the hearts of many others to the Cause but help them distinguish between the essential truths in the teachings and the fictions of their own making. He had already instructed Lua Getsinger to spend several months in Port Said, after her second pilgrimage in 1900, studying the words of Baháu'lláh with Mírzá Abu'l-Faḍl, for He could see that even she was suffering under misconceptions perpetrated by Kheiralla. Writing to May the previous October, Lua, who had been struggling to obey the Master's injunction to maintain unity at all costs, had confessed to her friend:

> Dearest there is some discrepancy in the teachings as given here by our Lord and Mirza Abdel Fadhl – and those given by Dr. Kheiralla – Mrs. Hoar will tell you about some things – and when I return to Paris I will try and make everything clear to my own darling girl.

The sad truth was that Kheiralla was not only using the Faith to extract money from the early believers but was filling their minds with arcane inventions of his own which bore little or no relation to the Cause of Baháu'lláh. His version of the teachings, based on the Gospels which he claimed were more suited to the Western mind, had distorted certain essential verities of the Faith and turned it into a quasi-secret society. Writing to May from Port Said on 25 January 1901, Lua confided:

> It was so beautiful to be in Acca while [Mrs. Hoagg] and dear Mrs. Cole were there for their hearts were turned fully to God and were just like clean cups waiting to be filled with the blessed Wine – which gives joy to the heart & life to the soul. And they did not wait in vain – for our Gracious Lord filled them to overflowing! . . . There

are many changes in the teaching and it is like beginning all over new – in fact I feel like a toddling infant as far as real knowledge goes – still I am trying very hard to live what I do know and that is making our religion a very practical one.

May was ready to learn and anticipated with intense eagerness the arrival of this new teacher sent to her by the Master. Lua, in her turn, could hardly bear to be parted from him when the time came. Between March and July 1901 she wrote to May from London:

I do not know why – but this parting from you all, was one of the most bitter I have ever experienced! It simply wrung my heart – and now to think of dear Mirza Abul Fadzl (the latches of whose shoes I am not worthy to untie) I am filled with sorrow too deep for words! Our Lord (rouhi fedah) told me that I must love Mirza Abul Fadzl as my own Father and I have always done so – but I did not realize how great and deep that love is – until I went to say 'good by' to him – yesterday – and then when I saw him again this morning – my heart broke! He is nearest to our Lord and more filled with His Holy Spirit than any one I know – outside of the Holy Family! Please convey to him my love, gratitude – and devotion and ask him to pray for me always.

Lua was not alone in adoring Mírzá Abu'l-Faḍl. In later years, when writing to the Kemp family, May recalled an episode in the course of that spring which illustrates how illumined she became and how much she learned from this great teacher:

One day on the streets of Paris in the early spring, I saw a little lame boy on a crutch holding a pussy-willow, his face lighted with rapture. I stood and gazed at him and he lifted his eyes to mine and our souls seemed to meet in mutual love and understanding in that moment of beauty. I told my great and learned teacher whom the Master sent to me, Mírzá Abul-Fazel, of this slight but touching incident and he said that out of such moments light is born, that out of that momentary contact of the spirit would unfold in the worlds beyond a whole life of meaning and purpose. The traces appear on this earth but the fruition is beyond, the seed of a loving deed, a warm and tender contact, a word of love and hope. A little service, a small sacrifice are but the traces here which like the seed will grow to mighty trees and bear imperishable fruits hereafter. Then how much more such lives as yours, spent in the service of the Cause of God, dedicated to Him, establishing an eternal foundation in this world whose superstructure shall appear in shining minarets and gems under the light of the eternal Sun.

She tried to share such moments with Sutherland too, for she was longing to be in harmony with him on a spiritual plane, to feel at one with him across space and time. She wrote to him of the unity that Mírzá Abu'l-Faḍl was able to spread around him, for she felt that such a bond with Sutherland would seal their love forever:

Is it not wonderful that as souls go toward God – towards the Light, they find their kindred spirits – and draw nearer together . . . [In] a friendship like ours no outside things make any difference – absence, distance – time & long silence do not affect that which lies deeper than these things.

But Mrs Bolles may not have been so happy about all these 'kindred spirits' sitting around in her salon. She frankly preferred Sutherland's company:

I wish many times every day that you were here with us – and we could talk and arrange matters as we used to, you understanding me and I understanding you. It used to please me very much that you relied on my judgement and I hope it may be so in the years to come, for I do try always to see things as they really are and I like balance in all persons.

Sutherland should have heard the warning bells; May had cautioned him already about her mother's desire to influence others. But perhaps it was the doorbell of 100 rue du Bac ringing to announce his brother's arrival. Edward could not have come at a more inopportune moment! Mrs Bolles told Sutherland all about it on 9 April 1901:

Your brother called yesterday but his visit was not quite as we would wish, as May had a young man to talk to about 'The Truth', Randolph was not well and I was going out; but I tucked your brother under my arm and took him off to see about some furniture, and then he went his way . . .

If she whisked him off with such alacrity, it may well have been in order to get him out of the apartment. Above all, Mrs Bolles probably wanted to avoid introducing Edward to their Persian guest. A man of consummate erudition, of spiritual refinement, and of true humility, Mírzá Abu'l-Faḍl was able to win Mrs Bolles' respect in the course of his stay, but she may have been concerned about his impact on Mr Edward Maxwell from Montreal just at that moment. Randolph provided Sutherland with a rather bedridden point of view one month later:

I am afraid that I have been a very irregular (to put it mildly) correspondent this winter; but then, as you know, old man, it has been thro' no fault of mine. Your brother has probably told you by this time of the plight he found me in when he was here; I had my face in a very bad condition not to mention that I was in very bad shape generally owing to the poison that had got into my system; and, as I was only just up and around the apartment in my dressing gown and quite unable to go out, I was not able to show your brother any attention of any kind, sort or description very much to my regret.

His mother made amends as best she could. She did all she could to charm Mr Edward Maxwell and invited him back to the apartment for a proper visit on another occasion. But her exasperation was evident in writing to Sutherland about it:

[T]oday he is coming to tea, and I hope he will dine with us, which he will do after May has found out what evening she will be free. Miss Barney with a Persian teacher and his interpreter and one or two others are just back from Acca or Haifa and I believe there are to be constant meetings for a few weeks . . .

If Edward thought the Bolles family rather odd, he did not immediately betray it. Sutherland was immensely relieved; one hurdle, at least, was overcome! Writing to May in April 1901, he told her that his brother thought she 'would be the making' of him and had spoken of her 'in a way that I have never heard him speak of any one else'; Edward had 'seen and felt the beauties of your soulful personality', he said. Such voluble praise from a man who was not easily impressed was rare indeed:

> Ed spoke very lovingly of you all. For you, my love, he has the great-est regard and respect and he is very glad that I have such a very fine young woman for my fiancée, and he considers me very fortunate. He congratulated me very nicely in a letter and in Montreal. And of your Mother, he spoke in terms of unstinted appreciation. He sin-cerely admires her and said many dear things about her and when I added to his many praises, he agreed with me. He spoke very kindly of Randolph and likes him very much, and when I asked him about Frank, he had good to say of him. In fact he found you all 'very charming people'; and for every virtue he enumerated I had many to add. It has been so pleasant to have had you all know him and it has added to my store of happiness and thankfulness.

Edward had delivered the engagement ring, of course. And May acknowledged it, according to Sutherland's letter, written on a Saturday in April:

> I was so glad that you liked the ring . . . The simple refinement of the design, to me harmonized with the essence of refinement and truth, that combined with sincerity and great-heartedness, are so noticeable in your loved character.

Writing to her again after his brother's return to Montreal, he expressed concern that she was so wholly engrossed by her Bahá'í work:

> Ed tells me you have been much occupied and I am thankful that you have had the great happiness of meeting Abdul Fadel (?). You will at least not teach in the evenings, will you Dearie? It is so nice to spend your evenings with your Mother and Randolph, having a relaxation and giving to them great happiness.

Randolph added a laconic reference to his sister's zeal in his letter to Sutherland:

Well, old man, it was a great pleasure for us to meet your brother – and I am only sorry we could not see more of him; however, I hope that we shall have a good chance to know him <u>well</u> some day. I can't say I do think he looks like you, altho' I think there is a slight family resemblance . . . I am glad that your work was so favourably commented on at the exposition; I know it deserved all the praise that it got . . . May is remarkably well, notwithstanding the tremendous amount of time and energy that she spends on her teachings . . .

Randolph may have been dubious about the 'tremendous amount of time and energy' his sister spent with their Persian visitor, Mírzá Abu'l-Faḍl. Mrs Bolles had begun to develop a certain affection for him as the days passed, and found him to be a most courteous old gentleman. But he seemed to have no intention of leaving Paris before July.

If there was to be no June wedding, Mrs Bolles was going to vacate the apartment and go to Brittany. Their affairs would have to be packed up and stored away again. The landlord needed them out by the end of the month, she warned.[35]

May had a dilemma on her hands. She knew, from everything that Mírzá Abu'l-Faḍl told her, that the Master had placed great hopes on her activities in Paris, and she had also received a Tablet from 'Abdu'l-Bahá stating that she should not leave Paris or its environs unless absolutely necessary.[36] She could not leave now.

But as a young, unmarried woman at the turn of the 19th century, she knew she could not stay in Paris either, all through the summer, without a chaperone. If her mother closed the apartment and left for Dinard, she would be expected to go with her, to avoid scandal. But if she did not obey the Centre of the Covenant, she would be courting something far graver than scandal. It must have taken considerable courage for her to tell her mother that *she* could go to Dinard with Randolph and Puck the poodle whenever she liked, but that May herself would stay in Paris that summer, and continue with her Bahá'í work until further notice. She records the consequences of taking such a stand:

---

35 In a letter written to Sutherland on 28 March 1901, Mrs Bolles confirmed that 'Randolph has not been well all winter and I shall hope to get away with him early in June, and if possible, I will rent the apartment for two or three months.'

36 This undated Tablet is in the Maxwell files; it is not the same as the Tablet quoted on pp. 131–2 above. In it 'Abdu'l-Bahá tells May that her teaching work in Paris is resounding 'like the sound of a bell'.

My dear mother, a broad-minded and beautiful person, yet with very natural maternal reservations, had written 'Abdu'l-Bahá[37] stating that this year was the last she and her two children – my brother and I – would spend in France, after an eight-year sojourn; that I was tired after the winter's work – alas! it tired her just to think of it! – and that she wished the Master to permit me to spend the summer with her in Brittany. 'Abdu'l-Bahá replied in a Tablet to me in which He said that on no account should I leave Paris! My mother was dumbfounded and very indignant. She told me once more that she could not understand my allegiance to this Man in a Turkish prison who interfered with our family life. Although my mother was a beautiful and gracious person – broad and liberal in all her views and who towards the end of her life reposed her whole trust in 'Abdu'l-Bahá – yet at that time she was greatly disturbed.

The tension inside the apartment at 100 rue du Bac no doubt rose with the temperature outside through the month of June. Mírzá Abu'l-Faḍl must have registered it without need of translation. He offered to write to the Master a second time when Mrs Bolles appealed to him to intervene on her behalf. May's record continues:

My troubled mother opened her heart to Mírzá Abu'l-Faḍl, who was frequently our guest, & whom my mother greatly revered, and for her sake he again wrote the Master about the coming summer months, fully explaining the situation. Again the Master replied, but this time He modified His decree, stating that I might leave Paris for one day! My mother then told me that I had made my own choice, as between her and a Turkish prisoner – that the consequences were upon me – that she intended to close our apartment, that no doubt my Bahá'í friends would look after me, and in this spirit of pain and anger, of utter blindness to the deep significance of it all, she and my brother left for the seaside.

---

37 There is a slight discrepancy in May's notes about this episode, another version of which states that it was she herself who wrote to 'Abdu'l-Baha: 'We were soon returning to America and my Mother had set her heart on our spending this last summer in France together. Thus I wrote to the Master asking for permission to leave Paris to spend those summer months in Brittany.' Given that 'Abdu'l-Baha responded with a Tablet to May herself, it might be that she added her appeal to her mother's.

Once the reply of the Master came, May had needed no further proof of Divine Will. She knew she could not budge. Her mother, on the other hand, had needed no further proof of diabolic influence. As far as she was concerned this so-called 'Master' was encouraging her daughter to violate all things she held most sacred. As May wrote in her notes: 'I knew the meaning of the Words of Abdul Baha when He said it is not the sacrifice of oneself in the path of God, but the sacrifice of the nearest and dearest that brings the greatest pain to the heart.' She must have been shaken to the roots of her soul as her mother swept off to Brittany in high dudgeon, trailing Randolph, Frank, and Puck behind her:

> Never shall I forget that hot summer's day when I went to the station to see them off. In the French compartment of the train two pairs of blue eyes framed in a window, filled with pain and sorrow, gazed their farewell with deep reproach and utter lack of comprehension. Those blue eyes – those two people had made up all the beauty, joy and meaning of life, until the Day I had beheld the face of 'Abdu'l-Bahá, for whom I had sought passionately from my very childhood – and the fact that neither knew nor loved Him, could not believe in the Advent of the Blessed Beauty nor take a few drops from this Illimitable Sea, was simply unbelievable. That hot summer's day the full force of this cruel separation sank deep into my soul. The platform heaved beneath me as the train moved away, and I spent the whole night in prayer and tears for them – on the floor of the tiny room I had taken.
>
> * * *

When the train containing her mother, brother and cousin pulled out of Montparnasse station, May must have been keenly aware of her disadvantages. A single woman in Paris, at the turn of the century, was alone in more ways than one.

She knew very well that her condition was of grave concern to her family. She guessed that her mother and brother probably thought she was in the grip of some strange mania, the victim of some dreadful cult. Although they were angry with her for opposing them, she was well aware that they were very worried about her too. On 12 August 1901, Randolph wrote a long letter to Sutherland from St Enogat:

You will see by the heading of this letter that we are back here again: that is, Mother, Frank, Puck and myself. We have been here about three weeks and are enjoying the change very much indeed after hot Paris. Unfortunately May is not with us. She is still in Paris, having had several pupils to teach, I believe, & as she does not seem to care for anything else nowadays except her religion, we have about given up trying to get her to do anything. We are in hopes that she will perhaps decide to take a rest soon, for she certainly needs a change very badly.

May was feeling torn. Her obligations were multiple, her loyalties divided, her loves seemingly opposed. She was, on the one hand, in a state of exaltation, almost ecstasy, because she was doing what 'Abdu'l-Bahá wanted: teaching the Cause, and expending every breath in her body to deepen the little group of Bahá'ís that summer. On the other she was acutely conscious of her vulnerability, her fragile health, her financial dependence and her sex, and knew all too well that she was not doing what those nearest and dearest to her wanted. By staying behind when they went off to Brittany, she had given all of civilized society every reason to misunderstand her motives and doubt her sanity.

She had no recourse but to turn to her Beloved and pray for aid, beg for protection, plead for His unfailing support. After spending that first night weeping in a hotel, May rose in the morning determined to fulfil her promises to 'Abdu'l-Bahá:

The next day was a Friday – our meeting day – held at the beautiful home of Mrs. Jackson on the Avenue d'Iena – and when she learned that my family had gone away, she put at my disposal a small apartment on the courtyard, back of her home. There I lived for one month, and it was during that month that the wisdom of His Command, the wonders of His Bounty became manifest. During those days we were immersed in the essence of the Covenant. His all-penetrating, all-surrounding Presence moved and directed our studies, our activities, our united servitude – day by day at the table of dear Mrs. Jackson we quietly conversed, deepening our knowledge and reinforcing our efforts.

Several of the souls who gathered round the table in Mrs Jackson's house over the next four weeks were among the immortals. One of them was Hippolyte Dreyfus, the first French Jew to accept the Cause in a country polarized by the notorious 'affaire Dreyfus', and according to Shoghi Effendi the first Frenchman in Bahá'í history to recognize the importance of the unifying message of Bahá'u'lláh at that critical hour. This distinguished man was unique in many ways. He was a true gentleman, of high refinement and broad intelligence. His mind was wide-ranging, his intellect keen, his command of language incisive and his soul eager and alert to the breezes of spiritual change. His translations of the Writings into French and his adventuresome travels to North Africa and the Far East were to gladden the heart of 'Abdu'l-Bahá in years to come. His audacity in helping Lua to secure an audience with Muẓaffar-u'd-Dín Sháh in the autumn of 1902 and his willingness to accompany her to the Elysée Palace Hotel when she submitted her petition to him on behalf of the Bahá'ís in Iran proved him to be an intrepid defender of the Cause. Writing to May at that time, Lua averred: 'Oh May you will never know what a great blessing and help Mr. Dreyfus has been to me! . . . You can't imagine how he has grown – and how wonderful he is!' Several members of Hippolyte's family, including his sister, also became Bahá'ís after he accepted the Faith, and his dynamic impact on the little group who gathered together in Mrs Jackson's house to read the words of their Beloved during the summer of 1901 was remarkable, as May herself recorded:

Day by day the believers and friends who still remained in Paris came to my little apartment, where the golden summer hours slipped by bathed in the burning rays of the Divine Revelation. The few translated Tablets, Hidden Words or other Sacred Writings were worn thread-bare, and seeing our plight, the Beloved sent that month the one destined to shed the light of Bahá in France through his marvellous translations into French of a number of revealed books of Bahá'u'lláh. Never shall I forget the overpowering impression of grace and power in the person of Hippolyte Dreyfus the first time he came to see me.

He said, 'I have come to learn what it is you have done to produce so remarkable a change in Edith S. [Sanderson]. She is not the same – she has found joy, serenity and a deep purpose in life' – and with his charming smile – 'how did you do it?'

He asked to know the tenets of a Faith which had, he said, transformed a friend of his. With fervour, simplicity, and, conscious of my utter ignorance in the face of such a scholar, putting my full trust in Bahá'u'lláh, as the Master had bidden me in Acca to do – I told him all I knew! He listened with courteous attention, deep interest at times, searching questions, and over all, a light veil of humour and slight scepticism.

When he arose to go he took my hand warmly and cordially and told me that it was no doubt interesting, that he did not recognize its historic importance, that he was touched by the ardour of my faith but that he did not believe in any force outside, or beyond natural forces, that he had never in his life experienced anything that would lead him to believe in Divine or spiritual influences. Then he left, saying he would come again at some future time. Within eight or ten days he returned, amazed & perturbed. It appeared he had been having a series of somewhat strange experiences governed by laws, or conditions, which he could not explain by natural forces, 'although he argued with himself for an hour or more seeking to prove their natural phenomena'. Frankly I was amused & delighted, having many times been an 'eye-witness' of the mighty, mysterious workings of Bahá'u'lláh, and I knew that this great soul was in the toils! Gradually, [he became] unable to resist his own experiences and the irresistible 'charm of faith'. Later, his rationalism being somewhat subdued, he began to read & study, and the priceless seed of faith germinated in his heart. And in due time he became the great beacon light of the Bahá'í Faith in France and in Europe.

Hippolyte remained a staunch Bahá'í, a true friend and a pillar of the French community until his untimely death in 1928. But the most famous of those early believers was the first Englishman to embrace the Faith of Bahá'u'lláh. Thomas Breakwell was like a comet that blazed above the skies of Paris at the turn of the century. None could equal his ardour and sincerity; none could match the fervour of his faith. His is the story that will be forever associated with the mystery of 'Abdu'l-Bahá's instructions to May to stay in the French capital at all costs that summer; his acceptance of the Cause was the fruit of her obedience. In her notes about the group of early believers, among whom were 'a number of teachers, now well known', she described the extraordinary circumstances in which this youth became a Bahá'í.

On 24 July 1901, just before Mírzá Abu'l-Faḍl's departure for America, May had written a letter to 'Abdu'l-Bahá thanking Him for the illumination imparted by this great teacher, asking Him to bless the few souls she was teaching herself, and confirming her intention to remain in Paris, according to His explicit instructions.

Oh! my Beloved,
. . . Tomorrow our revered and beloved guide, Mirza Abul Fadzl [sic], is leaving us and I long to thank Thee for Thy Great Bounty and Kindness in sending to Thy humble servants in Paris this pure and honoured servant of God . . .

I thank Thee in the name of all the dear <u>believers</u> in this City for the clear bright stream which Thou hast poured out to us thru the lips of Thy blessed servant . . .

My Beloved Master! At this time I am staying in the home of my dear sister Mrs. Jackson, and I have received from her the greatest love, kindness and hospitality. I humbly entreat for her, and for Thy pure and tender son, Sigurd Russell, that Thou wilt strengthen and confirm them in Thy Cause . . .

Sigurd Russell, a 15-year-old foster child of Mrs Jackson, was another of those who became enamoured of Bahá'u'lláh during May's stay in the capital that summer.

May recounts, in her notes, that after her family members had left for Brittany, '(a)lmost one month had swiftly passed before the full wisdom of 'Abdu'l-Bahá's command to stay in Paris became clearly revealed'. And then, she tells the breathtaking story of Thomas Breakwell:

. . . when one morning a friend who had just returned from America sought me out and brought with her a young man of such rare charm and vivid presence that the moment of meeting, as they stood at my door, left an indelible impression. In one flash he appeared to me as a veiled light, and Mrs. M. said, 'He was a stranger and she took him in.' We entered the little apartment and I found myself in the presence of Thomas Breakwell. The lady explained that they had crossed together coming to France, that he was interested in

Theosophy, that she knew I had kindred interests, thus she brought him to me. We spoke a little on spiritual matters but without mentioning the Cause, of his plans for a three-months' visit to European countries, and finally, when they arose to leave – he had looked at me often, with a strange searching intentness – he asked if he might come again.

He arrived the next morning, and standing in the same spot before my door I beheld him utterly transformed. The veil which I had seen over that burning radiant spirit had been torn asunder, and he entered like one in a dream. Standing before me he asked if I noticed anything strange about him, and I assured him that he looked very happy. He did not smile but, looking intently at me, he said that something strange had happened and that he did not know what was the matter with him. Reassuringly I bade him sit down and tell me. 'All the time I was with you yesterday I had a strange unaccountable feeling, and when I left I walked alone down the Champs-Élysées. You remember it was a warm, still day – not a leaf was stirring – when suddenly a wind rushed upon me and whirled about me with such violence that I could barely stand on the ground, then out of the wind came a voice saying, 'Christ has come again, Christ has come again, Christ has come again.' He gazed at me with wonder and a certain fear. 'Now,' he said, 'do you think I am becoming insane?' 'No, you are just becoming sane!' I exclaimed firmly – and then gently and joyously I sought to remove all his doubts and fears – and to impart to his blessed, receptive soul the wonderful tidings of the advent of Bahá'u'lláh.

It was a miraculous moment, and a sublime reward for all her trials. She continues:

For three days we spent many hours together while he drank ever deeper from the Life-Giving Source – while his whole life was changed. He threw away all his plans like playthings, and had but one single aspiration, one burning desire, to make the pilgrimage to Acca – to attain the Presence of his Master. It was just at that time that Herbert Hopper was about to visit the Holy Land, and he and Thomas Breakwell decided to go together, so at his request I wrote the Master begging for His permission and asking Him to send the reply to Port Said. Thomas Breakwell enclosed with mine the following significant supplication: 'My Lord – I believe. Forgive me. Thy servant Thomas Breakwell.'[38]

The impact of such faith could only be equalled by May's subsequent experience. She herself takes up the tale of what happened after Breakwell's letter was sent to 'Akká:

> As I wish to follow the thread of his incomparable story to the end, I will now briefly touch on my humble share & its immediate consequences. I mailed his petition to the Master, then walked over to our closed apartment to get my mail from the concierge, and my eyes fell on a blue cablegram, and on these words: 'YOU MAY LEAVE PARIS ANY TIME.' The hours that followed were fraught with such wonder & awe, such passionate love, such all-embracing yearning that the world might come under His blessed Shadow, and find everlasting joy and peace and eternal security. My feet were winged! I packed and prepared – sleep was a mere waste of the radiant hours before the morning train could take me to my family! When I arrived in the twilight I sat down with my mother and brother & told them all. They listened with absorbed interest, and when I reached the climax I read them the cablegram – my mother burst into tears, exclaiming: 'You have a wonderful Master!'[39]

* * *

All the time that she was nurturing the Bahá'í community in Paris, May was also writing to her beloved Sutherland in Canada. Even as she sought out receptive souls and taught the Faith to new seekers, she attempted to teach him too, long-distance, and to translate their relationship into spiritual terms. Throughout 1901 and up until early

---

38 Although May added: 'Later I learned that his plea for forgiveness was more that sense of shame and sorrow which comes to every soul in contact with divine light, with the all-revealing beauty and perfection of the Beloved,' Breakwell's appeal may also have referred to the child labour that was being used in the cotton plantations he was running in the United States.

39 This passage is taken from an original handwritten account by May Maxwell in the Estate papers of Amatu'l-Bahá Rúḥíyyih Khánum. A similar but different account by May Maxwell is published in *The Bahá'í World*, vol. VII (1936–1938), pp. 707, 709–11, and is entitled 'A Brief Account of Thomas Breakwell'.

1902, when the tension of waiting finally became more than either of them could bear, she struggled with the paradox of being the first disciple of 'Abdu'l-Bahá in France and a woman in love. For one of the greatest tests as well as the sweetest rewards of her life would prove to be William Sutherland Maxwell himself.

Over the seventeen months since Sutherland's departure from Paris, May did all she could to give him the strength to use their separation to forge ever closer bonds, and even more intimate connections between them. In doing this, she was following a well-established social as well as spiritual tradition.

But Mrs Bolles as well as Randolph might have been justified in suspecting that May had adopted a long engagement for reasons of her own. As time went on it appeared that she was doing everything possible to put off the wedding. Although the teaching work in Paris was one of the primary reasons for May's long engagement, her motives are both revealing of her faith and perhaps suggestive of her fears.

What mattered most to May and was her highest priority was her mandate from the Master: she lived to tell the world about the message of Bahá'u'lláh. She had already made this clear to Sutherland long before they ever parted. She was a born teacher and saw it as her primary task to educate him regarding the truth of the Cause. Writing to him on 21 December 1900, at the start of their long engagement, she sent him the following New Year wishes:

> [O]h! my beloved, how can I put into words all that I hope & pray that this coming year may bring to you! I shall pray for you on that day with such love & humility! that God will grant you the greatest blessing – that He will in His boundless Mercy descend upon you that which is best for you and give you the greatest happiness!

In order to resolve the potential contradictions entailed in the prospect of drawing apart if they were not united in spirit, May established separate spheres for herself and for Sutherland, and divided their roles accordingly. He was the practical one, and she the mystical; he was the artist and she was his muse; he worshipped beauty and she had recognized its source. A few weeks later, she wrote to him again on 18 January:

Every day brings me nearer to a realization of these wonderful truths, and this temporal life in the world loses its hold and gives way to a life of such love, such joy, such peace & beauty as I cannot describe.

The presence of Mírzá Abu'l-Faḍl in Paris that spring influenced May's personal correspondence profoundly. Since she was learning how to teach the Cause from this the greatest of all Bahá'í teachers, it was hardly surprising that her letters to Sutherland at this time were often thinly disguised Bahá'í talks. In fact it is possible that she was quoting the words of Mírzá Abu'l-Faḍl directly:

If you are imperfect my darling, so am I & we will help to perfect one another, and lead one another ever higher in whatever way God wills. Imperfection is the condition of the human race at present. I mean on this earth, for this life is only the beginning, and so we see man in a state of growth and development. Nature is God's Great Book, or Symbol – to teach us of the Eternal Kingdom of Reality. And if we watch and study nature & its laws and processes, we shall grow in true knowledge and understanding, for as we see trees & plants and flowers, so are we, the human creatures, the plants of His Hands – the flowers & trees of His Garden, and we are watered by His Mercy, heated and nourished by His Love, and the Breeze of His Spirit, and we should pray to Him continually, that we may grow strong and beautiful spiritually – for this is the only reality – the only lasting Life.

She may not only have been echoing Mírzá Abu'l-Faḍl but wanting to prove to 'Abdu'l-Bahá that her will was wholly in submission to His, that her love for Sutherland was in no way in conflict with her love for the Cause. Soon after Edward Maxwell's visit, when the June wedding was indefinitely postponed, she wrote:

In this letter[40] I am not going to say anything further about our marriage – for I feel that time, reflection & outside circumstances will reveal to us the Will of Our Beloved Father, in Whose Hands we, and our lives, and all our concerns repose – absolutely.

---

40 This letter is the last available from May Bolles to Sutherland Maxwell during that historic summer. No others between 3 May and 13 December 1901 have come to light at the time of this writing.

To Sutherland May was illustrating true submission while teaching obedience to the Covenant to the Paris Bahá'ís. She was trying to stir up the spiritual susceptibility of her betrothed while helping the new believers learn how to look for receptive souls, how to introduce the Cause, how to convey its truth with certitude. In fact, some of May's letters to Sutherland are living examples of how to teach the Cause. In May 1900, for example, she had written to him about the spiritual privilege of this Day:

> Do you love that glorious figure, back in the ages Sutherland? Has He seemed to you all your life very near and real and dear beyond anyone? Have you often thought how you would have loved Him had you been on the earth with Him, had He given you one glance from His loving eyes! I want you to know what that love is like dear, how it fills the heart with an intense devotion just like any other great human love, but higher and deeper and more self forgetful – we will go step by step towards all this light and joy, dear; and I long with all my heart for that hour to come.

Sutherland did not use the same vocabulary as May. The meaning of the word 'Master' for him was the 'Giver of all things' rather than 'Abdu'l-Bahá. The meaning of marriage was the basis of that very unity which she was so anxious to establish in the world; how could it undermine it? Looking towards the future, he saw, on the far horizon of 'Eternity', that there might be other stars in the universe besides their own small sun. He tried to tell her that they were just talking in different languages, but their goal was one:

> [I]n the morning of our joy, our hearts will be filled with a sunrise whose rays expand to infinity, thus will we start out in life and as rays do get wider, so will our horizon expand and new duties await us – our knowledge and experience ever getting wider, our light and our guidance ever coming direct from our Master and Giver of all things. And as our journey through life advances we are guided by this sunlight and if a cloud appears for a moment in the sky we know so surely of the great light that is behind it. And as the eventide of life approaches there appears on the horizon a star so faint at first but becoming more pure in its light as the moonlight pales.

This star is of a pure softer light, it leads us to the portals of Eternity, and on and onward we pass hand in hand – our eyes ever to this light that soothes and gives peace to our souls.

Sutherland's vision of the future was of himself and May, passing onward and upward, 'hand in hand'. But May's definition of love was anything but exclusive. She showered it on all and sundry. She saw herself not only as Sutherland's fiancée and would-be-wife but the friend, the guide, the living link of the Bahá'ís in Paris with 'Abdu'l-Bahá too. She was their bond with their Beloved, their brightest beacon in that City of Light. While she nurtured a special relationship with her betrothed, it did not stop her from expressing an equally tender affection towards her spiritual children.

* * *

Full justice cannot be done in these volumes to all the additional correspondence which May maintained in Paris during these early years.[41] But a few examples have been included below to illustrate the way in which she was teaching the Faith at this time. Although most of the letters she wrote are not available to this writer, those she received from the early Bahá'ís have survived and make fascinating reading in light of what was happening to her personally. For while her courtship correspondence unfolded with Sutherland, May was also writing and receiving love-letters from all to whom she taught the Faith.

Indeed, love seems to have been in the air in Paris at the turn of the 20th century. There was hardly a soul that May encountered at this time who did not in a sense fall in love with her, for her attachment to the Cause was like a magnet that attracted all who met her. Almost two decades later, in a letter addressed to the 'Beloved spiritual children of Agnes' on 19 November 1919, May wrote, 'Once the Beloved said to this servant – in her youth – *"There is in the heart of 'Abdu'l-Bahá an instrument which measures the exact degree of love for Him of every believer in the world!"'* A cursory glance at the correspondence she maintained with some of the early Bahá'ís confirms that the sheer intensity of her love for the Master caused others to respond to Him with equal intensity. She was, in a way, herself that instrument.

---

41 See 'The Maxwell Literary Estate', p. xix above.

Juliet Thompson describes May's impact on her contemporaries at this time:[42]

She was so fragile, so luminous. Her delicate, mysterious beauty glowed with a soft cool light. Laura had named her the Violet Star. She brought a special fragrance into our midst. Also, as I discovered later, she had a special gift of confirming people – a mysterious power.

Brenetta Herrman must have been entranced by May already, before she even heard of the Faith from her, for her letters are often passionate avowals. But after receiving a Tablet from 'Abdu'l-Bahá, her love rose to another level entirely:

My beloved sister, my teacher and my Ellice I greet you in His Most Holy Name Allah o' Abha!

I will not attempt to tell you how I felt when I opened your letter and saw the words written by our blessed Master to me – dear heart I am not worthy and for a moment the realization of my unworthiness almost killed me. I sat as one stricken and could neither speak or feel.

For the last ten or twelve days I have been almost burning up with love and the desire to do that work which it shall please God to send me . . . My Mother, my little Mother is near, very near, God give me knowledge to guide her to His face. My Father is far away for the time being at least, I feel from everything he says in connection with such subjects that it would be utterly useless to approach him just now. When one is filled with love how quickly people are drawn to you, really it is wonderful. I have met many, many people this winter, only for the one purpose of course, 'O friends consort with all the people of the world with joy and fragrance!' and all those same people have felt something, they did not know <u>what</u>, so gradually I am with God's dear help trying to bring them nearer and nearer to me until I can reach out my hand and say 'I have a Message for you my brother or my sister'. . .

Ellice I take you in my arms and whisper to you Allah'o Abha.

---

42 A note written to Marion Holley (Hofman) on 7 April 1940, as she was preparing the *In Memoriam* article for *The Bahá'í World* after May's passing.

One year later, in May 1901, Brenetta, who had returned to the United States, wrote to May again about the death of Minnie Hysler, whom May had cared for in Paris, and shared with her the good news that her mother had accepted the Faith:

Greetings to you dear heart and to all the dear brothers and sisters over the ocean, may our most gracious God bless and keep you all. We do not hear from one another often but our spirits are as one, is it not so dear?

Our little Min has gone from among us and I know you loved her dearly and will want to know about it all, but there is really not much to tell, she died on Monday May 27th after suffering agony beyond description and was laid away the following Wednesday . . .

Dear Ellice, I know you will rejoice with me when I tell you that my little Mother has really accepted the Truth and has written her letter. I pray to God with all my heart that you will soon be able to send me a similar message . . .

It was such an uplifting [experience] to see Miss Squires, what a wonderful and rare spirit she has, here in America that radiance is not visible often, and I fear we who live here lose a great deal of it by not being strong enough to stand alone, but she had just come home, fresh from your dear influence and inspiration, Ellice, Ellice there never was but one such teacher as you are, God bless you my sister . . .

May God the Infinite watch over you all and may He guard my Ellice with His Special Love . . .

It was as though love had made a magnet of May in those days. She was in love. She was the object of love. And to many who became Bahá'ís through her, May symbolized the love of the Cause. In one undated note to her, Laura Barney wrote, 'You are ever shining in the heaven of my thoughts. You are ever growing & living in the garden of my heart.' En route back to the United States, she wrote to May again on 29 July 1901, acknowledging how much she owed her for teaching her the Faith:

It is your sweet illumined being that led me to that lofty resting place, and through eternity my voice will ring forth my thanks.

When I look at the immense ocean, the thought that it is but as a drop
of water to the Creator, makes me dimly realize His endless Being.

Laura, like so many others whom May had taught, knew that the debt
of gratitude she owed her could only be repaid by teaching others in
turn. In fact, through May's example, the love between these early
Bahá'ís generated a great longing in their hearts to share the teachings.
From Washington DC, Laura wrote:

Violet Star,
    Every new soul I teach I always feel it is your tender voice saying
to my spirit – Elsa, it is the true life that I have given you to give
. . . How glad I will be to see you all in Paris. Dear one, I feel that
everything is going well, how could it be helped, when you are ever
praying for your children.

It was Lua who had set the standard for this quality of correspondence. As May's first teacher, she took every opportunity to awaken in
her heart the desire to teach the Faith. And she did this by evoking the
words of 'Abdu'l-Bahá with every breath. In fact May's correspondence
with Lua Getsinger, with Thomas Breakwell and with Agnes Alexander – Lua, who taught her the Faith and the two others, to whom she
taught it – was almost exclusively about the love of the Master and the
joy of teaching. Lua, who had been in the presence of 'Abdu'l-Bahá
in May's company during her first pilgrimage, wrote to her 'dear dear
Violet' on 27 March 1899 when the time had come for her too to bid
farewell to 'Abdu'l-Bahá:

Of course you must know how my heart was torn when I had to say
'good bye' and how it still aches. I dread to go back into the world
more than I can tell you, but I must, as my work is among the
people of the vineyard. Our dear Master has blessed me hundreds of
times more than I deserve – and the only way I can show my appreciation of the same is to devote my life in the Cause of God, to cut
my heart entirely from the world and be willing to die for the Glorious Truth! The day before I left 'The Master', Rooha Khanum and
myself visited the Tomb, and our Lord prayed especially for me that
I should receive the confirmation of the Spirit and be a successful

teacher. I have felt differently since that day, my heart is fairly melted by the fire of God's love, and now I see that never before have I had the real spirit of the great <u>reality</u>. I am ready now to meet anything the world has to say – regarding this teaching – and I am sure now that I can myself set the right example, which I know I failed in many ways to do in Paris. I trust you are still desirous of teaching, and that you will have great success wherever you are!

Two years later, in 1901, after leaving her spiritual 'child' in the company of Mírzá Abu'l-Faḍl, whom 'Abdu'l-Bahá had told her was her spiritual 'father', Lua wrote another spiritual love-letter to May:

My own little 'Violet',
    We arrived safely and are located. Had a smooth passage, the trip being without incident – except that during the whole journey I saw your tearful eyes and pale face ever before me – and I am afraid my eyes were at times somewhat tearful too.
    I realize your deep love and just how you feel tonight – for I measure your feelings by my own, as I am sure our hearts respond one to the other! Your flowers are on the table before me, and as I look at them this is what they symbolize! The Green leaves and stems – represent your <u>human</u> self – the Red Roses – your heart of rich love – the Pink ones – your lovely spiritual face – the Four Buds (there are but four) the 'Four Wings' of the spiritual power yet unfolded within you, and the fine White Flowers, the Breath of the 'Holy Spirit' which constantly surrounds you! The whole bunch together means – 'My Baby' My own little 'May Violet' whom I love better than I love myself – and oh, how much I miss you – and shall miss you as the days, weeks, months, and perhaps, years go by – ere I can fold you in my arms again – and look into your soulful trustful eyes, which have always seemed like windows of the other world to me! How sweet are the meetings, and how sad are the partings – which go to make up a page of life!

A few months later, on her return to her 'ain countrie' after her second pilgrimage and prolonged stay in Port Said, Lua wrote to May again on 27 July 1901, expressing her longing to share the message of the Cause with her own countrymen:

Well my darling, I am ready to begin my Lord's work – and came direct to Boston for that purpose. Mrs. Jackson's sister lives here and I am to see and teach her, and thereby open this city in the Name of our beloved Lord (rouhi fedah). It is very warm here, and most dreadfully hot in New York – but this we do not mind so long as we are doing our dear Master's work! We are only 'birds of passage' you know and I think we shall only light here for about one week then fly away to some other place – probably Detroit and from there I shall go to Chicago . . .

Many of the American Bahá'ís who accepted the Faith in Paris through May and then returned to the United States continued to write to her through the course of the following year. Marie Squires, who later married Herbert Hopper, affirmed[43] what so many of them felt, that May was their source of faith, their link with 'Abdu'l-Bahá:

You alone have helped me, you alone have been beside me and have led the way. You know I mean you accept [sic] Our Lord who I have never seen – You express our Lord to me. I have seen you go through things that He alone could have taught you to go through. So I have trusted as you trust and all responsibility has left me and all Faith that He was guiding has surrounded and strengthened me. When I say I have never seen Our Beloved (rouhi fedah) I mean that I have not seen His smile, or felt His touch as you have. It seems now as it never has before that I was going to realize these things for myself before long . . .

Later that same year, Marie Squires wrote to May again:[44]

You need no letters to know of my constant thought for you sweet-heart, of my great gratitude to God that I know you. You are my sweet Holy Sister that my heart ever beholds as its guiding star of sisters – . . . I have your picture on my desk and as I sat here yesterday one ray of sunlight fell upon the group but only your face was caught by it (the picture with the Getsingers) and you alone were enveloped in that bright light. It meant to me a great joy that you

---

43 29 January 1901.
44 24 November 1901.

shone so brilliantly even among such holy souls . . . Elsa Barney spent an afternoon with us . . . she was lovely – she made my family love her as well as the believers . . . I am expecting Agnes Alexander any day for a visit of a few hours any way, perhaps a day, she loves you so much. When I was in Chicago for one Sunday I saw our Beloved Brother – Mirza Aboul Fazl. Mirza Assad'Ullah Mirza Raffi and Khan. Mirza K. said all the believers are beautiful in Paris they have such a beautiful jewel Miss Bolles to teach them – Every one adores you my darling – To know you is to believe . . .

May's love towards her spiritual children generated their love towards each other. She showered encouragement on them unstintingly. Her support of Agnes Alexander, after she embarked on her historic voyage to Hawaii, is remarkable considering how much family pressure she was under herself, that summer of 1901:[45]

It is Sunday and you are on the great sea, on your way to work in God's beautiful Vineyard. Oh, my little girl, my sweet gentle Agnes, only God knows how I love you, how the image of your pure face as it was that last night with its radiant look of happiness and peace, is graven on my heart . . . I have thanked God over and over again that the Blessed Tablet reached you in time, so that wherever you go henceforth, you can feel that Our Great, Our Beloved Lord . . . has set His Eternal Seal upon you, has accepted you for His Own, and that He will move you, guide you, strengthen you & uphold you and surround you by His incomparable love, and His irresistible Protection.

This was the thought that consoled and upheld me that night after you had gone, when my tender little bird had flown from the nest of her Mother! I thought she is His Divine Bird now, and has flown away to seek her Eternal Nest in His Bosom . . .

Your humble sister and mother,
May Bolles

Soon after Breakwell's declaration of Faith in Bahá'u'lláh that historic summer, May wrote another letter advising Agnes Alexander on the best way to teach the Faith:[46]

---

45 1 July 1901.
46 27 August 1901.

My darling, be careful not to make the mistake of being too secretive or in any way <u>mysterious</u> about our Great Religion for this does much harm and causes much prejudice.

If people desire to know about it, even thro curiosity, we have no right to deny them, for it is God's Truth, not ours & He is able to protect His One Mighty Cause. Always remember that <u>nothing</u> happens by accident, there is no such a thing, so that if we meet anyone on our path, & they enquire, there is a reason and wisdom back of this event. Of course we have to use great judgement, & not deliver the Glorious Message to any soul until they are ready to receive this Word of Life into their hearts, but there is much that we can teach beside this.

For instance we can tell them the purpose of Our Religion, which is to unite all religions, & all people in a universal brotherhood . . .

My little girl, I hope my words, spoken out of my heart's great love for you, & with the utmost humility, confessing that I am but a helpless mote before the Glorious, the Omnipotent! I hope they may help you darling, far away in that land of His lands, working alone with all the fire & devotion of your soul for Our Glorious Lord! . . . He is with you. He upholds you with hosts of His Confirmation, and throngs of His Angels surround you, that you may become a door of Light, a pure sanctified channel of His bounty & Grace.

She often recalled Lua's words in writing to those to whom she had taught the Faith. In this letter to her spiritual 'baby' Agnes Alexander soon after she became a Bahá'í in 1901, she repeated what she had learned from her own spiritual 'mother':

As dearest Lua says, all our work in His Vineyard is on <u>ourselves</u>, to perfect ourselves day by day is the way to spread the Fragrance of Sanctity & diffuse the Breathes [sic] of God, & to deliver the Cause to the people. I know you have much to contend against, my precious, & I humbly ask God to strengthen you that you may overcome & win the victory & sever yourself from all else save Him, & receive His Confirmation.

A few months later, on 2 February 1902, she echoed Lua again in writing to Agnes:

I am longing to know all about your work in Honolulu. Always remember, my lamb, what was taught to Lua in Acca, that the work in the Vineyard of God varies greatly; it is not often that we can pick the ripe fruit; sometimes we have to cast out stones gently & patiently for a long time, or cut off bad branches, or fertilise the good soil with many prayers, but always & most of all to pour, pour the sun of Love upon the seeds & plants, for this alone will make them grow. We must give our love to all, & give it in the way they need it, warmly, fervently, tenderly, unchangingly, like the Love of Our Great Lord (may my life be shed at His Holy Feet!). I often think of Bedra Bey, the Turkish official who loves and adores Our Lord (rouhi fédah) altho he is not yet a believer, and for years Our Blessed Master has showered love & kindness upon him, showing him by every word, look and action that He loves him, sending him flowers & gifts showing forth in a thousand ways the beauty of His limitless Bounty. And this example of Bedra Bey is only one of so many that they could not be mentioned!

May's words to Agnes convey her longing to be united in the service of the Cause:

You will write to me my Baby, and tell your humble & loving spiritual Mother everything, that I may share your life & your world with you; we are <u>one</u> in the Holy spirit of the Glorious God, now & forever.

I clasp you to my heart & kiss you tenderly, my Darling. May God bless & confirm you & make you a dazzling Star of Guidance.

Another soul who wrote letters to May that reflected the vibrant love she herself showered on all who had the privilege of meeting her during that early Paris period was Edith Theodora MacKay. A talented singer, she was among the first to visit 'Abdu'l-Bahá, and never forgot the privilege. She was also one of the Bahá'ís who benefited from May's presence in Paris in the course of the summer of 1901:

My dearest!

H. Dreyfus is only coming back tomorrow – So, to my great regret I cannot be with you this evening – It was <u>so</u> good to see your dear shining face yesterday – I am getting desperate because I never see you enough! . . . If I dont have some new pupils soon – I dont know what I shall do – I am just burning to tell the Truth to the whole world! Is it not terrible to feel that way, and be able to do <u>nothing</u>! . . .So till Friday, my own angel – I am your's ever most humbly in the Love of Our Lord! . . .

When you came in the parlour yesterday when I was singing I felt the Spirit descend into me with such force, that I shook like a leaf!

In September, when Thomas Breakwell returned from 'Akká, Edith wrote to May again, overjoyed with the message she had received from the hand of the Master:

Beloved Sister, my own May!

Mr. Breakwell came last evening the bearer of such messages! My heart is overflowing with joy and a gratefulness beyond expression.

It seems as if for a moment, I had forgotten all my weaknesses, all my imperfections – to rejoice and be absolutely happy.

Oh the Divine Compassion the boundless Love of Our Lord! The Perfection bending down to lift the handful of dust that I am, by the hand with such words that are fit for angels! and the delicious suffering of a gratefulness that can never be great enough though I should go through fire and torture for His Name!

I know you have also received a Tablette from Our Blessed Lord (Rouhie fedah) and I hope you will grant me the joy of reading it sometime . . .

But Thomas Breakwell's letters to May were the most ardent of all. Following the pattern set by Lua and repeated by May, he too wrote to his spiritual mother from 'Akká on 8 September 1901, in the course of his pilgrimage; he too translated love into service:

My dear Teacher,

How can I begin to write you the joy I feel at being in Akka, and to see daily our dear Master. Now I realize fully the blessed privilege that has been granted me, and my heart seems ready to burst with joy.

I rejoice to tell you that I believe ten thousand times more than I did when I left Paris, for I thank God he has permitted me to see our Master from a spiritual standpoint, and with a spiritual eye, instead of in a material way. But it is impossible, as you know, to express one's feelings, although it is like being bathed in a sea of spiritual water, and it covers the whole body. The atmosphere also seems, and is, different.

I prayed God that he would teach me humility, and he is teaching me daily, for I never felt so deeply my imperfections and unworthiness. At times I feel as though I could throw myself at the Master's feet and cry for God's mercy, and indeed I will when I get a favorable opportunity . . .

I have also remembered all the Paris believers in his presence, as requested. All the believers here have a special liking for yourself, and the Paris believers . . . and they all wish to be kindly remembered to you.

I have had the great pleasure of meeting Mr. Hopper and Mrs. Brittingham, and to be with them here in the Master's house. That we all realize what a privilege this is you will fully understand. We dread for the time to come when we shall leave Akka. To the great sorrow of everyone here, the Master is not permitted to go to Haifa on account of recent troubles. This makes us realize to a greater extent the privilege we have of visiting him, and remaining in his house . . .

You must forgive me if I have written you a long tedious letter.

With many many kind regards to yourself, and all my Paris friends, believe me,

Your Sincere Pupil,
Thos. Breakwell

I do hope I will be able to visit Paris again, for I wish so much to see my Paris friends again, and to learn of you more of the teachings. I received from you a wonderful amount of spirituality, and many, many times think of you.

On his return to Paris, Breakwell burned with the love of the Cause. Six months later, it must have been clear to May that he was burning with fever too, for by then he was very ill, but the consumption from which he was suffering was not more infectious than his ardour:

My dearest, dearest sister,

How I praise God that I may call you by that name, and that we who have entered His Great Kingdom are all of one family, brothers and sisters in our Lord.

Dear Sister I write to tell you that I have followed your wishes, and the desire of my other brothers and sisters, and have placed myself in the hands of Dr. Gaube. He is the doctor for the family here; very clever, and a specialist on bronchial troubles; in fact, he is often called to go to other countries to give his special method of treatment. And so there is the great satisfaction of knowing I could not be in better hands. He pronounced my illness as chronic bronchitis, and says he can cure me, but on account of it being so chronic, it will take at least three months' treatment. I can continue my work, but must live very quietly.

Of course, dear sister, I have taken it in prayer to Our Lord, praying that He will bless the treatment I will take, and if it is in His Wisdom, that I may become well and strong again, so that I may be able to do more work in His Vineyard, for it grieves me so much to be so idle. I realize now, dear sister, so keenly, that a malady of this nature would preclude any active work in the service of our Lord, and believe now that it is God's will that I should use these means for my recovery (Inshallah).

I have also written to my father to send me the necessary money to carry me through, as he has written me several times of late that if I needed same, he could let me have it. But, my dear sister, I do want to thank you so much for your sweet offer in this respect, but as it will take many francs to pay for the medicine, doctor's fees etc. for the three months, it is better I should get it all at once, and thus my mind would be at ease. I thank God with all my heart that he has placed me in such a good home, and has opened up a way that I can take this treatment. Praise be to God! the giver of all things. I see but His Love and His Mercy through it all. Forgive my writing so much about myself, but I wished so much for you to know all, so that you may cease in your great love to be anxious about my health. God willing, I will follow the instructions of the doctor faithfully, and I trust in a few months to be able to mingle with my brothers and sisters more than I do now, and do more work for our Dear Lord.

I enclose you a letter received from Miss James, which gave me great, great joy. How happy I am to know she is well. When I can do any writing for you, <u>do please let me know</u>. That is a joy to me.

Breakwell longed to serve the Master and May was his direct link with the Master. In a Tablet to her received after his return to Paris, 'Abdu'l-Bahá writes:

Convey my greeting to Thomas Breakwell and say: Happy is thy condition, for thou hast made spiritual advancements; and I pray to God that thou mayest add with every moment to thy development, and become purely spiritual, and wholly divine.

He invariably shared the joy of receiving Tablets from the Master with May too. On 17 April 1902 he wrote her a note, enclosing a copy of one:

I long for you to read the Tablet our Beloved Lord so graciously favored me . . . Dearest sister this Blessed Tablet of our Lord had a marvelous effect on me, and immediately I felt His Presence, with all His Love, in my soul, and I was transported with an unspeakable joy . . .

If he could help May serve the Faith in Paris, he felt he might win the good-pleasure of 'Abdu'l-Bahá. Once, when she returned from a brief visit to the country, he wrote:

My dearest Sister,
My heart rejoices tonight because I feel that our Lord has greatly blessed you during your absence, and you have returned to Paris radiant and glorious. (Praise be to God!) You looked as though you had been bathed in His wondrous Oneness, Love and Holiness, and Miss Robinson also has caught its reflection, and it seemed to me when you first entered the room this evening, you had come direct from Acca.
Oh! my sister, if all in Paris could see, as I see, that beautiful Light of God, that is reflected in you, then they would acknowledge Him, and know that He had again bestowed His Holy Spirit on His chosen ones, to lead and give them light.

You are one of His chosen Ones, and to you this power has been given in all its fullness. When I see this Light reflecting through you, it strengthens me more than I can express, for I must confess sometimes I feel discouraged when I see that I have seemingly accomplished nothing in His Vineyard.

But I have asked our Lord to forgive me my weakness and selfishness, and that He will use me in His Service in any manner which seemeth best to Him, and that I may lose sight of this awful, awful Self.

I felt that I must write you these few lines, for my heart rejoiced so much to see you return to all of us so happy and radiant.

Humbly your brother, In the name of our Lord,

Thos. Breakwell

P.S. I have a typewriter now for a few weeks, so as to do some writing for you. I got it a few days ago. (How I will tell you when I see you.) I feel in this way I will be doing some real service for our Master, and that He wishes me to do it.

Since 'Abdu'l-Bahá had instructed May to stay in Paris, Breakwell must have felt that by helping her he might serve the Cause there too. In the following note written to her sometime in the early spring of 1902, he shares some joyous news about a new believer:

My dearest Sister,

Please forgive me for writing you again, but I must express my great joy that God has answered our prayers, and has brought Mr. Sprague into His Kingdom.

He returned to the house a new creature, telling me now he was convinced beyond any doubt, as while he was talking to you he saw your beautiful soul, and he said it appeared so radiant and bright, that he was awestruck, and for the rest of the evening it had a remarkable effect on him. I feel so sure he will make an earnest believer, and do a great deal for the Cause here in Paris.

Oh! my sister, the blessings of our Lord are coming so abundantly the past few days, that my heart overflows with gratitude to God, and I feel strengthened and confirmed in His Cause. My illness has been but a blessing in disguise, so, my dear sister, please do not feel anxious when God in His great love afflicts me.

Do forgive me for writing you so much of late. I could not resist expressing my joy that God has permitted our new brother to see that beautiful Light of His Spirit, which He reflects in His Chosen Ones. Praise be to God His Holy Spirit is again manifested in the world!

* * *

All through her long engagement with Sutherland, May remained first and foremost a lover of the Cause. Her dedication to the Faith was a guiding light to all who knew her during this time, as Emogene Hoagg averred in later years:

She was absorbed by it; she lived it; her entire time was taken up with teaching in some way. Her love for the Cause was an inspiration to all who knew her well. I feel that her profound and reverential love for the Faith, with her deep understanding of the Teachings, made of her an exception – a unique western example of the power of Bahá'u'lláh's Revelation.[47]

There is no question that without her helping hand some of the early Bahá'ís would have been rudderless and lost. But she was not immune to tests herself. In fact May's attraction to those whose spiritual search recalled her own sometimes led her down strange paths. In the years 1901 and 1902, she sometimes put herself in danger in her efforts to help others. To illustrate the extremes to which May sometimes expressed empathy, Amatu'l-Bahá recalls the fate of Lillian James in her memoir:

She [May] possessed great physical and moral courage. Once in Paris she heard that a friend of hers, a Bahá'í, who was a student of music, very poor and had been overworking, had had a complete breakdown. She went to her at once and found she had lost her mind entirely. The doctor told her that her friend was now danger-ously insane and that it was unsafe for her to remain with her alone. Mother, however, said she was not afraid and would watch with her

---

47 22 March 1940.

the night. The doctor warned her that if she fell asleep the insane girl would attack her. All night long she sat beside the bed, watching her patient, who seemed quiet enough. Towards dawn she felt overwhelmed with sleep and, fight as she did against it, she dozed off for a moment, only to awake and find the lunatic's hands strangling her. She told me she looked into the eyes of the mad creature quite calmly and normally, with love and tenderness, and the hold on her throat was relaxed and she was able to get her back into bed. No amount of effort would have freed her as Mother was small, weak and frail, the other quite out of her mind. For some reason they had not been able the previous day to remove her to a hospital; she was, however, after care and treatment, completely cured.

May herself wrote about this event in one of her letters to Sutherland, on 13 December 1901. But she did not tell him the details of this episode. She simply used the experience to illustrate for him the power of spiritual love:

> My own dearest Sutherland -
> I can only write you a little letter by this mail as one of my dear sisters, Miss James, is very ill and I am doing my humble share of taking care of her.
> I sat up all night with her a few days ago and God gave me the most wonderful & marvelous strength – & altho I was very tired the next day I was soon quite recovered. We are sending her home with a trained nurse & everyone has been so good & kind and loving & I feel so deeply grateful, for I love Lillian so deeply. I am sitting with her now, and I want to send these few lines to you – my darling – to give you my heart's love, and to tell you that I feel your beautiful pure spirit drawing nearer to mine in the wonderful love of God, and this is better unto us than any marriage on this earth . . .

* * *

The Bahá'í Faith had given May an identity over and above the traditional female ones. It had enabled her to achieve unusual independence for a young woman of her age and had given her psychological as well as spiritual wings. It had allowed her to carve out a 'space' of her own, priorities of her own, standards of behaviour beyond her obligations to her family. She wanted to make sure that Sutherland realized that she would never jeopardize this independence. In fact she had hinted as much in a letter written to him before his departure, on 22 September 1900:

> A few days ago we picked a great quantity of wild blackberries, & I made 14 pounds into the most delicious jam. I find I have not lost my hand in the cooking way, & I am so glad, for now I really care! I want . . . your wife to be the Best of home-women – but without being sunk in it! That I could never be.

And in her subsequent correspondence with her betrothed, who was busily planning their life together, she shied away from discussions regarding the buying of their future home:

> Dearest, what you say about taking an apartment now has set me to thinking & it seems to me that you had better wait. I would not reserve an apartment now if I were you until our future is quite clear – & would it not be better to choose it together when we go to Montreal, or would you rather have your wife's home already waiting for her? What do you think, my Sutherland? It has always seemed to me so much more ideal to choose the house together, then to furnish it together, & have it a growth & expression of both of us – do you agree with me? Tell me just how you feel.

As the weeks and months slowly passed, the language of her letters to Sutherland became increasingly abstract. In her letter of 8 February 1901, for example, she wrote:

> When I write to you, my own, I do not think of outside things that are only the shell, the symbols of the inward reality – I think & write of the love of our hearts that is like a spring, a fountain of pure waters – & of the deep life of our souls that is eternal – of our union – our aspirations – and our power & influence for good on every being with whom we come in contact – these to me are the only realities – & become more so every day I live. I pray to God so humbly & earnestly to open our hearts more & more to His light, to

His sublime Love, for without Him we are dead. God is the spiritual Love of which the sun we see in the heavens is an outward sign & symbol – when that sun shines on the earth it gives life to all nature – plants, trees & flowers, & they begin to grow. So it is with the Spiritual Sun, when it shines on the souls of humanity they awaken into new life, & begin to grow. There has been more growth & progress in the world in the last century than in all the history of the world in proportion up to that time, & in the last quarter of the Century than in all the Century – on this all historians are agreed – & this is for no other reason than that there has appeared in the world the Greatest Manifestation of God – the Highest Spiritual Light – Teacher & Guide – and the Power of the Almighty God is upon all mankind. We are so blessed to be at this time on earth – we are standing in the dawn of the light – that will flood the whole world.

That summer, when Thomas Breakwell and Herbert Hopper went to 'Akká, May evidently sent 'Abdu'l-Bahá some questions that bore directly upon her personal circumstances. Herbert's letter of 8 September 1901 provided her with His replies:

My dear Spiritual Mother,
     It is a great privilege to write to you from the house of our dear Lord and Master and even from His prison, as doubtless you must know of the order of the Sultan given about 15 days ago which confines him to the city of Acca, so that He does not even go with the believers to the Holy Tomb today. It is impossible to tell you now of the great blessings we are enjoying because, as the Master has said, we do not realize the greatness of the privilege as we will after we are gone.
     I have asked the Master the questions you wished me to and will give you a resumé of the answers now and when I see you in Paris talk more about them.
     First that believers are permitted to marry unbelievers.
     And as to prayers made at the Holy Tomb they were granted or are granted if the prayers are good for the one who supplicates.
     I was permitted to have a few moments private talk with the Blessed Master this morning and everything is settled for me in a general way but I hope to have another like opportunity before we leave.
     The talks of the Master are beautiful beyond comparison with

anything that I know of. Mr. Breakwell and I are together in the same house with Him.

* * *

By July 1901, the drama at 100 rue du Bac had reached its climax. It is impossible to know how much Sutherland was informed about it, but it is clear that he did not know that Mrs Bolles and Randolph had gone to Brittany alone when he wrote May a letter on 11 August. He believed she was already on the coast by then. As it was she did not leave Paris until the end of August and only spent two weeks in her family's company. Sutherland's letter must have arrived in her hands just before she left, exactly when she was teaching Thomas Breakwell about the Faith. He attempted in this letter to ground her theories about the Love of God in the soil of human relations:

> Your remarks about God are very beautiful. You say 'He is the only One worth knowing and loving' – Certainly Love for God is the highest form of Love, and 'true joy' and 'true life' are not given to us unless accompanied by that love. True fullness of life is not given to us unless we love God and our fellow beings. God teaches us to love him in many ways, direct and indirect . . . I think that it is God working within us that puts this beautiful love that trusts and that sees the good in our fellow beings, and enables us to make allowance for qualities that are capable of greater perfection. So that trust and faith are really signs of God's being in us. I think Dearest that we both see it in the same light.

And then on 8 September – quite unaware of the summer storm that had swept through Paris just weeks before, at the heart of which Breakwell had heard the stirring words 'Christ is come again! Christ is come again!' – Sutherland wrote to May about quite a different storm in which he had been caught, during a yacht race. It is strangely moving to read his interpretation of this event, which had seriously imperilled his life:

> In the very worst part of it I felt so united to you Dearest, I felt that everything would come out all right and in the little prayers that I silently offered up, you were foremost in my heart and thoughts.

A few months later, on 17 December 1901, May wrote to Sutherland about plans for their marriage:

> . . . your letters are such a joy & inspiration to me – they are becoming so full of spiritual light and strength & reality . . .
>
> Dearest – you ask me about the answer from Acca – so I can tell you now that it came the very day I sent you my last letter – & if you have kept that letter, & will read from where it begins – 'I love your companionship both spiritual and material' – & read to the end of the quotation marks where it says that our spirits will be as birds & fly away to the Eternal Kingdom . . . you will know the answer for these are His Words.
>
> He has greatly blessed us. He has promised to pray for us! And altho I must still delay a while our marriage yet this is in the Wisdom and Mercy of God. You see darling – that one of the principal things that keep people from turning to God is that they are satisfied without Him. They have what they want on this earth – then their souls are lulled to sleep, they are contented with human attachments & earthly interests – their lives pass away & they have lost the fruits of their labor – missed the whole purpose for which they were created in the very beginning – they have grasped the pebble & lost the diamond – the priceless gem!
>
> If you will think well upon this & consider the wonderful change & development in yourself in the past year – far, far greater than when you were with me my precious – then God will remove the veil from your eyes – and you will know that He Alone is all sufficient for us. He Alone is the Precious – the Beloved and able to fill our whole heart & soul & being with the Fire of His Mighty Love.

The trouble was that in the Tablet containing 'Abdu'l-Bahá's answer He had instructed her to stay in France without indicating for how long. He had urged her to wait a while before marrying for reasons that she could not sensibly offer to Sutherland. The original Tablet had been revealed in Arabic and the undated French version, probably translated by Ahmad Yazdi, one of the Master's secretaries at this time, had, according to May's letter to Sutherland of 17 December, reached Paris shortly before that date. It is evident from its present fragile condition, from the tears in the paper and the blurring of some of the words, that it must have been folded and unfolded, read and re-read by May a thousand times. This Tablet was intensely personal, specific to May's circumstances at that time, and relevant to her alone. It was highly unlikely that she would have shared it with the other Bahá'ís in Paris. Even though it made direct reference to Sutherland, she did not share it entirely with him either in the translation she cited in her letter of 17 December.[48] But she must have carried it around with her like a talisman:

O thou enkindled by the fire of the love of God,

I read thy detailed letter and noted its wondrous contents. Render thanks unto God that He saved thee from the affliction of His trials and delivered thee from the depths of the ocean of His tests. He enabled thee to be sincere in thy love of Him, independent of any one beside Him, attracted to His sweet savours, and manifesting His loving kindness. Rejoice, then, within thy soul, and be gladdened within thine heart for being the recipient of the grace of thy Lord, as He hath empowered thee to be attached to none other but Him. He is, verily, the True Protector, the All-Generous!

O Handmaid of God! Do not make haste in the matter, as it is better to wait a while in such affairs. Perchance that person's heart may be illumined with the light of guidance, and thou mayest draw him nearer the shade of the Tree of Life, and enable him to enter the Paradise of Divine Love. Tell him: 'I love thy companionship and fellowship in both the earthly and divine kingdoms, both physically and spiritually. Were we to be united in body only but divided in spirit, of what use and of what benefit would such a union be? Such intimacy would be an accidental illusion, not an essential reality. I would rather have a bond with thee in both the earthly and heavenly existence, in both body and spirit. Such a union would be divine and last forever. By its means we would soar like birds with the wings of divine love, gain admittance into the paradise of His Kingdom, build our nest on the branches of the Tree of Life, and sing wondrous and melodious songs of thanksgiving and praise in the realms above.'

Perhaps this person will be awakened from the slumber of negligence,

---

48 May had rendered into English, from the French translation she received, the exhortations of 'Abdu'l-Bahá to her in this Tablet. The translation in italics is an approved provisional translation from the Arabic.

and witness the signs of the bounties of thy Lord, which hath encom-
passed all the worlds.

    I turn in prayer to God that He may change thee into pure spirit,
shed upon thee the lights of Truth, free thee from all things, assist thee
to sacrifice thine entire being in the path of His love, and to forget
thine own self, thy body, and all thy corporal conditions. Thou wilt thus
become entirely spiritual, an incarnation of the spirit, an embodiment
of celestial light, a symbol of wisdom and one of God's angels that hath
come down from heaven.

Here then, was the reason for her delay. Here was the motive behind
her earnest hope to '*have a bond with* [Sutherland] *in both the earthly and*
heavenly existence'. She had clearly taken to heart the Master's advice to
'*not make haste*' and to '*wait a while*' before marrying. She was keenly
aware of His reasons for giving her this particular counsel. If she put her
personal desires before the needs of the Cause, how could she expect
Sutherland to be her spiritual as well as physical partner in life? How,
above all, could she expect to win the good-pleasure of her Lord?

* * *

May's entire being was attuned to the communications she received
from 'Abdu'l-Bahá. She longed for His words. She pored over them,
memorized them. Even when they only accompanied Tablets from His
hand that He was asking her to deliver to others on His behalf, these
precious words fed her, revived her, seemed to lift her into another
realm. On 24 January 1901, for example, He wrote:

> *O thou who art attracted unto God!*
>   *Verily, I remember thee in my prayer and supplication to God, and*
> *implore my Lord to make thee a flame of the Fire of the Love of God.*
>   *Deliver the enclosed letter to its owner.*
>   *May greetings and praise be upon thee.*
>   *'Abdu'l-Bahá 'Abbás*

She delivered the Tablet, but she kept the cover note as a precious
gift from the Master. Her soul was sustained by the encouragement
He showered on her, and her spiritual growth, which was a source of

inspiration to all who met her, was dependent on the exhortations that flowed from His pen. One can only imagine the impact on her of a Tablet such as the following, for example, which has survived, undated and in fragments, and tattered to shreds by repeated reading:

. . .

> Blessed art thou, for thou hast severed thyself from aught else save God!
>
> Blessed art thou, for thou hast been kindled by the fire of the Love of God!
>
> Blessed art thou, for thou hast been attracted by the perfumed breezes of God!
>
> Blessed art thou, for the service thou hast rendered to the Word of God!
>
> Blessed art thou, for the supplications thou hast offered to God!
>
> Blessed art thou, for the efforts thou hast exerted in propagating the Cause of God!
>
> I pray on thy behalf to make thee a lamp of guidance in that spot, a land heedless of the call of God.
>
> O servant of God! The Kingdom hath been adorned with the raiment of beauty, perfection, might, greatness, and glory; and from God's universal Revelation the veil hath been lifted, and lo, divine gifts, heavenly favours, wonders of the merciful Lord, celestial signs, wondrous symbols and holy tokens have appeared. These dazzle the eyes, astound the minds, rejoice the breasts, and attract the hearts of the onlookers.
>
> Alas! What a pity! For the servants and maidservants have become heedless of these divine gifts, and veiled themselves from these lordly favours . . .
>
> As to thee, be confident and well-assured, for the Lord of Hosts shall assist thee with the hosts of the Kingdom, and with the cohorts of the angels of confirmation from the Dominion on high.[49]

Another undated Tablet addressed to May from the early years contains a quite remarkable prophecy about her future rank and spiritual station:

> O thou maidservant who art attracted to the Kingdom of God and art announcing the glad tidings of the Beauty of the countenance of Bahá in those regions!

---

49 No copy of the Tablet upon which this approved provisional translation is based has been located at the Bahá'í World Centre; it was rendered from material found among the papers of Amatu'l-Bahá Rúḥíyyih Khánum.

Verily, I address to thee from this blessed Spot this message, through which thy soul will be gladdened, thine eye brightened, and thy heart rejoiced: Blessed art thou, O maidservant of God, for arising to proclaim the Word of God. Joy be unto thee, O thou brilliant leaf, for serving in the vineyard of God. Glad tidings be unto thee, O thou well-assured and believing soul, for diffusing the Fragrances of God!

Erelong will thy Lord enable thee to attain such a state of bliss as will be the envy of the queens of the world throughout the ages, inasmuch as the love of God is a glorious crown upon thy head, the brilliant jewels of which shall shine forth upon all lands. Its lustre, radiance and effulgence shall appear in future centuries when the signs of God will be spread abroad and the Word of God will encompass the hearts of all the peoples of the earth.

In a third Tablet addressed to '*the honourable Miss Bolles and her friends*', 'Abdu'l-Bahá refers to a photograph of the Paris group which had been sent to Him. Although this too, is undated, it must have been written sometime in 1901:

O ye illumined countenances!

It was in truth with great pleasure that I looked upon the picture which portrayed your noble selves. I found your faces glowing with the light of the love of God and each one of you bearing the tokens of His infinite grace. By my life, the glory of the All-Merciful shineth in your illumined faces and the signs of His guidance are manifest as though adorned with diadems of faithfulness. I am thrilled at an image so unique of a splendid group whose members have set their faces towards the Kingdom of the glorious Lord.

By my life, this message shall be for you a source of glorious pride throughout the ages and centuries to come. Therefore thank ye God for this gift and render praise to Him for this expression of faithfulness.

There was also a prayer of 'Abdu'l-Bahá revealed for the 'Five Leaves'[50] who were among the early believers in Paris and included some of the pilgrims who had just returned there on their way back to America from 'Akká. Their photograph, sent by Edward Getsinger to 'Abdu'l-Bahá,

---

50 May Bolles, Anne Apperson, Lua Getsinger, Julia Pearson and Brenetta Herrman were photographed during their reunion in Paris in April/May 1899, after the first pilgrimage.

had elicited this beautiful response.

> *O my God! These are the five leaves of the tree of Thy clemency and the five servants of the sacred threshold of Thy oneness.*
>
> *O Lord, surround them with the angels of Thy holiness and enable them to serve Thy Cause.*
>
> *O my God! Make their faces to shine with the incomparable light of Thy Unity.*
>
> *O my God! Fill their hearts with a boundless joy that wafts like unto a breeze from the Abhá Kingdom, that they may be wondrous signs of Thine appearance above the all-highest Horizon.*
>
> *O my God! Confer upon them the gift of Thy words and praises, that they may become distinguished amongst all mankind.*
>
> *O my God, they are the signs of the fire of Thy love, wellsprings of the waters of Thy mercy, tokens of the light of Thy providence, and shining stars of Thy grace. Grant them such blessings as Thou hast showered upon the saintly heroines of past ages.*
>
> *Thou alone art He Who hath the power to choose!*

How May's heart must have quickened each time she saw a postmark from Palestine on one of the letters delivered to 100 rue du Bac. How eagerly she would have shared its contents with the little group of Bahá'ís who gathered together in Paris over the course of 1900–1901. The Tablets of the Master meant all the world to her. She read them over and over again.

Only once did an envelope arrive whose contents may have disappointed her. It was in early 1901, when plans were being made for the little group of pilgrims to go to 'Akká, and May had asked permission to go with them. 'Abdu'l-Bahá's Tablet to her then had made it clear that she should stay in Paris:

> *As to thy request to come to this blessed Spot: for the present, it is necessary for thee to be there [Paris] and to remain with the beloved ones [believers]. Until the Cause of God is firmly established in that city, it is not permissible for the believers and the maidservants of the Merciful to disperse. Nay, it is necessary for all of them to assemble together and exert themselves to the utmost to diffuse the fragrances of God. When the opportunity presents itself, thou wilt be permitted to come.*

These words must have been engraved on May's soul. She had scruples about marrying without His blessing. The extraordinary circumstances related to the summer of 1901, moreover, proved for her the wisdom of the Master's words. His instruction that she should 'wait' in Paris that summer as well as 'wait' to come on pilgrimage, may have become a reason for her to 'wait' to be married too. This was confirmed when she received the subsequent Tablet from the Master, in which He told her plainly, *'Do not make haste in the matter, as it is better to wait a while in such affairs.'* Furthermore, another plan she had to try and go to 'Akká that October had also foundered. The challenge of applying for a visa from the Ottoman consulate in Paris was complicated, and the situation for the Master had evidently become too grave for Him to encourage further pilgrims from the West. It is not clear whether she had her visa application turned down or whether 'Abdu'l-Bahá Himself had discouraged her from coming. His wish was her command. If she could not leave Paris to go on pilgrimage then she could not leave Paris to marry either.

* * *

And now a second winter had almost passed, another spring would soon return and the summer of 1902 was looming. Mrs Bolles had remained in Paris to give Randolph one last chance to finish his diploma and to accommodate to her daughter's wish to serve her Master's will. The former, to her surprise, had fulfilled his side of the bargain and had even earned himself a medal,[51] but the latter was still in the same state of suspended animation as she had been one year before: engaged to be married but unwilling to commit herself to a date.

The time had now come for Mrs Bolles to make arrangements to return with Randolph to New York. Sutherland had conveyed his thoughts clearly to May in his letter of 10 February that he 'most certainly would not give [his] permission' for her to stay alone in Paris should they leave, to which May had promptly replied with the assurance that she would not do so.[52]

---

51 A note from Marie Squires to May written on 24 November 1901 from Illinois confirms that Herbert Hopper, her fiancé, had written to her from Paris that 'he had a medal, and your Brother also and that your Brother was through now, will you congratulate him for me – I am so happy for you all. I think so often of your dear Mother . . . I know how she rejoices in your brother's success – How she will some day rejoice in yours which is above all earthly joys.'

52 On 10 March Sutherland wrote: 'I was so glad to get your cable as it gave me great joy to

There was only one thing that could be done in the circumstances. Randolph wrote to 'Abdu'l-Bahá on his mother's behalf to explain the situation.

There is no doubt that the words of the Master were May's mandate for living. She must have longed that they might also become her mother's, for 'Abdu'l-Bahá had initiated the correspondence with Mrs Bolles Himself during this period and had written to her well before she availed herself of the opportunity to appeal to Him. In an undated Tablet addressed to her, He had called on her to witness the transformation wrought on May since her return from pilgrimage in early 1899:

O thou who hast heard the call of the Cause of God!

I adjure thee, by God! Hast thy young and honourable daughter ever been in the state wherein she is now? No, by God, for she was in one condition but now she is in another. Yea, she was human but is now heavenly; she was earthly but is now celestial; she was worldly but is now attuned to the kingdom of God. She was ignorant, silent, heedless and constrained, but now she is endowed with knowledge and eloquence; she is vigilant, rid of all attachments, attracted to the divine, enkindled, and fully aware of the remembrance of God. She is imparting the knowledge of God, directing the people to the path of salvation, bestowing the Spirit of Life, and spreading the Word of God throughout all regions. Her apathy hath been replaced by activity, her weakness by enkindlement, her stillness by wondrous utterance, and her heedlessness by a new spirit of alertness.

Doth not this amazing development satisfy thee, that thy vision may be illumined by the manifest Light? Hast thou ever heard of such a matter in past decades or generations? No, by God! The evidence is complete and decisive, the argument is clear and manifest, and the lights are shining before thine eyes.

Therefore be kindled with the fire of the love of God, make mention of Him, bear witness unto the appearance of His kingdom, and proclaim His bounties. Verily, this is best for thee both in this world and the world to come.

One can well imagine that Mrs Bolles might not have seen her daughter's transformation in quite the same light, at the time. But 'Abdu'l-Bahá

---

know that you were not to be alone in Paris and I feel that your mother and Randolph are very pleased and happy over it.'

continued to trust in her spiritual capacities. She was a good woman and loved her children; He knew that she had a pure heart. After the remarkable events of that fateful summer of 1901, there was a great change in Mrs Bolles. May wrote that she used to come into her daughter's room after hearing of Breakwell's acceptance of the Faith, with the shy request 'Pillows?' by which she meant she wanted to kneel down on the floor to pray with her daughter.

Whenever May received anything from the hand of the Master, her whole being thrilled with excitement. But to see an envelope postmarked from Port Said, and addressed to Mme Marie Ellis Bolles and Mr Randolph Bolles that spring of 1902 must have shaken her composure considerably. It contained two Tablets[53] which may have been written earlier but whose translations were dated 7 April. The first was addressed to Mrs Bolles herself:

> *O venerable lady!*
>
> *I have read thy detailed letter and noted its contents. I immediately wrote a letter to thine esteemed daughter so that she would obey thine orders, observe thy wishes, and act in a manner that would rejoice thy heart and brighten thine eyes. Thou shouldst thank God that He hath given thee an angelic daughter, spiritual and divine, whose worth thou shouldst appreciate. As she proveth her steadfastness, thou wilt behold from her that which will cause thy heart to soar with utmost joy and gladness, rendering thanks unto God at every moment for the celestial bounties He hath conferred upon her.*

The second was addressed directly to Mademoiselle Bolles:

> *O thou who art attracted by the fragrances of God!*
>
> *I beseech God that He may make thee a sign of guidance and a lamp*

---

53 The Tablets came with a note from Ahmad Yazdi, the Master's translator at the time, who wrote: 'Some time ago I received by registered mail, two letters from you addressed to My well-beloved Master (may my life be sacrificed to Him), which I duly submitted to His Holy Attention. Today, I have the honour of sending you the enclosed two responses from His sacred Presence, together with their accompanying translations . . .' The procedure of reception and response from 'Abdu'l-Bahá was slow at this time. After letters in French or English were received in 'Akká, they were sent to Port Said to be translated into Persian by Ahmad Yazdi, and then sent back for an answer. The Tablets of 'Abdu'l-Bahá then had to be sent to Port Said for translation and returned to 'Akká to be approved and postscripted by the Master. It could have taken at least three weeks between 'Abdu'l-Bahá's response and the reception of the Tablets in Paris.

enkindled by the fire of the love of God, to enable thee to spread the fragrances of the knowledge of God.

Know thou that the rights of parents are great, very great, and God hath compared them to His own rights. Thou must, therefore, please thy mother, obey her orders, and show consideration towards thy brother under all conditions, as required in the law of God. Thou mayest enter into wedlock with the one to whom thou art engaged, as there is no obstacle and the time hath come. And if it is the wish of thy mother that thou shouldst return with her to America, thou must accept this duty, for it is not fitting to remain alone in Paris. God will verily assist thee with the Spirit of truth and the power of the kingdom, and it will make no difference whether thou residest in Paris or in America.

O maidservant of God! Truly I am with thee and will be thy Companion at all times and in all places.

Rest assured that the grace of thy Lord is with thee, and that the spirit of power will enable thee to spread abroad the sacred and sweet savours of thy Lord.

Let nothing sadden thy heart, for soon thou shalt witness that which will delight thy soul and rejoice thy spirit.

The Master had added a postscript to the French translation of these letters:

Do all that is in thy power for the spirituality of thy fiancé, that he may become celestial and divine. After thy marriage, spare no effort in this, that haply his heart may be illumined by the light of the Kingdom. Thou art permitted to come alone to visit this luminous Spot.

The Master had given His consent for her to marry! But what did He mean by inviting her to come on pilgrimage *'alone'*?

* * *

Sutherland's reception of the Master's consent, written on 16 March 1902, indicates that May might have already received news from Haifa one month before. The Master's Tablet confirms that upon the reception of Mrs Bolles' letter, He had *'immediately'* written to her, but the absence of all correspondence from her and any other existing Tablets from 'Abdu'l-Bahá before the translated one dated 7 April leaves this issue somewhat uncertain. May's confession to Agnes Alexander, later that same year, of the emotional upheaval she experienced when 'Our Adored Master (rouhi fedah) sent me a Holy Tablet commanding me to go home to America and to marry the man to whom I was engaged' confirms that she was under great stress during this period. She evidently sent a cable to Sutherland immediately, however, and this message of 'condensed happiness' was confirmed by letter afterwards.

> Dearest – Your letter that brought me such good news yesterday was a message of great joy to me. You don't know how really thankful and happy I am and how grateful I am to Him in Acca who has been so good to us.
>
> I arrived home at about seven and opened the letter at the dining table and of course immediately read it, and my countenance was a tell-tale one, for Mother, who was there, said 'Good news, eh?'. She said I looked like Blythe[54] when he is pleased and I guess she was right, for I could not control my features. Well, Dearest, it was great news just as I expected and felt it would be ever since your cable of condensed happiness came to me. Do you know I am sorely tempted to take the next steamer and gallop over . . . but I will just hold on to myself and watch the calendar, the way a cat watches a mouse . . .
>
> Dearest – when writing to Acca – do convey my most sincere thanks and gratitude to your Master for his great kindness and help to us. Although our waiting long for one another has in some sense seemed hard, it has but served to make us better in all ways, and it has but conveyed to me a great knowledge and admiration of those qualities of trueness, strength, faith and gratitude that are the foundation of your being.

It is just as well that Sutherland accepted the news at face value and expressed his joy so simply, for in the weeks that followed her reception of 'Abdu'l-Bahá's consent, May was torn by conflicting emotions. She had yearned for His blessing, but may have feared that His hand had been forced, His permission extracted under duress. She longed to be married to Sutherland but may have felt that he had also forced *her* hand by threatening to arrive on her doorstep before she had the

---

54 Blythe was the first grandson in the family, son of Edward.

Master's authorization. And what of that precious opportunity of pilgrimage that had been offered to her in the postscript, on condition that she accepted *'to come alone to visit this luminous Spot'?*[55] Did this mean that if she was married she would never be able to visit 'Abdu'l-Bahá again? She may have felt guilty before, for putting the Cause before her troth to Sutherland, but was probably wretched now at the thought of putting him before the Cause. She was in a fever of contradictions.

Since she had already been under severe strain with all her Bahá'í activities for several months, her health broke down completely in March 1902. She fled from 100 rue du Bac to recuperate in the country. Edith MacKay, one of the few people in whom she may have confided and who evidently knew about her situation, wrote May the following letter on 5 March:

My beloved Sister,
　　I am with you day and night – do you feel it? I know what you are going through, and my prayers constantly ask God to unite our hearts so that we may be together, and help each other in His Light –
　　What suffering we must experience, what trials we must go through before we get the Confirmation of the Spirit! – That is what we think in this world – and all these things later will seem to us as mere grains of sand, compared to our everlasting Joy and Peace.
　　Yet, it is only by these trials, that light increases – and I feel now that my prayer and utterance should be, every time calamity attains me – Oh God – I thank Thee for this new mercy! This incomparable Blessing!
　　Your friend came to the meeting this evening – we read and talked, and she asked many questions, some of which were beautifully answered by H. Dreyfus – But we missed our Angel – oh so much! Who could ever replace your sweet presence – your inspired words, the light you shed every where you go? I pray God daily to become more and more like my beloved teacher.

55　This was a period of increasing danger for 'Abdu'l-Bahá under Ottoman rule. He was under constant surveillance as a result of the growing machinations against Him and had recently been confined within the prison walls of the city of 'Akká by edict of Sultan 'Abdu'l-Hamíd. Pilgrims who came to see Him had to do so one by one and with great circumspection. Although the situation improved a few years later, it would deteriorate radically when the plots against His life, which culminated in the Commission of Investigation, led as may be surmised from internal evidence to His writing the second part of His Will and Testament.

I trust I will see you Friday – Rest well in the Peace and Light of God – in the Beauty which is surrounding your spirit –

While she was away in the country for these few days, May also received a loving letter from her mother, dated 6 March 1902:

My dearest little Girl,

Thank you very much for the telephone message which relieved me very much and for your sweet little letter. I am very happy that you are better, for you were so ill, and although we miss you very much, we want you to stay until you are quite yourself. If you would like to have me go out there and stay with you – I would be more than happy to do so – for every moment you give me makes me glad. Although you were so ill those days—I felt a greater peace with you than I have for a long time – because you seemed nearer to me in every way, and I felt your love and tenderness and you, as you are really – my own little daughter, and I know your Master wishes it to be so. He loves you so much and he loves me – too – you know, and he knows how hard I try to be good and unselfish and how you do the same – *n'est-ce pas, ma petite cherie?* . . . God bless you – my little child – He has and will and we will all be happy and helpful.

Your loving mother

It is evident from the tone of this letter that something had brought Mrs Bolles closer to the spirit of the Cause; something had made her trust 'Abdu'l-Bahá at last. There is a suggestion in her affirmation that 'I know your Master wishes it to be so' that she finally felt 'Abdu'l-Bahá was 'on her side'. Perhaps her appeal was a reflection of her growing trust in Him. Perhaps His response confirmed her faith in Him.

Spiritual tests, however, were uppermost in May's mind. In the course of those same weeks, Lua wrote to her from Washington DC on 12 March about the crises faced by the American Bahá'ís after Kheiralla's defection. It is evident, from the lack of reference to it, that May's correspondence with her spiritual mother, unlike the one with her physical mother, bore no relationship to her personal dilemma:

My own May-Violet

I am in receipt of your most beautiful letter which made my

heart very happy and glad. I am with dear Mrs. Jackson and we are trying to promote our Glorious Cause here in this city. She has been a loving friend and mother to me through my tests and trials – and I love her devotedly. Dear Helen Cole came and spent a few days with us. She has come out of her furnace purified and beautiful – and she is not the same being at all. She is so strong and full of faith. But dear Mrs. Kheiralla has turned away from the Truth – and now we are all praying for her . . . This is a great time of trial in America. Dear do try and keep your children under the shadow of the Word of God for therein lies the safety of the world . . . We never know how soon our supreme test of faith may come so let us try very hard to help others through the ordeal and thereby prepare ourselves for it . . . Dear lovely Elsa is very firm in the love of the Master – and she and I are trying to unite and work for the Cause . . .

My precious May Violet – you cannot know how much your letters help me – how close I get to your lovely soul and pure spirit as I read them. Give my love to all of the Believers especially Theodora and her mother . . .

P.S. I love you more than I can tell you my darling precious spiritual child, and I want you always to pray for
Your Mother
Lua

In light of such severe crises of steadfastness among the early believers she knew, it is not hard to imagine how May might have construed her dilemma as a 'supreme test of faith' too. For more than a year she had been conscious that the American Bahá'í community had been undergoing severe trials. For over a year too she had witnessed some of her dearest friends getting married and in some cases drifting away from the Faith. One of her greatest ordeals was to find the way to tell the little group of Bahá'ís in Paris of her own impending marriage, and her imminent departure in the spring of 1902, without appearing to have broken faith with them, without seeming to have failed in her service to the Faith before all else.

Those who were far from Paris naturally rejoiced for her when they heard. Laura Barney, for example, assured her that 'Lua is in great happiness on account of the Master's words to you' and told May of her own relief at the news:

> The Master's Tablet to you filled my whole soul with joy – So Dear Sister your trial is over – thank God! These words from the Master's pen will give you the wings of strength that you yearn for to fly unto His Mighty Throne.
>
> I know dear one the torments that have gained[56] you this message – for I was the humble one who heard your sobs during these past months.
>
> I kiss you tenderly dear teacher and I salute you in the name you taught me 'Allaho Abha'.

But the Bahá'ís in Paris, who were going to lose her, felt very different emotions. She did not tell any of them until the last minute. Edith Sanderson wrote to May on 29 March advising her to share the news individually and 'not at the meeting', to lessen the shock that she herself experienced when she learned that May was going:

> May dear I was sorry to have to leave you yesterday as I did – that I could not have been braver than I was while in your presence for I realized all the time how I must be adding to your sorrow and burden. But it was a shock, and I could not control myself. Please forgive my selfishness May dear.
>
> It then seemed that in losing you we were losing all our strength. You have been our guide. You see May dear, you are so illumined and what is so clear to you is in darkness to us.
>
> My loss in your leaving us is great, but the loss of those who do not know is greater.
>
> But as you say, we must turn our faces towards our Lord – and know that since this is to be it is His desire and consequently for our good. So May dear I am trying to pick up my courage – seeing how brave you are about it – and am learning to say God's will is my will.
>
> I do hope to see you strong and well again by next Friday, and I think if you would tell all the Believers – but not at the meeting – you would feel the better for it.
>
> I say not at the meeting for it would be too hard on all of us –

---

56 The word 'gained' here is a Gallicism extracted from the French 'gagné', implying 'earned'.

Reactions like this could hardly have made the situation any easier for May. Thomas Breakwell's letter to her, for example, must have shaken the poor girl to her very soul. It is undated but was probably written soon after he heard the news:

My own dear Sister,

I have prayed our Lord to help me in writing this letter for I wish to express in writing my true feelings upon learning we were going to lose you, as I am afraid personally I would break down entirely.

First of all, my dear sister, I believe it will prove a great, great blessing to you, and that the spirit of our Lord will go with you to your new home, and that you will, through His Power and Mercy spread the Glorious News in Montreal, and wherever you go. You are needed as much in America as here, and the souls there are as dear to God, we know, as the souls in Paris.

Praise be to God! my dear sister we shall never spiritually lose you. This is my great consolation, for when we become believers in El-Abha we know we are all one soul, and whatever earthly ties we may make, we have but one Heavenly Father, and soon the time will come, when we will all enter this Glorious Oneness, and all praise and adore our Lord, not as brother, sister, husband or wife, but as new spiritual beings, living in the spirit, loving one another in the spirit, through the great and wonderful love of God, which will radiate every soul, and make us eternal. Praise, praise be to God! that this is what He created us for. What wonderful, wonderful love, to grant us such a gift!

My dear sister, I have begun to realize lately that it is God's wish that we should take on these earthly ties, and live simple, pure, beautiful lives, through His Mercy. Praying to Him that we shall love everybody, antagonize no one, speak ill of no nation or individual, but simply try to love all, and serve all. Then, too, my dear sister, our Lord has shown me that to lose self, is in a great measure, not to give our opinion of material things, and in ordinary conversation to listen, and not antagonize people by placing our opinions against theirs, even if we are right; in fact, to suppress our desire to express our knowledge of places, people, and things in general, when it will not advance the Cause, and perhaps start an argument. I have noticed that the greater portion of the hatred in the world, is caused simply because people express their opinions, and if they are not agreed with immediately discord and even hatred is created in their hearts. To lose myself in this way, my dear sister, I realize can only be done by the power of God and I pray Him for this earnestly and fervently. You, my dear sister, have through God's Love, been given this grace, and that wonderful sacrifice of self to others, and of listening to others.

Another lesson God has taught me recently. That is, He, and He alone, is the creator of this new Spiritual Kingdom. I am but a being created by Him. Have no power outside of Him. Can do absolutely nothing without He wills it. I realize that tomorrow He could set all France alive with His Spirit, and that I am not necessary for the advancement of His Cause. And so, my dear sister, I place myself as a supplicant before the Door of His Oneness, beseeching Him to let me work in His Cause, suffer for Him, and at last have the glorious crown of martyrdom. He alone can grant this, and none but He can give me the spiritual strength to remain faithful and firm.

Should none of these be granted me, I praise God He has created me, that I know that my Creator lives, and I shall beg for more love and gratitude to Him.

I mention these things, my dear sister, simply that you may know how my Lord has changed me, so that now, God willing, I can mix with the people of the world, knowing I am a Bahaist through the Mercy of God alone, and that the revelations He has given me were through His Great Love and Power, and that they do not make me superior in the least; that I was born of clay, and passed up through the material conditions the same as all humanity; in fact, my attitude to the world has been changed completely.

My dear sister, my prayers will go with you in the new life you will soon enter. I shall always, as in the past, supplicate a special blessing from our Lord for you. You know my great, great love for you in the Spirit of our Lord. In my soul you will always hold the highest place, the deepest reverence, and the purest and sweetest remembrance of my life. I feel what is going out of my life, although I have the spiritual consolation we do not part. You have been so much to me; always tender, always loving, and sympathizing with me, through the many spiritual conditions it has pleased God to put me through. I write you my feelings, because I could not express

An early group of believers in Paris, circa 1900: seated, front row, left to right, Mrs Emogene Hoagg, Mrs Helen Ellis Cole (cousin of May Bolles), Mr Herbert W. Hopper; centre, May Bolles; standing, left to right, Mrs Eliza Archad Conner, Miss Marie Squires, Mr Charles Mason Remey

*Phoebe Hearst, photograph
given to May Bolles' mother,
signed: 'Affectionately yours
P. A. Hearst, May 1889'*

*May Ellis Bolles and
Edith Theodora MacKay
in Paris, 1901*

Early Bahá'í group of Paris, 1901 or 1902: standing, left to right, Miss Elsa Bignardi, Mr Herbert W. Hopper, Miss Florence Robinson, Mr Hippolyte Dreyfus, Miss Berthalin Lexow, Mr Charles Mason Remey, unknown, Mrs Marie-Louise MacKay, Mrs Margarite Bignardi, Miss Stephanie Hanvais, Mr Sydney Sprague; seated, left to right, Miss Edith MacKay, Miss Holzbecker, Miss Edith Sanderson, Mr Sigurd Russell, Mr Thomas Breakwell, Miss May Ellis Bolles, Mrs Hanet, Miss Marie Watson

May Ellis Bolles

William Sutherland Maxwell

Announcement by Mrs Bolles of the marriage of W. S. Maxwell and May Ellis Bolles, 8 May 1902, in London

them personally, and although it will be several weeks before your departure, I now pray God's blessing on your journey, on the new ties you will make, on all your future life, and assure you, as in the past, you will in the future, always hold that high affection in my soul.

I pray our Dear Lord daily for each of us in Paris. That He will draw us closer together in the bonds of El Abha. That I may become as dust before the Believers; growing in affection for them day by day, and seeing in each one the beautiful Light shining in them. For I now realize, my dear sister, that the more love and light there is in my own heart, the greater beauty will I see in others, and if the Light burns not in my own soul, or reflects but dimly, to that extent will I see it in others. That I must love all, through God's help; serve all, <u>teach the truth to myself first</u>, and then through God's Bounty, try to teach others, and always be generous in thought, word and deed, not only to the Believers, but to all mankind. Thank God, He has created in my heart such a wonderful change in this way recently, that will I feel completely change me for the future. But with all I realize this is a Gift from Him, a precious Gift, and that I am nothing, have nothing, outside of Him. In a minute He has the power to cast me into the darkness, for He is God, and so I thank Him for these Bounties, praise Him for creating me, rejoice that He is my God, my Lord, and my Creator, and that with all His Power He is a God of Love, a God of justice, a God beyond all my praise or comprehension. I am happy, happy, happy, to be nothing, to serve Him as a being created by Him, to look to Him for all, to be bathed in His Love, and simply to be a creature loving and praising my God, my Creator, as I should.

May God richly bless you, my dearest sister, and I pray that He will grant you your dearest wish, that He will use you for the advancement and Glory of His Cause, in your future new home, and new surroundings.

Such anguish at her departure and such encouragement at her impending marriage put into words the conflict of emotions that May herself had been experiencing for months. It was at the root of her illness in the beginning of March and the reason she was paralysed all through April. Even her friends in Paris who were not Bahá'ís expressed the same sorrow at losing her and joy over her happiness at hearing the news. One of them, Elsie Stuart Pattee, wrote to her in March or April 1902:

> I wish I could see you now, at once, and throw my arms around you and tell you how sorry I am that you are going away; and yet how glad that you are moving swiftly on toward the most beautiful turning of the road that can come in a woman's life . . . I saw a picture of your fiancé, to-day, and by it I should say that you had made a perfect choice. Mr. Maxwell has a wonderfully fine face; a face that a woman might feel safe in giving her allegiance to, it seems to me. I most earnestly hope that everything that is loveliest and highest in this new relation may be yours, constantly and enduringly. I hope that every joy and sorrow will serve to bind you together . . .

Unfortunately, joys and sorrows seemed to be pulling her apart at that time. Indeed, the contradictions that May was experiencing just then marked her soul profoundly, and although the wounds healed in time, their scars still ached for many years to come. She begged 'Abdu'l-Bahá's forgiveness for abandoning the Bahá'ís in Paris:

> My Beloved – My Lord!
> . . . With my heart at Thy Blessed Feet I thank Thee for Thy Compassionate Tablet to this servant, and for Thy most Merciful Command. I entreat Thee to forgive my sins, to strengthen me to obey Thee, to become naught else but Thy sanctified servant.
> For sometime past I have been ill & weak in body. I humbly implore Thee to heal & strengthen me, that I may fulfill thy command, & be able to cross the sea.
> Oh! Most Blessed, Holy and Beloved Lord. I earnestly & humbly beseech Thee for my beloved spiritual children, my Brothers and Sisters in Paris, that Thou wilt cause our separation in the body to be a cause of unity & strength in the Spirit – that each one may become an illumined lamp, and that the Fire of Love may be enkindled & the Fragrances of Sanctity of the Glorious Lord be diffused.

On receiving her tearful supplications, the Master responded with infinite gentleness and at the same time challenged her and galvanized her spirits with these stirring words:

Be well assured of the favours of thy Lord, be resigned unto Him, and cross the ocean in full tranquillity and security. However, thou must show forth such steadfastness as will astonish the minds of those who are endowed with intelligence.

* * *

May had no idea how firm she would have to be in the future. But as Paris burst into flower that spring, marking the second anniversary of her love and the third of her faith, she was caught between extremes. February was a time of growing tension. March brought 'Abdu'l-Bahá's awaited guidance, and April proved the cruellest month indeed.

Sutherland must have sensed her condition from a thousand leagues away. He had been prepared to rush over to Europe in mid-February but despite his strongest instincts he had found himself unable to do so. It could not have been a worse time for work. Edward had to make several trips to New York and Baltimore just then, and Sutherland was left alone to run the firm. More and more draughtsmen were being hired at Beaver Hall Square[57] and the business was expanding rapidly. The brothers had carried out ten 'public projects for the Canadian Pacific Railway over the past decade and at least twenty private commissions', one of which, the Hosmer House, was being completed at that very time. As the quantity of their projects increased, the older brother was relying increasingly on the younger one to ensure their quality, and if Sutherland had gone to Europe in early 1902, he would have been compelled to break off vital professional engagements. Since there was so much at stake, therefore, he reluctantly submitted to Edward's counsel and, in spite of himself, obeyed 'Abdu'l-Bahá's injunction as well. Against his own will, perhaps, he was being governed by the Master's advice to May that they should not *'make haste in the matter, as it is better to wait a while in such affairs'*.

The 'good news' in May's March letter to him must have seemed like a blessed reprieve. She must have confirmed that she would come to America to be married in April rather than have him come to Europe. He wrote to her admitting that it was probably the best solution, in the circumstances:

---

57 The address of the Maxwell brothers' firm had become synonymous, by this time, with its name.

I used to be so annoyed at Ed and his common sense but perhaps it is the proper thing under the circumstances to wait and be married on this side . . .

But as the month dragged on, Sutherland began to have misgivings. May was supposed to be packing up for her departure, but she was apparently holed up in the country somewhere. On 20 March Sutherland began to change his mind about waiting:

I am thinking of taking a trip over next week but of course I will cable you if I decide and you will have the cable before this hasty line. I will speak to Ed about it . . .

Ed must have told him to hold his horses. If May could not get over by April, the wedding could take place in May, couldn't it? Sutherland was dismayed. There was something about this continued delay that he did not like at all. He vacillated between his brother's counsels and his instincts until 23 March, when he wrote to May again:

Dearest I so want you to hurry up your packing and come over; do try and be out very early in May. My common sense and my true feelings get on but fairly well, and each day my feelings say to me, why wait a day – why not fly away immediately, and let your heart be contented, and that monstrous old thing common sense drawls out knowingly – I think you will make a mistake, I know if I was you I would wait . . . And so on my tiresome common sense friend within me does counsel. And so Darling I say to myself one day, yes I will leave next Wednesday, and five minutes after, with a deep sigh – I resign myself to wait for you Dearest.

In this same letter, he dramatized for May the quandaries he was facing, talking to himself in an internal monologue as he tossed the pros and cons back and forth:

If you go over now you will arrive in Paris on April the third, you will spend a week or so there and then reside two weeks in London and then you will have a month abroad and will be back in Montreal or New York after having been absent two months and a half away.

And you must bear in mind that you have undertaken to have the Hosmer house ready for occupation the first week in April and that a hundred small matters need your personal attention, and if you go now Angus' furniture and interiors and carving will be left to hands that are less able to do these matters justice. Not to mention the expense of your journey.

As it turned out, he could not afford to leave just then. Work commitments did not permit it. But with every passing day it must have become increasingly clear to Sutherland that May was in no state to make decisions, let alone pack up her affairs after so many years in France, and move definitively back to North America. As he had so beautifully said a few months before, 'God made us human that we might exercise care of our fellow beings and ourselves.'[58] And it was evident that May needed care badly just then. By the last week of the month he was on the high seas and heading for Cherbourg. He arrived in Paris at the very end of April.

In the course of this month, when she was so overwrought, May also received a beautiful letter from Thomas Breakwell, written on 17 April 1902:

Allaho'Abha
Dearest Sister,

Please accept these few flowers, as a present from our Beloved Lord, as all things come through Him.

I realize, dear sister, all your suffering, and your great love to us all, and in spirit my soul seems to be going through with you those heart rendings at the thought of your leaving us, for you love us all so much.

I am glad I feel your sufferings, for, sister, it is a proof of that wonderful spiritual bond our Dear Lord has bound the children of El-Abha with, and I would I could at this moment bear all your sufferings for you; be weak, that you may be strong, and go through for you the sorrow of leaving us.

But, dearest sister, you have the most beautiful consolation, that we all love you dearly, and that you have been the means through God's Bounty, of giving us great spiritual inspiration and strength,

---

58 26 January 1902.

and through you we learned of our Beloved Lord. So our hearts are always yours, dearest sister.

May God keep you, may God bless and strengthen you is the earnest prayer of,

Your humble brother in the Wondrous Love of our Beloved Lord
Thos. Breakwell.

May's love for the Bahá'ís in Paris had met its match in that of Breakwell's. Canadians were still British subjects in 1902, but Sutherland still needed a residence permit to be able to register his marriage under British law. Ironically enough, by delaying his trip to Europe, he actually added to all the other expenses incurred by the wedding because he had to pay a fine for not having fulfilled this irritating requirement. Writing to Edward, *en route* to London on 3 May 1902, he sent last-minute instructions and apologies for the length of time it would take him to return, but could not help pointing out that if there were going to be extra expenses and time involved, it was his brother's fault. He too was under stress:

Dear Ed,

It is impossible to say how soon I will be home. May is progressing slowly. Owing to the Bolles having had but enough in hand to take them home – (we did not take steamer) I have advanced amounts so if I cable for cash you will understand.

I should have left six weeks ago when I wanted to. However all will come well but it will take time and care.

May and I send love to you.
Your affect. Brother
Willie

Note: Polish Peases floors if they need it. Have sent the papers.

There was one detail related to the wedding arrangements, however, which cast a slightly more comic light on these tense proceedings. When plans were finally made for the party to cross the Channel, May's brother discovered that quite apart from the mandatory two weeks' residence required for civil marriage procedures, there were also quarantine papers necessary if they were to bring Puck along. And since there was no time to wait for the poodle, Randolph had to remain behind in Paris. Although he had looked forward so long and eagerly to the marriage of his sister to his dearest friend, he missed the wedding because of the dog! Despite his absence, however, their long-standing friendship and his affection for Sutherland, which had begun in their youth, would remain intact until Randolph's death in 1939.

There was another slightly farcical episode, which occurred during the wedding ceremony and was destined to become part of family lore for years to come. Rúḥíyyih Khánum recounted that when her father was waiting in the vestry just before the procedures began, he was so nervous and fidgety that the rather rickety chair on which he sat himself down promptly broke under his weight. To his dismay, the 'big strong lump' of a Canadian, as he called himself, found he not only had to pay the additional fee for a special last-minute marriage licence but also the costs of repairing an antique chair! It was, as Edward probably let him know on his return, a costly wedding. But every penny spent was surely worth it, for those concerned.

And so it was, that between tears and smiles, the union of the happy pair was finally solemnized on 8 May 1902, in the parish of Christ Church, at Woburn Square in the Administrative County of London. Mrs Bolles signed the marriage certificate as one of the two official witnesses, and promptly sent a notice of it to her relatives on her return to New York. One can imagine her pride and relief in doing so:

Mrs. Bolles announces the marriage of her daughter May Ellis to William Sutherland Maxwell on May eighth, nineteen hundred and two, London.

In the course of their honeymoon, Sutherland wrote a letter to his own mother to make sure that she too had published an official notice about the wedding. He wanted to announce this long-awaited event to the whole world!

Did you put our wedding announcement in the paper? We were married in Christ Church, Woburn Square, London by the Rev. Glendinning Nash on May 8th at 4 p.m. . . .

After the high drama of their courtship, and the tearful climax of their wedding, the honeymoon itself was bound to produce some comic moments. May was in such a state that she actually expected her mother to accompany her on her honeymoon. Rúḥíyyih Khánum often told the story of how Mrs Bolles was trying to say goodbye to her daughter when May turned to her, horrified, and cried,

'But you're coming too, aren't you, mother?'

The truth had dawned on her at the last moment that she was actually going to be alone in Tunbridge Wells with this great hulk of a Canadian. When she begged her mother to join them, Mrs Bolles had loftily replied,

'Certainly not! You're on your own now.'

When Sutherland wrote to his mother ten days later, he sent her an update on May's health, and included a sketch of himself beside her bath chair as an indication of her condition and his own happiness:

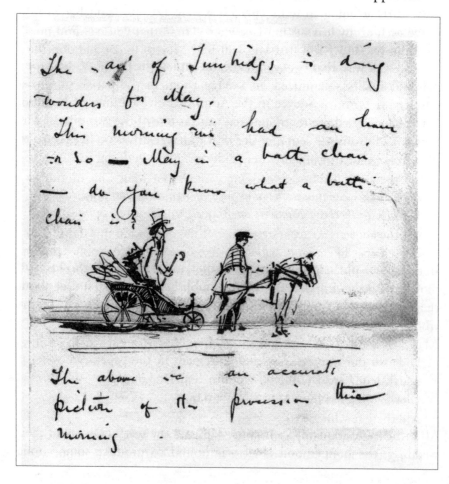

We are now in Tunbridge Wells in 'lodging' as they call it. We have three rooms occupying the first floor of a small house near the Public Common . . .

I gave details relating to our simple and beautiful marriage in a letter to Eddie. After our marriage we stayed in London for a week owing to May's not being well enough to stand journeying without losing any strength she gained. We have been three days here and she is gaining in strength and health.

Ed . . . did write to David saying it was very important that I should soon make for home . . . in any case I expect to hear in a day or so giving reasons. I simply cannot leave until we have stayed here ten days – by that time May will be much stronger and we will both be most glad to be with you all.

May is going to write you a letter today . . . I told her how you felt at my leaving and I now am certain that you will find me improved and I feel that you will find May to be an addition to your family – vying in importance with Blythe – I know that May looks forward to knowing you and being with you with most sincere pleasure.

Mrs. Bolles and Randolph and Mr. Puck (the wonderful pooch) left for New York yesterday via *S.S. Zeeland* of the Red Star lines, sailing from Antwerp . . .

The air of Tunbridge is doing wonders for May. This morning we had an hour or so – May in a bath chair – do you know what a bath chair is?

The above is an accurate picture of the procession this morning. The chair is like a large Baby carriage, only different. Rubber tired wheels – canopy etc. – small dapple grey pony – Welsh – small boy who walks and drives, and in the vehicle is the bride and walking along side is the groom.

May also wrote to her mother-in-law that same day, on 18 May 1902:

My dear Mrs. Maxwell,

Your boy has been writing you a long letter to which I want to add these few lines.

We are very happy and very grateful for our happiness, and he is so good to me! I know you must miss your son very much, but we hope to be in Montreal before long, and then I trust you will not feel that you have lost him, but that you have found a loving friend in me.

Sutherland has talked to me so much and so lovingly about you, and I hope to make him as happy as you do.

I am getting slowly stronger, and every one has been so kind to us.

Will you give my loving remembrances to all, and believe me to be most sincerely and affectionately yours,
May Bolles Maxwell

You will be glad to know that Sutherland is very well. I did not think to speak of it at once, as he is always so strong and well.

The young couple sailed for New York and Montreal soon afterwards. The next chapter of their lives together had finally begun.

1902–1914

With May's departure from Paris an epoch came to an end. Although she was to visit Europe several times in later years, with Sutherland and alone, her field of service would henceforth be concentrated in the Americas.

The Canadian chapter of the Maxwells' story began with a curious dream. On the first page of what appears to be an attempt on her own part some years later to write a history about the Faith in that country, May recounted her mother-in-law's strange dream just before she and her husband arrived in Montreal. With hindsight, it was to acquire great meaning for her:

It is strangely significant that on the eve of the return to Canada of those who were destined to be the first to raise the call of the Kingdom and herald the new Day that Johan Maxwell, the mother of William Sutherland Maxwell, had a very vivid dream. She was standing on the top of the Westmount mountain and saw the City of Montreal lying before her as a map of the Catholic Church. Gradually the horizon widened to embrace the Province of Quebec, and finally the uttermost boundaries of Canada. She saw clearly all the stronghold of Catholicism, its cathedrals and churches, schools and colleges and convents, the many institutions by which it had founded and nurtured and fostered the life of a great people for centuries. Then slowly it began to sink into the ground further and further until it was swallowed up by the earth and disappeared, and in its place a vivid fresh and verdant Springtime clothed far and wide the country in a new and living garment. She was so profoundly affected by this dream, the like of which she had never had, that she told her son and his wife at the time. From the beginning this continent became singularly blessed by the Mighty Confirmations of Bahá'u'lláh. One after another the heralds of the Cause visited Montreal. Sarah Farmer, Lua Getsinger, Thornton Chase . . .

She wrote no more of the history, but added a brief profile of Sutherland some time later that offers insights about her perception of her husband in the early years:

> This youth – who was destined to become one of the most brilliant architects in Canada – did not fully grasp the implications of this union with one who had been among the first pilgrims to the prison of Acca – who at that time had dedicated her life to the service of the Cause – and to whom the Master had said, 'I have accepted you as my own daughter.'

It had been difficult for May to part from a country and culture that had, to all intents and purposes, become her own. She had grown up in France and spent her happy days of childhood there. She had recognized the Cause of Bahá'u'lláh in France and met her love there. And after her first pilgrimage, she had come back to France, in the springtime of her heart and soul, and had taught the Faith there. The thought that those vernal days might never again return, the idea that she might have disappointed her beloved Master by leaving Paris too soon, the feeling that she had abandoned the fledging Bahá'í community that had been placed in her care, weighed heavily on her sensitive heart as the steamer drifted away from Europe.

Besides, May must have known that there were some among those precious souls in Paris whom she was destined never to meet again in this life. Her last supplication to the Master, on 26 April 1902, the eve of her departure for London en route to North America, was on behalf of His dearly-loved Breakwell:

Most Beloved Lord!
   I write to Thee on my last night in Paris to mention to Thee that Thy blessed servant Thomas Breakwell is ill, and to humbly entreat Thee to guide him to that which will heal and strengthen him, if it be God's Holy Will. He has severe bronchial trouble and coughs day and night, and at last, at the urgent entreaty of the believers, he consulted a good doctor. This doctor gave him a certain treatment

which has failed, and he now orders Mr. Breakwell to leave Paris, as the climate is bad for him. Thou knowest, Beloved Master, that Thy servant cares nothing for his body or his life, and he would not leave Paris lest Thou instruct him to remain here, and Thou knowest also that he is very poor, and has no means to enable him to do what is best for his health.

Oh! My Lord, he has a wonderful Spirit which Thou hast given him, and we love him greatly – all things are in Thy grasp, wilt Thou cause him to be healed in Thy Mercy!

This humble one leaves for America tomorrow, laying her heart & life at Thy Adored Feet, & thanking Thee and praising Thee forever.

She knew that Breakwell was dying. The dreaded news of his passing that same summer must have renewed the grief of leaving him, revived the pain of abandoning the Bahá'ís in Paris, and filled her with fresh chagrin. His death, coinciding as it did with her new life, must have broken open the old wounds once more.

Another event which probably caused her emotional turmoil took place soon after Breakwell's passing and barely six months after May had left the shores of France. It was Lua's trip to Paris that same autumn. This proved to be no ordinary visit. Lua waxed lyrical about it without giving May the details of her mission at first. But when the young bride finally received her letter dated 28 September 1902 she realized that her spiritual mother had been doing grand and glorious things in Paris, which she too might have been doing, if only she had stayed there:

I came to Paris dear to see the Shah of Persia, and after much trouble and difficulty I accomplished all of that – I obtained an audience with Him, after presenting a petition to the Grand Vizir, which he accepted from me and a copy of which Edward will send to you, also all the details of the reception if you will write him for them! . . . The Shah granted the first part of our petition, but could not promise anything regarding the release of the Master from Acca! . . . [B]y the time this letter reaches you I shall be on my way to Constantinople to see the Sultan & beg Him to release our Lord . . . Mr. Dreyfus, Mme. Jackson, Ellen Goin, Edith MacKaye, Edith Sanderson, and two other women American believers whom you do not know are going with me! Mr. Dreyfus and Mrs. Dashill and myself are going in advance of the others – about five or six days – as we cannot all arrive there at the same time, as it will create too much suspicion. Thus dear little May, I am now going to offer my life as a ransom that the Sultan will open the gates of Acca that the American believers may go there to see their Lord, and also that He will allow our Lord to go out of Acca as He was wont to do! Please pray for me dear that I shall be accepted, and that I shall be successful! . . . How I wish you were here to go with me my dear spiritual child – though it is best that you are not or you would be! . . .

What did May think when she read these words? What did she feel when she learned that Lua and Mrs Jackson and Ellen Goin and Edith MacKay and Edith Sanderson, and two other American women she did not even know, were setting off for Constantinople without her? Was she a little hurt, perhaps, by being excluded from such a glorious mission? Would she not have wished to defend the Cause too on behalf of the Bahá'ís of Paris instead of being marooned in Canada?

The longing for martyrdom was not unique to Lua alone. Many of the early believers, including May herself, had been smitten by this passion. Brenetta Herrman, the artist, was also intoxicated by the idea of sacrifice:[1]

> . . . I have prayed incessantly that if it were His will I might be permitted to have the way made clear for me to do some work in connection with the lives of the Glorious Martyrs – think dear sister of being given the permission to picture their lives and their last moments before going to Him . . . think of putting on canvas some of the noble deeds and acts of devotion by the Believers living in the world today – think of what use they would be were they brought to America and the people could see how others had willingly and with beaming faces given up their lives to the Cause . . . you can hardly understand how that one idea has dominated all others until it's the only thing I think of morning, noon and night . . .

The story of the martyrs in Iran was a living proof to the early believers of the truth of the Bahá'í Faith. They longed to give it credence through

---

[1] 6 March 1900.

their own acts: to give up everything, to sacrifice their all, to lay down their lives willingly and joyously for the Cause they so loved.

Perhaps May's letter to Agnes Alexander may give a glimpse of what she was going through in the weeks leading up to her wedding and for some months afterwards. It is undated but throws light on May's state of mind in late 1902 and 1903. She sent it from 184 Côte St Antoine Road, Westmount, the home of Mr and Mrs Maxwell senior, where the newly-weds first stayed on their arrival in Canada:

Agnes, my precious, let me tell you in a few words about things which have befallen this poor one in all these months when I have not written to you. Some six months ago, Our Adored Master (rouhi fedah) sent me a Holy Tablet commanding me to go home to America & to marry the man to whom I was engaged. Owing no doubt to the hardness of my heart, & stubbornness of my will, the effect of His Words was as a strong wind which uprooted the tree of my being & I became weak and ill, and suffered many things.

Mr. Maxwell came over & we were married in haste in London & after two weeks in the country, he brought me here, where I fell very ill. It was a deep cup of suffering which Our Heavenly Father gave me to drink & the light & joy & blessing which were hidden at the bottom of the cup were truly great & wonderful. *'In calamity is My Providence, in Appearance it is Fire and Vengeance, in Reality it is Light & Mercy!'*

The severity of May's illness can be gauged by Laura Barney's letter to Sutherland, written around this same time:

Dear Mr. Maxwell,

I have just heard through Mrs. Getsinger who asked me to speak of it to no one, on account of Mrs. Bolles that May has been or still is ill: –

I write to ask you to let me know if you think I could do anything for her. It would be very easy for me to go to Montreal and stay in a hotel for a couple of weeks if you think it would do her any good.

I know you will not feel that I am intruding, for you above all others can understand my deep love for May. If I am to come, just wire me . . .

* * *

Between 1902 and 1910,[2] from the addresses found among May's papers, it would seem that the Maxwells moved from house to house in Montreal three or four times. After staying with Sutherland's parents at 184 Côte St Antoine Road the young couple moved to Hope Street in 1903, to a little house belonging to Edward Maxwell. Then in 1904 they moved once more, to 494 Victoria Avenue, in Westmount, and in 1906 to 29 Bishop Street. Each move entailed an upheaval; each involved renovation and May often absented herself during these periods, either staying in Vermont with friends, in New York with her mother, or in Green Acre with Sarah Farmer and the Bahá'ís. This restlessness must have taken its toll on the young couple. Only in the summer of 1910 were they finally able to take up residence in their own home, which Sutherland designed and built himself.[3]

It was during the first years when they stayed with Sutherland's parents and then in the house of his brother Edward that the strain may have been the greatest. Sutherland had already warned May about the atmosphere of his parental home. In an undated letter[4] written in 1902, he described his father's character and contrasted it to his relationship with his mother:

> There is not the atmosphere in our house that I seek. There does not exist between my father and myself that feeling of comradeship and fellowship of sympathies that I wish did and there is not likely to exist that feeling. I have every respect for him and my opinion of his abilities is a good one, and my affection for him exists as it ought to. I presume I have always been too forward or aggressive or conceited or something. No such thing as a discussion or friendly argument is possible with him owing to our being constituted differently. I am afraid he is a little bit set in his ways, and he is sensitive and at times irritable. I have for more than a year had to bottle up my personality. I do not see him very much because I have my breakfast later

---

2 In one of her earliest letters written to Sutherland on 3 December 1902, Mrs Bolles wrote: 'I wish the house was ready for May now as I am afraid to have her stay in New York much longer, and she expected to go back to you on the 1st of December.'

3 The address, 716 Pine Avenue West, was changed by mid-1929 to the well-known 1548 Pine Avenue West.

4 Probably written on 9 Febuary 1902.

than the others and my luncheon is partaken of alone down town and I work until six every evening, and have dinner at about seven whilst the others dine at six. Mother is always with me at meals and our affection for each other is true, sympathetic and deep-rooted. Now Dearest you know just as well as I do that the effect of living this way upon a person is not extremely beneficial. My usual course is, if I do not feel in sympathy with anyone, to avoid being very constantly in their presence – and under no circumstances to show that I am not in sympathy with them. Now Dearie you will now realize that if there ever was any reason, besides our love, needed, that reason exists. I have hungered right along for your companionship and your Mother's and Randolph's. I have always sought, as friends, Americans, for their wholesome sympathetic optimism is the one thing that I absolutely need if I am to become what my humble attainments make possible.

The newly-weds stayed in this house for about a year. It could not have been easy. It was difficult for May to find her place within the Maxwell enclave. The divergence of temperament and culture between the two families was considerable. The Maxwells were cautious by inclination and did not readily express their affections. The Bolles, as May told her brother many years later, were exemplified by Mrs Bolles' 'broad & free ideas – her good-sense & courage – and her wonderful spirit of joy. She radiated a care-free and spontaneous joy which was like a remedy to all her friends.'[5] May had this same warm and outgoing personality. She must have done her utmost to draw close to her new relatives. With the exception of her mother-in-law and older sister-in-law, she probably received little open affection in return. She was more than ready to appreciate Edward's true-heartedness. When her health collapsed in late 1902 and she went to New York to recuperate, she was very touched by his coming to see her. Writing to Sutherland on 27 November she said:

Yesterday Eddie came & it was such great happiness to see his kind true face. He is coming again today . . .

---

5 May to Randolph, September 1935 from Stuttgart, Germany. Mrs Bolles, she added, 'taught me how to be happy – never to worry, like poor Muddie – to enjoy life to the full – each day – to live while I am alive!'

One can imagine that given the differences of personality among them, 'plain talk' would have been the last thing possible in the circumstances. May quickly learned that the notion of consultation, the importance of unity, the spiritual mandate to love others for the sake of God were not easy principles to share with people who were not, to put it mildly, 'in close sympathy with her religious convictions'.[6] Quite apart from the challenges facing any young bride in relation to her new in-laws, she was aware that the Maxwells looked askance at the Bahá'í Faith. It must have hurt her very much to sense their rejection of her beliefs.

She did not find a much warmer reception, either, in the privileged circles in which her husband moved in Montreal. It was not easy to find kindred spirits in the upper stratum of the Anglophone Canadian society. The *élite* who occupied the cocooned mansions, the country estates, and the private clubs which the Maxwell brothers were building in the Square Mile, or in Senneville and Saint Andrews, had little interest in the life of the soul. They were more concerned with social class and bank accounts. She had no friends among these wealthy wives of stockbrokers and railway magnates, these daughters of flour, paint and hardware empires, these sisters of banks and shoe companies and jewellery firms of early 20th-century Montreal.

Another cause for strain in the early years was the issue of language. The Anglophones of May's own class, with whom she had little in common at that time, were cut off by language as well as wealth from the bourgeois French-speaking families.[7] But May did not fit into Quebecois culture either. Her Parisian French was treated with suspicion by the Francophone families of Montreal and when she first arrived in Canada the colloquial dialect sounded a little uncouth to her. According to Rúḥíyyih Khánum, when the ship docked in the harbour her mother turned to her father and asked him what language the stevedores were speaking.

Sutherland was doubtless sustained by the routine of his work, by the familiarity of his culture, by the confidence he was gaining among colleagues, but she lacked anyone at that time who shared her interests, her priorities, her beliefs. As she confessed in a letter to Agnes Alexander, on 20 December 1904:

---

6   This phrase, which she afterwards crossed out, appears in the draft of the letter she wrote to Edward and Libby some time between 1905 and 1909.

7   Sweeny, 'Building for Power: The Maxwell Practice and the Montreal Business Community'.

Here, in Canada, the Cause is still in the embryonic stage – the soil needs much preparing, & altho I never withhold my tongue from mentioning the Appearance of God, yet few have 'attentive ears'.

Nor was the chill merely spiritual, cultural or psychological. May had been accustomed to temperate European living and her sensitivity to the severe winters was to become legendary in the family. One can just imagine what her hardy Maxwell relatives thought of this sickly woman Willie had picked up in France who could not even stand a bit of snow. Indeed, her correspondence throughout her life was frequently about the meteorological conditions as well as health and she went south every winter on the advice of 'Abdu'l-Bahá Himself.

* * *

May's need for a 'Divine Healer' of course lay at the root of her problems. She felt that unless her union with Sutherland was spiritual as well as physical, she would never be well. From the very start, she fretted over the fact that he was still not a Bahá'í. She felt that in granting His consent to her marriage, 'Abdu'l-Bahá had done so on condition that she do all in her power to illumine Sutherland's heart '*by the light of the Kingdom*'. And so she strove most earnestly. She struggled. She spared no effort. Predictably, all her letters to the Holy Land in those early years included a prayer that her husband might to enabled to recognize the truth of the Cause. In her correspondence with 'Abdu'l-Bahá, she repeatedly begged that his eyes be illumined, that he be awakened 'from the deep sleep of negligence':

> Therefore I beseech Thee to have mercy upon him and grant him the Light of Guidance, enable him to turn to Thee, and confirm him in the Truth; and I humbly implore Thee to sanctify me from him wholly, that I may love him sincerely, with <u>Thy love</u>.

She must have appealed to the Greatest Holy Leaf in the same terms too for the latter replied to May soon after,[8] telling her not to be despondent, not to be disheartened:

---

8   14 February 1903.

My dearly loved friend –

Many times I have desired to write you but as I do not know English I can only write you by the language of my thoughts and heart – and such letters I am constantly sending to you! I am longing for news of you, to know the condition of your health, and if you are happy, thus I have asked your spiritual Mother Lua to write for me a letter that we may once more get into communication with you! Our Lord 'Abdu'l-Bahá (rouhi fedah) always remembers you and He constantly speaks of you – hoping that you are sheltered under the wings of God's Mercy and secluded in the Arms of His Love!

O beloved friend, dear spiritual child of God – let not your heart be sad, and do not let trouble take possession of you – for you have attained unto that which will be of eternal and everlasting benefit to you throughout eternity! You have understood the Truth of God and have turned unto His Holy Covenant – severing yourself from all save His love. Thus you must ever be happy and joyful no matter what earthly conditions surround you. We humbly pray God to open the eyes of your husband that he may comprehend the Truth – and that both of you will be devoted servants to His Holy Cause. God is the Merciful and the Powerful, and I trust this great blessing will soon descend upon you. Be assured that we will ever remember you and pray for you in the Sacred Presence of Our Beloved Lord, also at the Holy Tomb of the Blessed Perfection . . .

May also prevailed upon Sutherland to write to 'Akká soon after their arrival in Montreal. According to Rúḥíyyih Khánum, when her father had asked her mother whether she had thanked 'Abdu'l-Bahá for permitting them to marry,[9] she had replied that he should convey his gratitude and his respects himself. He obviously did as he was told, because that September, the following Tablet arrived for him:

O my beloved one,

I received thy letter in which thou hast expressed thy contentment with one who hath turned unto God and prayerfully adoreth Him. Thy heart is gladdened by reason of thy blissful union with thine esteemed

---

9 This may have been in reference to his 16 March 1902 letter, in which Sutherland wrote: 'Dearest, when writing to Acca do convey my most sincere thanks and gratitude to your Master for his great kindness and help to us.'

partner in life, the handmaid of God, she who hath set her face towards the kingdom of God and is attracted to Him. Thou shouldst recognize her preciousness, because she will be a source of glory, of enlightenment and blessing to the entire family. She hath attuned her soul to the divine realm, hath freed herself from the promptings of self and passion, and hath become a devoted and merciful maidservant in the divine vineyard.

I pray the Almighty that thine inner sight may be illumined with the light of guidance, and that thou mayest become a heavenly sign in the world below and one of the sons of the Kingdom of God. This is better for thee than sovereignty over the whole earth.

'Abdu'l-Bahá's injunctions, in Tablets such as these, merely confirmed May's sense of spiritual responsibility towards her husband. He wrote her a Tablet too on the same day, in which He added a secondary message for Sutherland. As was often the case with His messages, His words were addressed to more than one person:

Give my greetings to thine honourable husband and tell him: God hath truly granted you a precious wife, the very daughter of 'Abdu'l-Bahá, whose heart is turned towards the Kingdom of God and attracted to His sweet savours. Thou shouldst appreciate how precious she is, so that God may confirm and bless this marriage under all conditions.

Sutherland certainly appreciated his precious wife. But May feared it was for the 'wrong' reasons. His soul needed to be surrounded by beauty, which was surely why he had fallen in love with May in the first place, but she felt it was not enough. His sense of composition, his feel for decoration, the grace of his furnishings, his rug designs and fittings – these were the ways in which his artist's soul sought for harmony and for meaning in life at this time. May tried her utmost to 'ripen' him with 'Love and Prayer', but he remained sceptical towards organized religion.

The couple had already been writing to each other for over a year about the relative merits of art and religion, about the need to balance body and soul. But there seemed to be no way of resolving their divergent opinions. Sutherland was interested in aesthetic questions, May in spiritual matters. He was preoccupied with the study of light on the texture of wood, on the sweet curve of an arch carved in stone. She was concerned about the state of the soul, the love of God and above all the importance of the Bahá'í Faith. But in the early years of their marriage, Sutherland was not very interested in the Bahá'í Faith. A year before in April 1901, he had described to her how he had conjured her presence in the office late one evening, to comfort his loneliness. In the process he confessed his highest ambitions, and his credo for living:

> [I]n business if we but seek to be successful, and great in the eyes of other people, we do debase the best that is in us, and that gloss that is not the surface but the heart and soul, is apt to become but a surface coating – a chameleon effect. To seek a competence, not deserting those principles and ideals that are vital to me, and doing unto others as I would like them to do unto me is what I strive for – sufficient time to live the life that we both hope for and believe possible and the companionship of the beautiful true woman that I love and that loves me so dearly is my ambition and to be all that you could want me to be – such is the sum total of my desires and with the guidance that is always offered to those who seek it we will try and live our lives truly and completely.

So when he finally had the companionship of that beautiful true woman he loved, Sutherland thought that was enough. May was his light, his life. She was his means of feeling close to God. What more did he want? He saw no reason to look for anything other than her, anywhere else. As he had already told her:[10]

> In many cases the true love and companionship of a woman is the medium through which we are brought nearer to Him. True love of any person or thing is based upon trust and faith and of course without these qualities any love would be but in name.

But although May could hardly, without self-reproach, fault Sutherland for being happy, she needed something more than a husband to be in touch with God. And she was convinced that unless he could glimpse the power of the Covenant, their love would never be fulfilled. Soon after their first wedding anniversary, which occurred while May was

---

10 11 August 1901.

away,[11] she wrote to him from Woodstock, Vermont, on this theme of spiritual union. There are many echoes between this letter of 12 May 1903, and the one she had written to him three years before, on 7 May 1900:

> This morning I received the beautiful letter you wrote me on our marriage day and it gave me such deep happiness. You are indeed changing Dearest under the Mighty Power of God's Holy Spirit – your soul is like a tree in the spiritual Springtime – all quickened, growing, budding and unfolding & in time you will bring forth flowers & fruits under the Hand of the Divine Gardener. Then we shall see the Words of Our Blessed Master fulfilled and you will become a Light & a Heavenly Sign amongst men. Inshallah!
>
> As for me I rejoice with all my heart for you my Darling – for God's Mercy & Bounty to you! for all His Great Kindness & Mercy to His humble servants, and I cannot express my love, my gratitude, and my humbleness to Him. I can only try to please and serve Him, and to make my Beloved Husband, my precious family, and all those with whom I am associated, happy thro' the power of Love and Unity shining from the Kingdom of God. My Sutherland – do you love to read about the Blessed Spirit – Christ, when He was on earth 1800 years ago? How a few only out of the many, could see with the spiritual vision, the Divine Light shining from His Presence – yet today the Light of His Teachings, the Glory and Power of His Spirit – are clear & evident as the Sun at noonday. In His Day He was despised, outcast, condemned & crucified – yet since His Departure He has been adored, obeyed and followed by millions upon millions of the human race & the sovereigns of the earth have bowed down before Him. The Word of a Prophet is the Word of God Almighty and It takes effect in spite of every obstacle, resistance, persecution or calamity. Nothing whatever can resist the Hand of God.

Later in August that same year, when she was in Green Acre, May shared the words of Mírzá Abu'l-Faḍl with Sutherland, appealing to him to join her at the Sarah Farmer Inn, as it was sometimes called, and spend a weekend with her there:

---

11 It was to become a recurring pattern. She missed many other wedding anniversaries too.

You know that the life of a human being on this earth is very short – the years fly by – and the opportunity is past – forever. You know that the <u>only reason</u> for a human being's life on this earth is to attain to the Knowledge of God – all else is nothing, all else passes away as a wind passes away. Now this is true at all times in the history of the world, then how much more true is it in this age – at <u>this time</u>.

For we are living in the greatest age that has ever dawned on earth – a time when every soul except those who are still sleeping is seeking for the True One – the Beloved Friend – and the Face of that Adored One is unveiled, the Light of His Glory is illumining every horizon – the Path of Salvation is <u>open</u> – the Living Water is flowing – the Door to the Kingdom is wide – & the bounties, blessings and favors of God are descending upon every creature. Everyone who seeks these bounties and gifts will obtain them – everyone who seeks them not will be deprived – and deprived not only here on this little earth – but throughout all Eternity!

You, my husband, have heard the Call of God – you have seen with spiritual insight His great signs in this Day – you have been guided to His Glorious Appearance and have believed in His Manifestation. Thank God for this incomparable gift which has caused you to take the first great step towards the Kingdom of God, and raised you from among the dead.

Now my Darling – you know what Greenacre is. Our Blessed Lord (may my life be His sacrifice) has revealed over 200 (two hundred) Tablets concerning Greenacre – and His Holy Spirit is upon all the people here, and every soul who comes here is blest – expanded, developed, unfolded and illumined with greater insight – granted deeper knowledge of Truth – quickened in spirit, attracted in heart, broadened in mind, and lifted to a greater height. All this you know – now let me ask you dear, if you think it is just to your own soul to give to it only a few days of this spiritual life? Do you think that it is right for you to sacrifice that which is so vital to you and to me & that which Our Lord has commanded all His servants to seek thro' the summer months – the blessings and incomparable advantages of Greenacre – for <u>anyone</u> – or <u>anything</u>?

In spite of the pressure of his work, her husband responded to her appeal; he came down to Maine in August 1903. What he thought of the experience can be inferred by the fact that she praised him for sharing it with his friends after he left:

> I was so pleased to hear that you tell people about Greenacre whenever you can & try to infuse into them a little higher thought & aim & life – & when we speak of the Truth – the Great Message of God to the world today, we will always take care only to mention it to those who are really seeking who are ready to receive it, for otherwise it only does them harm. As our Beloved Master (rouhi fedah) says, 'we must not pick the green fruit, but first ripen it with Love & Prayer, and guiding words, then when it is fully prepared & ripe we may gather it.'

May was not always governed by the wisdom she advised her husband to demonstrate. But it is touching to see how she encouraged him to teach the Faith to others before he had even formally accepted it himself. In doing so, she was, consciously or unconsciously, treating him as if he were already a Bahá'í, in the deepest sense. This was typical of her teaching method and the secret of her success:

> There is no work in the world today that can compare with this – it is the highest service we can render to God & I realize how fitted you are for this – for people love you so – your own beautiful, unselfish nature influences them deeply & they do not forget this influence which is the light of the Spirit . . .

* * *

Sutherland was a firm believer in work. The beginning of his marriage coincided with a decisive period for the Maxwell brothers and work was of paramount importance for them both between 1902 and 1905–06. They made an excellent team.[12] They were not only embarking on more and more prestigious projects but were expanding the scope of their work across Canada at this time. They were submitting plans for architectural commissions which in the past had automatically gone to American companies, and they were winning them too. They were

---

12 As Henry B. Yates recounts in 'The Lives of Edward and W. S. Maxwell': 'Edward was not only a fine architect but also had a keen business sense. He developed contacts with and entertained the many influential people he knew in business and government. William, on the other hand, had a remarkable ability for fine drawing and design.'

setting new standards in design from coast to coast. In fact, William Sutherland Maxwell was becoming known as one of the most talented architects in Canada and was making a name for himself as an interior as well as exterior decorator. Not surprisingly he was also listed, together with Edward, in the 1904 catalogue of the Royal Canadian Academy under 'Architecture and Design'.

May had every reason to be proud of her husband, of course. She recognized his talents and had the highest expectations of his genius. Rúḥíyyih Khánum always said that her mother was very supportive of her father's work. She remembered her sitting beside him in later years, looking with intense interest at his drawings and listening with total concentration to his explanations. She was a perfectly traditional wife in this respect, according to Amatu'l-Bahá, as he was a traditional husband. But there is no doubt that she was always urging Sutherland to see his work as a means and not an end, as an expression but not as the goal of his life. Whenever she praised his achievements, as she did about the Hosmer house in 1903, she used the occasion to pray that he would dedicate his remarkable gifts one day to a higher Cause:

> Yesterday I saw Eddie again, & it brought you nearer in one way, because I saw the photos – of the beautiful house! I cannot tell you how proud and happy they made me; oh! Darling, God has blessed you with a pure insight into Truth & Beauty and I beg of Him to grant you the Light of Guidance of which Our Dear Master spoke in His Tablet to you – that you may use these high gifts & qualities of soul & mind for God's service & glory, and become a light among men and a bright & gifted architect.

But in addition to his work for clients, Sutherland was much taken up with his own domestic arrangements at that time. He had been longing, for over a year, to design his own 'little home', built to his own liking and decorated with furnishings conducive to his taste. He was preoccupied with the choice of china and light fittings, by the texture of raw silk and the colours of curtains. The architect in him, however, must have been frustrated too, at times, with May's impractical suggestions:

> I wonder if you would mind my Darling not having any electric fixture in the dining room. It could be put in later if we wanted

it but will you let us begin by candles in low candle-sticks & . . . I think you ought not to have the lights placed in the bedrooms until we arrange the furniture . . .

May longed for a home too, but was primarily concerned to fill it with love and harmony, rather than French china and the right sort of lamps. She loved good clothes, but she was aghast at the thought of clothing a chair in expensive raw silk. She tried to point out that it was perhaps unjustified to spend so much money on, for example, curtains. She despaired when their letters became furniture inventories:

> You never mention God to me . . . and mention such vital matters as china – auctions – pictures!

It is hardly to be wondered at that May was so dependent on her correspondence with the Master. Without His Tablets, she would have had an even harder time in overcoming the tests of her early years in Canada. A word from 'Abdu'l-Bahá was enough to dispel her loneliness. Shortly after her arrival in Montreal, May received this Tablet which had been translated on 11 September 1902:

> *O thou who art attracted to the fragrances of God!*
> *Verily I read thy letter and thanked God for thy joy and happiness, as thou art pleased with thy revered husband. I beg of God to surround this union with a heavenly blessing, and to ordain for thy dear husband and thy dear brother a heavenly, spiritual and merciful gift which may lead to eternal, everlasting and spiritual life, and to infinite and heavenly distinction.*
> *As to thee: Flee not from the remembrance of thy Lord, the Merciful, the Compassionate, and diffuse the fragrances of God in that region.*

A month later, May received another Tablet from the beloved Master, translated on 17 October 1902, sending her once more the outpourings of His grace and praise:

> *O thou who art attracted to the fragrances of God!*
> *Verily I read thy well-composed letter containing wondrous meanings, and I thanked God and praised Him; for He hath safeguarded thee*

under His preservation and protection, delivered thee from the depth of tests and trials, and caused thee to be a proven, trustworthy and sincere leaf, devoted unto God. Thou wert as pure gold and didst enter the fire of tests. Thank thou God, for thou hast emerged sincere, sanctified, radiant and luminous in countenance, pure in heart, attracted in soul, as thou treadest the path of salvation.

Many a leaf hath been in a state of utmost attraction, but when wedded, she slackened and the fire of her divine love subsided. She occupied herself with the physical world, neglected the divine realm, set her affections on this mortal life, and dispensed with the Divine, eternal life. But as to thee, O thou enraptured maidservant of God: thou wast delivered from test and trials, and thy passion and devotion to the Kingdom of God underwent no change or alteration. And this is through the grace of thy Lord, the Compassionate, the All-Merciful.

O thou splendid and spiritual leaf! Gird up then thy loins, strengthen thy resolve, and arise with a mighty heart to promote the Word of God, to diffuse the fragrances of God, and to kindle the fire of the love of God in that remote region. Verily thy Lord will sustain thee through the hosts of His kingdom, the fragrances of His paradise, the breezes of His garden, the powers of His realm of might, and the potency of His Covenant.

Truly, I say unto thee: Every maidservant who ariseth in this day, inspired by the 'Mystery of Sacrifice' in the path of God, will become one of the stars of guidance in the supreme Horizon. All in heaven and earth will be illumined by her face. The angels of the Concourse on high will celebrate her praise, and she will be encompassed by the bounties of the Abhá Kingdom.

Convey my greeting and praise to thy dear husband, to thy noble brother, and to thy revered mother. I beg of God to ordain for them a light and mercy and an appointed measure of His wondrous grace.

'Abdu'l-Bahá's Tablets, filled with praise for herself and for her husband, may have enabled her to see that the differences between them were the very foundation on which their fortress of well-being was slowly but steadily being constructed. Their complementary natures would bring balance and untold blessings to them over time. After a while, May acknowledged a new stage in their relationship.

Indeed perhaps in the end May was also cured by her ability to laugh at herself. A hilarious experience in a hotel in Portsmouth, in 1904 or 1905, enabled her to see how much the companionship of this precious man in her life was worth all the rest:

> Oh! Sutherland. It has been a perfect nightmare, a hot, stuffy dirty room – such queer people – and a dreadful man in the next room to me, who has – under the semblance of kindness, annoyed & frightened me until I was so ill all night. Oh! how I <u>longed</u> for you – wept for you. I cannot travel alone to strange places – I do not know how to protect myself against the world. I do not want to speak unkindly of this man. I am sure he meant well – but why could he not see that I was a lady & let me alone. Poor soul. I pity anyone who is so barren of all sensibility & refinement. I was to have taken the 8.30 train this a.m. for Woodstock – but I felt too weak. Now I have decided not to travel while it is so hot, and until I am quite rested – & it is your dear spirit that has guided me so wisely – so I am going back on the one o'clock train to Eliot – & shall stay either at Miss Farmer's or some other quiet place for a few days. The <u>man</u> has gone out for the whole day – & I got some sleep after I knew that he was gone – & before he returns I shall be far away. I know I am absurd – but it is the heat, & because I am a little tired. Now – my beloved – do not be anxious – for it is <u>all over</u> & if it were not I would not write it – & when this reaches you I shall be in the sweet cool country, with dear friends. You know, Darling, I have such a terrible sense of humor that even thro' last night's horrors, I had to laugh at it all & myself for so magnifying the situation thro' my overwrought imagination.

Writing from New York just before returning home in 1905, she asked her husband:

> Do you think you can stand my peculiarities?

He evidently could. Throughout their early years of marriage when May was being treated by a string of doctors and trying to cure herself, Sutherland stood by her, supported her, sustained and encouraged her. He never lost faith in their future. In one of the rare letters from him that has survived from this difficult period, he wrote:

I want you to realize that treatment will help you wonderfully and I want you to have it. I know that our present condition is one of evolution and that the future promises the – evolved – union. Our faith in our Doctor and principally our faith in God are to be the active agents in this process. I want you to keep me in the closest touch with you and I want you to feel that our future is to be the fulfilment of the tablets of beauty that we received.

May had anticipated Sutherland's tender trust and touching certitude in the future when writing to Agnes Alexander, soon after her arrival in Montreal in 1902:

Day by day as I see my darling husband drawing nearer to God, being awakened from the sleep of his earthly life, and beholding, still with dim eyes, but oh! such a pure, true and loving heart, the first rays of Light of the Dawn of the Eternal Day which is breaking on his soul, as God permits me to be a humble witness . . . I know that the All-Loving has ordained a great blessing thro this union.

* * *

During their stay in the house on Hope Street, which Edward vacated between 1903 and 1904, the young couple were in close touch with Mrs Bolles and Randolph, who had returned to New York by then. The first November of their married life, when May was ill and staying with her mother, Sutherland received a note from Randolph, on the occasion of his birthday:

It is just about three years, I think this month, that you & I became acquainted; I remember so well the first time I saw you in the big 'atelier' sketching from a photo & I think I made the most of the occasion & called you a 'sâle-roman'. How time does go! And how strange it seems to think that now we are 'related by marriage'! You must be very glad to hear of May's steady improvement; she eats well now, & is picking up & beginning to look like her old self. If she could only begin to walk a bit, it would be a great thing for her.

Two years later, at Christmas, Sutherland received a book on Joan of

Arc[13] in memory of his student days in Paris. Recalling, with nostalgia perhaps, the time when his friend had been doing his drudgery work for him at the École des Beaux-Arts, Randolph inscribed the following dedication inside his gift:

> To my former 'nègre', present beau-frère, & friend – always, To Max from Randolph Bolles. New York, Dec. 25. 04.

He also received affectionate letters from Mrs Bolles, who was clearly missing her daughter and her son-in-law. Soon after their return to Montreal she wrote:

> Today I was trying on a hat. Randolph looked at me and said, 'For the love of Mike, what's that on your head?' I remarked with dignity that you had said of that hat that it was without composition, and he said, 'Well he was about right.' So I ripped it up and threw it away. How could I wear a hat without composition with such a dear old trump of a Max to tell me so. We send you and dear little May our very best quality of love and we miss you so much.
> > Devotedly
> > Your Belle Mère

But as this letter seems to indicate,[14] Mrs Bolles was not finding it much easier than May was to adjust to life in North America after living for so long in Paris. At this point in her life she belonged neither on one side of the Atlantic nor on the other. Although she took refuge in irony rather than melancholy, one can read her sense of homelessness between the lines:

> Dear old Max,
> How's the precious little wife? How is everything? Randolph and I find everything very amusing – happily – otherwise we would starve for people and things we love. Now we know from good authority why we feel as we do. There is not one street – one avenue – one anything that is not turned up. Houses coming down – others going up – underground, subway – they call it here – and consequently

---

13 M. Boutet de Monvel's *Jeanne d'Arc*.
14 Written on 23 June 1902.

malaria and sewer poison fill the air! You and May are lucky to be in Canada and I think your brother is so good to loan you his lovely little home.

We go next week to Newport – from there – I don't know where – but we are told to stay away during the next heat. How wise it is to listen to words of wisdom, for fevers are to be battled off.

Sadly, Mrs Bolles was unable to battle off sickness, and her physical decline was another reason for May's distress in the early years of her marriage. When her mother fell gravely ill in the course of 1904 and 1905, May was obliged to travel back and forth frequently to see her in New York. Since it coincided with Sutherland's attempts to renovate and to improve their rented home and May's own trials and tribulations, it is not surprising to find that the subjects of sickness and doctors, paint-work and plumbing dominated their correspondence. Mrs Bolles had already expressed her own feelings about May's frequent illnesses and absences in a letter written to Sutherland as early as 28 November 1902:

> You have been very good and very patient and I know you must have been very lonely, but if May goes back to you really well and no longer nervous, you will feel well repaid for the sacrifice you have made. At any time if you feel that she will be better for seeing me or her brother, we will go or she can come.

But as her mother's condition deteriorated, the visits became increasingly one-sided and it became more difficult for May to leave Mrs Bolles alone. In the course of 1904, she stayed with her mother for increasingly long periods, for it was now clear that Mary Martin Bolles, like her sister Charlotte, was suffering from cancer. Since the disease was too far gone by then, the treatment was hardly more than palliative. Writing to Sutherland in 1905, May tried to maintain her optimism:

> Mama is gaining steadily & the C.S.[15] treatments have nearly conquered the pain.

---

15 This would seem to be a reference to Christian Science, though there are indications that May also depended a great deal, until the very end, on homeopathy to cure her mother's cancer.

But the reports were soon more realistic:

> Mama is not at all well, but suffers greatly at times, & we do all we can to make it easier for her.

On another occasion she sadly informed Sutherland:

> Mama suffers nearly all the time & she says I am the greatest help & comfort to her – for which I thank God.

Towards the end of her mother's life, May's visits to New York were on a weekly basis:

> Dearest, I cannot leave Mama any more for more than a week or 10 days <u>at most</u> at a time. Her need of me is too great, and her sufferings too cruel.

When her absence from Montreal became quasi-permanent, May yearned for home. On 2 March 1905, after Sutherland came down to visit the Bolles family, she wrote:

> In a few hours you will arrive in Montreal, and I can think of nothing but my desire to take the train tonight, and to be with you, my Darling – tomorrow. But I know this would not be right – I must wait a little while and see how Mama gets on . . . Today [she] is free from pain, thank God. I will write you fully about her condition tomorrow.

A few months later, on a Tuesday in May 1905, she confessed:

> . . . the one thing on earth I want to do is to come home to you. The reason I feel that I ought to stay is this – Mama began the Littlefield treatment this morning (she does not know what it is of course as the doctor just told her it is a tissue builder he wanted her to use for a while). The powders are all numbered & dated & have to be taken at 8, 11, 3 & 8 promptly – mixed in a certain way etc.
> Brother might do all this but he does not & cannot take the care of Mama that I do – & if anything should happen during this

first week of the treatment – if Mama should have queer symptoms & refuse to take the medicine, or any new conditions should arise – I know that I <u>ought</u> to be here – for God has given me a special insight and power over Mama & if anything should happen thro' my being absent I could never get over it all my life. So what can I do? Next month I can get a nurse to take my place for a week or two, and thus I shall keep my health & be able to continue my care of Mama indefinitely. But I cannot do this unless I have periods of complete relief and of <u>being with you</u> – for sometimes it seems to me that the separation is beyond endurance.

John Harris Bolles had been estranged from his wife for nearly three decades and when her cancer was diagnosed, May tried to reconcile her parents. She became their go-between, carrying letters from one to the other, and through her efforts their relationship, after years of separation, revived towards the end of Mrs Bolles' life. Rúḥíyyih <u>Kh</u>ánum often used to say that the only thing that kept them apart at the end was that her grandmother was so wasted by sickness that she did not want her husband to see her.

Finally, when the pain became insupportable, the only relief for the sick woman was to have her daughter sit beside her, place a hand on her tormented breast, and pray. By then she was dependent on painkillers. In recording her mother's last days May wrote how she had asked for prayers to be said in Green Acre that August:

The group of 9 Bahá'ís met in Greenacre to pray for Mama. The next day, Sunday, the great cloud of suffering & sickness rolled away from her, & gave her respite for one day & night. From that time on a great change became manifest. A new and wonderful gentleness, meekness and sweetness breathed from my Darling. She was patient under the most cruel suffering – thankful for all that was done for her – gentle & docile in taking medicine or food. She was largely under the influence of codeine, so that she was like one in a dream. During those days she said, at different times – gently & thoughtfully as tho she were considering the matter: 'I am much worse – I feel <u>very ill</u>!' Again one morning she spoke of her Mother & said: 'Muddie said to me this morning: "look at the little graves".' Another time she said – 'My Father lived to a green old age.' Once as

I gave her the tissue builder she said – 'We did not give it to May & yet she did not die.' She asked me several times if the men standing at the foot of her bed had come to get her, and gently begged me not to let them take her away.

Several times she called Brother George, & spoke of 'the boys', & her mind seemed to go back to her childhood & all one night she called me 'Aunt Tousey'. When she was completely under the influence of the codeine she sang the little refrain of Chaperon Rouge which she had sung so much throughout her illness.

After Mrs. Foster left & got a trained nurse, with big eyes & glasses & a queer face – when she first came into the room Mama looked at her for a moment then turned to me & said firmly: 'Will you please take that cat out of the room'! Later in the day she kept looking at the nurse & then murmured, half to me & half to herself: 'You know those big things that fly thro' the air?' – meaning perhaps an eagle – & both remarks fit the nurse perfectly.

The morning I arrived my Darling said, as she turned & saw me, 'Oh! how lovely!' and a little later she said: 'When I woke up this morning I said, "You cannot escape God & His Angels," and I know I cannot for He sent you.' Every time I dressed her dear side she looked anxiously at me & said, 'How does it look?' & often sighed. The last few days of her earthly life she sighed so deeply, so wearily, so often – I shall never forget that sigh – for I often think that the breath of all humanity has become a sigh.

May was convinced that her mother drew closer to the Faith at the end. Writing to Sutherland in the summer of 1905, she told him:

I have just finished giving Mama a lovely cool bath, which the doctor said I might do every day while this intense heat lasts. I was up with her until 12 o'clock last night – Brother was at his class dinner and Mama was in great pain all the afternoon and evening, and the remedies which relieved her a few weeks ago have to be more than doubled in dose now. Her suffering seems to take my life with hers, yet during these fiery trials thro which we pass together the Power of God is so wonderful, His Holy Spirit lifts and envelopes us, and on the wings of my prayers she is borne over the fathomless sea of pain.

When her condition was at its worst, she sent a cable to 'Abdu'l-Bahá:

[A]fter I had cabled the Blessed Lord, she looked up at me with a face of such meekness & ineffable sweetness thro her agony, & said, 'How I suffer – God only knows how I suffer – but I suffer willingly now.' I have within my heart the assurance that with these words her beloved spirit passed into the Light – & there followed that deep oblivion – that semi-conscious stupor, from which she never roused until the day she died, Wednesday, August 23rd.

According to May, her mother recognized the station of Bahá'u'lláh before her passing. It had been a slow but steady evolution. From 1898 when she first heard of the Bahá'í Faith in Paris, Mary Ellis Martin Bolles had gone from a dismissive attitude to one of downright ridicule, from a sense of indignation to one of grudging acknowledgement, and finally from a reluctant acceptance of 'Abdu'l-Bahá's integrity to a dawning sense of gratitude towards Him, to a growing wonder at His spiritual powers, and finally to belief. Some years before her death, Lua, that perceptive soul, put into words the spiritual reality and the true nature of this woman:

. . . truly I think she is one of the finest characters I have ever met – and I am so glad I know the real true Mrs. Bolles & I shall always know her from now on. I think I shall never forget her love and kindness to us. She shows forth the deeds of a believer whether she says she is one or not.[16]

May was, in effect, her mother's spiritual mother too and remained faithfully at her side until the moment she passed away. Writing about her years later, she concluded:

And in the end of her dear life some years later – in those months of illness and great affliction – she gave her whole heart to God, testified to His Mighty Power, and found relief, strength and comfort only in the Greatest Name.

Some months before her death, 'Abdu'l-Bahá had written a Tablet to Mrs Bolles, which was translated on 18 June 1905.

---

16 25 July 1901.

O thou maidservant of God!

I perused the letter which thou didst dictate in a state of illness and sickness, and which was written down by the attracted maidservant of God, Mrs. Maxwell. Its contents were the cause of rejoicing, inasmuch as they described the services rendered unto thee by thy dear daughter. Daughters must render the utmost service to their mothers and must ever be the cause of their joy and happiness. I beg of God to assist her in that which will enable her to become a healer of the spirit and a minister to the spiritually sick; and that she may, day by day, deepen thy conviction, that thine assurance and trust in God may grow.

O thou maidservant of God! Thank thou the True One, for God hath given thee such a pure and noble daughter who hath turned her heart to God, is guided by the light of guidance and is attracted by the heavenly fragrances. She is engaged, night and day, in guiding others, so that she may illumine those who are in darkness, impart knowledge to the ignorant, give sight to the blind and bestow the power of guidance to the helpless.

Rejoice and gladden thy esteemed daughter on my behalf with wondrous Abhá greetings.

Soon after her mother's death, May wrote to 'Abdu'l-Bahá about her last hours. The original no longer exists nor is there any record of the Master's response. But a rough draft of May's letter, written sometime in August 1905, is included below:

Oh! Thou Great and Glorious Lord!

Through Thy Infinite Mercy Thou hast released the soul of my Beloved Mother from its prison of pain, Thou hast freed her precious spirit from its cage and hast permitted her to soar upward toward the Lights of the Eternal World!

How can I ever thank Thee! my tongue is dumb and my pen is impotent to express my thankfulness & gratitude. Oh! my Gracious Lord! Thro long months of mortal pain and great suffering she was brought at last to a condition of overwhelming constraint – then out of this fiery furnace her soul was born again, and brought forth shining wings.

In the last two weeks of her life on earth, 9 of Thy dear servants in Greenacre prayed for her, and during that time my Darling was changed, and from her being there emanated an inexpressable [sic] meekness, gentleness and humility, which seemed to this poor servant, as the dawn of the Eternal Life in her soul. Although partly unconscious much of the time, she seemed to know the end was near, & she had lost all fear, and lay, like a little child, in perfect resignation & trust.

On the day when I humbly sent Thee a cablegram August 18th, our beloved one had reached the culmination of mortal agony – and a few hours after the message was sent, she whispered to me: 'God only knows how I suffer, but I suffer willingly now!' These were her last entirely conscious words, after which she fell into a stupor, & suffered no more, until the final dissolution on August 23rd, when the Angel of Death bore her away, on the wings of Life. My Lord – my dear Mother for many months before she died, prayed earnestly & fervently, and worshipped each day in the Greatest Name; her heart was full of love, and she became patient and grateful.

On the evening she died the most blessed light, and heavenly peace descended upon us all. Neither my dear Brother nor I have shed a single tear – such is our gratitude to God, for releasing our beloved from pain; and in our hearts we have the full assurance that her heavenly joy & divine blessing immeasurably transcend her earthly trial & suffering. Since my Darling passed beyond our vision this transitory life seems a world of dream & shadow, and the Invisible Spiritual World is Brilliant, Single, Near and Everlasting, & my soul yearns and my heart aches for the Heaven of Thy Nearness and the Paradise of Thy Love. Truly I have tasted some drops from the Cup of 'I made Death to Thee as Glad Tidings!'

I humbly beseech Thee to grant to My Mother the utmost joy & an absolute spirituality, & that she may be accepted in Thy Kingdom. I beg of Thee to forgive all my sins towards her, & all my failings unto her, & grant us a spiritual union & ideal love whereby we may both draw nearer to the Most Glorious God. I beg of Thee to bless my dear Brother & my Husband; to enlighten & guide them; & to grant them the spirit of Faith & Love, and confirm them in the Blessed Truth.

With my fervent love, & humble salutations in the Name of God, unto all the Beloved Ones I humbly offer my soul heart [sic] to Thee, oh! My Lord.

* * *

May returned to Montreal to find Sutherland entirely taken up with his own interests. It was hardly surprising. He had adapted, stoically, to May's need to leave Montreal each winter and had busied himself with his own affairs so as not to miss her absences over these early years. During his free hours from work, he engaged himself in a variety of private and professional clubs. In addition to his curling, he played golf and his weekends were taken up by artistic activities. He gave drawing and painting classes every Saturday afternoon at the studio of Maurice Cullen, just a few doors down from his offices in Beaver Hall Square. He also maintained his associations with colleagues at the Arts Club every Friday where he played poker and billiards and talked about art and architecture till the small hours. Some of the members of the Arts Club were old friends and flat-mates with whom he had been in contact ever since his student days in Paris.[17] As his daughter recalled years later, he often spent 'the whole evening in a big cloud of blue smoke' with them. His interests were more and more removed from May's, even when she attempted to join his clubs. Writing to him in 1908, May cautioned him against wasting his time:

> Last night you were at the Pen & Pencil – and had a lovely evening I am sure. Do not exaggerate the importance of the Woman's Club lecture, I am a member & know that the preponderance of brain power is minus! Just be reasonable & do not sacrifice your precious time or eyesight too much for this primary Class!

As for May, her interests were less and less linked to her husband's and she threw herself increasingly into Bahá'í work during these years. Even though it was not easy, she attempted to take up in Montreal the task that she had dropped in Paris. She began to teach the Cause to the Maxwells and their cousins the MacBeans, to hold meetings specially for her

---

17 The flat in Boulevard Montparnasse was shared with Frederick W. Hutchison, the landscape painter who was studying at the Beaux-Arts with Jean-Paul Laurens at the same time that Sutherland was in the Atelier Pascal. 'Hutch', as Sutherland called him affectionately, returned to work in New York although he remained a close friend and a member of the Montreal Arts Club. Arthur Knox Hutchison, whom everyone called 'Artie', was another artist friend in Montreal. He was no relation to Frederick and had not studied in Paris, but worked with the Maxwell brothers on several projects in later years. He also married their sister Amelia.

relatives, to gather her friends together to discuss spiritual subjects, to go out, weather permitting, and visit those who might be interested in the Faith.

Amatu'l-Bahá Rúḥíyyih Khánum often told an interesting story about her parents at this time, a story she repeated in her formal talks as well as in private conversation. It concerned a great test which both of them faced not long after their marriage. It must have been some time in the early years of their married life. As they were seated together in their home, Sutherland had apparently turned to his wife and said,

'You are involved more and more in your Bahá'í work and I in my professional work; we are drifting apart.'

According to Amatu'l-Bahá, her mother was terrified at what these words implied. She was sorely tempted to rush forward and reassure her husband that from now on she would do as he wished. That was what a wife was supposed to do. That was what society expected her to do. But she steeled herself. She gently reminded him that, before marrying him, she had told him that the Cause of God would always come first in her life. She had warned him of her priorities. Then she quietly added,

'If I must, then I will go alone on this chosen path in my life.'

Sutherland was silent for some moments and then reached out and took her hands in his own. 'I will go with you all the way,' he said, softly.

Rúḥíyyih Khánum recalled her mother saying that this moment was a turning point in her father's spiritual life. May was convinced that her firm response to his remark was one of the reasons for Sutherland's recognition of the Faith. By taking this stand, she brought him, as it were, to a critical crossroads. He had to choose.

But it may also have marked a turning point in her life too. His statement must have forced upon May the full implications of her own choice. She had been married long enough by then to know how lucky she was to have a husband like William Sutherland Maxwell. She had witnessed many of her friends suffer from a lack of true companionship when it came to active participation in Bahá'í life. It was a very difficult balance to maintain. Most women fell into one extreme or the other, sacrificing everything for the Cause at the cost of their marriages or sacrificing the Faith for the sake of their husbands. Several of May's friends never found the companion who could go with them all the way; many opted for a life of solitary dedication to the Cause because of this. Not a few suffered from broken marriages. It was rare to be able to maintain an independent spiritual life from one's husband, Bahá'í or not. But Sutherland not only recognized his wife's right to such a life but was willing, despite his differences, to 'go with her all the way'. He was rare indeed.

Since she wrote to 'Abdu'l-Bahá about all the significant incidents of her life, she may have told Him of this one as well, for there is a beautiful Tablet of the Master addressed to May which seems to fit the circumstances. It is dated 6 June 1903:

> *O beloved maidservant of God!*
>
> *What thou hast written was perused. Thanks be to God that thy face hath become shining like unto pure gold in the fire of tests, and that thou didst remain unshaken by trials. Thou didst stand firm against a raging torrent and resist the onslaught of a mighty army.*
>
> *The wisdom of tests and trials in the path of God is that they cause the sincere to become firm and steadfast and the insincere to flee in all haste. Until this divine touchstone is applied, the luminous souls can in no wise be distinguished from those who remain immersed in darkness. That maidservant of God, having been protected from grave tests, hath become cherished in the Kingdom of God, and new confirmations shall erelong descend upon her.*
>
> *In that city and region where thou dwellest, thou must day and night perfume the sanctuary of thy soul with the fragrances of thy Lord and brighten thine eyes by beholding His mighty signs. Turn thy face then unto this sacred Spot and seek to inhale from it the fragrance of the Holy Spirit, to receive the breath of life, to illumine thy heart with the light of reality, and to loose thy tongue in praise and thanksgiving of the True One. Endeavour to shed the heavenly sweet savours, for therein lieth a magnetic power, a mighty force, which greatly reinforceth one's life under all conditions. When this favour hath been received thou shalt find the doors of the hearts unlocked and the cities of the spirits conquered! With one breath thou wilt perfume that region, and with one ray thou wilt brighten that country.*
>
> *Deal with thy husband with consideration; be as kind to him as possible, and advise him with all courtesy. He will come under the outspread shadow of the Cause and will obtain his light from the lamp of guidance. Give him a firm promise that, if he should believe, he will find his greatest happiness in both worlds.*
>
> *This is a promise which shall not be belied.*

'Abdu'l-Bahá no doubt was sure of Sutherland's brilliant future. Many of the Tablets He sent to May were addressed to her husband too. In one of these, revealed in her honour and translated on 13 March 1904, 'Abdu'l-Bahá wrote:

> *O thou blessed maidservant of God! O thou Mrs. Maxwell!*
>
> *Convey my longing and love to thy dear husband, and say: In this world, from the days of Christ down to the present time, although a hundred thousand kings have been seated upon the throne of earthly dominion, all have passed away and are no more. But the precious servants of Christ, although they were outwardly lowly, their blessed faces will shine brightly from the horizon of eternal might for evermore.*

It must have been in the course of this same year that May wrote to Sutherland about the wife of his cousin, Martha MacBean, who seemed to be attracted to the Faith. The 'Mary' she referred to in this undated note, possibly written in 1904, was a certain Mary Coristine who was also attracted to the Cause at this time:

> In a day or two I am going to give the Message to Martha MacBean, one of the purest souls I ever met – a lover of God, a servant of His Threshold. Will you and Mary pray for her Dearest? I find many people here interested in the glorious Cause. God grant that before another year is past an Assembly of faithful ones may be established, a rose-garden of unity may be adorned, and the roaring Fire of the love of God be enkindled in this land . . . How can I describe the love of God that fills my heart – that overflows it like a mighty river, flowing out purely, fervently, tenderly & compassionately to the whole world.

May was finding receptive souls at last and her teaching efforts were finally reaping some results. Best of all, she had succeeded in encouraging Sutherland to teach!

> The only proof I ask of your love . . . is that you shall light this flame in other hearts that through you this heavenly sunshine may be flooded upon other lives.

As it turned out, Martha Dewey, who married Stephen MacBean in 1901, became a Bahá'í before Sutherland himself. Martha was to become a pillar of the Bahá'í community in Montreal. In a beautifully bound, red and black leather Daily Memorandum Book for 1870, tooled in gold, which belonged to her father, May wrote, in her most careful hand:

William Sutherland Maxwell became a Bahá'í in 1904.

When Marion Hofman questioned Mr Maxwell in later years about when it was, exactly, that he had accepted the Faith, he identified the moment of belief as having occurred sooner. Indeed, it may have been a process which took several years, before and after the actual date of his declaration of faith. She quotes him as saying:

I guess it was in 1902/3. We had no stopwatch or timetable. I was not emotional about it. My reason recognized that this was – IT.[18]

It would seem that he recognized that 'this was – IT' sometime towards the end of 1903, for a letter written by Agnes Alexander to May on 15 January 1904 confirms:

Oh, May dear, I must tell you how filled with joy my soul was when I heard that your dear husband had become my brother in the Blessed Master.

In the course of 1904–05, May wrote a letter to Sutherland from New York in which she addressed him, significantly enough, with the Bahá'í greeting. This undated letter summarizes their relationship and illustrates how May taught Sutherland the Faith:

Allaho'Abha!

My dearest –
    Your blessed and beautiful letter came to me yesterday, and I do not need to tell you of the great happiness & peace that it brought to me. You always understand, my Darling, and deal with me so justly

18 Recorded by Marion Holley (Hofman) in March 1940.

and so tenderly that you restore my clear vision, and dispel those dark clouds. Someday, through the Mercy of God these clouds will go away forever – I shall be well in soul and body, and shall see only the light of Truth – but I could never attain this without you, and I need you for my life and growth, just as you need me for yours.

This letter you wrote me, and the one that came on Friday night – the one written in pencil, while you were sitting over the parlor grates, gave me such a deep insight into your heart and character, brought me into the closest contact and sympathy with your soul & your life. All that you say Dearest, about yourself and about me is true, & I realize it – and I want you to realize to what an extent my happiness is dependent upon this absolute union.

Whether it is because I am a woman, or because I am this particular woman, I do not know, but I know that the world of our marriage – to me – lies entirely in our two hearts & souls – independent of all external things or circumstances or people.

I mean that our marriage has nothing to do with our outward conditions directly – our home, our friends or families – the place we like or our occupations and interests – these are the scenery, so to speak – the channels of contact of our two souls, the accessories – but the reality of our marriage consists in an ever unfolding understanding & knowledge of one another – in an ever deeper love and sympathy, in an ever more complete and perfect blending of our two beings into one.

This is the path we have travelled, and are travelling together, is it not? ever nearer to our God, ever nearer to the hearts of our fellow beings – ever nearer to the sanctuary of one another's inmost souls and consciousness?

I have learned to understand what art, what your profession means to you – what a light it is to you, how through the channel of its beauty and truth, all beauty & truth reaches you, and this is as God made you, and I love you, just as God made you.

But I do not lose sight of the fact that the soul's relation to God is a direct one, which requires not material means or earthly medium, but is dependent upon the heart being turned to God – the soul seeking God, the mind being attracted towards spiritual realities – and that this is the first, single, essential & supreme station of every soul, entirely irrespective of any other state or condition or person, in heaven or earth. Everything else comes <u>after</u> this, & in a sense which we cannot realize too strongly – for everything else is temporal & non-essential. I know that you fully agree with me, and see as I do – for your letters to Our Blessed Master prove this, and your last beautiful letter to me shows me with each clear and profound analysis that while our focus is different, we are looking upon the Face of God. You have a true and keen insight Sutherland, and a well-balanced judgement, and I know of no two married people who are more admirably adapted to one another than you and I.

If you will make your utmost endeavour to shake off always & permanently those crusts, or (as you so aptly call them) those insulations which are a heavy encumbrance with which your family has endowed you, the light of your real self, your spirit will shine forth undimmed – your love will flow to me in a living stream, and in that light I shall unfold and blossom, and in that love I shall grow strong and full of joy, and the wings of my spirit will lift you and me above this mundane world, into the realm of spirit, the world of God. The people of this world stand all about us, ready to clip those wings, to pull us down to earth. My husband, in God's Holy Name I beg of you <u>never</u> – even through thoughtlessness – even in the smallest thing, to be one of these! Help me – help yourself, help everyone to <u>ascend</u> – to <u>aspire</u> – to overcome by the power of spirit – to live in the ideal! How did Christ – how did the disciples, how did the Saints of every age & nation – how did Joan of Arc subdue all earthly conditions – overcome all material obstacles, <u>transcend</u> the world and its people? Through the power of spirit, through faith in God – through <u>inspiration.</u> And to some souls this exalted atmosphere is their native air, without which they sicken and die. They <u>cannot</u> live in the atmosphere of this world, but they can live in this world and glorify it, when their souls are free to soar. You have told me freely your point of view – now I have told you mine – let us each cherish that which is sacred, that which is God given in the other – for He has given us to one another for this purpose – that we may love one another and serve one another in the highest aim and end.

May had already confessed to Myron Phelps[19] that when she had

---

19 The author of *Life and Teachings of Abbas Effendi* (New York and London: G. P. Putnam's Sons, 1903). His book became a classic of Bahá'í literature.

become sick in those difficult early years of marriage, her husband had been 'heavenly kind and tender to me in my illness. May God bless him!' She had also confirmed to Agnes Alexander, at the end of 1904, that her health was much better, adding:

> My dear husband is now a firm believer . . . and a few others have heard the Message and we are praying for them . . . I yearn with my whole soul to render to Our Eternal Beloved an acceptable service!

Finally she wrote to 'Abdu'l-Bahá that her suffering had been the source of 'the greatest blessing, for which I thank God' because it became the means of 'awakening my dear husband from the deep sleep of negligence'. One year later, on 9 March 1905, 'Abdu'l-Bahá acknowledged their spiritual union:

> O thou dear maidservant of God!
> I am very happy that thy marriage did not distract thee, for indeed, thou didst become more self-sacrificing and hast made progress. It is a sign of great bounty that thine honourable husband has allied himself with thee, and that thou hast led him to the threshold of God.

But there are possibly as many stages to the conception, the gestation, and finally the birth of the spirit as to that of the body. When Amatu'l-Bahá was writing her *In Memoriam* article about her father, she stated that it was not until 1909, when her parents were on pilgrimage, that Sutherland was really confirmed in his faith. Soon after this historic pilgrimage, May wrote to Sutherland, on 11 June 1909:

> I cannot be to you 'un camarade'! – a smoking man friend! But I am ever so many things much better to you! Wife – sweetheart – friend – companion – and your spiritual mother! Just think of it!

* * *

May's primary concern, after her husband's spiritual development, was to seek for souls who might be receptive to the call of Bahá'u'lláh and who would help her form a strong Bahá'í community in Montreal. She wanted to build the foundations of a 'Spiritual Assembly' in that city and become the 'spiritual mother' to many. At the same time as the Maxwell partnership was becoming well known, during those crucial months and years in the first decade of the 20th century when the firm of Edward and William Sutherland Maxwell was establishing its reputation for excellence and quality architecture with the most powerful financial groups in Canada, May Maxwell was constructing brick by brick and stone by stone, the first 'House of Justice' in the country, single-handedly, almost alone. Such an institution, of course, could only be the rudimental form of the administrative body it was destined to become, but its very existence, she knew, would have enormous spiritual consequences for Canada.

In addition to Martha MacBean, who became May's good friend, and whose children later attended the Montessori School in her home, another soul who became a believer through May's efforts at that time[20] was Percy Woodcock, an artist in his own right and someone whom Sutherland genuinely admired. Writing to May from New York in November 1904, he told her about his refreshing meetings with some of the Bahá'ís there:

My Dear Sister in El-Abha –
I was asking the girls tonight if they had written to you since our arrival but they said they had not. So I will take matters into my own hands and see that you get news . . .
Yesterday morning I started out on a hunting tour with the object of hunting up the MacNutts and succeeded, after three quarters of an hour on the street-cars, in finding them in a very lovely home – 935 Eastern Park Way, Brooklyn. I was fully compensated for my long journey by a right royal reception from Mrs. MacNutt, Mrs. Haney[21] and Mrs. — your dear little Spiritual Mother,[22] you know who I mean as I can't recall her name. Needless to say I found myself right at home and had a perfectly glorious time. Such a perfect spiritual blending as I never experienced before . . . Mrs. Haney is also a beautiful soul, so tender & true. As I sat talking to the two of them I felt as if I were in the presence of two disembodied spiritual beings instead of flesh & blood. They all made the fondest enquiries after

---

20 In 1904.
21 The mother of the Hand of the Cause Paul Haney.
22 Lua Getsinger.

you. Of course I told them of our many pleasant chats. And how you came to the station to see us off. . . .

Give my best love & esteem to Mr. Maxwell and by all means don't forget your dear self. Your brother in the love of God
Percy Woodcock

In the course of 1905–06 when she was away from home, Sutherland wrote to May and gave his favourable impression too of these early friends in Montreal:

I am so pleased that you met the Woodcocks and that the spirit with which you are surrounded is so beautiful . . . Mr Woodcock is a Canadian artist of note and his landscapes are very fine – refined, soft and feelingly skilful – no mere infatuation with the metier of his art – there is more – his canvasses continue to speak as it were. I confess I have seen but few of them but he is well thought of. I do not think that he is dependent on his art for subsistence so he works away in his own world, not the one the public lives in . . .

I had Martha and Stanley the night before last and they enjoyed the night's sleep – Martha now has the key of the back door so she can at any time make herself at home. Say your jelly 'jelled' – and many are the congratulations – Martha put the paraffin on and all is well.

Towards the end of her letter to 'Abdu'l-Bahá on 24 February 1906, in which May asked His confirmation for yet another move, which it appears was effected on her own insistence for the sake of her teaching work, she mentions Percy Woodcock:

My dear husband and I have now our home in the centre of this city so that we might be accessible to the Truth-seekers, and hold meetings. Oh! Beloved One! Thy Cause is spreading. Thy Call is heard – and thro' the efforts of Thy noble servant Percy Woodcock, many souls are seeking the Light of Guidance. We beseech Thee to accept the sincere ones, and confirm them in the Truth!

In the course of this year and the next, the activities in the house at 29 Bishop Street gathered increasing momentum. On 12 December 1907,

May wrote to Agnes Alexander about the gatherings taking place in her home, and some of her visitors:

> Recently my beloved spiritual Mother, Mrs. Getsinger has made us a visit of more than two weeks . . . and we had such beautiful meetings, my Darling, and the people came from all directions to hear Lua speak – & the interest & attraction were widespread & deep. We have an Assembly in Montreal, composed of 12 or 15 members – who meet every Friday night at our house.
>
> I say 12 or 15 because several come – and are deeply influenced who have not yet accepted. At Lua's meetings we had from 40–50 people, so we have much to do now in the Vineyard – to water and warm these precious seeds. We had a 19 day Feast of 15 people, and sent a greeting to The Master.

The Master's praise for the establishment of the 'Spiritual Assembly' in Montreal was great indeed. This truly was an achievement! When one considers just how many people May had been able to attract to the Cause by this time, one can understand how happy she had made the Master. They gathered together in 1906 and wrote a letter to Him, under her guidance, calling themselves a 'Local Spiritual Assembly'. In retrospect, this little gesture was just as significant for the future of the country as all the stations and hotels that were being built by the Maxwell brothers along the route of the Canadian Pacific Railway at the same time.

In 1906, a long Tablet, translated on 17 October, was received from the Master addressed specifically to 'The Spiritual Assembly of the Bahá'ís, Montreal, Canada':

> O ye friends of 'Abdu'l-Bahá!
> His honour Mr. Woodcock wrote a letter and in that letter he mentioned your names, asking divine favour on your behalf. While reading your names I opened my tongue in thanksgiving in the Threshold of Oneness, that He hath granted such favour and bestowed such providence. He guided the souls and pointed out to them the entrance to the Kingdom. Such confirmation deserveth thanks and praise, and such guidance is the most great bounty of His Highness the Desired One.
> Likewise, you must be engaged day and night, with all your soul

and heart, in thanksgiving and the glorification of His Highness the Desired One who hath created you in such a glorious period, made you the manifestors of guidance in the Day of the Lord, imparted to you the insight and enkindled your souls and spirits with the fire of love. Today the grandeur, the majesty, the splendour and the magnitude of this station is not clear and manifest because it is the time of seed-sowing and the beginning of the planting of trees in the orchard of the Merciful One. When that seed is grown and the tree reacheth the time of its fruition, then many harvests shall be gathered and all regions and kingdoms shall be adorned with its blossoms and fruits.

Ere long the Adored One of this providence will become the Beloved of the assemblages of the world and the rays of the Sun of Truth will illumine every house, every place and corner. At that time the greatness and superiority of the friends of God will become evident and demonstrated.

Consider ye! In the day of His Highness Christ, the grandeur and majesty of their Holiness the Apostles was not known. After three hundred years the loftiness of the station and the exaltation of their attainment became manifest. Ere long the result of the deeds in this cycle of Bahá'u'lláh will appear and every one of the friends and the maidservants will be crowned with a diadem whose splendid gems will radiate brilliancy and effulgence throughout cycles and ages.

Therefore, O ye servants of God and the maidservants of the Merciful One, do ye not rest for one moment! Do ye not seek any composure! Do ye not wish for any rest and ease! Endeavour and make ye an effort with all your heart and soul to spread the fragrances of Paradise, to raise the eternal melody of the Kingdom of Abhá, to establish the gathering of fellowship, to become assisted with the confirmations of the Holy Spirit; to clothe the temple of existence with a new garment; to bestow eternal life upon the reality of souls; to become a cause of the civilization of the human world; to characterize the bloodthirsty animals with the heavenly attributes and divine commemorations; to purify the world with peace and salvation, and to adorn man with the favours of His Highness the Merciful One; that perchance ignorance, animosity and strangeness may be removed entirely from among the denizens of the world, and the Banner of Reconciliation, Freedom, Nobleness and Oneness be hoisted; for the chains of existence contain countless links, each connected with the other. This connection is the cause of the appearance of the invisible powers in the world of the visible.

O ye real friends! Make ye an effort that this universe may become another universe and this darkened world find a ray of the Sun of Truth and become luminous and refulgent.

I entreat God that this favour may be realized and this unending outpouring become manifest and apparent, and the friends of God be confirmed by every bounty.

One of the names which must have caused 'Abdu'l-Bahá to unloose His tongue in praise at this time was surely that of William Sutherland Maxwell. He was among the first to identify himself as a Bahá'í in Montreal and became a member of the first 'Spiritual Assembly' of that city by 1906. It is all the more remarkable to consider that he did this at a time when his own career was at its height and the work of the Maxwell firm was expanding rapidly.

Within a few years, Sutherland was also listed as a member of the St James Club, the Pen and Pencil Club, the Canadian Handicrafts Guild and the Arts Club. Many years later, the Montreal writer and poet Leo Cox claimed that the Arts Club, located at 51 Victoria Street[23] just down from the offices of the Edward and W. S. Maxwell firm at 6 Beaver Hall Square, 'owed its very existence to the spirit and benevolent vision of William Sutherland Maxwell'. A few years later, he also became the President of the Arts Club as well as a Councillor of the Province of Quebec Association of Architects, an Associate of the Royal Canadian Academy, and an Academician of the Royal Canadian Academy. Throughout this period of creative and administrative activity, he continued to be a stalwart member of the Local Spiritual Assembly of Montreal and by the time he was elected as a Fellow of the Royal Institute of British Architects, as the President of the Royal Architectural Institute of Canada and the Vice-president of the Royal Canadian Academy, he had served on this Bahá'í institution for well-nigh thirty years.

Writing to him from New York on 7 May 1907 May used the occasion of their fifth wedding anniversary to remind Sutherland of the sharp contrast between the Bahá'í standards and the values of all the clubs and associations of his profession:

You will receive this letter tomorrow on the fifth anniversary of our

---

23 In later years, this address was changed to 2027 Victoria Street.

wedding day – and you will know that I am thinking of you with the utmost love.

I hope you are well Darling, and not tired or overworked for I know this is your busy time of year – and with the various competitions you have much to do. Do you have to work at night now? I hope not Dear – and that you get enough sleep. Last Friday night Gus Windolph and his wife dined with us, and he and I had a long talk about architecture and its practice in this City – there is so much dishonesty in everything – and the unknown architects have to work day and night to keep up at all. You are so fortunate to have such a fine field for your talent in Montreal and an opportunity to become known and respected both as a man, and as an architect. Windolph and Werner[24] have principles which are 'out of date' – as they say that to them a thing is either <u>honest</u> or <u>dishonest</u> – nothing between – but their friends laugh at them and say: 'Oh! yes – be honest certainly – but a man who is <u>strictly</u> <u>honest</u> now-a-days is a fool!' Is it not strange that the world is so corrupt? Yet it is not strange for this is the fulfilment of all the prophecies referring to the 'last days' – and as Bahá'u'lláh! (Glory to Him!) says: 'In this Day the Greatest Light and the greatest darkness prevail.'

May's other longing during those early years was to return to the land of light on another pilgrimage. Over eight years had passed since she had stepped off the boat in the little port of Haifa, eight years since she had made her way by carriage, in the company of Mrs Thornburgh, Anne Apperson, Julia Pearson and Robert Turner, along the deserted shoreline to the gleaming town of 'Akká on the far side of the bay. She had yearned to go back in early 1901 and had tried again in October of that year, without success; she had suffered heartbreak at having to leave Europe without availing herself of the Master's final permission to come. Memories of her unforgettable encounter with 'Abdu'l-Bahá had recently been revived by Mariam Haney, who wrote to May on 16 February 1906 about a meeting she had had with Mrs Hearst's butler, who had stayed a firm Bahá'í all these years:

> Last night we had the joy of having at our room two colored broth-
> ers; lovely, sincere souls – with clean, calm, illumined faces. One

---

24 Werner and Windolph was an architectural firm in New York at the time.

was Robert (Mrs. Hearst's servant) – and the other a Charles Tinsley – employed in a high-class cafe, but equally as radiant and firm in his belief. Robert told us much of the wonderful privilege and blessing which was his in making the Holy Visit. And as a treat to them, I read them your account of your Pilgrimage, which contains such a sweet reference to Robert. The tears just streamed down his face; and he said it was just as if he was <u>There</u> living that wonderful experience all over again, for he remembered all so well. When they departed, Robert said: 'When you write to Mrs. Maxwell, please give her my greetings, and tell her I never forget her, and am so glad to know her husband is a believer.' Robert has never wavered, and is firm as a rock.

May wanted to go back to the Holy Land with her husband this time, and to have Sutherland meet the Master face to face at last. He had promised her, when giving His consent to their marriage, that she could come on a second pilgrimage when her husband was confirmed as a Bahá'í, and so on 25 March (probably 1906), she sent a letter to 'Abdu'l-Bahá, asking if she could fulfil this expectation:

> My Beloved Lord and Master,
>   With all my heart I thank thee for Thy great Mercy and Bounty, Thy wonderful Love and Compassion! and I whisper to Thee in silence that which my tongue is unable to utter. I humbly beg of Thee to permit me to again behold Thy Face, to open the way for me to come to the Holy City & to present myself before Thee. Oh! this longing consumes my heart for something past nevertheless I await God's time in patience.

The permission was not given, however. Her hopes were dashed once more. It was at the height of the Commission of Investigation and 'Abdu'l-Bahá was in no position to welcome Western visitors to the Holy Land. Even if this had not been the case, it is hard to imagine how Sutherland could have left his work at this time; he simply could not have afforded to take such a journey given all his activities and responsibilities just then. But May could not resist writing to 'Abdu'l-Bahá a few months later. On 13 November 1906, after the Montreal Assembly was formed, she wrote another letter to the Master, once more expressing her yearning for reunion. This time, however, she tempered her request. The object of her prayer now was for spiritual proximity and not mere physical reunion with 'Abdu'l-Bahá:

> My Lord – My Beloved!
> Last night in my dream I was at <u>Thy Feet</u>! No earthly words can describe the heavenly joy, divine ecstasy, supreme attainment and incomparable Life that this poor servant found at <u>Thy Feet</u>. Others were near Thee, and around Thee – but I only clasped Thy Feet – bathed them with tears of love and joy – and raised my head to gaze upon the Beauty of Thy Face – to hear the music of Thy Voice!
> Oh! My Lord and Master! In my dream I tasted one drop of the reality of the spiritual life my soul may find with Thee – one drop from the Cup of Thy Love! Oh! rend asunder the veils of mortal sleep that keep me far from Thee! Oh! free me from the prison of the ego – from the grades of death – that I may come to <u>Thy Feet</u> – be forever at <u>Thy Feet</u> – in worship, love and adoration – be the slave of Thy Divine Threshold – and know no other bondage save servitude to Thy Blessed Beauty! Grant my prayer – if it be Thy Holy Will!

May's faith was touchingly human. No matter how earnestly she yearned for something, no matter how often she asked 'Abdu'l-Bahá to fulfil her wishes, she always submitted to His will in the end. And no matter how submissive her supplications, she was usually insistent, in the last analysis, when it came to asking again. Her requests always concluded with words such as 'if it be Thy Holy Will', but she made sure her own will was registered too. In a Tablet written to her in 1906, 'Abdu'l-Bahá showered His love and expressed His satisfaction with her:

> *O thou daughter of the Kingdom!*
> *In reality thou art attracted to the divine realm and set aglow with the fire of divine love. I am pleased with thee and seek help and blessing for thee from the threshold of the Abhá Beauty.*

On 4 June 1907 another Tablet was revealed for May by 'Abdu'l-Bahá:

O thou daughter of the Kingdom!

Thou art in my memory and art present in heart and soul in the assemblage of the Kingdom. I do not forget thee. I supplicate for thee from the favours of the Lord of this glorious Age, and of this new Century, abundant confirmations so that thou mayest find at every moment a new spirit and be the recipient of the outpouring of the Holy Spirit. 'And this, indeed, would not be difficult for thy Lord!'

The Master knew that the Bahá'í teachings would take root and flourish in Canada because of May. He was fully aware that her home was a beacon of spiritual light and was destined to become the centre of Bahá'í activity in that country as well as in the United States. She symbolized the standards of the Kingdom in that continent. The following winter, at the turn of the year from December 1908 to January 1909, she wrote a wonderful letter to Sutherland which vividly illustrates how she lived both in her world and somehow above it at the same time:

> I went to Juliet's to see the New Year in with her – with prayers and Tablets, and in that quiet studio, while all New York was in an uproar (which lasted from 8 to 3 or 4 o'clock!), we felt the love and peace of God descend, and for a while it seemed that we were in the Presence of that Beloved One in Acca. Brother had gone to a party at the Floris' – so he called for me at 12.15 and we saw the gay crowds on Broadway, confetti flying, horns blowing – parties in automobiles ringing huge bells – perfect bedlam!

Sutherland, meanwhile, was at the hub of the Montreal art world. The offices of the Maxwell firm were also home to several artists during the years 1906 and 1907. Laura Muntz, the Canadian painter G. Horne Russell, and the Des Clayes sisters – the best known of whom was Berthe – all had their studios above 6 Beaver Hall Square at this time. Maurice Cullen's picturesque studio was situated in the immense and freezing skylit attic, several doors down, at 3 Beaver Hall Square, which also served as Sutherland's 'atelier' for many years. And the Arts Club was situated at 51 Victoria Street in a building the interior of which Mr Maxwell redesigned several years later, providing modern comforts to what was essentially the re-creation of an Elizabethan hall. He designed not only the wall panels and ceiling of this historic building, but even the benches, bookcases, chairs, and the fireplace mantelpiece of what would become 'a quiet haven of bohemian zest and love of life'.[25]

Many of the craftsmen and wood and metal artisans responsible for the creation of the sculptures, carvings and stained glass for the buildings designed and built by the Maxwells in the first two decades of the 20th century attended Sutherland's workshops. The two brothers initiated a unique practice in Montreal when they gave credit to the contribution of the craftsmen who participated in the internal and external beautification of the churches, hospitals, schools and private homes they constructed. Believing in the close collaboration between architect and craftsman, they kept note in their account books not only of other firms and contractors who became their partners but also individual artisans and specialists in wood and metal work whom they commissioned to render their designs.[26] It was hardly to be wondered at that William Sutherland Maxwell was, as Rúḥíyyih Khánum attested in later years, 'adored' by his workers, for he accorded them the intelligent attentions of a diffident architect who was himself a genial artist; he treated them in a manner that 'commanded respect as well as affection'.[27]

But the union of the artistic aspirations of her father and the spiritual aims of her mother, the 'central point' which linked together 'the two arms of [their] swirling nebulae', as Rúḥíyyih Khánum so eloquently put it, became truly visible in the building of their house. This physical spot became the hub of both the spiritual and artistic worlds in Montreal and the home which 'Abdu'l-Bahá would one day call His own. This was where the Bahá'í community was born and became the cradle in later years of little Mary Maxwell. From 1907 onwards and for the next two years, Sutherland began to negotiate for the land, design the plans, and build the house on Pine Avenue. In February 1908, when the work was well under way, a Tablet of the Master arrived at their residence on 29 Bishop Street, addressed to Mr Maxwell himself. In praising the services of his wife, it was as though the Master were telling Sutherland that the home he was busy building in Montreal would one day serve as the physical lamp in which the light of the Covenant would blaze:

---

25 Quoted in Collard, 'All Our Yesterdays' (May 1962).
26 Pepall, in *The Architecture of Edward & W. S. Maxwell*.
27 Collard, 'All Our Yesterdays'.

O thou who hast turned thy face toward the Kingdom!

Although a delay hath occurred in writing, I can now answer thee. Couldst thou but realize with what love and attraction this letter is being written, undoubtedly thou wouldst soar on the wings of joy and happiness toward the pinnacle of glory, begin to sing and chant, and pour forth such a melody as to exhilarate and stir up the entire Dominion of Canada.

Thy respected wife, Mrs. Maxwell, is indeed a lighted candle. Know thou her worth. That maidservant of God shall shine forth in the spiritual gatherings in such wise as to surpass the fame of Mary Magdalene and St. Barbara.[28] *That lamp of the love of God is in truth aglow and will be the cause of thy glory in this world and in the Kingdom above. This gift is now hidden and invisible like unto the flame in the oil, but erelong it will turn ablaze. At that time thou shouldst render at every moment a thousand thanks for having had such a distinguished wife, who was the cause of thy guidance and carried thee away from this fleeting world to the realm of the Kingdom. In brief, I do love thee very much, for thou hast become the cause of the happiness of the heart of that maidservant of God and hast gladdened her heart and rejoiced her spirit. Appreciate thou her true worth, and at every moment offer thy praise, thanksgiving and supplication at the threshold of oneness . . .*

But this was not all. The beloved Master had added a postscript in His own hand:

Although in these days travelling to the land of the heart's desire is not permitted, thou and Mrs. Maxwell have permission to come.

How May rejoiced at these words! They must have caused her spirits to soar. She had been longing for such an invitation to come on pilgrimage and must have begged her dear Sutherland to make arrangements so that they might avail themselves of it as soon as possible. But it was not easy for her husband to liberate himself from his pressing obligations. He could not stop what he was doing, just because he had been granted permission to go to 'Akká. Edward needed him in Montreal

---

28 Christian martyr venerated from the 7th century, condemned to death for her Christian belief. Throughout the centuries she has been regarded as the patron saint in time of danger from thunderstorms and fire, and also as intercessor to receive the Sacraments at the hour of death.

to provide the finishing touches for the designs and oversee the start of a huge project that required his vigilant attention: the Legislative Buildings in Saskatchewan. Sutherland appealed to May for a reprieve. He asked her to wait for him, for a change. She must have realized the justice of his plea. Had he not waited two years for her? Had he not waited for even more years while she gradually adapted herself to married life? Did he not wait for her, faithfully, every time she left home and went to New York, or travelled to Green Acre, or met the friends in Portsmouth, Woodstock and elsewhere? And could she not wait a while longer for him to be ready to accompany her to the land of her heart's desire? Sutherland was working around the clock. The concrete foundations of the Saskatchewan Legislative Buildings were due to be set in place on 31 August of that year. After he had overseen the initial phase of the construction work, he promised to see if it were possible for him to take time off to travel to Europe and the Middle East. May bowed her head, and prayed. She acknowledged the pressure he was under, having to 'work so hard to make up for lost time'. Although she expressed the hope, four months later, that 'the rush is over now Sutherland Darling!', she was being optimistic.

On 19 August 1908 May wrote to 'Abdu'l-Bahá supplicating prayers on behalf of Herbert Hopper, one of the early believers who had accepted the Cause in Paris and had accompanied Thomas Breakwell on pilgrimage. He too had been suffering from tuberculosis and had just passed away after years of battling with the deadly disease. Just as she had done before, May served as a vital link between her spiritual children – whether in this world or in the next – and the Centre of the Covenant. In response, 'Abdu'l-Bahá wrote the following Tablet of consolation to Marie Squires Hopper and her child, comforting them in their bereavement:

O thou favoured maidservant of the Threshold of the Almighty!

Mr. Hopper had asked of me that he may hasten unto the place of sacrifice, give himself up as an offering to the Abhá Beauty and drink the cup of the most glorious martyrdom.

Praise be to God he was successful in his consecrated efforts and was assisted in serving Him. This is but martyrdom itself. This is the sacrifice of one's life in the path of the one true God.

The purpose is this: it was the wish of that departed one to sacrifice himself. Praise be to God that he attained unto this gift, was exhilarated with this cup of favours and hastened unto the invisible kingdom of oneness in the utmost joy and gladness. Now he is engaged in praising and glorifying the bountiful Lord, with wondrous melodies, in the gardens of the Kingdom. He became free from this earthly world and hastened unto the infinite realm of his Lord. He was released from this dustheap, found his way unto the divine Court, and became a nightingale in the rose garden of truth. He was freed from this contingent world and soared upwards unto the vast expanse and lofty heights of the Infinite.

Consequently be thou not grieved and let not thy heart be saddened. Follow the example of that glorious soul and walk in his footsteps, that thou might see him in the divine world and enjoy everlasting association and companionship with him.

In the postscript of her letter about the untimely demise of this dear soul, May had not been able to resist giving expression once more to her longing to see the Master. Although He had granted permission earlier when her husband was not free to travel, she begged 'Abdu'l-Bahá, yet again, to be allowed to come on pilgrimage:

Oh! My Lord, with the utmost longing, humility and meekness, with my heart subdued by Thy Love, and my tears flowing, I thank Thee for Thy Gracious permission to my husband and to me to present ourselves before Thee! This Favor is beyond Words! Wilt Thou, I beg, make us more worthy to attain this Gift and so increase the <u>capacity</u> of this poor drop that when she attains the Ocean of Thy Presence she may be lost and absorbed therein, and become naught but a wave of Thy Love forevermore.

And in September of 1908, a few weeks after the work had begun on Sutherland's magnificent Legislative Buildings in Saskatchewan, she received the following answer from 'Akká. It rang with affirmations:

O thou who art attracted to the Abhá Beauty and the lover of the Best Beloved!

At every moment I remember thee, turn in prayer to the divine Kingdom, and ask boundless aid for thee.

O thou dear maidservant of God! If thou didst but know with what bestowal and bounty thou hast been blessed, thou wouldst surely free thyself from the world, spread thy wings and soar in the atmosphere of joy and gladness.

The favours of the Abhá Beauty surround thee: What more dost thou want? The confirmations of the Supreme Concourse are at hand: What more dost thou seek? The grace of the Lord is manifest: What more dost thou ask?

He was telling her to ask no more: her wishes had been fulfilled. He was telling her to doubt no longer: she was certainly coming on pilgrimage with Sutherland. How His words must have uplifted her spirits and made her blush at the same time!

* * *

Mr and Mrs Maxwell set off on pilgrimage to 'Akká in the beginning of 1909. The exact date of their departure from Montreal is not known, but as Sutherland's letter to his mother indicated, dated 26 February 1909, they sailed from New York on 6 February, landed in Cherbourg on 13 February, and had arrived in Paris by the 15th of that month.

It was the epoch of majestic ocean liners. It was the period when it was fashionable for the wealthy on both sides of the Atlantic to voyage in style, and the elegance of the ship on which the Maxwells travelled anticipated the extravagance of the *Titanic*, which was to meet its demise just three years later:

Dear Mother,

We had a comfortable crossing on the German steamer Kaiserin Auguste Victoria – she is a floating city, 25,500 tons, and can carry over four thousand people, the crew numbering about 600. Our cabin was about 9 x 12 two lower berths and a sofa – a large modern clothes cupboard with drawers etc and two wash basins, steam heat, etc – The boat has a large dining saloon with round tables seating four to six persons – the first boat in which this system has been installed. – Among the special features of the boat are elevators, flower shop, news stand, information bureau, a gymnasium, a restaurant on the top deck (Ritz Carlton management) where one may have meals by paying (coffee 50 cents etc). Also on the same deck there is a winter garden where one may sit among palms, flowers etc. and drink coffee & wines etc and listen to a good orchestra. The ship has a 'German Band' which plays on the deck during the mornings and which plays on the stringed instruments at dinner time.

May was not sick and during the 3 last days she thoroughly enjoyed the trip – Cherbourg to Paris by rail was killing – left at 6.30 arrived at 3 A.M. – bed in hotel 4.10 A.M. – Paris was beautiful – and well kept and the traffic well governed – We changed our hotel owing to noise and found in the Hotel Madison ideal conditions. Our three days in Paris were pleasant but I did no sight seeing, being occupied during the afternoons with purchasing etc for our clients.

The trip to Marseille in the South of France was a dream, weather perfect, train ditto and the scenery quite enchanting – I never enjoyed any train journey so much – Marseille to Port Said was not enjoyable – boat of 10,000 tons, rough weather and English cooking. Port Said a revelation of Eastern life – all kinds of coloured men – Arabs, Sudanese, Turks, Egyptians, etc, long 'morning wrappers' in all colours, strange craft – eager boatmen – officials in gold lace red fez caps – etc, etc.

We are well installed in the Eastern Exchange Hotel. Intend seeing Cairo, Athens, Constantinople, Munich, Berlin, Paris, London and Montreal. May sends much love and I ditto to all – Affectionately Willie

They were accompanied on their journey by Louise Stapfer, later to become Louise Bosch;[29] she was their guest on this trip. There is no doubt that the voyage was full of emotion for them, for Louise had recently become a Bahá'í and the Maxwells were returning to Europe for the first time after many years. Their three-day passage through Paris was surely filled with memories and renewed acquaintances among friends in the American community. Their subsequent itinerary, through Marseilles to Port Said, must have revived intense recollections too, for May had crossed from Egypt to Palestine with the Hearst party when she went to see the 'Prisoner of 'Akká'.

---

29 In a later Tablet the Master advised May to remain close to this Bahá'í who came on pilgrimage with her and who He knew was destined to render such devoted services to the Faith.

A decade had elapsed since that first pilgrimage in 1899. A decade
had almost elapsed too since the couple had first met. May was now a
mature woman. She was also a married woman. She had succeeded in
nurturing the first 'Spiritual Assembly' of Montreal and had established
the Cause of Bahá'u'lláh in the Dominion of Canada. But although she
was the spiritual mother of France, she had not yet become a mother
herself. And although her husband had accepted the Faith as well as
making a name for himself in his profession, their childlessness must
have been a source of private sorrow to the couple. This pilgrimage was
destined to change their lives forever.

They arrived in the port of Haifa and made their way along the sea
shore, as was the custom in those days, to the fortress city of 'Akká.
At that time the Master was still living in a rented house next to the
Citadel, facing the sea. It was here, in the House of 'Abdu'lláh Páshá,
that May had stayed during her first pilgrimage and it was here again
that she came with Sutherland and they stayed for six days as His guests.

During those unforgettable days, two events of great significance
occurred, the first related to Sutherland, the second to May herself.
Rúḥíyyih Khánum frequently recounted the first to friends and pilgrims, and May herself has left a record for posterity about the second.

One day at table, Sutherland said to 'Abdu'l-Bahá:

'The Christians worship God through Christ; my wife worships
God through You; but I worship Him direct.'

'Abdu'l-Bahá smiled and said: 'Where is He?'

'Why, God is everywhere,' replied Sutherland.

'Everywhere is nowhere,' said 'Abdu'l-Bahá. He then went on to
demonstrate that such worship was worship of a figment of the imagination and had no reality; we must worship God through something
tangible and real to us, hence the rôle of the Manifestations. Sutherland
bowed his head in acceptance. The real seed of his faith germinated
from that hour.

As for May, she was immersed in an ocean of love by the Master
and surrounded with a thousand tokens of affection by the ladies of
His family. They well remembered that passionate young woman who
had come to the Holy Land with the first group of Western pilgrims;
they well recalled how vulnerable she had been and how transformed
by the Master. They must have been delighted to see her now in full
maturity, so beautiful, so happily married. They must have wondered at

her childlessness too, and talked of it, as women in a Persian household are so wont to do.

There is a moving note which May wrote many years later, on the eve of her daughter's twentieth birthday, about a significant incident which occurred while she was staying in the Master's home. The date of this letter is known – 7 August 1930 – but its recipient is not. Since it bears directly on the second important event which took place in the course of the Maxwells' pilgrimage, it is included below:

Despite all natural reserve and the great awe I feel in approaching you in such a matter, yet my heart and conscience so urge me to trust and confide in you that it must obey.

It is, after all, like so many of the strange and wonderful acts of the Master, utterly simple, born of His infinite love, mercy and divine compassion. Mary is now on the eve of her twentieth birthday, and about twenty-one years ago my dear husband and I, who had been married seven years and were childless, made the pilgrimage to the Holy Presence and the Shrines. We were there only a few days, and one evening, in the twilight, with a white veil the Beloved had wrapt around my head and shoulders, I had the little babe of Rouha Khanum in my arms. As I passed the Master's door on my way to show the child to my husband I saw in the gathering darkness the blessed Form standing at His threshold, and He called to me in a clear tender voice and motioned me to come – Rouha was by my side and the Master said: 'You like that baby? I will give him to you.' I said, 'But he belongs to Rouha Khanum,' and she replied, 'If our Lord gives him to you, he is yours.' Then I told the Master that twice I had had the opportunity to adopt lovely children but my husband would not. With that swift motion combined of love and action, the Master bade me enter His room, and setting all the waves of life in motion by His walk, He asked me if I would like to have a child – if I knew why I had never had a child – if I wanted one now!

I weep with joy and wonder as I recall the caressing penetrating tones of His voice, the light of His glance, the mysterious all-enveloping potency of His Eternal Spirit!

I told Him I could not have children but I was content in the Will of God. In ringing tones He said, 'This is not true; you can have children,' then suddenly half laughing half eager – yet with underlying gravity He said: 'do you want a child – shall I give you a child?' I replied, 'Whatsoever you desire for me – this is all I wish.' In a moment I found myself, Babe and all, clasped in His Holy Arms – His hands passed tenderly over my head. He said: 'That is the reply of my own daughter – be assured – be happy – I will pray for you.'

It was a mysterious moment and one that May herself would not fully understand till later. But it marked a great change, both physical and spiritual, in the lives of the couple. The radical transformation in their relationship can be glimpsed in a letter May wrote to Sutherland some years later, recollecting this pilgrimage:

> You know at what great sacrifice you took me to Acca – but the blessings that followed were untold! Our little Mary was one of them! You know how you wanted to leave Acca and visit certain centres of art & beauty – but 'Abdu'l-Bahá wanted you to stay in that Centre of eternal Beauty & light! As soon as you made that sacrifice you began to see and understand the Reality of 'Abdu'l-Bahá! Now the result of your sacrificing this pleasure trip . . . and giving me the <u>utmost</u> help and support on every plane has been that we have truly found a <u>new</u> <u>power</u> – and the words of Our Lord to you in that marvelous Tablet have been fulfilled! You remember He said He had the utmost love for you because of your love and kindness to His daughter & that a time would come when I would shine forth in the Assemblies of the World so that my fame would surpass that of Mary Magdalene & St. Barbara & that at that time your spirit would take a great flight & you would sing a melody that would enchant the denizens of Canada! Dear Sutherland – all progress – all attainment is thro sacrifice – we have been taught to consider sacrifice as something painful – but its real meaning is that we give up a lower thing for a higher – a lesser thing for a greater – it means unfoldment – capacity – life & joy!

It was a turning point in the lives of the Maxwells of Montreal.

* * *

May and Sutherland returned to Canada separately from Palestine. After spending one night at the Grand New Hotel in Haifa, on 13 March 1909, they sailed back to France via Egypt and then parted ways. It seems that Sutherland continued directly back home after reaching Marseilles, whereas May, who might have travelled later in the company of some English pilgrims, stopped off in France for several months to visit the Bahá'ís. Sutherland sent a postcard to his mother, dated 21 March, about his own travel plans:

> Dear Mother, Am on way home have had beautiful trip. Egypt was most enjoyable. Perfect weather, great architecture and art. Poor travelling connections have caused some delay. Shall get your plates. Love to all, Affectionately, Willie.

He had written to his father separately, from Marseilles:

> Dear Father, All goes well. May has been a good sailor. Saw this good looking girl yesterday. Affectionately, Willie.

The good-looking girl on the postcard was the Duchesse of Châteauroux, by Jean-Marc Nattier. Perhaps Sutherland saw a faint resemblance to May in her features, for it is hard to imagine why else he would have picked out such a postcard! He certainly visited the Musée de Longchamps in Marseilles, *en route* back to Paris, and may have seen other good-looking girls on canvas there too. But when he boarded the ship that was to take him back to Montreal, he left his own good-looking girl behind.

May stayed at 24 Avenue Carnot when she first arrived in Paris at the end of April, but then rented another, quieter apartment in which she stayed with Louise Stapfer and a maid until the beginning of July. During this period, she had much to occupy her. As she wrote to Sutherland on 9 May, some weeks after their parting:

> It seems a long time since I wrote you, and quite an age since I heard from you, Darling! but we are both so busy – each with our particular work, and I think that never before have we been so united – so close to one another in heart & soul. I know that you are enjoying your work immensely – and that it swings along easily under your master-hand – as you often say – even better alone than with

another to – well, I do not like to say interfere – but to confuse things a little! . . .

Do you have regular weekly meetings, and are they well attended? I am so much interested in all at home, and I am looking forward eagerly to being with you again . . .

Now you will be glad to know how well I am, and very busy trying to fulfil the wishes of Our Beloved Master. Laura Barney has gone to America, so we have the Tuesday meetings here. Mr. Woodcock and his family are here now, having just returned from Acca, and they have brought the heavenly beauty and calm of that blessed experience with them. I feel that the believers here are becoming more united, and that our love for one another is growing deeper and more real. Mr. Dreyfus is away also – he is finishing his military service. I am so sorry he is missing the Woodcocks for they are lovely people, and Mr. Woodcock is wonderfully developed since this second visit to Our Beloved 'Abdu'l-Bahá. I know that you live over in thought and memory those perfect days of love & light and peace in the Presence of Our Master, just as I do Darling, and we draw from that inexhaustible Source a mighty strength and inspiration.

The other dear friend with whom May spent time in France was Hippolyte Dreyfus. He wrote to her on 20 July 1909, thrilled at the prospect of her presence in Paris:

Just after writing you yesterday I received your telegram, and now comes your sweet letter. Yes you need not fear, May: there is not and never will be any misunderstanding between us; and I love above everything those impetuous words in which the spontaneity of your beautiful soul reveals itself. You must never refrain from telling me all your thoughts, and just as they come to you, for unexpressed thoughts might reach me still, and in a wrong way – I am so dull at times!

Now . . . you must first of all recuperate your strength, and for that, be sure that everything will soon be all right here . . . Have you seen my sister? She is in Paris you know until the end of this month; she is branched [sic]³⁰ on our telephone, and would be glad, I am sure, to do anything for you. If you needed some thing I hope you would not hesitate to call on her: she is often times of sound advice.

---

30 Literally a translation of "*branché*" from the French.

I cannot tell you enough how happy I am whenever I think of these last weeks in Paris where it has been my privilege to come so close to you, and whenever I realize that this spiritual union and this aim at the service of the Cause admits no separation!

Take good care of yourself, May, and count always upon me . . .

When May left Paris for a brief respite in Fontainebleau, Hippolyte wrote to her again, on 24 July, about his successful efforts to contact one of the Bahá'ís, in her name:

How glad I am that you have been able to leave Paris! I hope from the bounty of God that this change will soon make you feel perfectly strong, especially as now I have a handfull [sic] of good news to give you which will give joy and fragrance to your heart.

You see, it is you who have made me do the right thing. Not having heard any answer from Edith, I would not have written again, had it not been for your sake. And seeing that your letter to her did not make her write, I sent her another word in which I asked to see her to talk about you. Then she replied the next day that she would be pleased to see me at her Hotel. I could not believe my eyes, May, and was so happy I cannot tell you how: for I felt at once that all that was due to the heavenly influence of my Sign of the Invisible. How great and beautiful is your love, dear, to have been able to melt the ice . . . ! I went there this morning, but it was not necessary, as you suggest in your letter, to tell her once more to disregard personalities, and only look for the little amount of spirit that might be found in me, for our conversation, most cordial and calm, was just as if we had seen one another the day before, and we only spoke of you and of the Cause . . .

. . . So you see, dear child, if you come now, you will find every one happy and thankful, and it will be only rest for you, not work anymore! How sorry I am to have been the cause of so much trouble to you, but how happy that it has been through you that everything has been made satisfactory!

. . . Now, dear May, I must not forget that you are in Fontainebleau to enjoy the forest and not to read my broken english, and I hope that I will soon get a line from you full of the fragrances of the woods . . .

May was not only meeting with the Bahá'í friends and reviving their hearts; she was not only teaching the Faith as much as she could and encouraging Louise to go sight-seeing,[31] but she was also acquiring a Parisian wardrobe worthy of the wife of 'Lord Maxwell' as some of the Bahá'ís of New York jokingly referred to Sutherland. Writing to him on 25 May 1909, she confided:

> Several of my lovely new dresses are under way at Vickels. I have to finish my shopping – to see one or two friends – and then – as you say – Westward Ho! and oh! how happy we shall be my Hubby! Many people would misunderstand our separation – thinking that it was based on the same grounds of selfishness and indifference as that of many husbands and wives. But their thoughts are limited with the limitations of the circle and world in which they live and not one ray of that wonderful world of universal light and everlasting love to which God in His Mercy has admitted you and me has reached them. Our marriage is not based on uninterrupted physical contact – on a dull round of daily habits which the people call life, but which is only <u>existence</u>. – Our marriage is based on mutual love and understanding – on a spiritual union of the heart in love of God, on a broad human companionship full of sympathy, sweetness and great congeniality.

In her continuing remarks in the above letter, she confessed to Sutherland:

> . . . how I <u>thank God</u> for . . . a marriage which is my greatest source of <u>strength</u>, of <u>rest</u>, of <u>happiness</u> and <u>peace</u>! Oh! my Dearest, we will both try to be worthy of our great blessings, for God has been very good to us!

In signing off she asked Sutherland to give her love to the Bahá'ís in Montreal, and particularly to her older sister-in-law Jessie, who was

---

31 May gives a delightful glimpse in her letter of 9 May of her dear American friend's reaction to the art in the Salon of Paris and teases Sutherland too about his old artistic connections before their marriage: 'Louise is well and doing a little sightseeing. She went to the Salon and was disgusted, & Mr. Woodcock advised me not to go – he says it is a cesspool, and that one feels oppressed and degraded by the majority of the works. I saw your friend! Miss Wallace – the sculptress – who looked tickled & flushed (or blushed) when I mentioned you.'

closer to her than anyone else in the Maxwell family, except Sutherland's mother:

> Give my love to all the believers – Mrs. Cowles – Dr. Johnston – the Armstrongs & all – and give my love to your family, especially <u>Jessie</u>. In a letter which I had from you last week you spoke of Jessie being so well, and recovering so rapidly and I am very happy indeed – our lovely Jessie! I hope this rapid recovery means a <u>complete cure</u> – because it does not always mean that, Dear.

Unfortunately none of Sutherland's correspondence has come to light from this time except for one exceptional letter, which he wrote to 'Abdu'l-Bahá on 9 July 1909 after his return to Montreal. The difference in tone between this and his previous letters to the Master is marked. Although he was still responding to his wife's urgings, he was not under duress but wrote this time with a heart of crystal that scintillated spontaneously with the light he had received in the Holy Land:

> Dear Spiritual Father,
>
> My loved wife has written you from her heart and asked me if I wish to send a message to you. In all humility I join her and send you my humble greetings and thanks for the quickening power of love and understanding that is causing me to live and see as I have never done before. We are truly blessed in having access to this light of your manifestation and are in hopes that we may yet bear fruit of usefulness.
>
> The many talks that I have with your servant my beloved wife are a source of inspiration and real help to me and I know that all of this beauty is directly from you and my sincere and lasting gratitude goes out to you for this new light in my life. I pray that you may accept my humble thanks and believe me to be one who really is seeking equal to the capacity which is given unto me.
>
> Humbly Yours in Spirit,
>
> W. S. Maxwell

There is no further indication of his sister Jessie's health, which unfortunately did not improve in the course of the next few years. It was during this time that Sutherland received a curious letter from Sarah

Farmer. Writing to him on 31 March 1909, soon after his return from
'Akká, this eccentric and illumined lady invited the well-known Canadian architect to create a permanent summer cottage on her property
where his wife could come and teach the Faith. What Sutherland would
have thought at the time of this invitation to abandon the construction
of the Saskatchewan Legislature and come and build a log cabin on the
banks of the Piscataqua River, is unknown:

> Dear servant of El Baha!
>
> Do you remember the day you drove by the foot of Monsalvat,
> and, looking up at its pine-covered slopes, said – 'What a location
> for a bungalow with pasture rocks for its base, and broad piazzas!'
>
> Ever since that afternoon, I have seen that bungalow rising, but
> this is the first time I have been permitted to write you.
>
> Our Lord has said some wonderful and prophetic words about
> that hill-top on which He has promised to build a <u>Mashriqu'l-
> Adhkár</u> when the one now building in thought in Chicago is
> finished in wood and stone. He has told us that Monsalvat is to
> become 'a meeting-place of nations'. How would you like to help
> His words come true, by building there for your bride on her home-
> coming the bungalow, shown you in your vision? I will gladly lease
> the land to you on the condition that when you do not use it, it shall
> be at the service of the servants of El Baha and on the passing of
> yourself and your beloved, shall be a part of the Monsalvat property,
> dedicated to the bringing in of the <u>Placeless Kingdom of God</u> – the
> Kingdom of the Most Great Peace.[32]
>
> With this understanding also, I will give you the pasture-rock
> needed for the lower story [sic] and chimney (if built by you) and
> Norway pines to sustain the roof – rustic columns. My thought of
> this bungalow is of one large living room below stairs, in which
> (with the piazza for an overflow) your Flower of God could hold her
> services of love. A small addition in the rear could provide kitchen
> conveniences and bath-room. Dormer windows in the roof would
> give good sleeping-apartments for those who do not know the
> luxury of sleeping on the verandah.

---

32 Sarah Farmer's vision would in fact come true. 'Green Acre' was not only visited by 'Abdu'l-
Bahá Himself, during His trip to America, but became a regular summer home for Mrs
Maxwell in the years ahead, and a place where young Mary Maxwell was destined to grow
up and one day give Bahá'í courses herself.

Your goodness in receiving into your home and doing all in your power for our Elisheba,[33] when I had fallen by the way-side, makes me your debtor for all time. Hoping to hear from you soon. Yours in the service of El Baha

Sarah J. Farmer

There is no doubt that the heart of William Sutherland Maxwell must have been touched by the purity of Miss Farmer's motives. It is some indication of his forbearance, his nobility of character and his patience with human foibles, that with all his professional commitments and his very busy life, he always found time to respond to the requests of the Bahá'ís. He not only became involved in the affairs of the struggling community but also gave his attention to some of the struggling individuals in it, many of whom depended on his wife's charity. Lillian James, May's dear friend from the Paris days, also wrote to Sutherland during his wife's absence in Europe in order to repay some money that she owed:

I thank you for your kind response – I want to send this money now, as it is useless to put it in the bank for a few weeks, and so I will surprise Mrs. Maxwell when she returns. Please write me when you receive it. I hope I shall have the pleasure of meeting you some time. Yours very truly, Lillian James

Indeed, most of the Bahá'ís who knew May did not always have the pleasure of meeting, let alone knowing, her husband during those early years. He was a man of innate humility who sought at all costs to avoid drawing attention to himself. Unlike his wife, he was shy and retiring, but he was perfectly capable of participating in activities which were of personal interest to himself. On 25 May 1909, when his wife was still in Europe, he received the following letter from Lua Getsinger:

I see your name among the list of competitors for designs and plans for the Bahá'í Temple in Chicago and as I know an architect of some repute who will submit plans for same – providing you are really going to enter the Competition – I write to ask if it is true that you

---

33 The 'Elisheba' referred to in the last paragraph was Elizabeth Josselyn.

are making plans . . . He says he will compete if you are also in it but otherwise not.[34]

It seems that from Spring of 1909 to the following year, several well-known architects were making designs for the Temple in Wilmette. W. S. Maxwell of Montreal was listed as one of seven who participated in the competition at this time.[35] But although all plans had to be submitted by 1910, it was not until the Annual Convention of 26 April 1920 that the winner was chosen from the final three contestants. The description of the vote for the final winner was recorded in *Star of the West*. [36]

> Three architects were present in person, and to each of these, Mr. Charles Mason Remey, Mr. W. S. Maxwell and Mr. Louis Bourgeois, twenty minutes was allowed that each might explain his plans, etc. . . . The announcement was a clear majority for the Bourgeois model.

It is interesting, in light of this choice, to remember that when the beloved Guardian was decorating the Mansion of Bahá'u'lláh in the early 1930s, he chose to hang a photograph of Sutherland's design in one of the rooms. This was because 'Abdu'l-Bahá had shown a marked preference for it. Shoghi Effendi also included Mr Maxwell's model in *The Bahá'í World*, under which his caption reads:

> Design submitted by Mr. W. S. Maxwell, architect, of Montreal, Canada, for the competition for the Bahá'í Temple, held in New York 1919.[37]

It surely indicates the spiritual stature of William Sutherland Maxwell, to say nothing of his consummate professionalism, that although he was submitting proposals and winning commissions for some of the most important buildings in Canada at that time, although his distinctive style was being acclaimed and recognized throughout the country, he was not in the least perturbed at having lost this competition for the Bahá'í Temple. Nor was he offended by the length of time it took the

---

34 It is unknown who this 'architect of some repute' was.
35 *Star of the West*, vol. I, no. 4 (17 May 1910), p. 12.
36 *Star of the West*, vol. 11, no .4 (17 May 1920), p. 66.
37 *The Bahá'í World*, vol. VIII (1938–1940), p. 512.

Bahá'ís to come to a decision. A lesser man or a poorer artist would have taken umbrage at having his designs rejected, would have complained bitterly about the lack of professionalism in the Bahá'í community, but Sutherland was detached. Over the next twenty years, it was to a large part due to his scrupulous good counsel and professional advice that the Bahá'í institutions were able to come to their decisions on other projects.

On 3 May 1909, some months before May came back from Paris, her husband was formally elected as Chairman of an Architect Sub-committee for the Montreal City Improvement League and was invited to attend a meeting of the League Council at Loyola College. It is a wonder that he could have accepted civic burdens in addition to all his professional responsibilities at this time. It is hard to imagine how a man who was, as his own daughter often used to say, 'by nature a recluse', who was reserved and self-effacing by instinct, a lover of beauty, a con-noisseur of art, a person disinclined to indulge in words – how such a man would have had the patience, let alone the temperament or time, to spend hours on committees with the worthy burghers of the town. He must have had a remarkable degree of tolerance.

These were the golden years of the Maxwell firm and business was flourishing. In addition to overseeing the exterior designs under their construction, Sutherland was often commissioned by their clients to buy art objects for interior decoration as well, which entailed visits to the Anderson Auction Company in New York. According to Nancy Yates, 'The Maxwell Brothers architectural firm was a full service opera-tion that would design a home for a wealthy client right down to the table linens.'[38] Since his own home on Pine Avenue was also being built between 1908 and 1910, Sutherland often indulged his artistic sense by buying beautiful things for his private enjoyment while fulfilling his public commissions at Beaver Hall Square. As Nancy Yates attests:

> On their trips to the auction houses and dealers abroad to shop for their clients William and Edward would also shop for themselves and often came back with Old Master paintings, European and Ameri-can antique furniture and Oriental artworks to decorate their own homes. Both brothers became ardent collectors of art and antiques with William being the more passionate of the two and in the end owning a larger and finer art and antique collection. Their homes

---

38 See Appendix II.

were mini museums filled with items they had acquired in Montreal, New York and Europe.[39]

Sutherland was therefore extremely busy during May's absence but he must also have been missing his wife and was possibly disappointed to hear that she was not coming home as soon as expected. He might almost have anticipated it, though. She told him that she had been given a special mission by the Master:[40]

> I had expected to sail sometime this month as you know but it was not possible and I will tell you why – and of course you know that what I tell you is sacred. Our Beloved Master gave me a certain work to do in Paris, a very difficult and delicate task, of which I will tell you fully when I see you. The life of the Cause here in Paris was depending upon the success of this work, and I knew that if I obeyed 'Abdu'l-Bahá in every way that His Will would be accomplished. Nothing in the world but a Command of Our Master would induce me to leave you as I have done – to stay two or three months with the ocean between you and me – and as you know my love and devotion to you, you will know that in many ways it has been as hard for me as it has for you – this separation. Today I have been able to take the last great step in this work of the Master, and in a very short time now, through His Confirming Power, all will be accomplished, then I shall come to you at once.

May did everything in her power to nurture the remnants of the old Bahá'í community in Paris but it was clear that a new chapter had begun. The Faith now rested in the hands of the French Bahá'ís. One of the last letters she received before leaving France may have been from Hippolyte Dreyfus; it is dated 29 July 1909:

> If this is the last letter I am sending you to Paris, I can only tell you once more that my thoughts will accompany you on this journey, and my prayers will be with you until you reach home safely and happily. I hope that our spiritual union will always be so perfect that I won't

---

39 ibid.

40 Although there is no explanation of this 'task' in this letter of 25 May 1909, or subsequent correspondence, it may well have related to the disaffection of some of the early believers due to the continued influence of Covenant-breakers.

feel your absence, and that every now and then you will spread upon me the blessing and the mercy of your thoughts and counsels. My joy now is to think of the joy of all those who for so long have been deprived of your presence, and who are longing for your inspiring influence. If, with all my limitations and weaknesses, I can have a spiritual share in your work, it is more than I hope and that I deserve – But I know you won't withdraw from me the eye of kindness . . .

May had evidently told Sutherland about the English Bahá'ís with whom she had travelled and he must have encouraged her to pass through London on her way back home:

I think I shall leave Paris in <u>one month</u> from now and I will do just as you say about going to England for a week or ten days – to see the believers & visit the Hertz. I am not <u>keen</u> on going – in fact, I would rather sail from here – except for disappointing them – but I would like your opinion and advice . . .

I shall bring Millie & Jessie each a silk petticoat . . .

It seems that May's sister-in-law Jessie Maxwell may not after all have rallied from ill-health after their return from their pilgrimage. Hers was a slow decline, and one which was to take its toll on the family. In addition to worrying about her, another cause of distress for Sutherland at this time was his mother's death. Johan Maxwell passed away on 6 September 1909, barely five months after he came back. It must have been a blow, for Sutherland had always maintained a special relationship with his mother. It must have been a great relief to him too that May had returned to Canada before her passing. He doubtless took refuge in his wife's tender sympathy. Their pilgrimage together had drawn them closer than ever before.

* * *

Before May's return to Canada, Sutherland had already written his letter of thanks and gratitude to 'Abdu'l-Bahá, on 9 July 1909. But when she came back she herself received the following Tablet from the Master, translated on 2 September 1909, which she must certainly have shared with Sutherland:

O thou who art attracted to the Abhá Kingdom!

Thank thou God that thou wert quickened by the breath of eternal life, turned thy face to the Abhá Kingdom, and wert blessed with infinite bounties. Thou didst traverse mountain, land and sea until thou didst arrive at the blessed Spot, bowed thy head in adoration before the Holy Threshold and received the divine outpourings. Now, with an illumined face, a heart like unto a rose-garden, bearing divine glad tidings and a merciful spirit, and with high resolve, be thou engaged in the service of the Cause of God, a means to attract believing souls, and a channel to bestow eternal life to the heedless. Enable those who are deprived of His grace to comprehend His divine mysteries, and be an instrument to enable the spiritually destitute to receive a portion of the outpouring of the Kingdom . . .

Thy letters must reach here regularly. Convey wondrous Abhá greetings on my behalf to Mr. Maxwell and to the other friends.

Juliet Thompson, who visited the Holy Land that same summer, wrote glowing letters to May during the course of her pilgrimage, about 'Abdu'l-Bahá's love for her:

May, darling He said you were my 'mother'. He said I could never love you enough, He loved you so much. He said that to associate with souls like you meant my spiritual progress.

Several months later 'Abdu'l-Bahá addressed another Tablet to May, the translation date of which was 10 January 1910. It would seem from His references to past and present, from His recollection of her days in the East and her return to the West, from His comments about her spiritual state while she was in 'Akká and her condition during the months that followed, that He had been following her progress closely:

O thou maidservant of God!

Whilst passing some days in the East, thou wert a flame of the love of God. Now, assuredly, thou art even more aglow and illumined. Glad tidings must arrive from thee continually, so that they may be a cause of rejoicing of the friends and the maidservants of God in the East.

Convey greetings to thy beloved husband.

At about the same time, on 3 January 1910, May herself sent an historic letter to her father, John H. Bolles. In it she revealed her 'new glad tidings' and shared with him the physical nature of the spiritual quickening to which the Master had earlier referred. It would seem from the text of the letter that after her husband, her father was the first to know that she was pregnant:

> The love in which we are united in the Cause of God is of the spirit – & the world of light – & I could not endure to write of the months of suffering I have had – until I could share with you also their fruit – which is pure joy and bliss! With you first – I wished to share this sacred secret – that I shall soon be a Mother – and that this gift has come to me, like every other blessing in heaven or earth, from Our Beloved 'Abdu'l-Bahá.

The following day, on 4 January 1910, while May was sojourning for the winter in New York, she received a note from Juliet Thompson, one of the earliest of her friends to accept the Faith in Paris. They had evidently met the evening before, and talked, and although the subject is still concealed even in this letter, it is clear that May had told her of the impending event for which she had so ardently prayed:

> May, my most precious and beloved of all – save the Master! – you know, do you not, that of all the world I love you best, after our Lord? – For indeed you are my mother! . . . Since you told me your precious secret last night . . . I cannot imagine you more radiant and yet – you will be! – and how wonderful you will be, my beautiful May! – for think how that gift Crowns Every Woman – even the least conscious – the least awake! What then will you be!

The third person to whom May confided her 'precious secret' was another of her spiritual children, Agnes Alexander. She wrote a long letter to Agnes on 5 May 1910, telling her of her pilgrimage and relating the promise made to her by 'Abdu'l-Bahá. The letter ends with the following paragraph:

> And now my lamb I am going to confide to you a secret which is the sequel to what I have told you. Our dear Lord has favored

His maid-servant past all her hope, and by the pure showers of His
Bounty has watered the seed of life, and is bringing forth a child. In
a few months, Inshallah, the babe He is sending to my husband &
me will be born, and I beg for your prayers, both for the little one
and for myself – for I am not strong – nor young! and physically I am
passing through some trials – and this winter I had a fall which nearly
proved fatal. I have not told the friends – even the most intimate – but
I wanted you to know – and I know you will keep my confidence.

It was not long before the secret was out. May's protracted visits to New
York were soon explained by what she humorously called her 'protuberance'. But in a letter she wrote to her husband during her pregnancy,
she is clearly more worried about his condition than her own. He was
working around the clock to finish the house on Pine Avenue, in prepa-
ration for the birth of his child and in anticipation of his wife's return.
At the same time, he and his brother had also entered a very important
competition for the design of the new art gallery in Montreal in 1910,
which was to replace the original one on Phillips Square. It would be a
highly prestigious achievement for the Maxwell brothers, and Sutherland was under pressure to fulfil his side of the bargain. May, who must
have phoned before writing the following letter, could tell that he was
exhausted:

First darling – I am so sorry that you have that loss of voice again,
it shows that you are tired out and it almost makes me hate the Art
Gallery! I know you will smile at this – but Sutherland you must take
care of yourself. God has given you <u>health</u> – if you once really injure
or weaken it, you will never regain it in its fullness and vigor, and I
would rather we should be <u>poor</u> all our lives, than to have you suffer
anything of all that I have suffered through my body.

I am glad the house is nearly ready – and today I see Dr. Allen –
then he will tell me if he has to see me again and also the question
of my confinement will be settled – and if he says I may, I will come
home the end of this week – or a week from today. . . .

On Saturday night I went to my first meeting – my lack of proper
clothes and large protuberance has prevented my going! It was at the
Kinneys, and oh, it was so inspiring – and did baby & me so much
good.

In late May, while she was visiting her father and brother in New York, May wrote the following note to her husband. It is clear that her joy at this time was indescribable and she was determined to do everything in her power to protect the well-being of her baby:

> In the afternoon I saw Marion Nall & her new tiny baby – we had a delightful time – discussing the baby on her lap and the baby in my womb! for she saw at once! I know I shall never be a modern Mother. Marion adores her baby, & she is trying modern methods – not holding it much, not taking it up when it *yells*! etc. Mercy! I was not brought up that way – and I think I am not too much of a failure! I cannot see the sense in it all – but I must read and think and *pray* – in the coming months – and God will enlighten me.

Not surprisingly, May was having a difficult pregnancy. She had always suffered from poor health and to bear a child now, at the age of forty, was not easy. Her family were very concerned about her. Writing to his sister Ella on 28 May her father John Bolles confided:

> May is in the city now and expects to be confined about the middle of July, but has not yet fully decided to be in this city at that time, but may go to Burlington Vermont – she does not know the Doctors of Montreal well enough to feel like being there.

Given her weak constitution and the risks involved due to her age, she did finally decide to remain in New York for the birth of the child in order to be under the care of a homeopathic doctor. She had always preferred this method of medicine, her grandfather having been one of the earliest homeopathic physicians in New York. And so during the last months of pregnancy, she avoided travelling to Canada altogether. Rúḥíyyih Khánum used to say that her paternal grandfather often made caustic jokes on the subject of May's protracted trips to New York, and his jokes at this time were in rather poor taste.

However, nothing could have tarnished the joy of May and Sutherland at their baby's birth, which took place in New York, in the Hahnemann Hospital, at 657 Park Avenue on 8 August 1910. When the news was flashed through the Bahá'í community it acquired national significance. The following announcement was published in volume 1, no. 9, of *Star of the West* on 20 August 1910:

A LITTLE DAUGHTER HAS COME TO BLESS THE HOME OF
MR. AND MRS. W. S. MAXWELL OF MONTREAL CANADA.

But the greatest bounty for May was a Tablet she had received from
'Abdu'l-Bahá:

O cherished daughter of the Kingdom,

*Thy letter of 9 April 1910 hath arrived, and its contents attest to
the attraction and joy of the hearts and souls. Praise thou God for being
always in His Presence, fully intoxicated with the wine of His love.*

*Thanks be to God! Thy greatest wish to have a child hath been granted,
and what thou didst ask hath been realized, and thy friends and relatives
may thus be led to certitude and assurance. I ask God that thou wilt be
both the spiritual and physical mother of that luminous child, so that she
may receive her portion of the bestowals of the Sun of Truth.*

*Thou hast written that in New York the devoted handmaid of God,
Juliet, the well-assured handmaid of God, Mother Beecher, and the
enkindled handmaid of God who is ablaze with God's love, Mrs. Brittingham, as well as Mr. Woodcock and other friends, had gathered for
a feast, with thyself and Juliet serving as hosts. How blessed are ye for
having rendered such a service and for having organized such a feast!
Now, in Montreal, exert thine efforts to continue holding such feasts, as
these will conduce to the steadfastness and confirmation of the friends
and handmaids of God. Then will the fragrances of the divine rose-
garden be shed abroad and the quickening breezes of the Abhá Paradise
be wafted, causing the participants to be moved with boundless joy.*

*Give my kind regards to thy respected husband and tell him that
I give thanks to God that he is one in heart and soul with Mrs. Mary
[May], and that you have become like unto one soul. I hope that you
will both be assisted to serve this great Cause . . .*

*. . . Convey, on my behalf, to all the servants of God and to the hand-
maids of the Abhá Beauty, wondrous Abhá greetings. The Holy Leaves of
the family send their loving Bahá'í regards.*

*O maidservant of God, be well assured that through the grace of
God thou art mentioned in the Kingdom of God, and that in the sight
of 'Abdu'l-Bahá thou art most precious and revered.*

*William
Sutherland
and May
Bolles
Maxwell,
1905-6*

May Bolles Maxwell, probably 1905-6

May Maxwell, probably in Montreal . . .   *. . . and in New York, circa 1905-6*

Some of the early Bahá'ís of Montreal, circa 1905–6: front row, Mrs Pomeroy (mother of Elizabeth Cowles), probably Percy Woodcock, May Maxwell, unknown, Dr Johnson; back row, unknown, Elizabeth Cowles, Martha MacBean, unknown, Rose Henderson

Mary Coristine, her husband Walter Coristine and Sutherland Maxwell, with May Maxwell (standing)

The drawing room of the Maxwell home at 29 Bishop Street, Montreal, where they lived before they built their own home on Pine Avenue in 1906

Ladies in the Riḍván Garden, 'Akká, 1909: left to right, Louise Stapfer (Bosch), May Maxwell, unknown (photograph by W. S. Maxwell)

Travelling to 'Akká by way of the sea, May Maxwell and Louise Stapfer (Bosch), 1909

Photograph given to the Hand of the Cause Agnes Alexander by May Maxwell, with her handwritten note on the back: 'To dearest Agnes with love from little Mary and her mother'

It was evident that 'Abdu'l-Bahá too was overjoyed by the news. The newborn baby was the fourth Mary in a row to have been given this name in the Martin family and the third Maxwell of Montreal in this story. But she was the first child in the West to be blessed by 'Abdu'l-Bahá from the moment of her birth, and to be granted a *spiritual and physical mother . . . so that she may receive her portion of the bestowals of the Sun of Truth*.

* * *

As soon as May could travel after the birth of the baby, she went back to Canada. She was ready for a new life, and some time between August and December of 1910 she revealed her feelings in an undated note to her husband.

> For months I have been a vehicle of life to my babe – all the currents of my being flowed inward to her that she might be fully endowed – and every outward tie that was deep and vital was suspended. Now having passed thro' the last great ordeal I am returning to life with this treasure in my arms.
>
> As I have told you in all the deepest experiences of life where the fountains of life are freshest and purest I turn first to you – and so in these days and weeks with our sweet child you are more intimately associated with my love and joy than any other. I am learning from her how beautiful it is to become like a little child – so pure and happy, so loving and confiding toward every creature, so utterly unconscious of self – gazing upon the world from unfathomable depths of purity and trust. In the clear mirror of her soul I see reflected the exquisite traces of God.

By 2 March 1911 she was already ready, as she wrote to Agnes Alexander, to 'take up the threads where they have been interrupted by the birth and infancy of my baby girl'. Agnes had sent her a package which she could not find on her return home, in the upheaval entailed in adjusting to the new circumstances of her life in Montreal:

> So much of new and wonderful to me has been crowded into the past year, that I do not now remember when I last wrote you. Did

I write and tell you that I cannot find anywhere a package which Mr. Maxwell told me had come from you. It was, I think, before the birth of little Mary (in August) that something came from you – I was in the country and Mr. Maxwell told me of it – then I went to the hospital in New York – and was there for 3 months after the baby was born because at that time she was so weak and frail from improper nourishment that I could not bring her home. Then I got a good wet-nurse and came home – and the first thing I did was to search the house for your gift. Tell me what it was, dear Agnes – and how it was wrapped, for as the house is not yet settled, I still hope to find it. Was it something for the sweet child whom the Master has sent to rejoice our home? In a recent Tablet He said concerning her: 'In the garden of existence a rose has bloomed with the utmost freshness, fragrance and beauty. Educate her according to the divine teachings so that she may grow up to be a real Bahá'í, and strive with all thy heart, that she may receive the Holy Spirit.' How much more perfect I shall have to become before I can be worthy to follow this command. At Christmas I sent you her picture – with her little Mother and your little Mother! did it reach you safely? You guarded my secret so well – and no one knew until Nature proclaimed it, and everyone was so happy in the coming of this God-given child.

It was customary, at the time, for a middle-class lady who gave birth to hire a wet nurse for her baby. The German woman whom May brought back with her from New York had a little boy of the same age and an over-abundant flow of milk. Rúḥíyyih Khánum heard her mother tell the story many times of how her little Mary flourished while the poor baby boy suffered from colic. Unlike him, she grew healthy and happy no matter what the wet nurse ate. Her constitution promised to be strong.

As she moved into this new phase of life, May did not slacken her Bahá'í activities. In fact, it would seem that her Bahá'í activities had been transformed by her new phase of life. She appears to have experienced something of an epiphany; even the way she taught the Faith was metamorphosed by her becoming a mother. Writing to Sutherland from St John, New Brunswick, where she had gone – with her small baby and the wet nurse in tow – in response to an invitation to speak about the Cause from Mrs Mary Culver, the wife of the US Consul there,[41] May told him in glowing terms about what had happened to her:

I never once gave up hope that God would heal me in time and get me somehow to the hall – and then Himself speak to the people! I prayed incessantly for 2 hours – and then a divine force came and fairly lifted my suffering weak body – I dressed with care – to look as attractive as possible – this was all I could do for My Beloved – to give my whole self then He would do – all! I wore my white home-spun and new hat – & was all in white – and I looked so young and well & radiant that nothing but the Spirit could look like that – and no one dreamed I was in pain – and felt so light and strange and in a dream! I could not eat any lunch except a little mashed potatoes. There were about 100 men at a long table – too polite to stare but evidently interested in a woman speaker – fine intelligent men of the so-called upper middle class – with good faces and good cheer – and the spirit among them was so brotherly and natural and genuine that I felt happy and at home. Col. Culver made a brief and very fine introduction – and then amidst applause I arose and faced a long room full of men! Mrs. Culver and I were the only women. Oh! Sutherland, the thing I have dreamed of for years – longed for and prayed for was at last realized – and out of our united effort and sacrifice my darling – out of the fiery suffering and supreme effort, the greatest I ever made in His Path – was born a new power – the dawn of that woman that is to be – that He has always promised me! I was like a reed on which the Invisible One played a divine melody – I do not know what I said – it was as tho' I ceased to be entirely – and yet I was never in such full possession in my life. I was glowing – immersed in light – I was conscious only of the radiant effulgence of the Spirit filling all the room – illumining the faces & hearts of these men and we were all one – one spirit, one human family listening together to the Voice of the Ages! They said I spoke for 40 minutes, and then a narrow hidebound Methodist arose – he looked inspired & was deeply moved as he proposed a vote of thanks. He said that no words of his could express what they all felt so well as did the spellbound attention of the audience for 40 minutes. He said kind

41 Henry S. Culver was appointed US Consul in St John, New Brunswick in 1910, a post he held until his retirement in 1924; he and his wife were both Bahá'ís.

and beautiful things and I cannot tell you all the wonderful things some of them said later to me – & to Col. Culver. The dear Colonel is so happy he is walking on air – he feels that the effects of reaching this group in St. John will be very deep & far reaching – and I came home & thanked God – our Glorious, Merciful Lord – from the depths of my heart. I never felt your love and your spirit so near, my husband – my Sutherland – and I realized that the Message had never been given in Canada as God gave it yesterday – and that you and I have entered into a new relation, and a new life together – of <u>united</u> service and sacrifice.

Nor did she allow her links with 'Abdu'l-Bahá to slacken. During her early months of motherhood, she continued her correspondence with Him, receiving beautiful Tablets from His hand. At a time when all her attention might naturally have revolved around her own baby, she sought His guidance and was directed by Him to distinguish between the important and the most important, to keep her focus not only on the well-being of her child but also on the teaching and expansion of the Cause of God. In the following Tablet, translated for May Maxwell on 19 January 1911, 'Abdu'l-Bahá reminds her of her primary vocation:

O thou daughter of the Kingdom!

Thy letter was received. Its contents were like unto enkindled flames of the fire of the love of God, and thus were the cause of great happiness.

Thine utmost desire was to have a child, and while in 'Akká thou didst express this wish and request. Praise be to God, thy prayer hath been answered and thy desire attained. In the garden of existence a rose hath bloomed with the utmost freshness and beauty. Educate her according to the divine precepts that she may become a true Bahá'í, and endeavour with all thy heart that she may be born of the Holy Spirit.

Praise be to God that thy health is better. Now is the time to work with all thy heart and soul, to render service to the Kingdom, endeavour to have many spiritual children, and establish a heavenly household. For children of the spirit are dearer than physical children.

By early 1911, May had become the founding member and one of the four officers of the Mother's Clinic, referred to as The Colborne Street Milk Depot. It is interesting to note that Sutherland himself accepted to become its Treasurer, at a time when his work on the Musée de Beaux Arts in Montreal was at its height. He was involved, at one and the same time, in an organization that provided milk to needy children and the construction of one of the most prestigious buildings in Montreal. The Colborne Street Milk Depot continued its work until 1913, after which its name seems to have been changed to The Milk Committee of the Child Welfare Association. Sutherland continued to serve on this Committee, in the capacity of Treasurer, for the next several years. His concern regarding the infant mortality rates in Montreal is illustrated by the following letter, written in January 1915, which he received from the Medical Officer of Health in that city:

Dear Sir,

The year 1915 will, I hope see the continuation of our effort of the past year to abate the infantile mortality which has so long disgraced our City, although the work done last year has had a marked and gratifying result in this direction. The exact figures are not yet tabulated, but I may say that we have had a decrease in the number of deaths among children, apart from the fact that the temperature was, in the mean, less high than in the previous year. This was due no doubt to the good work done by the Pure Milk Depots, and in this connection I beg to express my sincere gratification for the work done by your organization.

May I be permitted however to say that there still remains much to be done and in this connection I beg to ask you if your organization could not agree with the other English Milk Depots to form a Central Committee on lines similar to that of the French Gouttes de Lait. This would, in my opinion, enable us to more accurately determine the ways and means to combat the infantile mortality, to improve our statistics and to distribute the depots in such a way as to render them easier of access to the population.

I trust that you will give your earliest consideration to this suggestion and that you will find a way to put it in execution.

Yours truly,

S. Boucher, Medical Officer of Health

May too was busy with her activities related to the needs of women and children, as well as with her Bahá'í lectures. The Milk Lunch Dispensary was a charity in which she continued to be involved until 1921. On 18 May 1911, she wrote to 'Abdu'l-Bahá about her reasons for engaging in this work in addition to teaching the Faith:

> My Beloved Lord, 'Abdu'l-Bahá,
>
> My dear Master, This maid-servant, with the help of Rose Henderson and other awakened souls in Montreal, has started classes for the education of Mothers, the care of babies, the distribution of milk and ice during the summer months. I have humbly undertaken this work for humanity as an offering to God in great gratitude for our child whom Thou hast given us.
>
> It is supported by voluntary contributions of friends – as I only give small contributions since Thou desired us to give all we can to the Mashrak-el-Azcar and the Bahá'í work.

Her father's praise of her charity work was delightfully laconic. Writing to May on 1 April 1913, John Bolles expressed his joy over the photograph she had just sent him of herself and the 'Fourth Mary', which he had shared with his brother and sister:

> My dear little Girl:
>
> The lovable picture of yourself and Mary is, and has been, a delight to me, and both your Aunt Ella and your Uncle Richard think it is very fine, and charming. At no time that I can recall, have I seen you wear your hair so much off of your forehead as it appears here, & while it detracts slightly from the more youthful lower forehead effect, yet it has an attraction of its own which cannot be diminished. There is nothing in the Reynold's or Gainsborough portraits, or those of Greuze, that give one, half so fair, half so winning.
>
> Of course I feel, as I have many times, like getting right upon a train for Montreal, but the time when I can go up there, to see you all, has not yet come, but I hope it will, some time this spring or summer. Mary has changed very much since her last picture, and since I last saw her, but remains quite as charming and lovable as 'a progressive'. You, Dear, begin to look more like your Mother, and what looks like a costume from the Court of Venice, especially in the sleeves and girdle, places you, I should say, quite close to the

Ducal Throne. Your noble charity, the milk lunch dispensary for babies, with the courses of lectures must take a great many of your days, and in a most happy way. Long live the Queen!

The following Tablet, translated on 18 June 1913, sets out clearly the Master's expectations and aspirations for May. He had his eyes fixed on her future. He knew in which Kingdom she was destined to play a role:

> *O thou daughter of the Kingdom!*
> *Thine eloquent letter was received. Its contents demonstrated thy turning unto the Kingdom of Abhá, thine attraction to the fragrances of God and thy firmness in the Covenant. I hope, through the assistance and protection of the Lord of the Kingdom, that thou mayest inspire steadfastness in every wavering soul and be so enkindled with the fire of the love of God that thou mayest burn away the veils of those whose eyes are covered . . .*
> *. . . Convey, on my behalf, the utmost longing to the believers of Montreal. I remember them always and seek confirmation and assistance from the bounty of the Holy Spirit on their behalf. I send special loving greetings to Mr. Maxwell. Do thou kiss both cheeks of thy sweet daughter who hath just begun to talk.*

* * *

The most exciting event for the Maxwell family, after the birth of their baby, was the news that they were given on 27 December 1911 of 'Abdu'l-Bahá's possible trip to America. In response to May's letter to Him, the Master replied:

> *O thou who art enkindled with the fire of the love of God!*
> *Thy letter was received, but I have no time to answer. In brief: God willing, I will set out for America next spring, and perfect and true joy will be attained.*

This auspicious announcement was the consummation of a dream, the fulfilment of the ardent prayers and cherished wishes of the early Bahá'ís in the West. As early as 1902, intrepid individuals such as Lua had undertaken the hopeless task of attempting to sue for His release from the Sultan of Turkey. Her hopes had been dashed, her dreams aborted on that occasion, but ever since the Young Turk Revolution in 1908 the believers in Europe and America had been hoping that 'Abdu'l-Bahá would be free at last to travel. Writing to Agnes Alexander on 2 March 1911, May had expressed this longing, upon hearing of 'Abdu'l-Bahá's sojourn in Port Said and in Ramleh, near Alexandria:

> Is not the journey of Our Beloved to Egypt a marvelous event? We hope that He may honor and illumine France – whether America receives this blessing or not is still uncertain. All are working with great longing and sincerity – and surely if any power can enkindle and unite the hearts it will be the hope of His Coming!

The believers in the West were understandably thrilled at the thought that the Master might be free at last after forty long years of imprisonment. Several among them, May included, must have asked Him, invited Him, begged Him to come and visit them. One can well imagine how her heart throbbed with awe when news came that He had boarded the *S.S. Corsica* bound for Marseilles on 11 August 1911, how anxiously she prayed for His health while He wintered in Egypt at the end of that year and the beginning of the next, and how generously she must have contributed to the £3,200 that was raised by the North American Bahá'ís for His ticket on the largest passenger liner in the world, whose maiden voyage was due to take place that spring. 'Abdu'l-Bahá returned the gift and embarked on the *S.S. Cedric* instead, which set sail on 25 March 1912, from Alexandria. He docked in New York on Thursday, 11 April 1912, just four days before the sinking of the *Titanic*.

It was hardly surprising that the arrival of 'Abdu'l-Bahá in the city of New York would have provoked such joy and celebration among the small band of Bahá'ís in that city. From the vantage point of history, it was also one of the greatest events in the life of the Master Himself. It was not only a high honour for the United States and Canada, but a symbolic blessing for the Americas and of vital consequence to the evolution of the Administrative Order world-wide. By this one act, 'Abdu'l-Bahá prepared the way for the writing of the Tablets of the Divine Plan which were to serve as one of the charters of the Covenant. By graciously accepting to set His foot on American soil He caused the spiritual life on that mighty continent to stir, and diffused the fragrances of the Blessed Beauty across the West. It was a journey whose effects were destined to be felt for centuries.

Juliet Thompson's diary describes 'Abdu'l-Bahá's arrival on the shores of America. Her famous record of this historic event indicates May's presence on that occasion. But although many Bahá'ís, as well as seekers and the curious public, were drawn to the Master as moths to the light when He first arrived in New York, Sutherland was not present. By a strange twist of fate, his father, Edward John Maxwell, died that very month.[42] He lost his physical father in Montreal at almost the same time as his spiritual Father arrived in the city of the Covenant.

There are many glimpses in Juliet's diary of 'Abdu'l-Bahá's days in New York. Soon after He arrived, Juliet records:

A few of us gathered in His rooms to prepare them for Him and fill them with flowers . . . About five o'clock He came . . . Lua, May, and I, for the first time together in the Glory of His Presence, sat on the floor in a corner, gazing through tears at Him whenever we could wrench our eyes from the sorrowful beauty of His face, silhouetted against the sky, gazing at one another, still through tears.[43]

She also recorded vivid stories about all three of them – Lua, May, and Juliet herself – who each in their distinctive ways served their Master with such devotion:

On this thirteenth of June, after Lua had chanted the prayer for Mrs. Hinkle-Smith, she and May came into the library, crossed over where I was sitting and stood behind me.

The Master looked up and smiled at May. 'You have a kind heart, Mrs. Maxwell.' Then He turned to Lua. 'You, Lua, have a tender heart. And what kind of heart have you, Juliet?' He laughed. 'What kind of a heart have you?' . . .

'An emotional heart.' He laughed again and rolled His hands one round the other in a sort of tempestuous gesture. 'You will have a *boiling* heart, Juliet. Now', He continued, 'if these three hearts were

---

42 15 April 1912.
43 Thompson, *Diary*, pp. 282–4.

united into one heart – kind, tender, and emotional – what a great heart that would be!'[44]

May was acutely conscious of the value of those sacred days. She kept records too, of every touch and every word associated with her beloved Master during His sojourn in the West. Among her papers is an envelope on which she has written: 'Almonds given me by the Beloved in N.Y.' There are two other undated envelopes from this same period containing: 'Flowers from the Hand of 'Abdu'l-Bahá' and 'Holy Hair of 'Abdu'l-Bahá'. She knew that she was living history at that time.

Amatu'l-Bahá Rúḥíyyih Khánum often told the story about one of her mother's visits to New York during 'Abdu'l-Bahá's stay in that city. When she arrived, the Master asked her how her child was, and where she was, for May had not come into His presence with Mary. She answered that as the little one was not feeling well that day, she had left her with her nurse in the hotel room.

'Abdu'l-Bahá looked at her in surprise.

'Your child is ill and you did not bring her to 'Abdu'l-Bahá?' He asked.

May instantly returned to the hotel and returned with her child. The Master looked at her lovingly and gave May an orange.

'Give her this and she will be healed,' He said.

The awed mother apparently allowed her child to hold the orange, but she did not let her eat it. She kept it for all time. After Amatu'l-Bahá's passing, the dried, wrinkled and black remains of this precious fruit were found wrapped up and placed in a box with the note signifying its history and recording its efficacy!

May had the privilege and the bounty of being in the presence of the Master in New York many times, but her crowning glory during this historic trip to the West was 'Abdu'l-Bahá's acceptance to pay the Maxwells a visit to Montreal. When she learned that He had accepted to come, her ecstasy was absolute, her joy complete. She sent the following letter to Him on 22 August 1912:

We have been so wonderfully happy by the glad tidings that 'Abdu'l-Bahá will visit Montreal, and we are all in the utmost joy and expectation! As soon as we hear from Thee the date of Thy coming

---

44 ibid. pp. 308–9.

we will announce it in the paper – and prepare a public meeting – and many, many people are already in joy and hope.

Mr. Thomas, the coloured Bahá'í from Washington, has spoken here in the coloured people's church – through him I also met them and gave them the Message, and Mr. Gantt, the Minister of the Church has offered his church to address the coloured people. We shall do all in our power to enable the people of Montreal to receive the utmost bounty and benefit from the incomparable blessing of Thy adored Presence – and we beg for Thy help and confirmation.

The answer she received must have caused tremendous joy to the couple. On Wednesday 28 August 'Abdu'l-Bahá cabled her from Malden, Massachusetts.:

> *YOUR LETTER RECEIVED. IN REALITY THOU ART ILLUMINED. WE LEAVE FOR*
> *MONTREAL FRIDAY MORNING.*
> *ABDU'L BAHA*

As Amatu'l-Bahá has so eloquently described in her memoirs, Sutherland's conservative nature made him reluctant, at first, to invite 'Abdu'l-Bahá to stay in their home. May, who adored the Master and had dreamed of having Him beneath her roof, did not insist. Sutherland must have sensed her disappointment. Two days before 'Abdu'l-Bahá's arrival, he had a change of heart. According to his daughter:

> When 'Abdu'l-Bahá consented to come to Montreal and arrangements were being made, my father explained to Mother that though He would of course be their guest, he did not want to have the Master in his home but would engage a suite for him at the Windsor Hotel. All his sensitive Scots reticence shrank from the publicity and limelight that would be thrown on him as the host of such an attention-attracting guest as the Persian Prophet and His entourage would constitute. Mother was heartbroken, but she did not remonstrate, realizing perhaps that such things cannot be debated but must arise from the heart. The day before the scheduled arrival of 'Abdu'l-Bahá, my father rushed into Mother's room, the largest bedroom, facing the garden and possessing three bay windows, and looking critically at her furniture declared: 'This is not good enough

for 'Abdu'l-Bahá, I'm going right down to Morgans to buy a new set', and rushed off and immediately purchased and had delivered a bed, dressing table and chairs in white-painted Louis XV style. One can only imagine how great was her joy that her husband of his own accord should have felt the longing to have the Master under his own roof. He himself met the Master at the train and begged Him to accept the hospitality of his home.

May must have been in a state of ecstasy when her Beloved finally entered her doors:

> In the fullness and splendour of a summer moon 'Abdu'l-Bahá arrived on the night of August 30th. As He entered the home of Bahá'í friends on Pine Ave., many watched from their windows to catch a glimpse of the white-robed majestic figure whose advent had been so eloquently heralded thro' all the press.

In her memoirs, she echoed the famous words uttered by 'that venerable and beloved figure' as He stepped in the house. She was to repeat these words so many times that it was as though they were engraved on the stones of the building:

> 'This is my home,' He said, 'All that is in it is mine' – turning with an ineffable look, He continued – 'You are mine – your husband and child. This is my home.'[45]

May recorded how the Master was cold and how they lighted the fire for Him. She described how He looked about Him and asked for the child soon after He arrived, how He told them not to disturb her when He heard that she was sleeping, adding: 'Dark indeed is the home where there is no child.'

A mighty commotion was set up by the presence of 'Abdu'l-Bahá from that day on. The fame of His address at the Church of the Messiah was spread abroad; there were constant telephone calls and large numbers made their way to the Maxwell home. Individuals begged to

---

45 When Rúḥíyyih Khánum wrote about her mother in 1940, she repeated a slightly different version of these words: 'When He entered it He said: "This is my home, you are mine, your husband is mine and your child is mine." ' May's own words have been retained as possibly more authentic.

be received by Him in His room and He received a good many. After three nights in the Maxwell home, He decided to move to the Hotel Windsor for the remainder of His Montreal visit, but meetings at the Maxwell home continued to the end of His stay in Montreal. Among His other activities during that historic visit were addresses to a gathering in Coronation Hall, associated with Jewish strikers, and to the congregation of St James Methodist Church.

Rúḥíyyih Khánum's biographical notes record more details of 'Abdu'l-Bahá's visit. She recalls 'How perpetually vivid in my Mother's mind remained the memories of those days He spent in her home.' She tells of how according to May, the banal day-to-day affairs in the Maxwell household acquired a strange wonderful glow of significance in the presence of the Master. She records how 'eagerly' and with what 'indescribable keenness of interest' 'Abdu'l-Bahá would look out of the window at the activities taking place on Pine Avenue in the morning:

As He stood there [on the landing of the stairs in the Maxwell home] watching the milkman on his daily round – the man delivering at each door-step the morning paper – early workmen on their way to work – what were His thoughts? What was the penetration of His all-knowing, all-searching spirit in these humble lives in their unconscious journey to Him! They glanced at His mighty prophetic Figure with wonder and traces of unconscious respect, & went their way – never, never to be the same again. The light of His glance had fallen on them – the warmth & power of His Spirit had for a fraction of time surrounded them in their daily rounds, their common destiny.

She describes how her mother was transported during those days into a state of ecstasy, a degree of devotion comparable to that of the early disciples, how she involuntarily identified with them, worshipping the Master as if He were Christ. No wonder 'Abdu'l-Bahá had to repeat over and over again for the early believers that His station was one of servitude – no more; that His honour, His glory, His highest aspiration was to serve His Beloved, and nothing else.

May was in a state of exaltation. It was just as well she had a two-year-old child to bring her back down to earth. Rúḥíyyih Khánum describes, in her incomparable memoirs, how 'maddening' her mother must have found her conduct at this time, and how mortifying too:

One day the Master, in the drawing-room, caught little Mary up in His arms and tried to kiss her; I say tried advisedly for He did not succeed as the small, strong, chubby and highly independent infant gave him such a slap on the face that the shock knocked the turban off His head! Then began a mad chase around the drawing-room in which the Master pursued the elusive and indignant child. Mother always said at that moment she could have gladly killed me. She managed to say, 'Oh 'Abdu'l-Bahá, she is very naughty! What shall I do to punish her.' By this time the Master had succeeded in catching and kissing me. 'Leave her alone,' He said, 'she is the essence of sweetness.'

She admitted, with her characteristic candour and forthrightness, that 'No good reports have reached me of my conduct during His visit' and then continues:

One day as He rested after lunch on a couch at the foot of His bed, Mother had quieted the whole household and particularly instructed me not to waken 'Abdu'l-Bahá on any account. Her back was scarcely turned when I rushed into His room and, going up to Him, pried His eyelids open with my small fingers, crying: 'Wake up, 'Abdu'l-Bahá!' It seems He took me in His arms and let me sleep on His breast. I was so attracted to Him that it was hard to keep me away from Him at all.

These wonderful stories, which Rúḥíyyih Khánum so often repeated to the Bahá'ís as well as her friends, bring to life the moments of 'Abdu'l-Bahá's visit in Montreal and make vividly real for us a time which, as she put it in her own words, it will be 'hard to recapture – and will as time passes, grow increasingly difficult to do so'. Another such moment was the historic occasion when 'Abdu'l-Bahá stepped through the doors of the Maxwell brothers' firm at 6 Beaver Hall Square. Amatu'l-Bahá has written in her notes:

'Abdu'l-Bahá visited Daddy's office; Mother introduced him to Miss Parent.[46] She said, 'I could not keep my eyes away from him – it is

---

46 Known fondly as AMP by all the Maxwells, Mrs A. M. Parent Brooks was the secretary of W. S. Maxwell for many years and a close friend of the family.

a face you cannot forget!' She said 'Abdu'l-Bahá turned to Mother and said: *'You can trust her.'* [This was brought out spontaneously when Amatu'l-Bahá came upon a drawing of the Master at Elizabeth Yates' home.[47]]

Many years later, in a letter to Leah Graham dated 27 January 1938, May herself referred to other words of 'Abdu'l-Bahá spoken in their Montreal home:

> I remember when the Master was in Montreal and there had been a strike for months in Dublin, women and children starving and a generally desperate condition. It had affected me very painfully; I slept little and could barely eat, and had that terrific helpless feeling, not knowing what to do about it. All this Sutherland told to the Master, begging Him to tell me that my attitude was all wrong; and as he spoke the Master turned very white and great beads of perspiration formed on His brow through His own agony and human sufferings; then He said, 'If more people felt as your wife does the world would not be in this dark and terrible state.' Then He added, 'However, you must strive to overcome these feelings, do everything in your power to help, pray, then leave it with God, because the world will grow steadily much worse, and if you suffer like this you will not be able to survive.'
>
> Nevertheless His Words opened a door of help to these strike sufferers, and on my return to Montreal I went to a very wealthy and prominent Irishman here, whom I had never even seen, burst into tears in his office, to his astonishment and mine, and asked him what he was going to do about it. Well, to end the story, he headed a committee to raise a fund which we sent to Dublin through private channels and which came just in time to succour thousands of women and children.

But the doors which opened wide to welcome 'Abdu'l-Bahá to Montreal that summer also had to part to let Him leave. Rúḥíyyih Khánum records in her memoirs that after 'this brief stay' of three blessed days in their house on Pine Avenue,

---

47 Elizabeth Yates was Rúḥíyyih Khánum's much-loved cousin and the youngest daughter of Edward Maxwell, her uncle.

He expressed the desire to go to a hotel, saying more people would feel free to seek Him out there than in a private home – a fact which of course was obviously true, particularly so in such a conservative city as Montreal. A suite was engaged for Him in the Windsor Hotel where He continued to be the guest of my father.

His departure from the house on Pine Avenue even had an impact on the servants:

> The cook we had at that time, though very capable in her own capacity, was a hot-tempered and somewhat irascible Irish woman. Mother was both astonished and touched when, on hearing 'Abdu'l-Bahá was going to the Windsor Hotel, she came to her and said, 'Ah, Mrs. Maxwell, why is He going away! Tell Him I will work my fingers to the bone if He will only stay!'

And so it was, on Monday, 9 September 1912, that the Master's wonderful visit to Montreal drew to a close. His departure marked the making of a shrine in that city and the beginning of a new spiritual epoch in the history of Canada. But He kept in touch with May as He travelled from city to city in America. Some time towards the end of October 1912, on His return to Washington DC from the West Coast, He addressed the following Tablet to her. His words show how much He missed his 'home' in Montreal:

> *O thou my daughter in the Kingdom!*
>
> *From the day of leaving Montreal until now I have not rested nor reposed for a moment. From morn until midnight I was engaged in heralding the Kingdom, and in numerous assemblages and meetings, even in the Jewish Temple, I raised the call proclaiming the Revelation of the Kingdom. Many a night I did not sleep, and on many a day, like unto a surging sea, I was in the utmost state of agitation. Praise be to God that in the great Temple of the Jews in San Francisco, proofs were produced to demonstrate the truth of Christ's divine Revelation, and all listened with great joy. No one objected. At the end of the speech, they expressed utmost gratitude. One said, 'I am ashamed to be a Jew, and I shall not be one hereafter.' Another Jew, when he met us on the street, said, 'Truly this speech was a speech of Isaiah the prophet.' Likewise others encountering us*

on the street expressed the utmost gratitude. One would say, 'Very good'.
Another would say, 'Very beautiful'. Yet another would say, 'Very nice'. In
a word, we are caught in the midst of 'beautiful', 'good', and 'nice'.

I am very pleased with the glad tidings of the exultation of the Cause
of God in Montreal and the unity of the believers. Convey wondrous
Abhá greetings to all.

On the 5th of November, we will possibly arrive in New York. I am
now on the point of leaving to depart for the East, for we have reached
Los Angeles on the coast of the Pacific Ocean. Now we must return.

Kiss on my behalf thy honoured husband and thy dear child.

When the arduous trip finally came to an end and the time for a final
parting drew near, the beloved Master, in His mercy and compassion,
permitted His lovers to gather round Him, to be with Him to the last.
He allowed them to come from north and south to bid Him farewell
before He left the shores of America. On Saturday, 9 November 1912
May received the following cable from Washington DC:

WE WILL ARRIVE IN NEW YORK MONDAY NIGHT. THE TIME FOR SAIL
IS NOT YET SET. YOU AND FRIENDS HAVE PERMISSION TO COME TO
NEW YORK. ABBAS

On 5 December May stood with the rest of that small band on the pier,
watching the Cedric drift slowly out of the harbour, her eyes fixed on the
dear white handkerchief that fluttered from the deck and finally faded
from sight. She had no reason to believe that it was the last time she
would see the Master of course, and could not have borne the slightest
premonition of such an absolute farewell. But 'Abdu'l-Bahá would surely
have known it. And her sensitive heart would have sensed His sadness
too at this physical parting. In His loving-kindness towards her, and as
a sign of His special affection for this faithful maidservant, 'Abdu'l-Bahá
sent the following cable to May from England on 17 December 1912:

SAFELY ARRIVED LONDON. REMEMBERED ALWAYS. GREETINGS
MAXWELL KISS BABY. ABBAS

It was as though He were permitting May to keep her eyes fixed on
Him long after His ship disappeared on the horizon.

Although the departure of the Master from the shores of North America left a void in the hearts of those who were devoted to Him, it nevertheless infused a renewed zeal and dedication in the Bahá'í community in that continent. It confirmed their faith; it broadened their horizons. It galvanized their souls to have seen the Master with their own eyes and heard His words with their own ears.

May encouraged all to whom she taught the Faith to go on pilgrimage and meet the Master. She would often ask permission for them to do this, and her letters to 'Abdu'l-Bahá were filled with supplications written on behalf of seekers. Whenever replies arrived, whenever the outpourings of divine grace were received from His hand, she showed them to the other believers in her little community in order to encourage, sustain, and guide their souls, as well as her own. Translations of the Bahá'í holy texts were few and far between in those days; publication and dissemination of the scriptures was rare, and so it was only logical that May would have shared extracts from the Tablets she received from her Beloved with the members of the Montreal community. These spiritual children were no less dear than her own child.

* * *

It is clear that the birth of little Mary had greatly enhanced the awareness of both parents in matters related to early childhood development. In addition to serving as the Treasurer of the Milk Committee, Sutherland's active concern for children in general and his little baby daughter in particular may be illustrated by his membership in the City Environment Committee, another of the ancillary groups set up under the Child Welfare Association. The Souvenir Handbook for the Child Welfare Exhibition, held in the Drill Hall, Craig Street, Montreal in October 1912, states that this Committee was devoted to the far-sighted objective of

> . . . ideas, both in this city and in other lands, for improving the physical environment which surrounds the child, and thus making it possible for him to grow up healthy and wholesome, and with fulness of life.

Some years later, in the middle of World War I, Sutherland wrote to

286

May in September 1915 about a road accident involving a child. His comments illustrate how far-sighted he was even then, and how aware of the needs and rights of children:

> Adelaide must have suffered intensely but as you explained it was not her fault. Children will do these things and the cities need playgrounds – the street is no play place for any child. With the increased use of motors there will come a time when the matter of playgrounds will be driven home to humanity.

This new-born awareness regarding the needs of the child brought both May and Sutherland into contact with a wider world of friends and acquaintances. May, who was never one to lose contacts, kept her links with people she had befriended during those days of Mary's babyhood. Many years later, on 19 March 1926, she wrote to Dr Anna Louise Strong, recalling their friendship in her usual spontaneous manner, and seeking to revive it. This woman, who had been the Director of the Exhibit in Montreal, was someone with whom she had done child welfare work before World War I and the Russian Revolution swept them apart:

> Dear Anna Louise: Do you remember me, I wonder? I have never forgotten you . . . and have only lately finished reading your delightful book about Russia. Do you remember the splendid work you did years ago in Montreal? I have been longing to see you ever since I heard you have come East and questioned every likely person as to your whereabouts . . . if there is any chance of my seeing you before you return to the West or to Russia, we can arrange such a meeting. I would dearly love to see you if only for half an hour.

In addition to being deeply involved in caring for her little girl during this time, May continued to nurture new contacts and was engrossed in the task of spiritual education in her community. She threw herself into the teaching work. She increased her efforts, occupying herself day and night with the propagation of the Faith. Her dedication to her Bahá'í work was matched only by her love for her husband and her child. Eagerly, enthusiastically, she shared with the Master her plans and intentions, her vision as well as her achievements for the proclamation of the Cause in Montreal. On 21 March 1913, 'Abdu'l-Bahá wrote in answer to her letter:

Thy letter was received. It showed the happiness of thy heart, the utmost purity of thy motives, and thy determination to serve the Cause of God, and thus it imparted joy and delight. It is my hope that through the power of thine attraction the souls in that city may be quickened, and that the rays of the Kingdom may spread abroad and illumine that region . . .

As regards thy vision, it signifieth that the light of the Kingdom of God shall rise above the horizon of that region with the utmost brilliancy and splendour.

Convey on my behalf to Mr. Maxwell, thy revered husband, my warm regards. Kiss likewise on my behalf thy beloved daughter on both cheeks.

That year, Sutherland attended the Fifth Annual Convention of the Bahá'í Temple Unity Foundation at the Masonic Temple, New York City. His presence there was recorded as a 'visitor'; he was in New York in the spring of 1913 en route to London. Ever since Roger Fry had introduced the work of the Post-Impressionists to Britain in 1910, the English art scene had been in ferment. Everyone in the world of art and architecture was talking about it; everyone was experimenting with new styles. Painters such as Vanessa Bell and Duncan Grant were beginning to develop a whole new fashion of interior decorating and their work was doubtless of interest to the Maxwell brothers. Sutherland may well have wished to keep up with recent developments in design and would probably have been keen to see whether recent fashions in this field were to the taste of his clientele. The firm had constructed studios on Clarke Street, in 1911, for the Montreal branch of the Worcestershire-based Bromsgrove Guild of Applied Arts which was linked with the Arts and Crafts Movement in Britain, and it was important to stay in touch with the latest trends.

By a curious coincidence, the same year that Sutherland visited London, Roger Fry established his Omega Workshops at 33 Fitzroy Square, inspired by the belief that the creative joy of the artist and craftsman should go into the making of articles for everyday use. It was a philosophy which Sutherland himself strongly supported in his own ateliers in Montreal. As Nancy Yates affirms,[48] he had already begun to collaborate in 1911 with the Bromsgrove Guild of Canada, a group of Montreal artisans affiliated with the English guild of the same name.

---

48 See Appendix II.

They were, in their day, Montreal's finest wood-crafting and cabinet shop, specializing in hand-built furniture which Sutherland himself designed, based on historical English, French and Italian models.[49] Other collaborators of his were Paul Beau, an outstanding Canadian metal craftsman of fine hand-hammered brass and copper, and the well-known sculptor George Hill, who carved Sutherland's designs on furniture and panelling. Several other artist friends[50] were commissioned to carry out murals in both private and public buildings being constructed by the Maxwell brothers during these pre-war years. In view of the importance he placed on craft William Sutherland Maxwell became a member of the Canadian Handicrafts Guild.

He attended several art exhibits in London in 1913, just before the war broke out, one of which was the Annual Exhibition of the Royal Academy and the other the Exhibition of the Royal Institute of Painters in watercolour. Here he bought a copy of *The Preece Collection,* a catalogue of Persian figural ceramics and faience, in which he wrote 'May 1913, during my visit to London'. It is clear that at the same time that he was becoming more involved in Bahá'í activities, Sutherland kept his finger on the pulse of the art world, both classic and contemporary.

He also kept a hand on his golf clubs, it would seem, and was an enthusiastic golfer as well as a creator of golf courses at this time. Shortly before his daughter's third birthday, during a relaxed moment in one of the golf clubs he himself had designed, he made a sweet little drawing of her, which he entitled 'Mary', and on the back of which he wrote: 'W. S. Maxwell Kanawaki Golf Club, adjoining Adirondack Junction'. This particular Golf Club was one that he often visited when he had time. Writing to May on 3 September 1915, he said:

I am going to Kanawaki today as Monday is a holiday and I shall have lots of open air exercise and swatting the ball. Goodness but

---

49 See for example this description of a large private House in Montreal: ' "The fittings and furnishings reflected the most fashionable tastes found in grand North American city residences. Each room had its own stylistic character conveyed through its colour, furniture design and architectural motifs." The drawing room was decorated in the style of 18th-century France. The breakfast room was inspired by the English Regency period. The billiard room "decoration offered one of the best Canadian examples of the ideals of the British Arts and Crafts movement, which emphasized handcraftsmanship, the use of simple materials, reference to local traditions and the integration of the crafted arts with architecture." ' Yates, ibid., quoting Pepall, 'City Houses', p. 137.

50 ibid. The artists included Maurice Cullen, Frederick Challener, Frederick Hutchison and Clarence Gagnon.

it would be lovely if you were here and we could go somewhere together. The weather is absolutely perfect. I wish I had a letter from you right now, I want to hear so much about you – what you think, are doing and if you are happy and sleeping well.

During the very cold months of Canada, May took refuge in Boston and New York, not merely to escape the cold but to spread the warming messages of 'Abdu'l-Bahá among the new American believers there. But although 'Abdu'l-Bahá Himself had advised her to avoid Montreal during the winter months, the place seemed to have changed for May since the Master had passed through it. No matter how inclement the weather, nor how cold the culture, 'Abdu'l-Bahá had fixed her sights on the spiritual destiny of that city which could, if only she fulfilled her obligations, become ablaze with the love of God. During her husband's absence in London, the following Tablet, translated on 21 May 1913, was received by May:

> *Thy letter was received and its contents imparted utmost joy, because it indicated firmness and steadfastness in the Cause of God, holding fast to the Covenant and determination to uphold His Testament. It is my hope that Montreal may be quickened by the breaths of the Holy Spirit, and thy face may become radiant with the rays of God's Covenant, and the Cause of Bahá'u'lláh may spread in such wise as to make that city the envy of other cities.*
>
> *Convey utmost respect on my behalf to thy revered husband, Mr. Maxwell, and show infinite love on my behalf to thine illumined child. Kiss her face anon, and at other times her hair. I beg of God that this little child may become great and glorious in the divine Kingdom.*

It is evident that she corresponded with the beloved Master about her activities in the City of the Covenant too, for shortly afterwards, in a Tablet translated on 10 July 1913, He responded to her with these soul-stirring words:

> *Thy detailed letter was received. Indeed, it was not a letter but a spiritual rose-garden in which the flowers of inner meaning and significance sprang forth and from which the sweet fragrance of the love of God was inhaled. As I have no time I will write in brief. The believers of New*

York are my companions, as they are intoxicated and exhilarated by the wine of the love of God. It is 'Abdu'l-Bahá's hope that the fragrance of musk and amber may become so diffused that all senses may become perfumed, that the power of the Abhá Kingdom may dawn and cast its splendour upon all regions, and that the continent of America may from shore to shore become an Abhá Paradise.

Praise be to God that thou art enkindled by the fire of the love of God and attracted by its magnetic power. It is certain, therefore, that thou shalt provoke a tumult and excitement in Montreal, and that the standard of the oneness of the world of humanity will be unfurled.

Convey wondrous Abhá greetings to all the beloved of the Lord and the handmaids of the Merciful.

Kiss thy beloved child on my behalf. Kiss her face with the utmost love, then her hair.

Convey respectful and loving greetings to the honoured Mr. [Maxwell].

Under the protection of Bahá'u'lláh I have reached Port Said. All the inconveniences of the journey are forgotten . . .

A few months later she received another Tablet from Him, most probably written from Ramleh, Egypt. It was translated for her on 30 September 1913 and reflects the degree of 'Abdu'l-Bahá's trust in her, His certainty in her faith. She was truly that pure and selfless channel through which over and over again He regenerated and revitalized the gatherings of the friends. Her utter devotion, love and servitude to the Centre of the Covenant was mirrored in her words and her actions. The love she had in her heart for the people was a reflection of the love she had for 'Abdu'l-Baha.

O thou candle aflame with the fire of the love of God!

. . . During my stay in America I continually encouraged thee to advance in the Kingdom of God. I ever expect that with each passing day a new confirmation may descend upon thee, and that thou mayest become so illumined as to enlighten a vast multitude in that city [Montreal].

Convey my warmest regards to the respected Mr. Maxwell, and likewise embrace my little daughter and on my behalf kiss her on both cheeks.

* * *

At this time, in addition to her teaching work in both Canada and the United States and the engrossing responsibilities of motherhood, May's activities were primarily centred on raising money for the building of the Mashriqu'l-Adhkár in Wilmette. Her correspondence, from as early as 1910, shows her involvement in this project. It was uppermost in her thoughts and a priority among all her other activities during the last years of the Master's life. Her deepest desire was to finish this sacred edifice during the lifetime of 'Abdu'l-Bahá. The following excerpts from her letters to the Master portray her ardent concern for its completion:

5 May 1910
My Beloved Lord 'Abdu'l-Bahá,
    Thou wilt soon have tidings of the great Temple Convention held in Chicago, of the Presence and Power of the Spirit of God – of a love and union hitherto unknown on earth save only in the Abode of our Beloved, in Acca! . . .
    Oh! My Lord and my God! I humbly thank Thee for this wonderful Convention in the Western World, for Thine Infinite Mercy, Bounty and Compassion to all Thy servants and for the outpouring of Thy Spirit upon all mankind in this Wonderful Day.

30 April 1913
My beloved Master,
    The wonderful Bahá'í Convention closed yesterday . . . Thy servant Ali Kuli Khan spoke in words of fire concerning the necessity of building the Mashriqu'l-Adhkár during the lifetime of 'Abdu'l-Bahá on earth – he made an appeal to the innermost heart and conscience of every hearer for the utmost <u>sacrifice</u> for the immediate building of this holy edifice . . .
    I humbly submit to Thee this question: Is the central building of worship to cost one million dollars and must the plans be drawn up for so large and expensive an edifice, or is it acceptable that we build to half a million or less and begin <u>within one year</u>.
    Oh! My beloved! I know that many feel as I do that <u>any sacrifice</u> is possible to build the Mashriqu'l-Adhkár in the light and

splendour of the Day of the Covenant, but where is the inspiration to sacrifice for a building which shall come after the Sun has set!

5 August 1913
My Beloved 'Abdu'l-Bahá,

The meetings here have been very spiritual and united and we have arisen to fulfil Thy Command to collect money for the Mashriqu'l-Adhkár. We have decided that every member of the [Montreal] Assembly shall contribute not less than one dollar a month (those who can afford it can give more). We are writing to all of the Assemblies in America asking them to do the same. If this suggestion is put into effect there will be some 50 to 75 thousand dollars raised annually . . .

She was herself a steady, continuous and generous contributor towards the building of the Temple; her donations to its Fund continued till the end of her life. A letter addressed to her sister-in-law on 17 January 1930 touches on this point:

We were all so disappointed not to have seen you during the holidays as we had fully expected to do, but we had to give up all our plans on account of the Temple as Sutherland, Mary and I after consultation decided to give every available dollar in that last big drive for the Temple and forgo an expensive holiday.

The Mashriqu'l-Adhkár, for her, was the outward symbol of the true teacher: listening before speaking, embracing differences rather than insisting on distinctions, and spiritually restorative. How she yearned to see this mighty edifice completed. How she longed to see its doors opened to the public, attracting seekers from far and wide. In 'Abdu'l-Bahá's Tablet to May translated on 18 June 1913 He included specific reference to the question in her letter of 30 April 1913. One can imagine to what a degree she would have been committed to the project after receiving such instructions:

As to the matter of the building of the Mashriqu'l-Adhkár, that is, the matter of beginning the building thereof: A considerable sum of money must decidedly be prepared in order that work may be begun; that is, at least two or three hundred thousand dollars must be ready. And, most assuredly, if it be built in the Days of the Covenant, it will be more joyful and more heart-rejoicing; but this is difficult. Now be ye engaged in collecting contributions.

And she was not alone in her commitment. In addition to submitting his own designs for its construction, her husband was active too in raising money for the Temple Fund. During his attendance at the Fifth Annual Convention of the Temple Unity Foundation, in New York on 28–29 April 1913 when he was en route to London, Sutherland had contributed vigorously to the consultations taking place about the ways and means of meeting the need of the budget for this mighty enterprise. His suggestions were later recorded in *Star of the West*:[51]

The Chairman then called on Mr. Maxwell of Canada to speak.

Mr. Maxwell: We cannot expect to build the largest building in the world, but we may build the most beautiful; it should be one of beauty and permanence rather than size. Although two million and six million dollars have been mentioned, I think $500,000 is a better figure. The New York Public Library and other famous buildings in New York were under construction for eight or ten years. The completion of the Mashriqu'l-Adhkár will be, perhaps, five years in the future, and would mean the raising of $100,000 a year. Now if there are 5,000 Bahá'ís in America, and that number will be increasing, and each gives on an average of one dollar a month, that ought to cover our needs. If you can get a hundred thousand dollars the first year, it ought to be very much easier to raise that amount every succeeding year.

Mr Maxwell's suggestion was adopted by the Montreal Assembly,[52] and a letter to this effect dated 13 September 1913 was sent to 'all of the Assemblies as well as the *Star of the West*'.

Statistics can be dangerously seductive. In fact, it took the Bahá'í community of North America another 40 years to raise funds for

---

51 *Star of the West*, vol. 4, no. 8 (1 August 1913), p. 139.
52 *Star of the West*, vol. 4, no. 11 (27 September 1913), p. 194.

and complete the Temple, which was constructed in various phases, at an overall cost of some US$2.6 million. Although William Sutherland Maxwell's assessment did not seem unreasonable at the time, he underestimated both the budget necessary and the years required to complete a project of this magnitude. His point of view was limited to professional experience. As one of the senior partners of a successful architectural firm, bolstered by a powerful network of clients and a thriving economy, he had no reason to include sacrifice in his calculations. But the Temple had to test the spiritual as well as material commitment of the Bahá'ís; it had to challenge them to fix their sights far further than five years. And its construction depended not only on the contribution of one dollar a month on the part of each believer, but also on the will of God.

World War I, whose rumblings had been heard faintly but with ominous persistence over the past decade, was approaching ever nearer. The earliest tremors that had already been felt in far-away Japan and Russia and in North Africa would soon be threatening Europe. Once the dull embers of these dying empires kindled the blazing antagonism of nations, the impact of the war would reach the shores of North America and greatly impede the construction of the Temple.

But William Sutherland Maxwell would learn much from this experience. He would also contribute a great deal of advice, provide invaluable guidance and offer his recommendations to the Bahá'ís on the subject. His correspondence with the secretary of the National Spiritual Assembly of the United States and Canada concerning many aspects of 'the Bourgeois contract' would continue through the next several decades. His vital role in the construction of another mighty edifice on Mount Carmel would be marked by the experience.

1914–1922

The year 1914 marked a turning point for the Maxwells of Montreal, as it did in the history of humanity. The war that was destined to shatter the fortunes of many during the next four years, eroding empires, erasing boundaries, eradicating economies and eliminating whole generations, would not leave the Maxwell family untouched. The words of the Master uttered in their home in Montreal such a short while before were to prove prophetic for the planet: humanity was indeed 'out of touch with God' and despite all 'Abdu'l-Bahá's prayers that 'strife and enmity may be banished, warfare and bloodshed taken away', one of the worse conflagrations in human history was about to undermine the very foundations of civilization. How saddened, how grieved He must have been at this time of crisis.

May surely sensed it when she received this Tablet, translated on 21 March 1914, from Haifa. 'Abdu'l-Bahá was bowed down by the pressure of work, crushed under His responsibilities. Although He continued to pour out His love and encouragement to her, she must have realized how much He was suffering:

> O thou who art attracted with the love of God!
> A long time hath passed and I have not written thee a letter, but I have not forgotten thee. My health was in the utmost weakness and my physical powers exhausted, and correspondence was thus impossible. Now, praise be to God, through the bounty of Bahá'u'lláh I have regained my health to a degree, and hence I am writing to thee. Spend thou thy time as much as possible on matters which conduce to the joy of heart and soul, that at every moment thou mayest find a new spirit, in every day discover a new power, and in every night light a bright candle and become a fountain of living waters to revive the souls of men. May thou become a tree of Paradise and yield the choicest fruits.

Convey to thy respected husband the most wondrous Abhá greetings

. . .

Kiss thy dear, sweet daughter on my behalf.

The Master wrote this letter to May on Naw-Rúz day, the year the war began. But in fact, there had been more than the Naw-Rúz feast celebrated in Haifa that day. A wedding had just been celebrated in the Master's house between Fatimih Tabrizi, a young woman born and brought up in the prison-city of 'Akká, and Mírzá 'Alí-Akbar-i-Nakhjavání, a well-known Bahá'í from the Caucasus. That same month, May received another Tablet from 'Abdu'l-Bahá concerning Fatimih's sister, Zeenat Tabrizi. 'Abdu'l-Bahá told her that He was sending this young woman to Montreal to be married to another great servant of the Cause, Dr Zia Bagdadi of Chicago. Since her sister's wedding had taken place in His home in Haifa, the Master told May that Zeenat should be married in 'my home in Montreal'.

It was an historic occasion, the very first Bahá'í wedding to be solemnized in Montreal, and it was also a joyous one, for it had been arranged and blessed by the Master Himself. But it was not the first occasion that 'Abdu'l-Bahá had intervened to arrange marriages between Bahá'ís. During the grim early days in 'Akká, He had asked permission from the Blessed Beauty to allow weddings to take place among some of the prisoners, in order to lift the atmosphere of gloom that had enveloped them. Many had fallen sick from typhus and had died soon after they arrived; the Purest Branch had fallen from the roof of the citadel during those first difficult months and had died in excruciating circumstances, and 'Abdu'l-Bahá felt that the hearts of the poor exiles needed to be cheered. It was as though He wanted to create a joyful excuse to counteract their sorrows, to have a feast to help them endure the ongoing fast of their tribulations. And He did the same at this time too. Was He arranging marriages once again on the eve of the looming crisis of World War I?

Zeenat arrived on the steamer on 29 April 1914 and the wedding took place in that blessed house on Pine Avenue soon afterwards, amidst much joy and excitement. It proved a very happy marriage though sadly short-lived. The two sisters were widows longer than they were wives, for Dr Bagdadi, like his brother-in-law 'Alí-Akbar Nakhjavání, died in the prime of life. But the blessings of 'Abdu'l-Bahá had long-term effects. When Zeenat Bagdadi came to the Holy Land in 1977 at the invitation of the Universal House of Justice, she was able, with her crystalline memory, to help refurbish the House of 'Abdu'lláh Páshá in which she had lived and grown up. In her conversations with Amatu'l-Bahá Rúḥíyyih Khánum, both the bride of those bygone days and the little girl running around the house on Pine Avenue also remembered her wedding in 'Abdu'l-Bahá's 'home' in Montreal. On 9 February 1998, Amatu'l-Bahá herself recalled that happy occasion from a child's point of view:

> I remember very distinctly, in almost a photographic manner, the marriage of Dr. Zia Bagdadi to his wife Zeenat. Indeed, she was sent by 'Abdu'l-Bahá to be his wife, and in addition to this important event in their lives, it was very important and a great thrill for me, little Mary Maxwell, as it was the first time in my life that I was allowed to 'sit up' and not be put to bed before sunset, and could see the wedding, which I remember as clearly as if it took place last night.
>   Dr. Bagdadi had on a dark suit and she had on a nice white bridal dress to the floor, which I have a vague recollection my mother may have provided for her. My assumption, probably based on fact, is that my mother outfitted Zeenat in her white wedding clothes . . .

But the skies darkened as summer drew near and funerals soon followed the wedding feasts. Although the war itself would erupt out of a seemingly clear blue sky, the clouds of sorrow were already gathering ominously above the Maxwell home that June, when May sent 'Abdu'l-Bahá the sad news that her father was dying.

John Harris Bolles had endured many difficulties in life. His letters depicting some of his privations combine melancholy with a kind of gallows humour:

> With me child! humour seems often to be born of sorrow. A God sent gift, sent to me sometimes, to enable the mind to turn from the wear of sorrow, and get a needed relief. So, if it seems to come at times, at most unfitting moments, it has not the same source as levity.[1]

---

1   22 May 1906.

Although his prose betrays a certain leaden quality at times, which may explain why his wife (whose spirits were so much more ebullient) found him tedious company, John Bolles evidently loved writing. In April 1906, for example, he described with relish the conditions in Missouri where he was prospecting 'close to the Kansas line, where the old confederates still <u>brag</u> about the War, and a stranger is obliged to believe that they were victorious.' He describes the insalubrious mines where he was drilling for zinc and lead ore – 'no place to stay, or to eat, or even to sit down, unless in the saddle. The land lies low, wet, & is frequently flooded with heavy rains, and as a residence should not be considered, unless one joined the shaking Quakers and took one good meal daily on Quinine.' And finally he describes where he was lodging:

> The queer looking frame house I 'live' in, is called an Hotel and is conducted by an old Union soldier (J. A. Loop) and his wife 81 years and about 70 yrs. respectively. It is not possible for me to eat most of the food that is piled upon plates, but as they have soda crackers I can get along pretty well, and the old soldier means to do what is right and his wife keeps things clean, but is almost perfectly deaf and quite irritable . . . This house goes to sea nearly every night – or in the mornings – and then, when it comes to anchor, I 'set' the pictures on the walls straight again. From the changes that I have to make to get things on level base lines, I think the old lady sees 'up' with one eye, and 'down' with the other[2] . . . Write me pretty soon, Dear! for it is lonely here.

One month later, in May 1906, he wrote to his daughter again on the occasion of the 'fourth anniversary of your marriage'. Before praying for her happiness he tells her with self-deprecating wit of the pain he was experiencing from kidney stones:

> I suppose you will consider that a miner who carries his predilections for collecting stones, so far as to set up a crystal factory in his kidneys, is going at least a step further than is ordinarily considered professional, and I will endorse that view of it, so far as to say that it

---

2   Interestingly enough, Rúhíyyih Khánum may have inherited her grandfather's obsession with straightening picture frames. She had an unerring eye for symmetry and its lack, which seems to have plagued John Bolles too.

is not within my plans to continue it . . .While the laws of crystallization are a most interesting and wonderful subject of investigation,
and comprise the most beautiful constructions, it does not now
appear to me that the kidneys are the wisest place to manufacture
them, and as an engineer I protest against the insufficient channels
provided for their expulsion . . .

John Bolles had never really found his place in society. An engineer with
a propensity for literature and meditation did not fit into the 'norm'.
Most people, as he told his daughter, 'do not seem to understand a
man who, for the most part, is silent when he is not writing'. After
the death of her mother, May was able to spend more time with this
quiet, thoughtful man. Each time she went to New York in the winter
she arranged to be with him. It was as if she were trying to make up for
the loneliness he had experienced without his family all these years. In
January 1909 she wrote to Sutherland:

> I had such a happy time on New Year's Eve that it did me good.
> Daddy took me to dinner at the Café Martin where we had a deli
> cious dinner, heard good music, and watched the merrymakers. My
> little Daddy was so happy it did my heart good to see him and I
> thought of you Darling every moment.

Two months later May was seeing her father as frequently as three times
a week, and on 14 March he told his sister Ella:

> She is a sweet child, a loving daughter and has been the only comfort
> I have had here in my absence from home.[3]

On another occasion when Sutherland went down to New York for his
own work, he not only visited the Bahá'ís but took time to be with his
father-in-law too:

> I am in Daddie's room and I am writing this to you, then I shall go
> to the Grand Central – then meet Randolph at 5:50 . . .
>   I want to tell you what a lovely time I had at the meeting this
> morning. I met so many of them after the service and they were

---

3   14 March 1909.

so cordial and all asked after my Pennie.[4] The speakers were Mr. McNutt then a Dr. Thatcher of Chicago who spoke eloquently and convincingly; both speakers spoke of the need of not thinking of the personality of the Master and Bahá'u'lláh. It was simply fine and how you would have enjoyed it.

Daddie seemed well and has been sleeping well and we have had a long talk on mines etc. – shall tell you all about it.

Unlike his brother Richard, who had a shrewd business sense and an indomitable energy, John was not interested in making money and avoided the hustle and bustle of entrepreneurship. May's father had his feet planted in the alluvial mud, but he was an idealist at heart. Writing to his daughter on 13 April 1913, when his son was also in Montreal, John Bolles summarized contemporary politics:

> For the hour, our country is peaceful, and the Democratic Administration appears to be discreet and equal to the situation. If that condition of peace will continue, without our Capitalists resorting to oppression and crimes, I think we will gradually become a decent people with prosperity.
>
> Give my love to all, and kiss the blessed babies for me.

Although they were very different in temperament and talent, her father might have reminded May of her own husband in the way he first reacted to the Faith:[5]

> I received the little pamphlet of Baha U'llah teachings, but cannot accept all that he puts forth, as I think there are many roads leading to the same final Home, and many, without any human teacher, or any teacher in human form, who are well on their several roads, differing in their routes, but all leading to one terminal.

According to Rúḥíyyih Khánum, her mother always said that her grandfather accepted the Faith at the end of his life. Perhaps as time went on he realized that the message of Bahá'u'lláh was exactly what he himself believed after all: that there were indeed many roads leading to 'the

---

4   'Pennie', from Penelope, was Sutherland's term of endearment for May.
5   2 April 1906.

same final Home', but that 'Home' was ultimately one and the same. When 'Abdu'l-Bahá passed through New York on His journey to the West, May made sure that her father had the privilege of meeting Him. He was addressed by Him and affectionately embraced by Him and this meeting, according to May's expressed opinion, was what finally confirmed his faith.

He suffered greatly during the last year of his life. He began to lose control of his right arm and was unable to write legibly. One of his few surviving notes, written after a visit to Montreal on 18 June 1913, reveals how tenderly he loved his daughter, how scrupulous he was about money, and how he knew that his end was near:

My dear Little Girl:
We all reached here comfortably altho' the night was very cold. When I came down town this a.m. Jeanette was skirmishing for rooms with a roof garden, and probably found them at about $35.= per week, at 'The Bonheur'– I found your letter, gentle, sweet, loving as usual, with the check for $80.=, intending to return the $70.=, and divide my careless loss of $20.=, but I could not consent to such a sacrifice, and herein enclose U.S. Money Order No 730917, of this date for Ten Dollars to your order. I most heartily and affectionately thank you with my devoted love. You have always been the same loving and devoted child, that has filled my heart with peace, comfort and content, and with love. I shall, pretty soon, it may be, be waiting with your Mother for you and all those we love. Must close to catch this mail, but not until I tell you that I and we, had a most happy stay at the charming home made for you, by your well loved husband, to whom and to Randolph I send my hearty, sincere love. Gently I kiss you Dear, my beloved daughter, my little girl, with the greatest love.
Your devoted father
J. H. Bolles

The following year, on 14 June 1914, May asked the Master to pray for John Bolles:

My Heavenly Beloved,
I am again in New York but I have come to be with my dear

father who is dying. His face is calm and illumined with the light of that beautiful world beyond. Oh! my Lord, my Beloved! I humbly beg of Thee to pray in His behalf – that he may be submerged in the Ocean of Divine Forgiveness and Mercy, and attain a place in Thy Kingdom, under the Shadow of Thy Protection. Oh! Thou Centre of the Covenant!

How grateful May must have been, how comforted she was when a response arrived from her Beloved in answer to her supplications.

> *O thou daughter of the Kingdom!*
> *Thy letter was received. In regard to thy dear father, rest assured that in the Kingdom of God the brightness of his countenance is great indeed. I will ask forgiveness for him at the Divine Threshold. Be thou assured.*

Some weeks later, on 10 July 1914, her father passed away, from cancer of his right arm, which accounted for the shaky handwriting he had suffered from for some years.

* * *

May must have realized, in retrospect, that her father was lucky to have died when he did. With the onset of World War I, 'Abdu'l-Bahá's warnings finally became a grim reality. No one could have imagined the horror of it. No one could have conceived the moral cost of so much cultural and political complacence until all of western civilization began to sink, as it seemed, like another *Titanic*, into the muddy battlefields of Europe. As stated in the masterful analysis prepared under the aegis of the Universal House of Justice:[6]

> When the great conflagration did break out . . . the nightmare far surpassed the worst fears of thoughtful minds . . . The statistics themselves remain almost beyond the ability of the human mind to encompass: an estimated sixty million men eventually being thrown into the most horrific inferno that history had ever known, eight million of them perishing in the course of the war and an additional ten million or more being permanently disabled by crippling

---

6   *Century of Light*, pp. 31–2.

injuries, burned-out lungs and appalling disfigurements. Historians have suggested that the total financial cost may have reached thirty billion dollars, wiping out a substantial portion of the total capital wealth of Europe.

It is hardly surprising that the Maxwell firm was also affected. Amatu'l-Bahá Rúḥíyyih <u>Kh</u>ánum often spoke about the impact of World War I on her father's and her uncle's business in Montreal. As the real estate market slumped all over Canada and the United States, the building contracts and architectural commissions at 6 Beaver Hall Square dwindled correspondingly. What made the situation particularly awkward for the family was that catastrophe struck just shortly after Randolph Bolles finally made his dream come true of working with the Maxwell brothers. He had moved up to Montreal from New York, together with his wife and family, shortly before the war broke out. Several of John Bolles' letters in the course of 1913 refer with joy to the fact that her brother Randolph was now close to May, and that the children in the family were growing up together. But with the onset of World War I, when no one wanted to construct anything higher than trenches, prospects for the Maxwell brothers as well as Randolph Bolles, began to look grim.

It was at about this time, soon after John Harris Bolles died, that Sutherland received a proposition for work from May's uncle, who was living in Jacksonville, Florida. Several years before, Richard Bolles had bought some 500,000 acres of Wetlands at $2.00 an acre, with the understanding that the State of Florida would drain the land. Since then he had been auctioning off tracts of undrained swamp to prospective farmers who hoped to make their fortune in what was being advertised, at the time, as the 'Tropical Paradise' of the Everglade Waterways. When the government failed to drain the land, two court cases ensued in 1913[7] – the judgement being that Richard Bolles was found to be 'an honest man'.

---

7   The first case 'was settled in November 1913, with the court allowing Bolles to keep the $1,400,000 already paid him, but prohibiting him from collecting any further funds until the State had fulfilled its contract to drain and survey the Everglades lands. Bolles was arrested on 18 December 1913 and tried the following March – he was found to be "an honest man". He continued to maintain that he believed what federal and state officials said about the Everglades, and that his opinions rested on the many substantial investigations already conducted to assess the possibilities of Everglades drainage and reclamation' (from *Reclaiming the Everglades*).

By the time World War I broke out, it had become increasingly difficult to sell off land parcels or promote the illusory promise of the Florida Fruit Lands Company. When Richard suggested that 'Max' and Randolph might act as his promotional agents, he was evidently hoping to take advantage of the demand for agricultural products during the war to stimulate further sales, which had dropped off dramatically since the court cases. He wrote about his proposal to Sutherland on 17 September 1914:

> Dear Max,
>
> I am sorry to learn that your business has temporarily come to a standstill, and I am afraid that all kinds of enterprises in Canada must be slow in recovering unless there is a speedy ending of the war . . . It occurred to me that it was quite possible if your business continued dead through the winter, you would like to take a hand in the business down here . . . It may be that I will need assistance in the office and on the outside in supervising or in making sales, and in either case there is no one whom I would prefer to you as an assistant or a possible partner . . . I have written to Randolph to the effect that if he is not actively occupied this winter that it might be well for him and in the interest of all of us to start in on cultivation of Sec. 14 Twp. 53 S. Range 40 with the assistance of a successful farmer whom I can control, and possibly unite with it some interest in this business with headquarters at Miami . . . I would . . . thank you to frankly discuss with me your own and Randolph's views, and predilections.

Sutherland's answer to his wife's uncle, dated 15 October 1914, is a combination of tactful caution and courteous gratitude. After modestly indicating his own areas of incompetence, he makes it clear that he is not accepting the position because of financial need but because of a desire to be of assistance at a time of difficulty, and indicates that he is accepting the proposal because of his personal interest in the region. He withholds all judgement on the thorny issue of the Everglades:

> Dear Uncle Rich,
>
> I have delayed replying to your letter of Sept. 17th inst. until I was in a position to know definitely if I could leave Montreal, in case you thought I could be of any service in Florida. Matters are

now so fixed that I can go to Florida and help in any capacity you think me capable of – as matters stand it would appear practicable to stay away for the winter, and it might turn out that I could let architecture go for an indefinite period. I have no dislike whatever to business, but it would be useless to consider me as a bookkeeper or as tied down to minute clerical work, but if you think there is an opening for me in any constructive or directing capacity, the work would be interesting and I could work hard and am supposed to be persevering and a bit of a fighter if necessary . . . My financial position at the present time is such that I can live and meet my indebtedness such as current living and land payments etc., but naturally everyone is living economically. I do not ask you to make me an enticing proposition; I am going to go down there and help out in any way because I am interested in the Glades – and realize that the present is the difficult time for you . . . May and Mary are well and return this week much benefitted by their Summer, and May is pleased at the prospect of my possibly going South. Please write me very frankly regarding the whole matter of going South, there is no reason why you should feel that I should be offered a soft-soap . . .

It might be well to remember the context in which this episode was taking place. The great expansion West, which had been at the cost of the Native American peoples during the 19th century, had by this time given way to skirmishes for property among the whites themselves in the last remaining unclaimed areas of the United States. This scramble for swamp and desert was characterized by raw capitalism rather than by the spirit of adventure associated with frontier settlement. Richard Bolles was no different from most businessmen of his day, or indeed ours, who look for ways of being financially shrewd. There were no regulations, laws or federal controls in force at the time to control land speculation, and his wealth would not have been considered ill-gotten by his contemporaries, let alone ecologically tainted.[8] Sutherland would have felt it perfectly justifiable, therefore, to see the situation for himself.

As it turned out, Randolph decided to join him in the venture, and the two brothers-in-law left their wives and children together in

---

8   It may be well to remember that contemporary scruples on such matters would not have been roused had it not been for the economic as well as environmental disasters of the 20th century, such as the Everglades.

Montreal during the first year of the war. Although their architectural partnership never worked out as planned and although the Everglades project too was aborted soon afterwards, one of the benefits of World War I was that the Maxwells and the Bolles spent some years in close companionship, a bond that was to have long-term effects on the next generation.

Sutherland's activities with the company included recruiting other people to the Everglades project too. On 5 November 1914, he wrote to his wife's uncle citing a possible Canadian agent and confirming his own travel plans to come south with Randolph:

> Dear Uncle Rich,
>   I have appointed Mr. W. W. Grant, 120 St. James, Montreal, Canada to be an agent of the company . . . Randolph and I are well and leave Sunday night for New York, spend Monday night there so Randolph will not get fagged out, and on Tuesday[9] we leave for Jacksonville.
>   Yours Sincerely,
>   W. S. Maxwell

But finding agents did not prove easy. Sometimes it was even disastrous. Earlier that autumn, soon after leaving Montreal to embark upon this new venture, Sutherland had written to May from New York on 24 September 1914, telling her about the possibility of a position for Hans von Liemert,[10] a young German who had married Isa Robertson, one of little Mary's first governesses. As a result of anti-German sentiment during the war, von Liemert found himself without work and was desperate for some kind of employment. Sutherland confirmed the difficult circumstances Hans was in when responding to May's suggestion that he might work for her uncle, but retained a certain scepticism regarding their friend's ability to fulfil the specific job expectations:

> Von L. . . . has about $40 clear and no job. Uncle Rich thinks Von L. can go to German settlements and do well. Von L. is enthusiastic about the Glades – and the prospect appeals to him – but I cannot

---

9   5 November 1914.
10 He became a Bahá'í just before World War I and is mentioned in a Tablet of 'Abdu'l-Bahá received by May in 1914.

say for certain if he will be a land agent or our star boarder and furnace man for the winter.

Shortly afterwards, he commended May on her plan. Things were looking hopeful:

> Von L. called this afternoon and it looks as if he would leave next Friday authorities permitting. He is quite keen on 'this subject' and I think will get on – even if he gets on the land of some lettuce and potato expert. So I am delighted at his determination. He will make for Arverne and good luck to you all. Get busy with the cold-cream etc. Your ideas are excellent.

But in the end the project was aborted. The Everglades provided no refuge for von Liemert and his bride and May's efforts to help the young couple came to nothing. The reasons are not explained by Sutherland, but just how difficult their circumstances were can certainly be inferred by his letter to May written in September 1915:

> It is too bad that Hans and Isa had such a hard time – and I want you to tell him how deeply I regret the trying conditions and to convey my congratulations and best wishes. Isa acted with great decision. It must have been a very difficult thing to do. It is not possible to get Von Liemert a job in Montreal in fact we could not get him into the country – Austrians are practically all interned.

Prejudices in Canada were strong during the war years: an illustration of just how strong can be found in the story Rúḥíyyih Khánum used to tell about a neighbour's dog which she always played with during World War I. She had christened it 'Kaiser', and remembered scandalizing the neighbours during the war each time she ran out into the street calling for it. The sorry fate of von Liemert can only be imagined if a dog's name could provoke such ire.

The circumstances for Sutherland were not much easier during the Great War. He was anything but a travelling salesman and the agents he recruited were not much better off than himself. One of May's letters written to him some time in early 1915 indicated the irony of his situation and the extremes to which he was being driven:

You seem to be skipping around a great deal – how funny to have a football player as an agent?!

Given the circumstances, she was anxious to keep in touch, wherever he went:

I hope you left your Chicago address at the Hotel in Detroit – asking them to forward any letters – or if you did <u>not</u> (which I think you should do <u>every place you go)</u> please write the Hotel at once and have them forward the letter to you.

But as it turned out, the experiment was mercifully short-lived and Sutherland was back in Montreal by 12 March. All he gained from the short period that he spent in the United States, between November 1914 and March 1915, appears to have been a business card which identified him as the Vice-President of the 'Okeechobee Fruit Lands Company, 1010 Bisbee Building, Jacksonville, Florida'. But whatever he may have thought of the Everglades project, he did his utmost to approach the job for which he had been engaged with the thoroughness, the responsibility, and the meticulous attention to detail that was the hallmark of his character. He made 50 pages of notes, in alphabetical order, for a booklet of promotional materials, and prepared detailed descriptions of fruits, vegetables and other items deemed necessary to convince prospective customers of the value of buying property under water. His lists included:

Agents Appointed, Agents Recommended, Advertising, Avocados, Bananas, Canadians, Cattles, Corn, Crops, Farms and Wheat Planted, Fertilizers, Melons, Oranges, Paw Paw Tree (Papaya), Population Data, Potatoes, Prices, Quotations, Sugar Cane, Useful Tables, Tomatoes, Water.

After a few weeks on the job, he was very grateful to come home for Christmas, as indicated by his postcard to May on 19 December 1914 from Jacksonville, Florida:

I am so sorry I cannot get time to write a letter. I am coming home for Xmas. That is my good news. Am delighted at prospect. All well and booklet is out. Can't put all my good feelings on a postal but send much love, Sutherland.

He rattled across the country from one cheap American hotel to another. The delightful letter he wrote to his wife on 10 February 1915 shows how his sense of humour remained intact despite the uncongenial nature of the work:

> I have had a punk week – appointed no agents. Toledo spoiled by campaign of Real Estate Board against the purchase of outside property; Kendallville spoilt because a 'Mississippi Lemon' had been foisted on the town folk; Goshen – found a man who may take up an agency. Elkhart – two men are interested but nothing doing now, perhaps next fall – and tonight I resume my confab with another man who may get really interested.
>
> I have taken to doing one night stands, not half bad you know, get all this fuss and feathers off in one day – and the $2 American hotels all included are hot stuff. Went to the Orpheum last night, audience about 92. Quite amusing – the usual line of stuff but minus the tang and finer tinsel. Thought I had all the good things working to my benefit in Kendallville: The country life so simple and inspiring. The avenues of tree-lined dove-cots. Such romantic street lamps and the moonlight!!! To cap the climax my room was no. 19. Well I had it all doped out that the Toledo hoodoo was a thing of the horrible past. I slept like a 3 year old, felt sure you were recovered, and stepped out at 9.30 a.m. to conquer – I used my finest brand of eloquence on the rubes[11] and returned at 5 p.m. to the dainty Hotel Kelly to settle up and sneak out to Goshen.
>
> Well Goshen got the better of my dope and the hotel at $2.50 per was a treat, everything clean, splendid food and cooking and a gala lot of young dames, all in white, to slide the pork and beans to you.
>
> Now I am seasoned. I take the whole show as it comes – if I do well – 'tant mieux' – if not – why the weather's good anyway etc.
>
> Well Darling I think of you ridiculously much, for the cultivation of a good opinion of wife and family send me on this circuit.

---

11 rube - a country bumpkin, hick, yahoo, yokel; someone uninterested in culture.

His absence certainly raised him in the good opinions of his five-year-old daughter. In a letter addressed to 'Abdu'l-Bahá at this time, in which May supplicated for prayers on behalf of her brother, his wife and many of the Bahá'ís and friends in Montreal, she added a message from Mary to the Master:

> My little girl says: 'Tell Abdul Baha that I love Him very much, and when my Daddy comes home I am going to ask him to take us to see Abdul Baha!'

But there was at least one occasion, in the course of his peregrinations across Indiana and beyond, when Sutherland must have been grateful to be on the road. When the Panama–Pacific International Exposition took place in San Francisco in January 1915, he was able to fulfil the wishes of 'Abdu'l-Bahá by being present and was listed as a participant under the 'International Bahá'í Congress – A universal movement having for its purpose the bestowal of economic, social and spiritual unity upon the world of humanity'. The Master had greatly encouraged the Bahá'ís to take part in this event. As early as 12 July 1911 He had sent a Tablet to Mrs Ella G. Cooper, saying:

> *Regarding the Exposition of 1915 which will be inaugurated in San Francisco, America, undoubtedly from now on the Bahá'ís must arrange and prepare ways and means so that a great number of them may be present on that occasion.*

He had also written to Mrs Helen S. Goodall on 14 April 1914, repeating this hope:

> *The believers of God from now on must think about going to the Panama–Pacific International Exposition. Everyone goes to the Exposition either for amusement or recreation, or in the hope of obtaining commercial benefits. But you, who are the believers of God, enter the Exposition with the desire to summon the people to the divine Kingdom and hope to receive the breath of the Holy Spirit.*

There were sixteen Vice-Presidents appointed at the Exposition: William Sutherland Maxwell was one. Although neither his temperament nor his talents were suited to the Everglades job, he must have been glad that it enabled him to attend the Exposition.

Richard Bolles himself did not live long after the Everglades project foundered. He was already one of the wealthiest men in Florida when the government sold him 500,000 acres at $2.00 an acre, but by the time he died, in March 1917, the 'Everglades King' was a millionaire. His heart attack, shortly after boarding a train en route to Jacksonville, made the national headlines but his impact on the family fortunes lasted considerably longer. His generosity towards his niece and nephew was unstinting, and the legacy he left them played a crucial role in their lives. May and Randolph received almost half of their Uncle Rich's inheritance between them.

In stark contrast to this material legacy, May received a Tablet from the Master which was to be one of the last she had until the end of World War I. It had been written from Tiberias, a town on the shores of the Sea of Galilee which served the many rural settlements in the region, one of which [12] 'Abdu'l-Bahá had acquired in the early years of His ministry and harvested until the end of His life. His systematic efforts in overseeing the planting, reaping and storage of the wheat from this settlement during World War I was to prove invaluable in saving thousands from starvation.

The onset of the war, which proved disastrous for the old world, brought forth a founding charter for the new one. The international crisis relieved 'Abdu'l-Bahá of certain onerous duties in His daily life and granted Him the essential solitude required to write His Tablets of the Divine Plan. But His Tablet to May, translated on 1 June 1914, gave no hint at that time of the spiritual harvest which the war years were to reap. He simply acknowledged the faith of a new believer,[13] and sent her His enduring love:

O thou candle of the love of God!
    Thy detailed letter was received and it brought the utmost happiness. It was a brilliant proof of thy firmness and steadfastness and a conclusive evidence of the brightness of the fire of the love of God; especially as it conveyed the news of the faith and assurance of Von Liemert. I have answered his letter, and the answer is herein enclosed for delivery to him.

---

12 Adasiyyih.
13 Reference to Hans von Liemert.

313

From the day that I left America I have ever supplicated God on thy behalf, begging for thee infinite protection and assurance, so that in that city thou mayest be a centre for the Bahá'ís, for the assemblage of the spiritually minded and for the guidance of a vast multitude; that to the thirsty thou mayest be a fountain of life, and to those who are lost a path to salvation; that to those who are withered thou mayest be a source of joy and gladness, and to the lifeless impart eternal life.

Convey warmest regards to thy respected husband, Mr. Maxwell.

Kiss thy darling daughter on my behalf on both cheeks.

Convey utmost love and kindness to each and all of the believers on my behalf.

* * *

The onset of World War I also marked the fourth birthday of little Mary Maxwell. She was no longer a baby and her distinctive character, her strong will, her bright intelligence and vivid personality were already well formed. The challenge of raising this little girl and of educating and training her abilities to the maximum, both intellectually and morally, would preoccupy her parents for the next 20 years.

Eight years later, in 1922, when May was in New York, she wrote a story for her daughter, which captured something of her emerging character during those war years. She called it 'Story of Mary' and dated the first page 15 September 1922:

This book is called Mary because it is named after its little heroine, and because there are probably more little girls named Mary than any other name in the world, and because Mary has been the name of some of the best and loveliest women that have ever lived.

I have written this story because I believe there are many children who would love to read about another child full of all the joy and sweetness and imagination of childhood.

This story just rambles through the years of her childhood and a good part of it she will tell herself as you will see.

Although Mary was born in New York she is a little Canadian girl and has spent most of her life on the mountainside of a large and beautiful Canadian City.

As soon as she could toddle on her fat sturdy legs she would go out to play and be swallowed up from view in those huge snow banks higher than the tallest man which often characterize the Canadian winters. She could stay out for hours in the coldest weather and would come in caked with snow, her fat cheeks like red apples, her blue eyes lit with joy and tell her mother quite seriously that she loved the snow better than anything in the world.

Her little voice was sweet and clear, she always spoke very distinctly, and from her earliest childhood used the most remarkable language. When she was about three years old she remarked with a pleasant smile to a guest, 'I only live for these Canadian winters' and then added cheerfully, 'I am really very sorry for those children in New York and Boston who have to scrape around to find a little snow to slide on.'

One cold winter's day Mary built a beautiful snow fort opposite the bay window of her home. She was the proud possessor of several flags of different nationalities, and being without patriotic bias and taught to respect them all, she would plant sometimes one, sometimes another on her fort.

On this occasion she chose a pretty little American Flag, a favourite with her because it was made of silk.

Soon after Mary was called into dinner and the little flag blew and waved in the bright sunshine unchallenged by kind passersby, until two well-dressed women appeared.

It was during the terrible war when people's feelings were sensitive and their actions not always reasonable, and the women stopped and indignantly glared at the flag. I will not repeat what they said nor what they did to that little flag for one should never repeat disagreeable things. And because it is the only instance in all the years I have lived in Canada that I have seen an unfriendly spirit shown toward the United States. After these women had gone Mary was very quiet. She went out and played as usual all the afternoon but something was working in the background of her little mind and at supper time it came out, she fixed her eyes on me . . .

The writing ends here and no more pages have been found. We have no idea of how May would have told the rest of the story. But like so many other fragments in this tale of the Maxwells of Montreal, it is precisely its unfinished nature that engages us. According to Rúḥíyyih Khánum, she had been much exercised as a child by why these grown-ups had broken her flag. Their disapproval of the United States of America for not having entered the war was a notion so far removed from her concerns that the look of puzzlement she fixed on her mother that evening lingers across the decades and interrogates us still today. Why indeed should politics have any relevance to a child's game? May faced many such looks as a mother in the decades ahead. She had to answer many such imponderable questions.

By 1914, the question of schooling was of primary concern in the house on Pine Avenue. May had always been interested in children's education but it was now a practical and not just theoretical issue. Years before, on 19 September 1900, she had exchanged thoughts on the subject with Sutherland during his Italian tour, when she had written a story for him which had been relayed to her by her cousin Frank:

> Frank was telling me yesterday of a man who has adopted a little girl, and educated her on a system of his own, by making all her lessons play, & so attractive that she loved them, and the result was that at the age of 3 years, she can read write & speak in three languages! I am sure that in this wonderful time that is coming in the world the whole system of education will be changed, and everything we learn will be spontaneous & happy. And it will be so different – for we shall learn to <u>see</u> – to understand, & to <u>do</u> as never before – instead of accumulating a mass of dry facts called knowledge.

In reply, Sutherland had written back on 24 September 1900:

> Frank's account of the three-year-old is remarkable. I hope the child will be not only a prodigy but some day a woman of genuine talent.

Like many parents, May and Sutherland doubtless saw in their own daughter too the signs not only of a prodigy but a potential 'woman of genuine talent'. She was an unusual little girl with an independent mind and indomitable will. She was, moreover, articulate from a young age, for like many single children she had received a great deal of attention. Unlike the traditional 'Victorian' child who should be seen but not heard, her parents had encouraged young Mary to speak her mind. She was, May noted, 'Never afraid of anything – interested in

May Maxwell with Mary

*May Maxwell and Mary,
about 4 or 5 years old*

*Mary Maxwell sitting on the lap
of her maternal great-uncle,
Richard J. Bolles*

Mother, daughter and grandfather: May Bolles Maxwell, Mary Sutherland Maxwell and John Harris Bolles. Mary is wearing a string of beads given to her by ʻAbduʼl-Bahá

Mary Maxwell with Kaiser, the neighbour's dog which she always played with during World War I

Mary Maxwell and her cousin Randolph Bolles, Jr., in front of the Maxwell home at 1548 Pine Avenue, Montreal

Mary Maxwell holding Randolph Bolles, Jr., aged about 3 and 1, circa 1913

'Mary was just five years old when this picture of her bursting through the daisy beds was taken,' wrote May Maxwell

Mary Maxwell, outdoors in snow and ice, near her house in Montreal. As she remarked in later years, 'I loved eating icicles.'

everything', and while this characteristic often caused difficulties over questions of discipline, May was able to recognize in such traits what she took to be signs of 'an intellectual analytical interest'. When she fell into a creek, for example, Mary told her mother, 'It was an accident, on purpose to see if I could swim.' On another occasion, according to May, when she had behaved improperly towards her father, Sutherland had said:

> Do you understand, you have got to show more respect to me because I am your Father.

To which the precocious child had famously retorted:

> Why should I respect you when you are not respectable?

On yet a third occasion, which Rúḥíyyih Khánum often recalled, she turned tables on her mother too. Having kept May waiting for a long time, and after many warnings and remonstrances, little Mary was finally punished for her lack of punctuality. May deprived her of the right to say the healing prayer with her, a privilege the child evidently cherished. She had wept bitterly on hearing of it and had protested that her actions did not, in her opinion, merit so severe a punishment. As May recorded, she turned severely on her mother saying:

> You must not punish me so much for such a small thing – I am only little and young and I don't know the hard things about life yet. You must only punish me a little bit for little things, and a lot when I am very bad.

And she continued, in injured tones, to echo her mother's own reproaches, telling May that God would not be at all pleased with her if she drove the love out of the heart of her own child! The story captures perfectly the method of reward and punishment which characterized May's treatment of her daughter. It also typifies the latter's sense of justice, and her keen capacity to observe as well as to imagine.

Little Mary exercised these talents through her love of animals, which started very early. According to her mother:

... she started when she was very little to draw pictures of these darlings of her heart ... When she began to talk she told me of an animal that always lived on the stairs on a red carpet. This strange creature was called Laudrios and he was more real to Mary almost than her Father & Mother. Often as we went upstairs she would remark – 'See Laudrios sleepin'' or 'don't step on dear little Laudrios' and I would hastily step to one side. This feeling about animals was stronger than anything in her life and everything else was subordinate to it.

In another episode in early childhood, the child dictated a letter to Santa Claus, requesting – among the other more traditional objects – a pet monkey, a tame kitten and a little puppy dog. She also asked for a little goldfish, a chicken and a parrot. She loved to watch animals, to protect them, and to collect them. May noted that on one occasion Mary told her, 'A large fat caterpillar was crossing the side walk, "not near enough to step on", she added in a hurried parenthesis to relieve any anxiety I might feel as to its fate.' Another time when she was no more than five years old, she had brushed aside parental summons to return into the house, with the impatient response:

Schut, stop your nonsense don't you see I am watching that grasshopper!

May also noted that one day she had come in out of the rain 'wreathed in smiles and worms' and on another 'covered with green caterpillars'. During this same summer of 1915, she came running in from the garden in the evening, cradling a toad in her two palms and crying in excitement and delight:

Oh! God! She is so good to me! She showed me where to find the toad in the dark & helped me to catch it!

It is not surprising that with a mother like May, Mary should have found it natural to use a feminine pronoun to identity the deity: May was doubtless her daughter's first means of knowing God. And it was understandable that such a child would not fit easily into traditional moulds ... No wonder, therefore, that May sought out the latest and most advanced methods of education for her daughter. It was clear to both parents, as Mary grew up, that she needed an avant-garde and creative education. Although she hired a governess for her child, as would have been expected in that society and time, May therefore looked for one who would assist her in establishing one of the earliest Montessori schools of Canada in her own home.

It may be well to remember that governesses were part of a social class as well as a particular epoch in the West. Up to and including World War I, it was the norm for a child born into a middle-class family to be raised by a private tutor in her home. World War I not only changed the concept of war forever but created an upheaval in concepts of class. It also brought about a great change in the role of women. Obligatory education for the masses in Europe and North America, such as became the norm in England and France in the late 19th century, was often associated with the great movements of social reform, intended to raise the lot of the poor. But it also became more common for girls of all classes to be educated after the war. Schools for the daughters of impecunious clergymen and impoverished gentility in the 19th century gave way to the cult of 'new women' in the 20th.

May, however, had become a mother late: she remained quite traditionally 'Victorian' in some ways, although she was advanced in others. She was high-minded when it came to questions of social welfare and education and often made friendships with those who shared with her a desire to 'do good' and perform charitable works for the disadvantaged.[14] When a cousin of Sutherland's, Sarah Maxwell, had sacrificed her life to rescue children in the burning school of which she was the principal, seven years earlier, May had been greatly affected. She had been one of the first American Bahá'ís to contribute towards the Bahá'í Tarbíyát School in Teheran, and was to sacrifice money for many years towards scholarships for some of the needy students in that establishment. When the time came for her own child's education, it was natural

---

14 A classic example is the acquaintance she struck up with an Englishwoman, Josephine Moore, on board ship from Alexandria to Marseilles after her pilgrimage, who wrote to her on 29 April 1909 from Cheshire to say: 'Miss Bleckly has talked much of you, & I have promised to take you round to see them when you come & stay with us on your way home. My friends at the "Settlement" in the slums are all anxious to make your acquaintance for I told them I had an American friend, interested in social work, coming to stay with me. I have been down fairly often since my return. I have visited the five crippled children I am supposed to have under my eye, & I was at the big monthly party for the cripples last Sat. Also I have been sent to talk to & amuse various sick persons.'

that she should want to go to all lengths to find a befitting school for her in Montreal that would also be of benefit to other children.

The year the war began, May turned the top floor of her own home into a kindergarten and engaged a trained Montessori teacher from New York to teach there. She used the space which had until now been called 'The Studio' for this purpose, and enrolled about eight children under her roof. Some of them, like the MacBeans and the Bolles who were living in Montreal during these years, were members of the Maxwell family; others were children of the neighbourhood and came from less advantaged backgrounds. The system of education evolved and taught by Maria Montessori of Italy was new and revolutionary at that time, and this school established in the home of the Maxwells was one of the first of its kind in Montreal.

Throughout the years that she was travelling for the Faith, or was obliged to go south for her health, May Maxwell hired a series of govern-esses, such as Isa Robertson, Doreen Barwick and Miss Mousley, who ran the nursery school and then gradually took over the private tutor-ing of her young daughter Mary. As her letters show, May took a keen interest in what her child was learning. Unlike most women of her class and culture, she educated her daughter long-distance, both morally and spiritually. Indeed, both parents corresponded with Mary from the time that she was very young. May sent her letters through the intermediary of the governess long before Mary could read or write. Indeed, she may have done this to give the child an incentive to read and write. The earli-est note which has survived was written when Mary was not yet three:

> Here are two pretty cards for your album. I hope my little girl is very well & happy – Give my love to dear Miss Mousley & Isa. Love & kisses from Mother

The second was written when she was almost four:

> My darling – Your dear Teacher wrote me a lovely letter & told me you are so well & happy, & such a good little girl. This makes me very happy and I send you all my devoted love & kisses and I am longing to see you.
>
> Your own dear
Mother

Sutherland wrote to Mary too, on 30 January 1915, when she was five, during his peregrinations in the United States for the Everglades project. He scribbled a note to his little daughter from Hotel Gibson in Cincinnati, Ohio, on the back of a coloured postcard depicting an elephant in a parade, with a howdah on its back:

> Dear Mary, Daddy did not see this because it is winter. How are you getting on with the School and how is little Ritta? Daddy is doing a lot of travelling and living in Hotels. Tell Mother he goes to Detroit on Sunday night or Monday. Wish you and Mamie were with me. We would have a lovely time. Send love to you and Mother. Daddy.

When she was answering Sutherland, May conveyed his daughter's reply:

> Mary says: 'Give Daddy my love & lots of kisses' . . . (she) is quite well again – & so <u>pretty</u> – she speaks of her dear Daddy always with such tender love –

The notes May received from Mary during her absences were distinguished, even through an intermediary, by candour and humour:

> Daddy is well, Isa is well, I am well. The gold fish does not look well to me.
> Love and kisses mother dear,
from Mary

In addition to a governess, little Mary was accustomed to having at least one maid as well as a cook in the house. The maid to whom she was closest was her faithful Emma Replisch, who was German and attended to Mrs Maxwell's personal needs as well as being a nanny for her child. But in the middle of the war, during the summer of 1915, a terrible episode occurred in connection with this maid.

May herself had not been at all well that year. The cause can only be surmised from a letter written by Mr Maxwell to 'Abdu'l-Bahá on 12 March 1915 on his return home from the States. In it he despairs for his wife except through the Master's intervention. His letter, unusual for him, is a naked plea for the Master's help:

Beloved 'Abdu'l-Bahá,

It is a long time since I have had the honour of writing to you, but daily you have been in my thoughts and have influenced my life; for all of which I am sincerely grateful.

Your messages to the members of the local Bahá'í assembly have spread fragrance and joy among us. Particularly the message addressed to the Bahá'ís, in which you say the war will soon terminate. This will indeed be a great blessing to humanity. This apparently senseless conflict will surely bring us the Peace and understanding of your glorious message to mankind, in which case we shall gain infinitely more than we have lost.

I wish particularly to supplicate for my beloved wife who has had to suffer from physical ills to an extent that causes us all to feel most deeply for her.

You know this part of her trouble and the suffering it has caused her and the extent to which it has prevented her teaching in the Cause.

I beg of you to tell me in what way she can be cured of her troubles. Mrs. Maxwell wanted to go to see you but the war conditions and financial ones have rendered this almost impossible of achievement.

You told her that she would be well after she had her 'Boy'. It would in every way be a great blessing if this should happen.

If you will honour me with your advice I shall be very grateful and shall know that I have received direction that will be the true guidance.

Little Mary is a joy to us and thinks of you very frequently. She loves you with a deep and true love and understanding.

I send you my homage and respectful love and trust that you may be with us for a long time. At no time have we needed you more than in these trying days. Your Obedient Servant,

W. S. Maxwell

The reference in this letter, to May being 'well after she had her "Boy" ', is a prophecy of 'Abdu'l-Bahá's on which Mrs Maxwell had evidently pinned her hopes. She must have interpreted it literally.[15]

---

15 As May later understood and interpreted it, this prophecy would not be realized until 22 years had passed. The promised 'Boy' was none other than Shoghi Effendi, and May's 'wellness' was related to the Covenant.

May was in a very weakened condition and needed a change of air at this time. So she went to the seaside that summer, with her little girl and her German maid. She went to Arverne-by-the-Sea, in the New York City borough of Queens, and rented a cottage on the Rockaway Peninsula where she could convalesce. Her little girl could play on the beach while she rested and Emma could take her on walks along the boardwalk every day. But one day, Emma disappeared. She never came back from her walk and was simply nowhere to be found. Amatu'l-Bahá many times related the chilling story of how the police came to their cottage some time later and asked her mother to identify the body of a dead woman retrieved from the sea.

It was a terrible shock to May. She was too ill to get out of bed and so she sent her five-year-old child to respond to the summons instead. It is astonishing, in retrospect, but there were many such instances in Mary Maxwell's upbringing which defy the norms. She was a pampered and cosseted child in some ways, and in others she had to cope at a very early age with grave adult problems. Rúḥíyyih Khánum used to always say:

I was not afraid at all, but I never forgot the face of our German maid.

She would often repeat this story to emphasize how her mother had brought her up to face death. They had several long talks about it then and later, which her mother recorded for posterity. She described how Mary had told her, at that time, that when she died she believed that her heart would go to 'Akká and live with 'Abdu'l-Bahá. She noted on another occasion that her daughter had confided to her that she thought when people died their outside skin peeled off and their inside 'tender skin' went to God! It is surely an affirmation of May's faith in immortality that she encouraged her daughter to speak of death and think about it. She wanted Mary to accept the dissolution of the body as a natural part of life, as a process which united all things in the cycle of creation. She encouraged her to feel connected to every living thing because each living creature also died.

Rúḥíyyih Khánum also recalled another episode when, at the age of five or six, she demanded to be taken to a funeral. The husband of an old Bahá'í friend, Elizabeth Van Patten, had taken his life, and when the hearse passed by on the way to the cemetery little Mary insisted on going too. If all this was natural, she wanted to be part of it. As Rúḥíyyih Khánum later noted,

> I raised such hell the day of the husband's funeral . . . that [Elizabeth Van Patten] begged mother to let me come! which I did & can remember standing beside the open grave, watching everything!

This little girl was evidently preparing herself for difficult tasks ahead.

* * *

At the mid-point of World War I Lua Getsinger died. On the eleventh day of Riḍván, 1 May 1916, May's beloved spiritual mother passed away and the bittersweet associations of the most holy festival of Riḍván must have had a particular poignancy for May that year. The loss was irreparable. The deep love which had been established between the two women from the moment that Lua gave the message to May in 1898 had never wavered, and their friendship had symbolized the essence of fidelity, the gauge of true faithfulness for almost two decades. May had followed the news of Lua's historic trips all these years and had rejoiced over her sojourns in the Holy Land. She had witnessed how faithfully Lua had tried to obey 'Abdu'l-Bahá – in avoiding conflict, in following instructions – and how tirelessly she had worked to dissolve the jealousies engendered by her services. When the Master reached the shores of North America she had stood beside May to welcome Him and in her latter years, when Lua became the target of gossip in her marriage, May had remained loyal to her. Although she may not have known of Lua's destitution in India until too late, and had no idea of how grave was her condition when she finally fell in her tracks in Cairo, their spiritual bond had remained unbroken to the end. It must have shattered May to learn of her death.

Lua had left a glorious legacy for those to whom she had taught the Faith. Martha Root quotes May's story about how '[o]ne day in Paris, at one moment's notice [Lua] gave up her trip to London and gave up her tickets to give the message to one man, because he wanted to hear it from [her]'.[16] That love of teaching as well as her undeviating firmness

---

16 *Star of the West*, vol. 8, no. 9 (20 August 1917), p. 117.

in the Covenant was Lua's greatest gift to her spiritual children. Even though May was a year older, their relationship had always been that of mother and daughter. In the early years, when she was still in Paris, Lua's long letters, expressive of love and pride in May's achievements, often addressed her as: 'My darling baby "May-Violet"' or 'my little "Wood Violet"' – 'my own dear little girl' – 'my star and my heart's dear child'. When in March of 1901 Lua was in the Holy Land again and met some of the new believers who had come on pilgrimage from Paris, she wrote these words of praise to May:

> How happy I am to have met and made this visit with so many of your dear pupils. They are all an honor and glory to their 'Heavenly' Teacher, and she – thank God is a star in my crown. Oh my own dear, little Violet – I praise God and thank Him that through you so many have been guided into the Kingdom; may your light continue to shine brighter and brighter and each day may your soul become more and [more] illumined by the Beauty of our God and the incomparable Perfection of our dear Lord and Master . . . My darling, I had thought to see your dear face very soon, but now it seems that great pleasure is not to be mine yet – this is as God wishes – and whatsoever He desireth for me, with that I am content.

May understood Lua instinctively. She shared her passionate desire to protect the Cause. Despite Kheiralla's defection, she remained its staunch defender at her side and Lua always knew that she could trust May's firmness in the Covenant. But she could, in addition, depend on her friendship too, on her understanding as a woman. When she returned to New York on 15 August 1901, she confessed as much to May:

> My heart is full of trust in God and full of faith in my beloved Lord, so I rest secure after all while the storms rage on. Besides I have the love of my dear husband to shield and comfort me! Yet, sometimes I yearn for <u>you</u> – I cry out for you – for you are the only one, outside of God – with whom I find it safe to be natural! . . . I still miss – oh so greatly – a <u>human</u> sympathy from one who <u>knows me as I am!</u>

Later, on 12 March 1902, Lua sent May another note. She could not love her enough:

I love you more than I can tell you my darling precious spiritual child, and I want you always to pray for
Your Mother
Lua

The failure of her petition to secure the release of 'Abdu'l-Bahá when she had an audience with the Shah in Paris surely added to Lua's sense of inadequacy. The Master's intervention, stopping her from proceeding as far as the Sublime Porte with this petition, must have made her fear that all her efforts to help were merely hindrances to the progress of the Faith. Knowing Lua's propensity to blame and chastise herself, May often praised her and expressed the wish to emulate her. Some time in 1904 or 1905, for example, she wrote these words of appreciation about Lua to 'Abdu'l-Bahá:

My Lord I have seen Lua! Just for an hour we met here in N. Y. and all my being is changed and my soul is stirred to the depth by a mighty power. Oh! Lua! Lua! thou art that wonderful woman, thou art the miracle of God's very Creation. There is no one like her, not one, and it is not of her outward being I speak, but of that mysterious Creation of the Spirit of God. In this world of dust, she is alone, amidst these fleeting forms and shadows she is eternal, radiant, spiritual. Even the most beloved & enkindled believers are torches giving forth a mingled & unsteady flame, but upon the being of Lua is enthroned an effulgent moon, whose rays will penetrate the deepest gloom, whose warmth & radiance will melt the cold heart of the world. . . . Have mercy upon me, my Lord & my God! that I may walk in the footsteps of Lua, my Mother . . .

At other times she would supplicate 'Abdu'l-Bahá to extend His grace to Lua, would plead on Lua's behalf because she knew how her friend agonized over her unworthiness, how keenly she doubted herself. On one occasion a Bahá'í brought Lua news from 'Akká saying that 'Abdu'l-Bahá had praised her with words like these:

Lua is to be revered among women. Her love & devotion to the Cause of God is great. She is most acceptable as a true loyal & faithful maid servant. She has encountered tests. She will experience

326

them and in the end God will say 'Well done thou good and faithful servant enter thou into the joys of thy Lord.' Lua is the material
martyrs are made of – she must not worry or be unhappy she must
rejoice evermore!

Doubtful of the veracity of such high praise and distrustful of herself,
Lua wrote May an abject letter from where she lay sick in a sanatorium
in Washington, describing the 'whirlwind of tests' in which she had
been caught and begging for assurance: 'Oh May I may be wrong . . .
but please tell me if He really did say [these words] regarding this poor
unworthy servant. How I have suffered, May, since I came home only
God knows – and I don't want anything told me about Acca that is not
true . . .'[17]

May's feelings towards her spiritual mother were often maternal too.
She longed to protect this soul who burned with such ardour, for she
understood her sensitivity, her vulnerability, her self-doubts as well as
her great faith and fortitude.

When 'Abdu'l-Bahá came to New York three years later and instructed
Lua to go to California, May appealed to Him on her friend's behalf,
for she was aware of how desperately hard it was for Lua to be separated
from her Beloved at such a time.

> I am writing to mention to Thee with great tenderness & devo-
> tion my spiritual mother, Lua, whose heart is breaking through Thy
> divine decree. She has accepted it – this bitter cup of separation
> from Thee – she sacrifices her life that other souls may live – she is
> the Mother of the Occident – but I do humbly implore Thee to take
> away her sorrow, to make this bitter sweeter than honey, and this
> sorrow the essence of joy and happiness. Thou art Able!

And on 14 January 1915, a year and a few months before Lua's death,
May supplicated 'Abdu'l-Bahá again – 'Let me humbly mention to Thy
heart of Infinite love the name of my beloved Mother Lua!' – for she
was aware of how shaken her dear friend had been when her husband
initiated divorce proceedings against her. Lua had suffered cruelly from
scandal over the years. Her constant activities and travels for the Faith
had placed a severe strain on her relationship with Edward and when he

---

17 20 April 1909.

demanded a divorce, after returning to America from India, the blow was very great indeed.

May must have realized later that Lua's loneliness during her last days had been a living martyrdom. She had indeed achieved her heart's desire to sacrifice her all for the Cause. She was crippled by ill health and destitute of all comforts; her marriage was in shreds and her reputation tarnished by gossip. But poverty was nothing, humiliation was meaningless compared to her separation from the Master and her fear of losing His good-pleasure. On 28 October 1914, cut off by the encroaching war in Egypt from all those she loved best in the world, Lua wrote to Louise Bosch:[18]

> One thing has never changed however – and that is my love for you – May – Mariam and Mary and also Juliet. I may never hear from you or see you again in this world but I <u>know</u> that throughout eternity I shall love you . . .

Towards the end of her life, she lamented her separation from May in particular:

> I have not heard from May since I left America. When you write her will you tell her that I love her more than ever – and am so glad she has such a good husband, such a lovely home and blessed child! I seem to see her <u>always</u> surrounded with these blessings – the gifts of 'Abdu'l-Bahá and I am so glad for her <u>that they are hers</u>! May she realize – of course she does – their value! Remember me to her and say 'When you think of Lua – <u>pray</u> for her – don't trouble or bother to write, she understands and wishes for you now, as always, a life crowned with supernal joy!'[19]

---

18 Quoted in Metelmann, *Lua Getsinger*, p. 283. Lua's closest friends were May Maxwell, Juliet Thompson, Mariam Haney, Mary Lucas and Louise Bosch. She repeatedly expressed her love for them in her last letters and deplored the fact that she had not heard from them. The connection between herself, Juliet and May was particularly special and is best symbolized by the story of the Robe of Bounty. Amatu'l-Bahá Rúhíyyih Khánum often referred to this dress, which had been given to Lua by the Greatest Holy Leaf, the cloth of which had been associated with the person of the Blessed Beauty. Once when I was helping Amatu'l-Bahá clean and air her precious old things, she showed me this white dress and spoke to me of it. After her passing, the whole genesis of this garment was found written up among May Maxwell's papers. Doris McKay, who had been spiritually nurtured by May Maxwell, also wrote about the 'Robe of Bounty' in her memoirs.
19 ibid. p. 285.

It was a plea that would haunt May in the years to come. Lua had provided her with many other salutary lessons – not only about obedience, about detachment, and about self-abnegation – but also about the need to balance the love of the Cause with wisdom in marriage. When the Faith was entirely sacrificed to a marriage or else used as an excuse to avoid its responsibilities, the results could be devastating. Several of the early Bahá'ís, like Anne Apperson who had been on the first pilgrimage, had ceased to be active over the years because their husbands, who did not share their beliefs, either were absorbed by their professional pursuits or opposed their wives' connections to the Faith. Others, like Lua who returned from that pilgrimage ablaze with the desire to serve, were married to men who shared their beliefs but whose Bahá'í activities were so all-consuming that they became a substitute for professional and material responsibilities. At the time, divisions in gender roles were the norm in Western society and naturally found themselves reflected in the Bahá'í community, but the Maxwells were a rare example of a conventional relationship that achieved spiritual equilibrium in this respect. May and Sutherland both loved the Faith but expressed that love in very different ways, which allowed for a balance in their lives. May must have known, when she heard of Lua's marital troubles, that there but for the grace of God might she have gone, were it not for Sutherland's patience, his sense of responsibility and his emotional stability.

Lua sensed her end was near. The following letter, written on 9 February 1916 from Cairo, three months before she died, may be the last that May received from her:

My beloved May-Violet,

Yours of Jan. 8th rec'd. I am so glad to hear from you again after such a long time; what joy your tender words have brought my heart you cannot know. May God bless you, my dearest child for your loving remembrances of one who is so unworthy; and the thought that you still bear in mind that first night we met in Paris, nineteen[20] years ago, touches me deeply. We have both lost many who were and are dear to us since then and gained much through the bitter, sad experiences. But as you say, what does it all matter, so long as we get nearer the Great Central Heart of Reality thereby; everything is passing and soon in the onward march of events becomes

20 Actually they met in 1898.

transmuted into something better . . . The final goal to be attained is 'Severance from all else save God', and in His great Mercy He puts each one in the place where the painful process may be quickest and best accomplished. Hence I am in Egypt, and you are among the snowdrifts of Canada . . . Oh May – please, as you love me now pray that I may attain to the greatest and sincerest desire of my heart – which is <u>to do and be as He would have me.</u> And only He knows to what station He has called me! If I cannot attain it, all I ask is to sacrifice my soul – that you may all succeed where I fail. How I love each and every one of you only He <u>realizes</u>. God bless and keep you & yours. Love to Sutherland and Little Mary.

Yours in the Covenant of Love,

Lua

One month later she wrote to Elizabeth Nourse, saying 'A voice is calling me – and I must obey! It is insistent of late! It comes from far, and when I arise to answer it will take me to a country whose shores my feet have not yet trod. The journey will be long and lonely . . .' May was to hear that voice too and never forget it. Her tribute to Lua Getsinger written on 25 May 1916 echoes its plangent tones:[21]

'Lua has ascended to the Supreme Concourse' – those are the words I heard. For hours I have seen Lua, the woman, the child, all love and tenderness, dying far away – alone. Far from the land where she sowed the seed from the Atlantic to the Pacific – from the land where she arose like the dawning star heralding the light of Bahá'u'lláh in those days when the Occident lay frozen in the grasp of materialism – and far from those who should have loved her and cherished her as a priceless gift from God. I could only see her frail form, her lovely, sensitive face, her pleading child's eyes. I could only hear the cry of her soul, her yearning for sacrifice in the Path of God. Without home, money, or any earthly hope or refuge – after her years of suffering, service and sacrifice she attained her supreme desire [and] lay, at last, a martyr!

Then I saw no longer the bruised and broken reed trodden and crushed to earth, whose fragrance shall perfume all regions. I saw

---

21   *The Bahá'í World*, vol. VIII (1938–1940), p. 643.

the victorious Lua, majestic in her death – the Lua who shall live through all ages – who shall shine from the horizon of eternity upon the world when all the veils which have hidden her today from mortal eyes have been burnt away. As Kurat-ul-Ayn was the Trumpet of the Dawn in the Orient in the Days of Baha'u'llah so Lua Aurora shall wave forever and ever the Banner of the Dawn in the Day of the Covenant. Even as her age and generation knew her not, seeing only her mortal frailties – so future ages and cycles will love her – adore her – venerate her blessed name – and strive to walk in the path of her utter servitude, severance, and sacrifice. The passion of Divine love that consumed her heart shall light the hearts of mankind forever and forever.

Great and wonderful were her qualities – in her own person she bore the sins and weaknesses of us all, and redeeming herself she redeemed us. She broke the path through the untrod forest: like the grasshoppers, she cast her soul and body into the stream and perished making the bridge by which we cross: she was a Niobe all her days, washing our sins in her tears: she was burned to cauterize our wounds. 'Abdu'l-Bahá said that when one soul should arise and become severed from all else save God, that soul would open the way for all to attain. I believe that the last time Lua left her Beloved 'Abdu'l-Bahá she died to all save God and took the 'step of the soul' by which the spirit of truth and reality dawned in the Cause in America. In fulfillment of His Holy Words, the light broke forth in Boston in the autumn of 1915: its rays were reflected in some souls throughout America and other parts of the Occident, so that at that time the believers began to enter on a new era of spiritual consciousness, and here and there the fire of Divine Love and reality of unity became manifest. The outcome was the bursting into the realm of possibility – the building of the Mashriqu'l-Adhkár, the outer sign of the appearance of the inner spiritual temple.

Those who were present at the Holy Convention realized that the reality of the Cause of Bahá'u'lláh had at last appeared in America, and on that day when the Divine Outpourings reached their height, many realized that the Spiritual Temple had come into being. Is it possible that on that day Lua attained the utmost longing of her soul? That in the laying of that first stone the mystery of sacrifice became revealed and her death was the consummation of her life?

Lua was buried in Cairo next to her own beloved teacher, Mírzá Abu'l-Faḍl. They died within two years of one another and shared one common monument in a dusty cemetery, which May was destined to visit in years to come. Her grief surely echoed that which assailed 'Abdu'l-Bahá, according to Ahmad Sohrab, one of the secretaries of the Master, when He finally received the news of Lua's passing a month after her death:

> Since that day I have heard Him more than a hundred times exclaiming with a moving voice: 'What a loss! What a loss! What a loss!'[22]

But when Sohrab later quoted the Master's words about the 'Mother of the Occident' to Juliet Thompson, in his letter of 15 October 1916, it was the radiance of Lua's spirit, the liberation of her soul and her characteristic joy which he said was remembered by Abdu'l-Bahá:

> *She is very happy in the Kingdom of God! She was one of the best teachers of the Cause. An eloquent tongue, a severed soul, a detached heart were hers. Although she passed away from this material world, she is living in her spiritual children. Their love for her must increase. I loved and taught her . . .*[23]

* * *

Nothing could have consoled May for the loss of Lua at such a time but the gift of the Tablets of the Divine Plan. They arrived like a burst of light out of the darkness of the war and illumined the path ahead, showing the Bahá'ís a way out of the mire. The first eight of these luminous Tablets were penned between 26 March and 22 April 1916. The final six were revealed between 2 February and 8 March 1917. And the two which were addressed to the Dominion of Canada were sent directly to Montreal and received by May herself on 19 August 1916.

It is wonderful to consider that at the very time when Europe was engulfed in senseless conflict, when internecine war was ravaging the fairest regions of that continent, and one by one the nations were being pulled pell-mell into the bloody fray, 'Abdu'l-Bahá, the Divine

---

22 *Star of the West*, vol. 9, no. 19 (2 March 1919), p. 228.
23 No copy of the Tablet upon which this approved provisional translation is based has been located at the Bahá'í World Centre; it was rendered from material found among the papers of Amatu'l-Bahá Rúḥíyyih Khánum.

Exemplar and Centre of the Covenant, was revealing His Tablets of the Divine Plan and constructing the foundations of a new world order in complete contrast to the mayhem around Him. Since the war that was raging precluded the festivities appropriate for the hundredth anniversary of the Birthday of Bahá'u'lláh, 'Abdu'l-Bahá revealed these priceless Tablets to coincide with it instead. They were destined to launch a spiritual campaign of world-wide peace across the globe. They marked a turning point in the regeneration of mankind.

They also marked another turning point in May's life. They became her charter to travel. They interpreted history for her in an urgent light and emphasized for her the absolute necessity not only of teaching but of spreading the message of Bahá'u'lláh far and wide. She entered a new sphere of service after reading these Tablets. From that moment until 'Abdu'l-Bahá's passing, five years later, she did not rest but moved restlessly, back and forth, across North America, galvanized by His call. She had travelled before, of course, to New York and Green Acre, but had done so primarily for family reasons: to see her mother, her father, her brother and his wife; to spend her summers in the country with her daughter and her husband. This time she travelled for the sake of the Cause alone. It must have been in part due to her extraordinary response to these precious Tablets that she later earned the title of 'distinguished disciple' of the Master and one of the 'heroines of the Formative Age of the Faith of Bahá'u'lláh'.[24]

Ever since she had arrived in Canada as a bride in 1902, May's Bahá'í activities had all been limited to Montreal and to the east coast of the United States, with the exception of her short trip to New Brunswick earlier. She had taught the Faith either privately in her own home or in public meetings as a speaker whenever she travelled for health or family reasons, but she had always remained in this closed circuit. After the reception of the two Tablets for Canada, however, at the end of the summer of 1916, she started to move further afield. She began to go far from home and started her journeys from coast to coast. The Tablets of the Divine Plan not only opened the cage door but taught May how to fly.

On 13 October 1916 she gave a public speech at the Red Men's Hall

---

24 Shoghi Effendi, cable of 2 March 1940, and letter of 15 April 1940 to the National Spiritual Assembly of the United States and Canada, in Shoghi Effendi, *Messages to America*, pp. 38 and 40.

in Edgartown, Massachusetts on 'The Message of Universal Brother-hood', a subject that must have sounded contradictory and at the same time strangely relevant as the echoes of universal enmity were being sounded across the world. According to *The Vineyard Gazette*, which described her as 'a charming speaker' and published a report on the event the following week,

> Mrs. Maxwell . . . spoke with much feeling of the great catastrophe of the age, the universal war, in which Christian nations, worship-pers of one God and followers of one Lord, are slaughtering each other on the battlefield.

On 11 December 1916 she gave another public talk on the Bahá'í Faith in St John, New Brunswick, one of the Maritime provinces in eastern Canada, where she travelled with Grace Ober. This trip to a different province in her adopted country marked the first of many journeys over the next decade and a half.

According to a newspaper article in *The Troy Record* about this time, 'Mrs. William Sutherland Maxwell addressed prominent women of Troy on the "Bahá'í Revelation".' She had also attended and addressed the Eighth Convention of the 'Bahá'í Congress' as it was then called, from 29 April to 2 May 1917, and had spoken with great eloquence, as Louis G. Gregory reported in *Star of the West*:

> A friend from Canada voiced the oneness of the world of humanity in so wonderful a way that one might well have thought our beloved 'Abdu'l-Bahá was using this wonderful soul to convey a message to the Convention. 'We are one in purpose,' she declared. 'It is such happiness to know that we are all one, one in origin, one in destiny.' This message was realized in spirit and in truth.

When speaking to the friends, Amatu'l-Bahá often referred to an important Tablet of the Master's which had inspired her mother in her teaching work and in her travelling. It had been addressed to May Maxwell in the early years of the century and must have been quoted by her often for her daughter to know it so well. It sounds almost like the Master's mandate to May when she left the Old World to travel to the New. It became His personal charter to her, the lodestar and the compass of her journeys across America and Canada. It symbolized the spirit of her talks, the hallmark of her services.

> *Thou hast written that during this summer thou art intending to travel to different parts to deliver the glad tidings of the kingdom of God. I hope that thou wilt be confirmed. Whensoever thou desirest to explain and expound a passage from the Holy Bible, turn thy face toward the Divine Kingdom, supplicate for assistance, and then immediately open thy lips. Undoubtedly the confirmations of the Spirit will descend upon thee.*

May was not alone in her response to 'Abdu'l-Bahá's Tablets of the Divine Plan. In the 31 December 1918 issue of *Star of the West*, a report bears witness to the way in which all the friends had been set astir and a great ferment of activity had started in the North American community. May was in the forefront of these early travellers, but she was in good company:

> The teachers are starting forth to scatter broadcast the seeds of the Kingdom . . . So have Mrs. Maxwell, Miss Jack, Mr. Gregory, Mr. Tate, Mr. Remey, Mrs. Hoagg, Mother Beecher and others in the East and North and South.

* * *

Just weeks before the Tablets of the Divine Plan reached May in the summer of 1916, a personal Tablet addressed to Sutherland arrived too. 'Abdul-Bahá had dictated it three days after receiving what appears to have been another request for prayers from Mr Maxwell on behalf of his wife, at the midpoint of the Great War. The first appeal had been written on 12 March 1915; the more recent one on 11 April 1916. William Sutherland Maxwell evidently wrote to the Master more than once but many of his letters, including this last, have not yet been traced at the time of this writing. In His reply, which Ahmad Sohrab translated on 27 June 1916, it is touching to note the way 'Abdu'l-Bahá refers to Himself as May's 'kind father':

> *To his honour Mr. Maxwell, Upon him be greeting and praise!*
> *O thou real friend! Thy letter dated April 11th was duly received.*

Thou hast written regarding the maidservant of God thy respected wife. This news imparted sadness but it is hoped that through divine providence and favour and the prayers of this kind father she may become wholly recovered; for that maidservant of God in her first trip to ʿAkká became exceedingly sick and the physicians became hopeless on account of her health. Praise be to God through prayers she became well. I hope that the same thing may now occur. Regarding the house that you intend to acquire for the summer season or rent for the whole year, it is very acceptable.[25] *That maidservant of God is very near in the Kingdom of God; for she has no other aim save God and no other intention except summoning the people to the Kingdom of God. The fact proving this statement is that she invited Mr. Harlan Ober to Burlington, so that he may deliver a talk in the women's club. She must be happy over this, for he gave an eloquent speech. Concerning your presence in the Holy Land: these days it is impossible. Whenever the way is open and the means are available in order to travel with ease and comfort, you have permission to come. Convey my utmost kindness to that respected maidservant. I beg of God that like unto a candle she may become enkindled in that region with the Fire of the Love of God and the light of the Knowledge of God. Kiss on my behalf the two cheeks of the little girl, the beloved Mary.*[26]

By a strange twist of fate, this Tablet from the Master reached Sutherland's hands soon after he had been afflicted by another grief. His wife's health had begun to rally, but he had been much saddened earlier that year by the loss of his beloved sister, Jessie Gertrude Maxwell, who died on 19 February 1916 after a long illness of almost ten years. Their relationship had evidently been a close one and Sutherland had been keeping May informed of his sister's deteriorating condition for some months past. On 23 September 1915, he wrote to her when she was in New York:

I was out to Jessie's last night so was Ed and Libbie. She was quite cheerful, due to her having had a glass of champagne. She takes a pint each day. She is hopeful of her recovering and it is best that

25 A reference to the lease of the house in Arverne, Long Island, where May stayed in 1915.
26 No copy of the Tablet upon which this approved provisional translation is based has been located at the Baháʾí World Centre; it was rendered from material found among the papers of Amatuʾl-Bahá Rúḥíyyih Khánum.

such should be the case. Millie is nervously worn out and says why do we not do something. The fact is she cannot abide Dr. Day and his professional manners. The facts are Lafleur was called in – no favorable pronouncement. Nurse said Lafleur has made mistakes – all of them do as we know. Springle called in, got busy Xray etc and will give her some treatments.

Unfortunately neither the treatments nor the X-ray results were very positive. A week later Sutherland wrote to May again about his sister:

I saw Jessie last night. She was poorly – some sleeping & stupefying powder had the kind of dope that upsets the stomach but they will not use that kind again. Libbie and Ed called – Xray shows pleurisy – they did not draw off much fluid as there was some blood in it indicating some rupture or other – if the support of fluid was removed a worse condition would have developed. I asked if you were writing. She loves you and your letter will help her very much.

May must have suggested that her husband might talk to Jessie about the Bahá'í belief in immortality. In another letter he wrote during this period, he told her that it had not been possible to raise the subject. He might have been influenced in this regard by the characteristic Maxwell reticence. And he may well have been right:

I had one chance to talk with Jessie regarding 'Abdu'l-Bahá but did not do so, felt it would have caused her to think of death – other times were not favorable – I shall try to do as you ask and think I can bring the matter about naturally.

May, who greatly loved this sister-in-law, had written the following note to her in French some time before:

Remerciez Dieu de vous avoir donner [sic] un pareil frère! C'est lui qui est le cause de l'honneur éternel et de vous toute votre famille dans ce monde actuel et dans tous les mondes invisibles![27]

---

27 'Thank God for having given you such a brother! For he is the cause of eternal honour for you and your family in this world and in all the unseen worlds!'

After Jessie died, the words of 'Abdu'l-Bahá, addressed '*To his honour Mr. Maxwell*', must have been a consolation for Sutherland. His sister had passed away, but through the *divine providence and favour and the prayers of this kind father'* his wife had been revived.

* * *

In the course of the next few years May's services to the Cause multiplied. In 1918 she was appointed to the Committee for the Compilation on the Most Great Peace, and was also a member of the Executive Board of Bahá'í Temple Unity, serving again on that Executive Board for the years 1919 and 1920. She was a delegate to the National Convention in 1920, and continued to be elected in this capacity in 1925, 1929, 1931, 1934 and 1937. Amatu'l-Bahá often used to joke about the number of times May attended the National Convention, saying:

> Either my mother was a delegate from Montreal or Mr. Robinson was. Mother, because she could afford the train ticket, and Mr. Robinson because he worked for the Railway Company and got the ticket free!

She served on the National Teaching Committee from 1921 to 1925, 1927 to 1930 and 1932, for much of this time as either its chairman or secretary. She was secretary for the period 1927–1930 when there were many travelling teachers (circuit teachers). The logistics of travel, alone, were very time-consuming. Her correspondence with the friends in fledgling communities in small towns, as well as in more established communities in the United States, is a remarkable record of her indefatigable commitment and effort in this vital work.

May's calendar for the years 1919, 1920, and 1921 was full of activity and constant movement. During 1919 alone, her recorded trips are as follows:

- In January and February she was in Boston.
- The 21 March issue of *Star of the West* reports that 'Mr. Randall and Mrs. Maxwell are speaking to the new centers in the East', which would suggest she had been in that circuit in February.
- In March she was in Washington DC.

- In April she was in New York City attending the 11th Annual Mashriqu'l-Adhkár Convention, at which she served as one of the four members of the Convention and Congress Committee of the Executive Board.
- From 26 to 30 April she was a participant in the grand affair of 'The Unveiling of the Tablets of the Divine Plan' in New York, and on 28 April she addressed the 5th Session of the Bahá'í Congress at the Hotel McAlpin, in New York City, on 'The Seed Sowing of the Ages'.
- In the month of May, for just a week or so, she returned to Montreal.
- But by 24 May she was back in Chicago speaking at the Central States Second Bahá'í Teaching Convention.
- On 10 June she was in Toronto for one week, a visit which marks the beginning of many more teaching trips and activities in Toronto.
- By 16 June she was back in Montreal, remaining there until September when she left for Green Acre.

The following year, 1920, was equally full. Her activities included her attendance at the 12th Annual Mashriqu'l-Adhkár Convention in New York City, as a delegate, between 26 and 29 April. She was in constant motion.

In 1921, the months of January and February were as usual spent in New York, and then she attended the 13th Annual Convention in Chicago and addressed the friends there more than once. It was at this Convention that she met Keith Ransom-Kehler, later to become the first American martyr, in Persia, and a Hand of the Cause of God. This friendship was one of the most cherished and lasting ones in the lives of these two heroic women. There is a sweet note in Keith's handwriting, addressed to May at the Auditorium Hotel, Chicago, which reads:

Beloved, will you have the kindness to extend the invitation for Saturday night to Mr. Bagdadi? The party includes you, Jenabe Fazel, Mr. Sohrab, Mr. Baghdadi, Mr. Vail and my husband.

A few months later May requested permission to make the pilgrimage together with Keith and her husband. Writing to May from Persia many years later, on 20 March 1933, Keith recalled the occasion in 1921 when she and her husband had accepted the Faith:

> In the meantime, my twelfth spiritual birthday, May third, has come. How Jim and I sat in your dear presence and as you spoke embraced His Blessed Faith is a recollection springing up into everlasting life. Ours is a relation that will never die, according to the Master's promise . . . Two dozen letters are sobbing to be answered. I'm sorry to send you anything so bald as this, but such is the lot of mothers.

Seven months later, on 27 October 1933, while still in Persia on a mission for the beloved Guardian to alleviate the increasing measures being taken to suppress the Bahá'í Faith in that country, Keith passed away. Following her passing, Sutherland was asked to design a monument for her grave. In May's letter of 9 February 1934 to Sutherland, she expressed her deep feelings about this:

> I know you will make a masterpiece for the monument of our beloved Keith, soaring, unique and significant like herself, and I am so grateful to the N.S.A. for giving you this opportunity because she was so close to us all, and I often feel her overshadowing influence.

By 24 June 1921 May was back in Montreal, and in the month of August the Maxwells of Montreal finally joined Sutherland's brother Edward at Maxwelton Farm, in Baie d'Urfe, Quebec, Canada. It was a rare lull in her busy schedule and one that must have been particularly appreciated by her husband.

During these same years, while his wife was travelling back and forth and attending to her Bahá'í duties, Sutherland too was very busy. He took advantage of the lull in his architectural activities at the beginning of the war to take up painting again, in addition to his Bahá'í services, and was soon exhibiting his works in galleries.

- The 1916 Royal Canadian Academy catalogue listed an entry by him that was a nostalgic echo of the past, a pastel entitled 'Street Scene, Dinan Brittany'.
- One year later,[28] he participated 'as a delegate' in the 9th Annual

---

28 *Star of the West*, vol. 8, no. 10 (8 September 1917), p. 130.

Convention held in the Hotel Brunswick, Boston, Massachusetts and was appointed to the 'committee on resolutions'.

- For two consecutive years following, in 1918 and 1919, he was
  the Vice-President of the Royal Canadian Academy and also
  listed under the 'Council' that first year.
- In April 1918, he was elected as the 'alternate' delegate from
  Montreal to the 10th Annual Bahá'í Convention at Auditorium Hotel, Chicago, Illinois; and the year after, in 1919, he
  was appointed as a member of the 'Decoration Committee'.[29]
  His wife, who was the delegate in 1918, gave a talk entitled
  'The Irresistible Movement Toward World Federation'.[30]
- That same year Mr Maxwell, in addition to Bahá'í and professional work, submitted a patent for a light-proof container
  which he had invented for photographic plates and films. The
  one-page description which accompanied this submission,
  dated 10 May 1918, is entitled: 'A MEANS OF TRANSFERING PLATES
  IN DAY LIGHT FROM A PLATE HOLDER TO A DEVELOPING TANK'.

Since both parents were evidently very busy during their little girl's
first ten years, it is only natural to wonder what she was up to at this
time. Who was looking after her? What was she doing? How was she
being trained and educated? And what were some of the challenges her
parents faced as this daughter of theirs grew up?

* * *

Between 1916 and 1921, at a time when the Tablets of the Divine Plan
were first being implemented in North America, May wrote dozens of
notes and letters to her daughter. And over the years, as she grew up
from childhood through adolescence, her daughter also wrote dozens
of notes and letters back to May. As time went on father and daughter
also exchanged as many letters as husband and wife. The majority of
letters which have survived are May's own; they not only bear witness
to a mother's sacrifice for the sake of the Cause, but also reflect the
impact and influence of that spiritual sacrifice on her husband and her
child. Since they were apart for weeks at a time, this correspondence

29 *Star of the West*, vol. 10, no. 4 (17 May 1919), p. 55.
30 *Star of the West*, vol. 9, no. 4 (17 May 1918), p. 42.

also illustrates the humanity, the familiarity, and the singularity of the bond between the Maxwells during these formative years. Many years later, on 3 May 1926, when her daughter was on pilgrimage at the age of 15, May wrote a letter to Mary about these absences:

> Some day when you are married and know the sweetness and pain of motherhood, you will realize more fully that however often I have been compelled to leave you since you were a little child, for the sake of this great Cause in which we are united; and however lonely you may have often been, you never suffered alone, because I was always with you, I felt for you more deeply than you can ever realize, and it is out of the pangs of this mighty motherlove that my spiritual motherhood to you has been born.

While Mary was growing up, however, May tried to hide her 'pangs' from her little girl. This was the greatest challenge that she faced: to balance her duties as a mother against her obligations to the Cause; to reconcile her child's needs with the need to train her child. In many of her letters, she tried to show her that physical separation could bring them closer to each other spiritually. It is noteworthy that May should have deployed the same arguments with Mary as she had done with Sutherland in the past:

> My darling Mary –
>   Mother feels very near to her little girl all the time – especially when I have the joy of telling the people about 'Abdu'l-Bahá. And now I am in Canada! so that is one step nearer home, and you, my darling!
>   Yes, I shall be home a week before Xmas if God wills – and I am well and able to come and what a happy heavenly time we all shall have! Have you got any secrets yet? I have <u>two</u> secrets about Xmas!
>   Thank Isa[31] for her beautiful letter which came today and tell her not to read this part out loud to you as it is a secret! (Isa – darling – please find out by tactful remarks whether Mary wants a white doll's sleigh – or something else & then tell Sutherland or you get it at once – or they will all be sold.)

---

31 Robertson, governess and Montessori teacher.

I hope my little girl is well and happy and I am <u>longing</u> to see you and hold you to my heart – my own sweet child. Give my love to Molly. I love her very much – & ask her if she has any Xmas surprises. Give my love to Daddy & tell him I hope he is not working too hard on that house & I will write him soon. How is dear Kaiser?[32] With all my love & kisses, your own dear

Mama

Mary often replied. She was evidently allowed to type letters to her mother with her governess's help. One such letter, written without intervention, affords a glimpse of the child's creative spelling when she was between 6 and 7:

Dear Mother,
I am sending you A little pickture that Ima
de for you this morning Ihope you are getting better plea
se come home soon.
With love and kisses,
Your loving little [signed] Mary Maxwell

It would be difficult for any mother to read such an appeal and not rush home immediately. It must have been painful for May. But although she was influenced by her age and culture, she was also striving with heart and soul to follow the Master's guidelines. 'Abdu'l-Bahá's prayers, she was convinced, had given her this baby; He had blessed her little girl from her earliest childhood with His smile. And when His glorious Tablets of the Divine Plan were received at 716 Pine Avenue West in Montreal, May never doubted her priorities. She knew that if her daughter was to fulfil her potential and attain the summit of 'Abdu'l-Bahá's wishes for her, then she, May Maxwell, her mother and the mother of the Faith in Canada, should respond to His call herself, follow His Charter, and do everything in her power to obey Him.

But such high principles did not always translate easily into practice. When she was far from home she must have missed her and worried about her too, for she could not always ensure that she was being properly controlled. The following winter, on 19 January 1917, May sent another letter to her daughter. It had presumably been written after

---

32 the dog, see above, p. 309.

a telephone conversation which may have provoked something of a tantrum at the Montreal end. Six-year-old Mary clearly wished to commandeer the telephone, and had not taken kindly to giving it up to her governess! May's letter, in addition to evoking her child's passion for pets, is replete with moral guidance and example. If a little dog could be jealous, how much more might a little girl. Reading between the lines, one can imagine how the child would have idolized her absent mother, and how difficult it would have been to be her governess during those years.

My darling Mary –

It made me feel very sad to know that you cried today – because you know dear Isa would not do anything to make you unhappy & as I told you over the telephone I had to speak to her about the meeting & important things.

You must be a very happy little girl because you have everything to make you happy, and yesterday I saw some poor children here who were so cold they had not enough clothes to keep them warm, & they looked thin & poor and I longed to help them.

It is lovely that you can have Kaiser and I am sure you are very kind to him. Does he keep quiet at night and not disturb Molly?

What do you think I did last night? I lay down to rest with all my clothes on – & went to sleep, & slept eleven hours! And woke up all dressed – boots and all! ready for breakfast! Wasn't that killing? Tell Isa she must come here sometime & get a good long sleep.

Yesterday I saw a little white curly dog like doodles. I tried to get him for you but I could not find the owner. Would you like a dog like that – or do you think Kaiser will be jealous? Don't forget to feed your gold fish darling.

I miss you very much, but I am glad I came because Mrs. Van Patten needs me so much – her first words to me, when I came by her bedside were – 'You look like an angel from Heaven'! and this is not because I am an angel of course – but because Our Beloved 'Abdu'l-Bahá sent me to her when she is so ill & needs His help.

I have not seen Norma but I shall soon, & then I can tell you about her. But all the Van Pattens & also Betty Shaw asked about you. God bless you my own sweet little girl. You are the beloved little daughter of 'Abdu'l-Bahá, & He loves you.

I send my tender love to you & Isa & my heart is at rest because I know you both live every moment in the sunshine of His Great love.
With kisses from
Mother

Instead of feeling guilty about her Bahá'í services and being torn between these and her maternal duties, May tried to implicate little Mary in her journeys, to involve her in everything she did. She tried to exemplify for the child what it meant to be a follower of Bahá'u'lláh. She molded her character and instilled in her a deep commitment to the Cause by naming and defining her activities as Bahá'í. Some time in the autumn of 1918, she sent her daughter the following undated letter:

My darling little girl –
What a big page to write on to a little girl? But you are so big now, and I am wondering why you do not write to Mother? Ask Daddy to hold your hand while you write me a little letter – because I love you so much my darling, and I long to have a letter from you. Are you having lessons every day and learning to write to Mother?

Soon I am going to travel in Canada for 'Abdu'l-Bahá – to tell all the people how God has sent His Messenger into the world today to save the world from darkness and destruction and bring all the people into the light, so that they may know God and love God, and serve God, and everyone be good and loving and happy. So you must pray for me – that I may help all the people by teaching them about the Blessed Báb, the glorious Bahá'u'lláh, and Our Beloved 'Abdu'l-Bahá.

I am so glad you had a lovely halloween party. Tell Isa that whenever she writes me to let you know so you can send me messages, and always keep in close touch with Mother – the way Miss Mousley used to do – and I want you to see Miss Mousley because her heart is full of love my darling & you love her so much. Let Isa & Daddy both read this letter and keep my little girl's heart in touch with <u>Mother's great love</u> – and <u>all love</u> – for this is <u>life</u> itself. There is a dear little girl here who sends you her love. God bless you my beloved child, my darling Mary. With love to Isa & Daddy, your
Mother

But all the exhortations in the world could not lessen a child's longing for her mother. Although Mary imbibed deep from this cup of sacrifice from an early age and vindicated her mother's most earnest hopes for her in regard to her own relation to the Cause in later years, the correspondence between them is peppered with references to her loneliness, to her longing for her mother's return home. And the ache did not lessen, either, when she grew up. As late as 1932, when she was 22 years old, Mary was still writing to May to say, 'Dearest I must see you soon. I am beginning in spite of my mature years! to get lonesome!' In another letter written during her twenties, she confessed to a sentiment that might even have been akin to a very natural jealousy at having to share her mother with so many other Bahá'ís:

> It is marvellous the way you are always a haven of refuge to all. I wish I could do a little of that creeping into your arms business! I could stand an awful lot of it! What oceans of things about the Teachings and everything we will have to talk over when we meet!

The arts of proximity in remoteness, of reunion through separation, were well-exercised by May. Her daughter grew to be an adept at them too; she had no choice. Had she succumbed to a sense of victimization instead, had she resorted to blame, she would never have achieved as much in her life, or been able to overcome far worse crises of loss. But while her mother's arts strengthened her to face the tests ahead, Rúḥíyyih Khánum still looked forward, with an undiminished yearning to 'sit on a pink cloud' as she used to say, in order to talk with her mother for the rest of eternity.

The highlight in their lives between the years 1916 and 1919, for both May and her daughter, must surely have been the reception of the Tablets of the Divine Plan, and these were anything but conducive to sitting! Even if she did not completely understand what they were about when the first of these precious documents arrived in her mother's hands in 1916, Mary was certainly conscious that May's travels were linked to them. In fact, they marked her own formal début in the Cause, for she was an active participant in the ceremony for their unveiling which took place at the end of the war. Ahmad Sohrab's letter of 31 March 1919 records the plans for this historic programme:

The Tablets . . . are written on parchments in the most beautiful Persian handwriting and gilded. They are now in the hands of a Committee to be framed in the most exquisite and tasteful manner. At each session of the convention, one of these Tablets will be read and then it will be unveiled by some pure and heavenly soul . . .

The Tablet of Canada will be unveiled by the little daughter of Mrs. Maxwell, little Mary, and the Tablets of the other sections of the United States will be unveiled by just such dear sweet souls who may embody in themselves the pure ideals and freshness of the Kingdom of Abhá. To this part of the program I give the greatest importance because all the poetry – loveliness and joy embodied in these Tablets must be represented in that angelic soul who will unveil that Tablet . . .

Mrs. Maxwell's daughter is going to be dressed in a beautiful soft pink silk dress for the occasion and as she advances toward the platform to unveil the Tablet a strain of soft music will be played.[33]

Little Mary Maxwell must have advanced towards the platform very beautifully indeed. Having a public figure for a mother, one who often gave lectures and spoke in Bahá'í meetings, she must have learned how to behave in the limelight from a young age. Rúḥíyyih Khánum had a dramatic presence and a natural flair for theatre which she must have inherited from May. And she greatly enjoyed the pleasures of the wardrobe. But while these traits were to stand her in good stead in the future, they must have made it all the more challenging to raise her when she was a little girl. While encouraging her social poise and public confidence, May had to inculcate humility in her young daughter and also train her to bring herself to account each day. She had to teach her the art of dressing the soul as well as the body, of acquiring those attributes and moral qualities that would grace her spiritually as well as physically on the stage of life.

May was attuned to her daughter's sensibilities; she knew all about her little childish loves and hates; she was aware of her strengths and weaknesses of character. And as a mother she had to find ways of encouraging the former, gently and lovingly, even as she curbed the latter, calmly and firmly. She had to give her daughter the benefit of

---

33 Mary Maxwell and Elizabeth Coristine shared the honour of unveiling the two Tablets to Canada. Elizabeth was the daughter of Mary Coristine, an early Bahá'í in Montreal.

the doubt without indulging her egoism. It was not an easy balance to achieve. The only standard she had, the only measuring rod she could use to establish the lines of demarcation between justice and mercy, reward and punishment, was that set by 'Abdu'l-Bahá. May was always reminding her daughter of 'Abdu'l-Bahá:

My darling Mary,

Mother has been thinking of you so much ever since the night I left you on the train. At first your dear little face was sad, but I know that my little girl turned her heart to the Beloved 'Abdu'l-Bahá, and the moment we do this we are filled with His glorious light and happiness.

My darling, I feel that more and more every day you are becoming a real Bahá'í, a true Bahá'í – which means that the deep love for 'Abdu'l-Bahá is in your heart and you show this love to everyone around you, by being so kind and sweet, and doing everything to make others happy.

When you were only a very little girl you told me that you found that the real happiness, the greatest happiness came from making others happy. So many of the dear Bahá'ís at the Convention spoke of little Mary, and how much you have improved. I hope you feel well and are entirely rested, and I want you to write me darling and tell me just how you are – & if you are well and very happy. I want you to be radiantly happy & shed this light in other lives. I want to know how dear Isa is, if she is more rested and eating & sleeping well. Today Mrs. Cowles is going to Montreal with our dear dark Brother Mr. Tait, and I want you to see him dear & talk to him – for he is a glorious soul.

How is Daddy? Do you have happy times together? How is Aunt Jeanne, Uncle Randolph & the little cousins? and don't forget to tell me all about the birds – the turtles and the fish. I am writing John Bassett, and I am going to tell him that if he hears of a dog to let me know. Give my tender love to Daddy & Isa and with devoted love & kisses to you, I am your own dear

Mother

May also tried to provide her daughter with comparisons, without arousing her jealousies. In a letter written to Mary from Chicago, in the early twenties, May draws a vivid picture of another single child, the daughter of Dr Zia Bagdadi, little Parveen:

> She is four years old and is like a spark of light, so intelligent, so sociable and knows the Cause so well. Someone asked her 'Who is 'Abdu'l-Bahá?' She said, 'He is the greatest Branch.' I bought a very pretty little present for her and one for a little girl I know on Pine Ave. I asked her to come up to my room and get it and as she walked along the hall she said, 'Oh my God! Oh! My God! I am going to get a present.' She is adorable and you would love her and she wants to come to Montreal to see you, but I think her parents would not lend her to us for a month.

She praised her daughter too in addition to exhorting her to do better. She identified closely with Mary's little victories but used every opportunity to remind her of the standards of the Faith in relation to her failures. Whenever possible, she tried to show her the larger picture before responding to her small concerns. The following letter, written when Mary was 9 years old, in March 1920, is a masterpiece of metaphysics in which the need to improve her writing skills is wonderfully intermixed with the death of mice and the meaning of immortality.

> My darling Mary,
>
> Last night your dear letter, so beautifully written, and covered with kisses came to me here. It had been forwarded from the Hotel in Boston, because I came here to New York a few days ago to see Laura and Hippolyte Dreyfus-Barney, because they are my spiritual children, and they were going to sail away to Europe to teach the Blessed Cause – and I would not see them for years. Also dear Harlan and Grace [Ober] sailed the same day to go to see Our Beloved Lord and Master – and then they are going to Persia for the Cause. They left their dear little boy, Aziz, with Mrs. Randall – so he can be a Brother to their little boy.
>
> I am sorry the little mouse died my darling, and I know you must have felt badly, but we Bahais do not feel sad about death, because we know that life is eternal – and the life of the little mouse will go on in other forms, and finally become a part of some human being and that human being has a soul that will live <u>forever</u>! Isn't that wonderful!

Why is Jip[34] only pretty well? Is he not <u>very</u> well?

Now Mary about my coming to Washington I have been very disappointed but I am not well enough to come. I had to come to New York on business – as well as to see these dear friends, and it has tired me so much that I know I cannot go to Washington. But how would you like to come spend your Easter vacation with me? You write me yourself or get your dear teacher to write, and tell me when your vacation begins, and if you want to come spend it with Mother. I am going to see two doctors tomorrow – specialists, and see what they tell me and then if they think it best I shall go to the little house of Richard at Kendall Green [Massachusetts]. He sent you his heart full of love in his last letter. He would simply be overjoyed if you would write him & send him some of those lovely kisses. His address is: Mr. Richard Mayer, Tangerine, Florida. If the doctors think I need a warmer climate I will go to Washington – but if not I will go to Kendall Green and you can come. So let me know darling.

With all my devoted love and as many kisses as you can stand from your own dear

Mother

Please write to Daddy & Richard. This is the way to show your love and it is good practice for you and someday you will be a great letter writer like your Mother! I mean a <u>many</u> <u>letter</u> writer!

How prophetic these words were to prove!

* * *

Many years later, in 1935 when May was travelling in Europe with her grown-up daughter Mary, she wrote a letter to her brother, Randolph about their own mother, Mary Ellis Bolles. They had both become parents by then; they had raised their own daughters who by then had both grown up. By evoking the spirit and qualities of their mother, May wanted to remind her brother not only of the best in Mrs Bolles, but also of the heritage they shared. She and her brother had proven their mother's words to be prophetic, when it came to how they interpreted parental roles:

---

34 the dog – sometimes spelled Gyp.

Mother used to say there are two kinds of parents and altho' they both love their children I call one kind a good parent – the other bad. The first kind loves their children with a <u>selfless</u> love – it is the <u>children</u> they love – such parents sacrifice their own wishes – hopes – desires & happiness for the <u>children</u> – that the children may find <u>themselves</u>, the highest & best in them. Then she said the bad parents (& she used these very words) keep the children for <u>themselves</u> – some utterly sacrifice the lives of their children to themselves – others are good to them, but in their <u>own way</u> – they never know what the children really want or long for. They never really know their own children![35]

For the most part, May was utterly self-sacrificing as a mother; she never tried to 'keep her child for herself', in the sense her mother had deplored.

Health had been May's constant concern throughout her life. During her middle years when her insomnia was endemic and she was very tired, she grew obsessed with Mary's sleep patterns. Writing to Sutherland from Boston on 7 January 1919, she appealed for his help:

You cannot imagine how I need your letters – and to know all that those who are so dear to me are doing, especially my heart is sometimes troubled about Mary and I long to know if she is really well, sleeping well, and not getting tired . . . I have some terrible nights. Last night I was awake until 5 this morning – so I do not feel able to go to N.Y. with Emogene today . . . I would rather travel alone anyway – because everyone tires me . . . I have written to Mrs. Francis this morning telling her some things about Mary – because when Mary is slow and dilatory & trying it is <u>only because she is tired.</u> Please do not let her get so tired – are you devoting some time to her each day? do you take her motoring. Oh! please keep in closer touch with me & close to Mary – Sutherland I cannot carry my burden alone.

In another letter to Sutherland, written during this same period, May wrote:

---

35 May Maxwell to Randolph Bolles from Stuttgart, about September 1935.

I hope you found Mary asleep so that she was not disturbed by the meeting, and as soon as you can write and tell me that she is going to <u>sleep</u> before eight every night & getting eleven hours sleep – I shall be very greatly relieved – because her condition does trouble me. Be sure and tell Mrs. Francis she must sit perfectly still in another room while Mary goes to sleep as the slightest sound rouses her – and then it takes her hours to go to sleep. Will you also dearest – say the prayer you say for me every night for Mary <u>instead</u> – do not pray for me – but for her – as I know I shall be better as soon as she is.

Rúḥíyyih <u>Kh</u>ánum often said that her mother was so fixated on the subject that it caused her a great deal of trouble later. For many years she was convinced that she needed absolute silence to sleep, and it was not true.

May also believed that her daughter, even at the age of 10, should be exposed to less rather than more stimulation and should not attend more than three or four hours of schooling a day. When Stanwood Cobb advised her otherwise, May replied:

Dear Stanwood,

Thank you and Ida so much for your kind and prompt replies to my letter. I can see your school is indeed Baháʼí – for its foundation is <u>love</u>, and your kindness and consideration of the parents serves to strengthen those sacred bonds of <u>unity</u> which is the only constructive force on earth – and in the lives of the coming generation. I wish to cooperate with you all in my power – yet I am truly afraid to let Mary attend school in the afternoons – if she has three or 4 hours in the morning is it not better for so nervous & mentally active a child just to <u>vegetate</u> the rest of the time? You know Luther Burbank says modern schools (<u>not like yours!</u>) are the best system ever devised for the destruction of the nerves – & of true intellectuality – our public schools etc. & the length of the hours he utterly condemns. I am not <u>set</u> in this matter but am open to conviction. Would you mind waiting until after Easter vacation – then I can probably see you & talk it over. I am so glad you & Ida are so happy! With all my love to you both

May

May is not the only mother to have felt that her child had unique needs. The question of schooling has always been a thorny one for concerned parents, and many children have been more or less the victims of adult educational experiments. But in light of May's hesitations to expose her daughter to afternoon classes, it might be well to remember that an only child, accustomed to private governesses and experimental methods of education, might not have readily adapted to a traditional curriculum anyway. As it turned out, little Mary only survived one term at Stanwood Cobb's school. She was utterly miserable, lost weight while she was there, agonized about the possibility of her mother dying in her absence, and was finally brought back home.

Her other exposures to school life over the next five years would prove to be equally short-lived. Nor did the problem of following a fixed curriculum in her studies become any easier with the passage of years. One of the consequences, which Rúḥíyyih Khánum herself candidly confessed, was that her spelling was idiosyncratic, to say the least. Young Mary's habits, when it came to home study, were as irregular as her school attendance. The governesses who were supposed to teach her to read and write and to tutor her in the rudiments of education, came and went through the doors of the house on Pine Avenue in bewildering succession. A summary count indicates at least ten governesses were engaged by the Maxwell family between 1914 and 1927. They survived for longer or shorter periods, like the cook and housemaids, depending on how well they were able to manage the independent-minded daughter during her mother's absences.

When May wrote to her 'Darling Little Girl' from Hotel McAlpin in New York on 5 February 1922, it is clear that she was not only trying to exert her influence on a wilful child, nor just attempting to exhort her towards the acquisition of moral and intellectual discipline, but was also advising her governesses on how and what they should teach her. It was probably the only way she could do it, for this strong-minded daughter would not have listened to any other authority than her mother's.

I was delighted to receive your letter which was certainly very interesting, and I was sorry to miss Mrs. Currie's beautiful recital of which you and Daddy each wrote me such interesting accounts. I was very much amused to hear how 'Gip' and 'Blackie' disturbed your night's sleep, and I hope you have been sleeping well and that you are getting on splendidly with your piano.

Do you practice at least a half an hour darling every day? because I want you to make real progress, especially as when we take this long trip to Haifa your piano study will be interrupted so I want you to have a good foundation now.

I also want Miss Brown to give you a ten or fifteen minute spelling lesson every morning out of your Bailey Manly spelling book which is either in your bedroom or the dressing-room, and you must write the words down and each day go over the words you learned the day before with Miss Brown, and really apply yourself to learn to spell, for it is really terrible for a child of your age not to spell better.

Also you must practice writing every day with Miss Brown. Show her your book in Arithmetic and let her give you similar sums every day. Also she must read to you for at least a half an hour every day the Canadian History in your book of knowledge.

If Miss Brown cannot do all this for you I shall arrange with Miss McShane but I see no reason why Miss Brown cannot give you these simple lessons of which I spoke to her before. At that time you were not well enough to study because your eyes were troubling you but now they are better and you must not lose a day, because unless you apply yourself now to a little study each day it is going to bring years of very hard work in the near future. If you like you can ask Aunt Jeanne to let little Randolph come up every morning at half past ten and have his lessons with you. Aunt Jeanne could try this for a few days and see how he gets along and Miss Brown will find it much easier to teach two children than one. I am sure Aunt Jeanne would be willing to give it a few days trial and see how it works, and Miss Brown can give Randolph the kind of sums and spelling he is used to and give you yours. She is intelligent and will know how to adapt the teaching to each of you.

Did you get the funny papers I sent you and the box of fudge? Now I am sending you a beautiful little green handkerchief to use with your green party dress and you must be careful not to lose it. I am always thinking of you and your happiness my darling and I am going today to see about the boats to Haifa and then we can talk it all over with Daddy.

I hope that you had a good meeting on Sunday and that the

children had a good class, and I know my precious lamb that you say your prayers every night.

Mother is feeling very well, and shall probably go to Washington for a few days before going home. Give my loving greetings to Miss Brown, my devoted love to Daddy and with my heartful to you my dearest, I am your own

Mother

Little Miss Mary was growing up to be an iconoclast and wanted to do things her own way. Like most precocious children, she was also developing into something of an autodidact. Her mother did not feel this to be a handicap at the time. If Bahá'u'lláh wanted to raise up a new race of men, then her daughter was going to be the first woman among them. But May's daughter always considered herself an ordinary human being like everybody else. To illustrate this, she used to repeat the story of a little boy she met on her travels many years later. During her visit to the home of a young Bahá'í couple, she noticed that their son was staring fixedly at her from across the room. Finally, the stare lasted for so long that she asked him what the matter was.

'Why are you so important?' the child guilelessly inquired.

Rúhíyyih Khánum was slightly taken aback. But not for long.

'Because there is only one of me,' she told him simply. 'There was only one Guardian of the Bahá'í Faith and he had only one wife and I was that wife and so that's the only reason I'm important. Otherwise I would not be important at all.'

This paradox exercised her all her life. It was one that she ironically referred to as the relationship between supply and demand, which she claimed was the only lesson she had ever learned from her brief study of economics.

In later years May admitted that she may have been at fault in encouraging the illusion of singularity in her child. She wrote to her from New York in 1925, saying that she may have been wrong to indulge her so much in this respect:

. . . there is nothing harder in life than not to conform to the common life of humanity; to be an exception, to be different in all those things which pertain to our every day life is a great mistake.

But at the time it was hard not to make such a mistake. And it has to be admitted that Mary was unique in many ways. As one of the few Bahá'í children in Canada, and the only one of such prominent parents, she was an exception to the rule and would have been known, as well as loved, admired, and possibly even envied by her peers. What other little girl in the Western world had rested her head on the breast of 'Abdu'l-Bahá and been allowed to sleep there? It would have been difficult for any mother, least of all May, to treat this bright and beautiful girl as though she were no different from anyone else. It would have been hard to ensure that such a child would follow the rigours of disciplined study, let alone pursue the private arts of self-assessment.

* * *

By her own account, Mary Maxwell was fully grown by the age of 12, and towered above her mother. She was already 'in charge' of the household at that age, but though she was physically mature she was still far from being the adult that she may have looked. May was keenly conscious that in spite of outward appearances, Mary was vulnerable and in many ways naïve. A little note written to her mother on 8 March 1922, while May was still wintering in New York, betrays the touching combination of child and adolescent that she still was at that age:

> Dear Mother
>   I hope you are well and happy. I am well but lonesome for you. When are we going to Haifa? . . . Dear Mother I love your present of that beed [sic] bag . . .
>   I think Miss Browne is leaving [because of a small disagreement about one of Mary's pets] but I cryed [sic] and said I was very sorry. Please do not be mad with me. Lovengly [sic] yours
>   Mary

Animal rights had always been more important to Mary than human ones. May recalled in her notes that once, when Sutherland had read to her a sad account of an accident in which a man, a woman and a child had all been killed crossing a track in a carriage, she had burst into tears. 'Oh mother, was the poor horse <u>killed</u>?' she had cried, for the human beings were only secondary to the story: the real tragedy, in Mary's mind, lay elsewhere. At other times, she saw no difference between animals and human beings. If one could say, 'Shut up, you pie-faced mutt!' to a dog then, as May recorded, her daughter saw no reason not to say the same thing to a person too.

May used Mary's love of birds and beasts for the purpose of moral training. Animals became the means by which she taught her daughter about the value of truth telling, about the importance of honesty in her dealings with others, about the harm caused by detrimental influences in her life. In a letter written to her on 17 August 1922, for example, May tried to address the problem of her daughter's choice of friends in a manner that would not ruffle the feathers of the 12-year-old. By recalling the ideal first, before warning her against unfortunate realities, she was able to emphasize the positive while cautioning her against negative models of behaviour:

My Darling Mary:

Your beautiful letter came last night and I was very happy that you could write such a letter. Not only was there a great improvement in the writing and spelling, but you express yourself so clearly and the letter is very truthful, straightforward and frank.

These qualities I have tried to cultivate in you because our beloved 'Abdu'l-Bahá says: 'They are the foundation of all character.' He says when a soul is truthful and sincere, frank and honest a beautiful character can be built on that foundation, but if a person is untruthful and deceitful and insincere that it is very difficult for them to come to anything good.

The reason I write about this particularly darling is because I want you to be protected from certain influences in life, and a great part about the influence in our lives comes from our companions and associates.

You have always been surrounded by these good influences in your home with your father and mother, and 'Abdu'l-Bahá said it was a Bahá'í home and must be kept always under these good influences, and as you are the little daughter of that home and the little mistress of that home when mother is away, I know you will always help to keep it pure and beautiful so that 'Abdu'l-Bahá's spirit will always be there as He said it would.

You know what a wonderful unity you and I have always had and how, as you say in your letter I have always trusted you, and I want you to have this same deep unity with your father just as I have with him, and we shall both always trust you and you must be sure of this and never be afraid to confide everything to both of us. Now I understand perfectly about all these troubles with Donnie and Eva, they are just children's troubles and perfectly natural, and each of you has your faults and each of you has your qualities . . . But Mary you are only twelve years old and mother is very old and naturally knows more about life, therefore you must believe me when I tell you that the influence of a person is often something which we feel without their saying one word.

For example, suppose you take a dog that has a good pedigree and has been brought up in a lovely home where he has been kindly treated and has been trained and has good manners, and is friendly and affectionate with everybody, and compare him with a mongrel dog who has lived in back alleys, been beaten and kicked about, had no proper training and so forth, you will see that that common dog, compared with the other one, will have very bad traits of character. He will be afraid of everybody and everything, he may be cross or vicious, and if you bring him to the home and make him the companion of the good dog, unless he is just a little puppy, you cannot change him. On the other hand you will begin to notice that the well-bred dog, especially if he is young, will begin to take on all the bad ways of the other. This is a law of nature . . . it is exactly the same with human beings. . . .

There are some people who tell lies just to make trouble and this is very wicked . . . Now when a person talks to you kindly and lovingly and shows you where you are making a mistake or doing something that is not quite right, you are perfectly just and honest and reasonable. You are willing to admit it, you see your own mistake and the trouble is all over. For instance, you admitted to me over the telephone that those boys you used to play with in Montreal and also Miss Brown had put some wrong and ignorant ideas into your head, and that you were going to try and get rid of all that, and that you and Eva would not talk of these subjects any more . . . But when I talked to Eva over the telephone she immediately began to defend herself like the poor little dog that was afraid of everybody.

May had earned the right to deploy animal metaphors when it came to training and educating her child, for she had allowed her little girl to have a great many of them. The house on Pine Avenue was home to many pets, as were the various hotel rooms in New York, Washington and Chicago where her daughter stayed with her. This only child had many little brothers and sisters in the animal kingdom. So May was not exhorting her in a theoretical manner, as many parents do, when she deployed allegories to teach Mary about moral truths. She was speaking to her in a living language that she knew the child respected. She was talking in a way she knew Mary understood, for she had inherited her mother's wonderful ability to anthropomorphize. As late as 1931, when her daughter was almost 21, May was sharing little glimpses with her of the natural world that resonated with humanity:

> I longed for you this morning when your beautiful pool in the sunshine [was] flecked with the shadows of the poplar trees, and full of beautiful pond lilies and pads the boys brought me, when two large black mackaws were drinking from the clear water and walking around and around it, in sheer delight and obvious admiration at this new acquisition, a lovely clear pool of water all to themselves!

As another letter makes clear, written the following year, on 12 April 1932, Mary's love of animals was evidently inherited. May and Sutherland had cats and dogs from the time that they were married and many of May's letters to her husband in the early years were laden with advice about the diet and exercise of their pets. Even though burdened by a myriad other matters, May still found time to worry about Mary's pets too. Her concern, in the circumstances, was nothing short of remarkable:

> Tomorrow is the day to feed the turtle <u>without fail</u>, one heaping tablespoon of minced meat, and please keep him in just the right amount of <u>fresh</u> water. He needs constant care because he cannot ask for himself.

A note she scribbled when her daughter was about 10 years old reveals that she had to protect the animals in the house from being looked after too diligently at times:

Mary dear! do not feed kittens before 9.30 I have fed them at 8 & their stomachs are swollen & hard. It will kill them to overfeed them –

Although in later life Amatu'l-Bahá used to turn to her friends in mock appeal and make them swear, with widened eyes, to say nothing in the future about her menagerie of cats, dogs, parrots, rabbits, guinea pigs, monkeys, chipmunks, chinchillas, turtles, snakes and even alligators on the loose, to say nothing of a mongoose, her respect for and love of animals was well known throughout the Bahá'í world and appreciated by many. It brought her close to innumerable people and enabled her to befriend many strangers. It bound her to those whose language she did not know, whose culture she did not share, and heightened her sensitivity to the unspoken. She used to say that animals gave her energy, that they transmitted a life force to her that enabled her to give more to others.

Amongst her scattered notes for the writing of *The Maxwells of Montreal*, Rúḥíyyih <u>Kh</u>ánum wrote several lists of chapter headings and jotted down the subjects that she wanted to include in the book:

When I write the biography 'The Maxwells of Montreal' I am going to call one chapter (on me) 'People, people, people' – all my pet anecdotes re travels, etc.

In an earlier note, she had wanted to call another chapter 'AH . . .' It would be, she wrote,

. . . all about animals & wild places. The 'AH . . .' when you are going to pounce on a frog or something you see you can catch. The 'AH . . .' when you suddenly draw a deep breath & dream you could go to that island, that mountain – it might be possible to fulfil that dream!

She used to say, laughingly, that she knew very little about theology, but a great deal about zoology. It was a telling distinction. She was wonderfully rooted in reality and prided herself on having her feet planted firmly on the ground. Her identification with the voiceless and oppressed of the world was a higher, spiritual form of this same empathy. Her freedom from the obfuscation and intellectualization associated with a priestly caste was its hallmark too and would serve to protect the Cause of God during the critical years after the Guardian's passing. Her mother never crushed or thwarted these instincts in her daughter. Instead she nurtured and preserved them. Her patience in doing so was exemplary, her insight acute. Many years later, on 6 January 1938, Rúḥíyyih Khánum wrote to May rather ruefully from Haifa:

> . . . I hear the friends recall my donkey riding, tree climbing, snake charming past! If they only realized there are such tremendously more important things in life I do, plenty of spiritual tree climbing and am learning to ride my own ego! and perhaps to charm the snakes of tests.

Rúḥíyyih Khánum often described her mother's method of balancing liberty and self-discipline. After allowing her leeway for a certain length of time and giving her free rein to do as she wished, May would often summon Mary into her bedroom and proceed to analyse, scrupulously, ruthlessly, and unrelentingly, but in calm and tempered tones, every act of egoism, every gesture of selfishness, every word she had uttered and deed she had committed in the course of the preceding days which was not in accordance with the standards of the Faith. Amatu'l-Bahá used to say that this rigorous technique of spiritual accounting caused her agonies of self-recrimination. As she wrote in her earliest attempt at her mother's biography in 1940, she used to wish her mother would inflict any form of punishment on her other than this quiet and uncompromising recitation of her misdeeds, this calling of her to account:

> . . . every now and then, when she felt you had had enough chance of improving your weakness in some direction and were doing nothing about it, she would sit down and give you a lecture on the subject of yourself that would reduce you to microscopic dimensions of self-esteem. I seldom got these lectures but when I did I would just sit and listen and feel myself steadily diminishing in worthiness as she quietly enumerated my foibles and shortcomings, until I was reduced to abject despair and tearfulness. Finally she would say 'Now darling, don't cry about it. I don't want you to be unhappy, and anyway crying won't do any good. You must just see

361

these things in yourself and try to improve and overcome them.'
It was like a spiritual spring cleaning. She treated me to it whenever she felt I needed it – as indeed she did with her husband, her
spiritual children, and those in whom she took a deep interest –
sometimes even the servants! I used to think as a child that I would
rather have a whipping than one of those self-revealing talks, given
with no anger or malice, designed only for the good of my soul. This
manner of scolding – if one could call it such, was an indication of
her profound ability as a teacher. She reached the inmost soul. She
made you face up to your own weaknesses, a thing most of us abhor
doing and indeed many of us never do do at all. After it was over no
trace of it remained. She would kiss me and we would go do something else – ten to one something kind and pleasant to take away the
taste of the bitter pill!

This early training did not stop as young Mary grew from childhood
to adolescence. May continued to draw her daughter's attention to her
failures right up to her twenties, in the same calm and loving manner.
Writing to her on 8 November 1933, for example, she catalogued the
consequences of Mary's apparently callousness towards some of her
young admirers at the time, adding:

> Mary dear, I may as well tell you all the painful things at once, and
> then we can talk it over, because I do not want you to get any over-
> sensitive reactions. The only way to correct our weak points in this
> critical hour of the Cause, is to courageously face them and then set
> in with the power of God to cure them.

In another letter too, written to her during the Depression, she reminded
her daughter of her many blessings and suggested an antidote to help
her acquire contentment:

> This is not said with any reproach, my precious, but the suggestions
> of self are so subtle and I am constantly and daily meeting them in
> myself and trying to get the upper hand once and for all of that ter-
> rible enemy. I use every day, sometimes twice a day, for all of us the
> prayer to be delivered from self, beginning, 'Keep this sinner clear
> from the stranger'. It has a marvellous effect . . .

Such habits of self-accounting would stand Mary in good stead in years to come. The love of her mother meant more to this child than all the world and the thought of losing her good-pleasure was a strong check on her natural egoism.

* * *

May's own longing for 'Abdu'l-Bahá's good-pleasure was equally passionate. She did her utmost to win it and His joy and pride in her activities during the last years of His life have been well-documented. In the following Tablets to May, translated on the dates indicated (the first two translated by Shoghi Effendi), we read:

1919, February 9th
  I ever remember thee and shall never forget the days I have passed in Montreal and in New-York. I pray God that such days may be made again possible.
  Convey to thy respected husband, longing greeting on my part, and kiss thou the cheeks of thy beloved daughter.

1919, July 25th
  Thou hadst written concerning the convention which thou art going to establish in Canada in the months of September and October. This is highly advisable and I pray God that thou mayest be confirmed and assisted. But this is conditioned upon thy taking care of thy health and the providing of whatever conduces to thy comfort, health and prosperity.

1920, June 27th
  Though others have very often spoken of thee in their letters expressing their joy over thy praiseworthy services to the Kingdom of God, yet no letter directly from thyself hath been received. Verily, thou didst put forth effort and self-sacrifice at the convention more that what thine energy permitted. Therefore thou art being praised by the Supreme Concourse and encompassed by the bounties of the Kingdom of Abhá.
  Extend the utmost love and kindness, on my behalf, to every one of the friends and the maidservants of God, especially to thy honoured husband, Mr. Maxwell! I think always of him and supplicate heavenly

confirmation for him. I hope that he will, day by day, progress and attain to that which is his greatest longing.

With the utmost longing do thou kiss, on my behalf, thy dear daughter on both cheeks. Though she is now a little child, yet I hope that she will grow old in the Kingdom of God. If there is no obstacle and the means of travel are prepared, thou art permitted to make a trip to the Holy Land, if thou wishest. All the members of the family are very eager to meet you

In a Tablet which the Master addressed to Juliet Thompson on 14 May 1920, He refers to

Mrs. Maxwell is in very truth a mercy from God and a token of His grace. In assisting the friends she is self-sacrificing, and in firmness in the Covenant she is a heavenly example.[36]

In another Tablet to Juliet, revealed on 21 June 1920, He again refers to May:

My dear daughter Mrs. May Maxwell is in truth spiritually illumined. She hath no thought, and uttereth no word, save it be in the service of the Kingdom of God.

May herself attested many times that only God's mercy and His grace could have transformed such a weak creature as she was to a handmaid of His threshold. 'Abdu'l-Bahá told one of the early pilgrims from France regarding May Bolles: 'God chose the weakest instrument to manifest His Power.' How else, with all her handicaps and weaknesses, could she have followed such a punishing schedule and become such a successful itinerant teacher during these years? How could she, physically ill for much of her life, turn into one of the great public speakers of her age? She was radically transformed through 'Abdu'l-Bahá's Divine Plan and became a mature woman of radiant eloquence and shining certitude.

With this Charter the Master charged her to proclaim the glad-tidings of Bahá'u'lláh, and she obeyed. He advised her, when she had to speak about the Faith, to pray first, to turn her heart to Him, and

---

36 No copy of the Tablet upon which this approved provisional translation is based has been located at the Bahá'í World Centre; it was rendered from material found among the papers of Amatu'l-Bahá Rúḥíyyih Khánum .

Dr Zia Bagdadi and his bride Zeenat, 1914. They were married in the Maxwell home. 'Abdu'l-Bahá had told May that Zeenat should be married in 'my home in Montreal'. (Photograph from Star of the West, vol. 5, May 17, 1914)

Carrie L. Kinney, called by 'Abdu'l-Bahá 'Vaffa', with May Maxwell

Juliet Thompson and May Maxwell at Green Acre

A family picture: two young girls, front left to right, Mary Maxwell's cousin Elizabeth Maxwell and Mary; others, left to right, Stirling Maxwell, May Maxwell, Mary's 'Aunt Milly', Jean Maxwell and Blythe Maxwell

Atelier of Edward and W. S. Maxwell, Architects. Sutherland Maxwell is standing to the far right in the first row; his brother-in-law Randolph Bolles is in the back row, third from the right; seated in the centre is Miss A. M. Parent, 'AMP', secretary to Sutherland Maxwell

The Colborne Street Milk Depot, an organization founded by May Maxwell to provide milk to needy children; Sutherland Maxwell served as its Treasurer.

At the unveiling of the Tablets of the Divine Plan, 29 April 1919, Mary Maxwell (seated, centre) and Elizabeth Coristine (seated, right), unveiled the Tablets addressed to Canada. Seated to the left of Mary is Bahíyyih Randall

be assured of His assistance. And she followed His instructions to the letter. As long as she felt that she was fulfilling His will, she had the will to live. And when He died, her will died with Him.

It happened suddenly, despite the signs of impending decline. May was not ready for the news. She had been eagerly anticipating her third pilgrimage. Hippolyte Dreyfus had written to her from Tunis on 27 April of that year telling her that he and Laura 'expect to go home by the beginning of June, and Insha'allah visit the Master in September'. She too had been planning to go to the Holy Land, with her daughter this time. In reply to her request for permission, she had received the following Tablet from 'Abdu'l-Bahá, translated on 16 August 1921:

> *Thy letter was received. The contents indicated that thou hast the utmost love towards Mr. and Mrs. James Kehler and dost ask permission to come together and be honored with a visit to the Holy Threshold. For thy sake I give permission . . .*
>
> *Extend my great respect to thy husband, Mr. Maxwell, and cherish thy dear child on my behalf.*

In her generosity towards Juliet Thompson, May had also offered to take this dearly-loved friend with her to the Holy Land as her guest. But Juliet was tied down and could not go at the time when May was given permission. As a result the pilgrimage was postponed to a later date. Too late.

May was at her home in Montreal on 28 November 1921 when the news came. Rúḥíyyih Khánum often spoke of that terrible day when they heard of the Master's passing. She said that she and her father were down in their library and May was resting upstairs in her room when the phone rang. They heard it being picked up. There was a brief silence, followed by a heavy thump. When they ran upstairs, they found May lying on the floor. She had fainted and when she was revived, it was only to faint again. A friend had phoned her and had said, without preamble:[37]

' 'Abdu'l-Bahá has died.'

---

37 The way this devastating news was conveyed to May made her extremely sensitive to how the friends might hear of it. A note written to her that same year by one of the older Bahá'ís, a certain 'Florence' in Pittsfield, New Hampshire, on 3 December bears witness to the efforts May made to protect others from the same shock at a time when she was still reeling under its impact: 'I wonder if you can realize how much your personal note containing the news of the cablegram received at N.Y. means to me. I should have felt like one almost cut off from the Cause I so love, if I had been obliged to wait until I read the message in the Star of the West some time hence.'

May's world eclipsed with those words. The last time she had had such a severe collapse had been in her youth, in France, when she had despaired of ever finding the truth. This time she succumbed because she felt she had lost it again. She had despaired, at her departure from Paris, that she might have lost the good-pleasure of her Lord, and now she was devastated by the thought that she had lost the Master Himself and would never be able to seek His good-pleasure again. 'Abdu'l-Bahá had protected her from her worst fears but where was He now? He had blessed her with permission to go on pilgrimage, but she had missed the chance. Had she failed to serve her Beloved adequately? Had she been denied the sight of His dear face because she no longer deserved to enter His presence? Was she eternally cast aside? May was overcome with self-reproach and self-recrimination. All the anguish of the past, the lost chances, the sense of failure, the fear of having made the wrong choices, assailed her again with the accumulated weight of decades and of death. She feared that by delaying her pilgrimage she had not only deprived herself but her daughter too from meeting 'Abdu'l-Bahá.

One of the few letters from May that have survived from the period just after the passing of 'Abdu'l-Bahá was written to Juliet on 3 December, just five days after she received the dreadful news. It may have survived only because it appears to have never been sent.

My Beloved Juliet: –

Your dear letters and messages have come deepening the love and unity that is now identical with this sacred consciousness of His Presence, this emanation of His Being upon the whole earth.

Your spiritual strength is wonderful and I can only walk with my hand in yours, and arise with you and all His near and dear ones, for it is as though I had never known grief before, as though I had learned for the first time what pain and anguish mean. I cannot look into my own heart for a moment, and I seem to live only in the presence of the Believers. In them He lives and I find Him only in their nearness and love.

It is as though in the twinkling of an eye all things were changed, everything is swept away except reality, we are no longer separate entities struggling through the human veils toward each other, when the veil of His Temple was rent He lifted us into the Temple of His Being.

I feel as you do, my darling, that there will arise from this most mysterious change, for which He made the supreme sacrifice of all that is, a new activity, an activity arising from these unfathomable depths of His love and oneness within us, which shall appear spontaneously from every heart and unfold with a perfect collective power and momentum . . .

It was hard for May to keep her hold on the positive aspects of this 'mysterious change'. She was too easily engulfed by its negative consequences. The absence of 'Abdu'l-Bahá in the material world made her feel forsaken and forlorn. She received a letter from Juliet, dated 2 February, evidently trying to reassure her, to comfort her, to construe meaning out of coincidences:

> Beloved May – in looking in my old diary of <u>1912</u> – I find that the day the Master gave me the rose-water for you and sent me to you was <u>Nov. 28</u> – just ten years to the day [sic], Dear.

She was trying to evoke memories of the Master so that May would feel the touch of His forgiveness and His mercy from the past. But He was gone, and the present had lost Him forever. May could not forgive herself and broke down in fresh tears.

Two days later, on 4 February 1922, she pulled herself together sufficiently to write a letter to Rúhá, one of the daughters of 'Abdu'l-Bahá:

> I am ashamed to speak of my own sorrow, combined with the most bitter remorse, in the face of your most sacred grief. Let me only say that the realization that I did not go to the Master, and that I will never again see that Blessed Being on this earth has nearly crushed out my life. You know I was coming in the Autumn and all my plans were made, even to take Juliet with me, but there were so many obstacles in her way at that time that, alas! I waited for her and lost the opportunity forever. I will not speak of this again . . .
>
> I am making arrangements to sail with my little girl as soon as possible and I hope that it may not be long before I can attain to that Holy Spot and cleanse my Soul in those healing waters . . .

The root of her disability is hinted in this letter. The thought that she would 'never again see that Blessed Being' was more than she could bear, but it seems from her own words that she had not considered the possibility of turning, instead, to the one whom that 'Blessed Being' had appointed in His Will and Testament.

Despite her grief, she managed to travel to Chicago that Riḍván. She was even able to speak to the friends on 23 April 1922 at the Auditorium Hotel. Her theme – 'the new springtime of the oneness of humanity'[38] – illustrates how hard she must have been trying to pull herself out of her depression, how earnestly she was striving to overcome herself. But she could not do it alone. It was clear that she needed spiritual as well as psychological assistance. Sutherland was certain that Shoghi Effendi was the only one who could save her. Dr Zia Bagdadi, whom she met at the Convention, urged her to write and ask for permission to visit the Shrines. But with every passing day she grieved more at the finality of the Master's passing, at the stark reality of what it would mean to go to Haifa with Him gone. She delayed writing to the Guardian. And once he left for Switzerland that summer, she may have sensed only a great void in her heart and a terrible absence at the centre of her faith.

All was darkness before her. Sutherland was at a loss as to how to help her, for May recoiled now from the idea of pilgrimage. He urged her to write and ask the Greatest Holy Leaf but she shrank from doing it and felt herself wholly unworthy. He tried hard to convince her to make this journey in the company of a maid and their 12-year-old daughter, but to no avail. He would have taken her to the Holy Land himself, he told her, just as he had come to Paris to marry her twenty years before, but he was carrying too many heavy responsibilities on his shoulders.

It was a particularly critical juncture in the life of William Sutherland Maxwell. The passing of 'Abdu'l-Bahá, coinciding as it did with the aftermath of World War I, not only shook his domestic calm and disrupted the peace and order in the house on Pine Avenue, but also signalled the end of a significant chapter in his professional life. In the middle of one of the biggest projects ever undertaken by his firm – the construction of the West Wing of the Château Frontenac in Quebec City – Sutherland's brother Edward was diagnosed with terminal cancer. This partner in his work, this mentor and guide in his profession, this close companion in the world of art and dear brother who was seven years older than himself, had always had a profound influence on Sutherland's life. He had not only been responsible for his education

---

38 *Star of the West*, vol. 13, no. 4 (17 May 1922), p. 72.

but had become the mainstay of his career as well as the senior partner in the Maxwell firm. His sickness was a severe shock to their business relations as well as a painful blow to Sutherland personally. It must have been terribly hard for him to realize that their lifelong partnership was coming to an end. The fact that Edward's sickness lasted for more than a year and he was watching his dear brother fading before his very eyes must have made it even harder for him.

When he cabled the Holy Land in the summer of that year, begging for prayers for May, he must have been at his wit's end. It was one of the darkest moments of his life. For at the same time as worrying about his brother and the future prospects of the firm, Sutherland was obliged, during the next seven months, to travel back and forth to different cities – to New York, to Washington DC and to Baltimore – where his wife was thought to be on her death bed. May had tumbled into a spiral of despondency. Her instructions to Sutherland regarding what he should do and how he should act in the event of her death must have been deeply distressing to him. Her thoughts circled obsessively around her daughter.

Amatu'l-Bahá Rúḥíyyih Khánum several times spoke of the terrible impact on the family of those days.

A letter from Rúḥá Khánum written to Sutherland on 8 July 1922 testifies to the concern felt by members of the Master's family at the news of his wife's illness. It indicates to what extremes this very private and discreet man had been pushed to beg for prayers from the Greatest Holy Leaf:

> We were shocked when we first received the telegram about her serious illness. The Greatest Holy Leaf and all the Holy Family went to the Holy Tomb and read the Healing Tablet for her . . .

Two months later, on 6 September 1922, a letter from Dr Zia Bagdadi to May, replying to questions she had written to him on 1 September, helped her to see what she had been experiencing during this terrible time. A true physician, he placed an unerring finger on the pulse of her pain and described her condition:

> All afflictions, troubles or calamities, whether physical or spiritual, are of two kinds. First: troubles that we bring upon ourselves, which are indeed divine calamities and punishments. Second: troubles that

result in blessings: 'My calamity is my providence'. Your trouble is of the second type, not the first. 'When the fire of love becomes intense, the harvest of reason becomes consumed.' Your mind or reason was to a certain extent consumed because of your intense love to [sic] the Beloved Master and this became manifest after His ascension. Nabil, the poet, drowned himself after the ascension of Bahá'u'lláh. Hadji Mirza Seyed Hassan Afnan drowned himself a few days before the ascension of 'Abdu'l-Bahá because he did not want to see that dark hour! Ismail Agha, the faithful gardener, cut his own throat at the Shrine of 'Abdu'l-Bahá, because the harvest of their [sic] reason was consumed. In like manner, you are in the same class of the faithful ones and you are going through the same test as the sincere ones have gone through. Yet 'there is ease after difficulties, and happiness after sorrow'.

As that terrible summer gave way to autumn, May slowly groped for her equilibrium. It is clear that her trusted friend, Dr Bagdadi, was responsible for helping her recover some measure of calm. Like Sutherland, he encouraged May once more to turn to the Shrines to assuage her grief; he tried to remind her that she had not been abandoned, that she was not alone, and that there was someone there in the Holy Land from whom she should ask for permission to go on pilgrimage:

> In regard to my humble suggestion for you to sail for Haifa. I thought that the Holy Land where the Sacred Shrines of Bahá'u'lláh, 'Abdu'l-Bahá and the Báb are, is the place where your heart and soul would be calm, quiet and at peace. Nevertheless, I suggested to take a permission from the Greatest Holy Leaf and if she approved of your journey, then there could be no doubt that the desired good results would be obtained . . .

This gentle reminder by Dr Bagdadi must have been helpful and comforting. Earlier that spring she had responded to an invitation to visit Haifa from an individual member of 'Abdu'l-Bahá's family, but Dr Bagdadi was reminding her that she could only go to the Holy Land if she was invited by the appointed Head of the Faith. Over the summer, her grief had paralysed her so much that she could not bring herself to do anything but think of death, but he was reminding her of the binding power of the

Covenant and of the Master's Will. He was recalling for her that although 'Abdu'l-Bahá had passed away, the Guardian had been appointed in His stead, and that although Shoghi Effendi may have been absent from Haifa, the Greatest Holy Leaf was at the helm of the Cause. It was possibly his timely assistance that enabled her to find the courage to write a letter to the Greatest Holy Leaf that autumn. Although there is no copy amongst her papers, the answer, dated 12 December 1922, has survived:

> O lover of the Truth,
> The contents of your letter of the 9th October 1922 were perused with happiness and joy; we could read within those lines the wonderful devotion and sincerity that you bear towards the Beloved Master 'Abdu'l-Bahá. We have experienced it time and again that there is no greater force in the world that can bring about wonders except the unique dominating power of the Spirit of the Master which guards the devoted friends of God the world over. The greater the unity of the believers the greater is the expression of that Divine Power . . . special prayers were rendered on your behalf at the Holy Shrines seeking for you blessing and Grace . . .

It is remarkable to consider, in retrospect, that many of May's letters to Mary dated August and September 1922, and filled with the most telling guidance and sensitive counsel, were written in the aftermath of this crisis. Somehow, she found the energy to meet with the Bahá'ís in New York again that autumn, and was picking up, even long-distance, some of her activities. On 27 October 1922 she wrote to Sutherland from New York, telling him that she was feeling a little better. How relieved he must have been to read all her instructions to him; how glad he must have been that she cared enough to write of such matters again. She expressed the same sentiment:

> Oh, how homesick it makes me to be with you all but I am so thankful I can take this interest in it.

But even when May was so deeply depressed and Sutherland so sadly oppressed by work and grief at his brother's rapid decline, neither of them forgot their responsibilities to the Faith or to society. It is remarkable to note how much they were both engaged in reaching out towards others at this time. They were, if anything, as heavily engaged, as wholly implicated, and as committed to their responsibilities towards the world around them as they were burdened by their personal concerns. Two examples may suffice to illustrate this.

On 18 August 1922 May wrote a letter to William Randolph Hearst, the newspaper magnate. From the content it is evident that she was discharging the responsibility and trust which 'Abdu'l-Bahá had given her, in 1920, to convey His words to Mr Hearst. One also distinctly feels that she was making sure she had carried out the instructions of the Master before her demise.

Dear Mr. Hearst: –

You will naturally not remember me although your Mother was a dear friend of mine, and my Mother, since my girlhood.

You also know of your Mother's interest in the early days of the Bahá'í religion, and of a small group who accompanied her to visit 'Abdu'l-Bahá.

I remember that at that time 'Abdu'l-Bahá spoke of you and of the possibilities of your great future, and as the influence of this great educator of humanity has become so universal, and his impress so deep on the hearts and minds of people – I feel that I cannot longer delay in communicating the following message to you.

It was my wish to see you and speak to you, and in passing through New York last winter I made the effort, but you were away.

Two or three years ago in a letter to a friend of mine, 'Abdu'l-Bahá said it was his hope that your newspapers would become the first newspapers of America, because they stood for the rights of the people, and that it was his wish that the blessed name of Hearst (referring to your Mother and her wonderful life) should become perpetuated and immortal.

In a letter to me about a year before his death 'Abdu'l-Bahá wrote: 'Say to Mr. Hearst that it is my hope that he will come entirely under the Shadow of Bahá'u'lláh.'

As I am at present in this city very ill, I felt that I must discharge this trust which 'Abdu'l-Bahá left with me, both because of the love I have always had for your Mother and because of my sincere sympathy with all your deep and far-reaching services for human progress.

Amatu'l-Bahá Rúḥíyyih Khánum always added, whenever she told this story, that her mother never received any response to this letter. One month later, however, on 12 September 1922, Mr Maxwell did receive a letter from the Secretary of President Harding in response to a letter of concern he had written, apparently on behalf of the Montreal Spiritual Assembly, to the President of the United States of America after hearing the news that the First Lady was suffering from kidney failure:

> My dear Mr. Maxwell: The President has seen your message and he asks me to convey assurance of his very grateful appreciation. He will be glad to tell Mrs. Harding, at a suitable time, of your expression of sympathy and interest.
> Sincerely yours, Geo B. Christian Jr., Secretary to the President.

At the end of November that year, when May was slightly better, an old friend who was a wealthy industrialist and owned his own private train, offered to transport her at a slow pace back from New York to Montreal. She was so fragile by then that she could not bear rapid movement, but Seward Prosser was happy to come to her rescue. He had been a family friend of the Bolles' many years before and was possibly one of May's most ardent admirers from the time of her youth. When Marie Squires had returned to America in 1901[39] she wrote to May from Illinois saying, 'Mr. Prosser came to see me in Englewood and he asked so much of you, he loves you so tenderly.' The faithfulness of this friend proved to be unfailing.

Once Seward Prosser helped May home, she evidently improved enough to consider the possibility of pilgrimage at last. Most important, she found the courage and the spiritual resources to ask if she could come. 'Abdu'l-Bahá had granted her permission to return to the land of her heart's desire, but since He was no more, she now turned to the Guardian, and humbly asked again.

Early the following year, on 29 January 1923, she received a cable in response. Shoghi Effendi's answer was brief and to the point:

MOST WELCOME TO HOLY LAND.

It was an invitation to begin anew.

---

39 Her letter, dated 1 July 1901, was written before she married Herbert Hopper.

Some Reflections on the Maxwell Family in Scotland and Canada from the 1700s to 1902

by
Henry Yates[1]

The Scottish origins of the Maxwell family

The Maxwell family is a significant part of the history of Scotland. The ancient and honourable house of Maxwell is considered to be one of the most distinguished in Scotland. It is believed that in the twelfth century, the family was founded by Maccus, son of Undwyn. The name Maxwell, or Maccus, is thought to be of Saxon origin. Maccuswell or Macceswell, meaning Maccus's well or pool, was the first form of the name, and over time became Maxwell.

The Maxwell family in the 18th and 19th centuries in Scotland and Montreal

Family history in the 1700s is rather sparse but begins with a female, a Wilson, born in circa 1765 who married a Maxwell, probably in Jedburgh, a border town about 40 miles south-east of Edinburgh. To this

---

1 'This summary was compiled in January 2007 from information from my personal knowledge and from family documents in my possession. Other references used are: (1) *The Architecture of Edward and W. S. Maxwell*, published by The Montreal Museum of Fine Arts, 1991; (2) 'The Maxwell Family', a family tree handwritten by Henry Yates in Montreal in 1981; (3) *Maxwell History and Genealogy*, by Florence Wilson Houston, Laura Cowan Blaine, and Ella Dunn Mellette, published by Press of C.E. Pauley & Co., Indianapolis Engraving Co., Indianapolis, Indiana, 1916. This book contains information about the Scottish origins of the Maxwell family and the Maxwells in the USA' (note by Henry Yates).

couple was born a son, Edward Maxwell, in 1805 at Jedburgh. Agnes Reid, born in 1806, and Edward Maxwell married on 31 December 1824 in the same town.

Edward was a joiner and carpenter. In 1829 he sailed to Montreal from Scotland, probably spending four to six uncomfortable weeks on a small sailing ship about 120 feet long. No doubt he was required to supply his own blankets for his bed and some food. His wife and at least one child most likely came the following year after Edward had arranged for living accommodation. In 1830 a letter was addressed to Edward as follows: Edward Maxwell, Joiner, Montreal, North America, c/o M. A. Stevenson, Grocer, Montreal.

In 1830 the couple lived on St Gabriel St, St Anne Suburb, which was near the harbour of Montreal. They attended the Gabriel Street Presbyterian Church, one of the few Presbyterian churches in Montreal at that time; many of the residents were French-speaking and belonged to the Roman Catholic Church. Nine children, some not reaching adulthood, were born to them.

The Victoria Bridge was completed in 1860, built across the St Lawrence River from Montreal Island to the south shore. This significant railway bridge, built of steel on stone piers, was one of the longest bridges in the world. The Prince of Wales, eldest son of Queen Victoria, came to Montreal to officially open this bridge. A large wooden platform was built for the occasion and the chief builder was none other than Edward Maxwell.

Both Edward and Agnes are buried in Mount Royal Cemetery in Montreal, Agnes dying in 1865 aged 59 and Edward dying in 1876 at the age of 71.

Of Edward and Agnes's nine children, their fifth child, Edward John, was born in Montreal on 20 February 1836. He lived in Montreal his entire life and on 29 April 1861 married Johan MacBean of Montreal. The Minister was Reverend Alex F. Kemp, of the Knox Presbyterian Church.

Johan's parents, William and Johan (Sutherland) MacBean had been married in Aberdeen, Scotland on 25 July 1822. William was born in Fochabers, a town on the River Spey 57 miles north-west of Aberdeen. As a young man he took up residence in Aberdeen, walking there from Fochabers. William and Johan immigrated to Montreal in 1832, the city then having a population of 32,000. The MacBeans had eight children, the seventh being Johan who was born on 7 September 1836 at St Henri, an inner suburb of Montreal.

Edward John was also a carpenter and builder, following his father's craft. In 1862 he founded the E. J. Maxwell Company, which purchased hardwood from Canada and some wood of rare species from other countries. This wood was then milled into refined lumber for sale to builders. In the 1890s Montreal became prosperous, with much building taking place, and the E. J. Maxwell Company prospered too. This company was well respected in the lumber business and remained in the Maxwell family until the 1970s.

Edward John built a large house on Côte St Antoine Road, probably in the early 1860s. Then it was located in the fields about three miles west of Montreal, but is now Westmount, an inner suburb of the City. This impressive house still stands.

Edward John and Johan were parents to four children, two daughters, Jessie Gertrude and Amelia Johan, born 2 March 1862 and 29 May 1863, respectively, followed by two sons, Edward, born 31 December 1867 and William Sutherland, born 14 November 1874.

It is assumed that both boys were either tutored or attended local public school near their parents' home. At the age of 14 Edward informed his parents, to their disappointment, that he was quitting school to study architecture, but knowing the determination of their son, they had no option but to accept his decision. He apprenticed with an architect in Montreal, Alexander Dunlop, who was somewhat accomplished, but little has been written in the architectural records about him. He designed a large structure, St James Methodist Church, on St Catharine St West now located in one of the commercial areas of Montreal. This church still stands as a prominent structure. Edward was with Dunlop from about 1882 to 1888. Architecture was not then taught at Canadian and probably American universities and young Canadians were encouraged to apprentice at American architectural firms. In 1888 Edward was in Boston at the well-known firm of Shepley, Rutan & Coolidge, the successor firm of H. H. Richardson. Richardson (1838–1886) had a short but brilliant architectural career, developing the well-known shingle style, particularly for country houses in New England. Also he designed many prominent buildings in America.

In 1891, Shepley, Rutan & Coolidge sent the able young architect to Montreal to supervise one of their commissions, the Board of

Trade Building. A year later Edward was still acting for Shepley during continued construction of this building. This job was extremely significant for Edward because he came in contact with many of Montreal's prominent businessmen in commerce and industry, particularly in the Canadian Pacific Railway Company and some major banks. Montreal was then the business capital of Canada, with over 60 per cent of the influential and wealthy families living in what was called the Square Mile. In early 1892, at the age of 24, Edward opened his own architectural firm with the reluctant blessing of his Boston employer. Many of Montreal's prominent residents, with whom he had come in contact at the Board of Trade, recognized his architectural abilities and his good character. He began designing large houses for them, many of which still exist in the Square Mile, and some are owned by McGill University.

In about 1895, Edward was engaged to a lady whose name is not recorded. In that year he was ill and recovering at his parents' home. By chance his third cousin, Elizabeth Ellen Aitchison, living in Potsdam, a small town in upstate New York, was visiting her relatives in Montreal. Oral history relates that Edward saw her beautiful face through the crack of his bedroom door and recorded a vivid mental image. They were married on 15 December 1896 at the First Presbyterian Church in Potsdam.

Edward designed a small house attached to his parents' house that had many distinctive features including an oval dining room and a large seashell design over the front door. The happy couple lived in this house, which still stands, until 1902 when they moved to a substantial house of his own design at 3480 Peel Street in the Square Mile.

Elizabeth and Edward were the loving parents of four children, Blythe (b.1900), Jean (b.1903), Stirling (b.1905) and Elizabeth (b.1908), all growing up at the Peel Street house that remained in the family until 1955.

William's architectural apprenticeship began in his brother's firm in 1892. With Edward's encouragement William trained at a large architectural firm in Boston, Winslow & Wetherell, from 1895 to 1898, at which time he returned to Montreal. He became attracted to the French Beaux-Arts style of architecture and by October 1899 he was in Paris.

There he lived at 83 Boulevard Montparnasse, the same address as the highly acclaimed Canadian painter Maurice Cullen. William was not registered as a student at the École des Beaux-Arts, but he became a student at the atelier of Jean-Louis Pascal, a leading Beaux-Arts archi-tect. This large atelier was essentially a private school of architecture with both French and foreign students, and provided an opportunity for stimulating exchange of ideas. William was a talented artist and had a skill for drawing that made him ideally suited to the École des Beaux-Arts concept of considering the architect as an artist.

William met May Ellis Bolles in Paris in 1899 and they were married in London on 8 May 1902. That same year they became residents of Montreal.

Edward's architectural practice was highly successful, and in 1901 William joined the firm as a partner, with the firm's name being changed to Edward and W. S. Maxwell. This was a fortuitous event, for they were both talented architects with Edward having an astute business acumen and William having an exceptional artistic ability. The twelve years to the beginning of World War I were extremely prosperous in Canada and the Maxwells obtained numerous major commissions across the country, particularly in Montreal, that resulted in their firm having one of the most influential architectural practices in Canada.

APPENDIX II

The Artistic Achievements of William Sutherland Maxwell

by
Nancy Yates[1]

William S. Maxwell (1874–1952) is best known as an outstanding architect, not only of the Shrine of the Báb but also as a partner, with his older brother Edward, of the largest and most preeminent architectural firm in Canada during the first quarter of the 20th century. Although his architectural talents were great he was also 'a man whose interest in every aspect of artistic expression in all ages and cultures was universal and profound'.[2] He was a passionate collector of European, Canadian and Asian artwork and antiques and possessed the second finest Japanese print collection in North America after J. P. Morgan in New York. He also had a great love of books and his collection of art, architecture and first edition books was one of the best in Canada. An extremely gifted artist, he always had a sketchbook with him to paint and draw his surroundings locally and on his many trips within Canada, the United States and Europe. Seventeen of his sketchbooks

---

1   Nancy Yates is the great-granddaughter of Edward Maxwell. She is an appraiser in Fine and Decorative Arts, specializing in 19th–20th century European, American and Canadian paintings, works on paper and sculpture, and is a member of the Appraisers Association of America. She obtained her Bachelor of Arts degree in Art History from the University of Toronto, and continued her education at New York University with courses in Appraisal Studies and Fine and Decorative Arts. For some ten years she was associated with Christie's International in Toronto and Christie's East in New York. After the passing of Amatu'l-Bahá Rúhíyyih Khánum, Nancy was invited to Haifa by the Universal House of Justice to go over all the fine and decorative arts of W. S. Maxwell which were in the possession of Amatu'l-Bahá. In six months she was able to prepare a thorough and detailed report and catalogue. Nancy presently resides in New York.

2   Letter from Mary Maxwell Rabbani [Amatu'l-Bahá Rúhíyyih Khánum] from the Philippines to Irena Murray, Montreal, 23 July 1989, quoted in Murray, 'The Old Craze of Buying Books: The Libraries of Edward and William Maxwell', p. 40.

still exist along with over 200 paintings, watercolours and drawings. His contribution to the artistic community in Canada was significant as he was either the founder or president of several art clubs and institutions which promoted Canadian artists and the arts in general. He also took great pride in cultivating relationships with leading artists and craftsmen who collaborated with him on many architectural commissions. He could best be described as a renaissance man; as his daughter Mary Maxwell Rabbani states, he was 'fundamentally . . . a scholar and a creator and very much of a recluse. He wasn't interested in social life, but he had a passion for everything to do with art and architecture. He had a knowledge that was literally encyclopedic.'[3]

Early training: Montreal, Boston and Paris

His love for architecture and the arts was most likely influenced by his older brother of seven years, Edward (1867–1923), who after briefly apprenticing for an architect in Montreal upon graduating from Montreal High School, spent three years (1888–1891) training in the architectural firm of Shepley, Rutan and Coolidge in Boston. This firm was the successor to H. H. Richardson (1838–1886), who was the leading architect in the United States until his death. Edward gained an extensive knowledge of draftsmanship and design in Boston, which was unattainable in Canada at the time. American architects were highly influenced by the École des Beaux-Arts of Paris which emphasized a knowledge of the history of architecture along with a strong sense of design and also encouraged the artistic collaboration between architects, painters and sculptors. This Edward brought to Montreal when he started his own architectural firm in 1892 at the age of 24 and employed the Canadian sculptors Henry Beaumont and George W. Hill. He later went on to provide studio space above his office, at 6 Beaver Hall Square, to Canadian artists such as the three Des Clayes sisters, Laura Muntz Lyall and George Horne Russell.

William's love for drawing must have started young. The earliest known dated works by him (January 1891) are six small pen on paper drawings he copied from Tristan Ellis's book *Sketching from Nature* at the age of 16. They consist of four small drawings of people along with a sketch of a sailboat and one of a watermill. His earliest known

---

3   ibid.

watercolour is dated May 1891 depicting a landscape scene of trees in a field. He appears to have been self-taught at this young age and learned by doing pen and pencil sketches of drawings he found in books and magazines, mostly of men and ladies in fancy dress. There are several known examples dating from 1892 and 1893. At this time he also worked as a draftsman (1892–95) in his brother's Montreal architectural firm, where his natural talent to create elaborate and detailed architectural drawings was cultivated. Not only was he surrounded by the stimulation of Edward's bustling architectural firm but also by the artists and craftsmen with whom Edward associated.

With the encouragement of his brother, William went to Boston (at the age of 21) to further his training as an architect. He worked in the office of Winslow and Wetherell from 1895 to 1898. His real talent for decorative domestic interior design blossomed as he worked on drawings for office buildings, hotels and private homes designed by the firm. His daughter, Mary Maxwell Rabbani, said of him: 'They found that he could draw beautifully, so they gave him all the details of the buildings, the cornices and so on.'[4] He writes to his brother in 1895, 'I have been working a good deal with Henry Forbes Bigelow lately and am now carrying out a large country house for him, he seems satisfied with my work . . . He is a very clever young fellow and knows more about planning, designing etc. than anyone else in the office.'[5]

He also attended drawing classes in the evenings at the Boston Architectural Club and would frequently sketch details of Boston buildings. On the weekends he occasionally took sketching trips to nearby Marblehead, Massachusetts and Portsmouth, New Hampshire. There is a series of still life watercolours dating from 1898 (age 23) that one would assume were painted while in drawing class. Two sketchbooks also remain from his Boston years.

He had a great love for books, which continued throughout his life. As an architect in training it was important to study the history of architecture and this was mostly achieved through books, which he avidly collected. In his letter to Edward from Boston in 1895 he writes: 'I have been getting on very fairly down here, have attended classes (2) at the Atelier and have learned considerable thereby. I have caught my old

---

4   Interview by Professor John Bland with Mary Maxwell Rabbani at McGill University, Montreal, 19 November 1980. From the files of Mary Maxwell Rabbani, Haifa, Israel.

5   Letter from W. S. Maxwell, Boston to Edward Maxwell, Montreal, 16 March 1895. From the collection of Mary Maxwell Rabbani, Haifa, Israel.

craze of buying books etc . . . You asked me to look out for new books. I can confidently recommend the following – Nash's Elizabethan houses, 5 vols., original edition . . . and "L'Architecture Française", 7 vols.'[6]

In February 1899, at the age of 24, William left for Paris to study for a year and a half in the atelier of Jean-Louis Pascal (1837–1920), a leading Beaux-Arts architect closely associated with the École des Beaux-Arts. One of Pascal's students recalled, 'His ideal was architecture that was and looked distinguished.'[7] Many of the leading architects in the United States studied there, including several at the Boston firm of Winslow and Wetherell (where William was apprenticed). He lived at 83 Boulevard Montparnasse, which was the same address as the Canadian painter Maurice Cullen (one of the first Canadian painters to paint in the Impressionistic style) who later painted murals in Montreal private homes designed by Edward and W. S. Maxwell. William wrote to a friend: 'Paris is delightful and I wish I could prolong my stay for years.' [8]

William's artistic talent and love of drawing made him ideally suited for the training required in the Beaux-Arts method where the architect was considered first and foremost an artist, with the emphasis on exquisitely executed drawings and plans. This can be seen in one of William's most well-known watercolours entitled 'A State Barge', depicting an elaborately decorated bow of an old sailing ship. It may have been a practice exercise executed in 1900 for an entry for the Prix Rougevin, a competition for the rendering of ornaments in an architectural context. It was later exhibited at the Art Association of Montreal, Spring Exhibition in 1901. Another example is a watercolour rendering, painted in Paris, titled 'Salle des Fêtes' showing a front and side elevation of a classic Beaux-Arts building modelled on the Paris Opera House. The detail and design on this study are beautiful, emphasizing symmetry, grandness and classicism, and incorporating symbolic sculpture, all perfect examples of the Beaux-Arts style.

Now that William was in Europe he must have marvelled at seeing the buildings he had only read about in architectural books. In April

---

6   ibid.
7   Francis Swales, a former student of Pascal, quoted in 'The Teaching of Architecture at the École des Beaux-Arts', in Chaffee, *The Architecture of the École des Beaux-Arts*, pp. 61–109; and in Pepall, 'The Education and Training of William S. Maxwell', p. 31.
8   Letter from W. S. Maxwell to G. A. Monette, Paris, February, 1900, Province of Quebec Association of Architects correspondence, 06-P-124-1, in Pepall, 'The Education and Training of William S. Maxwell', p. 30.

1900 he went on a sketching trip in northern France with his soon-to-be brother-in-law, Randolph Bolles, visiting Compiègne, Pierrefonds, Soissons, Rheims, Laon and Nyon. He writes to May Bolles:

> Randolph and I arrived at about three o'clock at Laon which promises to be very interesting as seen from the station. We both made straight for the cathedral as soon as the choice of hotels etc. was completed. I, almost as soon as I saw the building, started to do some uncalled for criticizing, beautiful Rheims with its lofty nave and innumerable attractions has quite spoilt me for the "smaller fry" – although my enthusiasm did not rise to the occasion, do not let me give you the idea that Laon is not interesting . . . [9]

After completing his studies in Paris he furthered his education by travelling through Europe to sketch well-known architectural buildings. Six sketchbooks exist from this time. In June he went to the Loire Valley region of France, visiting Tours and Amboise. In July he travelled to the Normandy region, visiting St Denis, Rouen, St Maclou, Coutances, Caen and Bayeux, and in August he went to the Brittany region, visiting Dinan and St Malo. In August he passed through Lucerne, Switzerland on his way to Italy, where he spent two months visiting Milan, Brescia, Verona, Venice, Padua, Ravenna, Bologna, Pisa, Pistoia, Florence, Perugia, Assisi, Rome, Pompeii, Caseria and Naples. His sketchbooks from this period show beautiful pencil renderings of details of many cathedrals and important buildings and contain copious notes on the architectural aspects of each. On one drawing from Caen he notes: 'Stunning old little church – remarkable for interesting details here and there. Odd patched up plan. Staircase suggested by interesting detail. Good Francis 1st work on exterior.'[10] He also filled his sketchbooks with scenes of the cities and towns he visited.

---

9   Letter from W. S. Maxwell, Hotel de le Bannière, Laon, France to May Bolles (Maxwell), dated 19 April 1900. From the collection of Mary Maxwell Rabbani, Haifa, Israel.
10 W. S. Maxwell sketchbook, July 1900. From the collection of Mary Maxwell Rabbani, Haifa, Israel.

Edward and William Maxwell architectural firm, Montreal 1902–1923

In late 1900 he returned to Montreal and in 1901, at the age of 27, joined his brother as a partner in his architectural firm. He brought to the firm his outstanding talent as a skilled draftsman executing beautiful drawings and plans. His great love was ornamentation and decorative details such as cartouches and cornices, trophies and swags used to decorate the interior and façades of buildings. He had a sure sense of composition and a remarkable feel for decoration. This led him to not only work on the decorative elements of the buildings the firm was designing but also to submit drawings for furniture, rugs and fittings (plaster, carved decoration, etc.) to be installed inside the structures. He formed a collaboration in 1911 with the Bromsgrove Guild of Canada, a group of Montreal artisans affiliated with the Bromsgrove Guild in England that hand built furniture and created intricately carved interior panels in the tradition of the Arts and Crafts designers of England. In its day they were Montreal's finest wood-crafting and cabinet shop. The Guild executed William's furniture designs, based on historical English, French and Italian examples, to be placed in public buildings and private homes completed by the firm for the remainder of its existence. Another artist collaborator was Paul Beau, an outstanding Canadian metal craftsman who provided fine hand-hammered brass and copper pieces for the firm's buildings. The firm of Castle & Son provided stained glass, furniture, rugs, wallpaper and draperies for a number of private residences. The well-known sculptor George Hill was asked to carve decorations on furniture and panelling for two private residences. Several artists were commissioned to carry out murals in both private and public buildings: Maurice Cullen, Frederick Challener, Frederick Hutchison and Clarence Gagnon. William greatly enjoyed the companionship of the artists and craftsmen with whom he collaborated, and worked closely with them to execute the decorative aspects of buildings. His daughter, Mary Maxwell Rabbani, recalls that 'her father had a close working rapport with these artisans, who "adored him" '.[11] He placed great importance on the work of craftsmen and became a member of the Canadian Handicrafts Guild.

---

11 Interview with Mary Maxwell Rabbani by France Gagnon Pratte and Rosalind Pepall, 1 April 1989, Haifa, quoted by Rosalind Pepall, 'Craftsmen and Decorative Artists', p. 48.

The wealth of the Maxwell brothers' clients allowed them to pay for handcrafted work by these highly skilled craftsmen and as a result the workmanship in their buildings was outstanding. One of the most beautiful private residences designed by Edward and William was a home in Montreal for James T. Davis, a prominent building contractor. More than any other home they designed, this one was a showcase for the many artisans and craftsmen they worked with. 'The fittings and furnishings reflected the most fashionable tastes found in grand North American city residences. Each room had its own stylistic character conveyed through its colour, furniture design and architectural motifs.'[12] The drawing room was decorated in the style of 18th-century France. The breakfast room was inspired by the English Regency period. The billiard room 'decoration offered one of the best Canadian examples of the ideals of the British Arts and Crafts movement, which emphasized handcraftsmanship, the use of simple materials, reference to local traditions and the integration of the crafted arts with architecture.'[13] Maurice Cullen painted three murals for this room that were incorporated into the panelling. Artisans created a stained-glass panel for the entrance door, hand-carved wall panelling, brass door handles and plates, fireplace tiles and the billiard table. Edward was the more outgoing and social of the two brothers and he was a very astute and enterprising businessman. Montreal at that time was the financial and social capital of Canada and he entertained and mingled with the Montreal elite, building friendships with them and acquiring commissions through his connections. Mary Maxwell Rabbani has said of her uncle: 'He painted well, he drew well, he was a sound and fine architect. He was not only the architect but the engineering principal in the firm with a sound head for figures and engineering.'[14] William was more introspective, a true artist and designer, more interested in executing plans and designing decorative elements and furniture for the jobs Edward acquired. As their roles evolved, Edward, although a good architect, spent an increasing amount of time dealing with the business side of things and William became the main design influence.

As Edward and William's partnership developed over the years, their strengths complemented each other and their firm grew to become

---

12 Pepall, 'City Houses'. p .137.
13 ibid.
14 Interview by Professor John Bland with Mary Maxwell Rabbani at McGill University, Montreal, 19 November 1980. From the files of Mary Maxwell Rabbani, Haifa, Israel.

the largest in Canada, employing 56 draftsmen. The firm practised all branches of architecture: residential, institutional, commercial and civic, specializing in the dominant Beaux-Arts style which emphasized classicism. The brothers' timing was fortuitous as Canada was a young, rich country at the turn of the century, in need of many monumental public buildings as well as new mansions for the wealthy elite – builders of the Canadian Pacific Railway, founders of banks and businessmen. It had been routine for Canadians to bring in architects from Boston and New York, but Edward and William insisted for the first time that Canadians could and should win competitions to build public buildings in their own country. This they did to great success, winning competitions to design the breathtaking Parliament building for the Province of Saskatchewan in Regina (1908), the Art Gallery for the Montreal Art Association, now the Montreal Museum of Fine Arts (1910), and alterations and additions to the Château Frontenac Hotel in Quebec City for the Canadian Pacific Railway Company (1919). These commissions set new standards in design for Canadian architects.

There were many other important commissions including:

1903 – Canadian Pacific Railway Station and Royal Alexandra Hotel, Winnipeg
1905 – Alexandra Hospital, Montreal
1906 – Church of the Messiah, Montreal
1910 – Dominion Express building, Montreal
1911 – Palliser Hotel, Calgary

They also designed private residences (50 in total) for their clientèle, who were the leaders of Canadian finance and industry of the period, in Montreal and its surrounding countryside as well as St Andrews, New Brunswick (a wealthy summer retreat). They used a variety of styles to suit their clients' wishes, such as the American Shingle style (popular on the Eastern Seaboard), rustic Adirondack style and the Château style.

It was not long before William's talents were acknowledged by his peers and he was elected an Associate into the Royal Canadian Academy of Art in 1909, an Academician in 1914, and in the 1930 catalogue is listed as its vice-president for the 1929–30 term;[15] a patron of the Beaux

---

15 Royal Canadian Academy catalogues of 1930–1937 (excluding 1934, which is not available to the author) list W. S. Maxwell as vice-president; that he was also vice-president in 1938 is confirmed in Murray, *Edward & W. S. Maxwell: Guide to the Archive.*

Arts Atelier in 1912; a fellow of the Royal Institute of British Architects (FRIBA) in 1928; a fellow of the Royal Architectural Institute of Canada (FRAIC) in 1931 and its president in 1934;[16] and a Councillor of the Province of Quebec Association of Architects in 1908, becoming its president in 1914. In 1935 he was honoured with the presentation of the King's Jubilee Medal for Architecture on the occasion of the Twenty-Fifth Anniversary of the Accession of His Majesty to the throne.

The Maxwell Brothers architectural firm was a full-service operation that would design a home for a wealthy client right down to the table linens. This would entail either designing the furnishings to be made by local craftsmen or going on shopping sprees to mostly New York and occasionally London and Paris to acquire antique furnishings and paintings to decorate their clients' homes. In New York they would frequent the Anderson Galleries auction house, later to become Sotheby's. William also used his connections with leading artists such as Maurice Cullen (his friend and well-known Canadian painter) to paint murals in a few of the mansions in Montreal they designed for the barons of Canadian industry.

On their trips to the auction houses and dealers abroad to shop for their clients William and Edward would also shop for themselves and often came back with Old Master paintings, European and American antique furniture and Oriental artworks to decorate their own homes. Both brothers became ardent collectors of art and antiques, with William being the more passionate of the two and in the end owning a larger and finer art and antique collection. Their homes were mini-museums filled with items they had acquired in Montreal, New York and Europe.

Sadly, Edward died of cancer at the young age of 56, which must have left a large void in William's life. They were not only brothers and partners in their architectural firm but also firm friends who shared a love for the arts. They were both family orientated and conveniently lived around the corner from each other, which made it easy for family members to get together. William's daughter, Mary, was two years younger than Edward's younger daughter, Elizabeth, and they became more like sisters than cousins, growing up so close to each other. Mary Maxwell Rabbani has said, 'We were a very close family and remained very close all our lives. Elizabeth and I were very, very close, just like

---

16 Letter of 9 April 1934 from W. S. Maxwell to Mason Remey.

sisters.'[17] They took up painting at a young age, no doubt influenced by their fathers, and had a lifelong appreciation for art and antiques, with a habit of frequenting auction houses and antique dealers.

William carried on the architectural firm after Edward's passing, forming a partnership with George Pitts, an engineer and architect from McGill. The new firm was called Maxwell and Pitts and remained in existence until William moved to Haifa in 1940. They completed projects such as the Château Frontenac, that had been started with Edward, and acquired their own commissions; but without the brilliant business acumen, enterprise and skills of Edward the firm never flourished as it once had.

In 1991 the Maxwell brothers' architectural achievements were recognized by an exhibition titled 'The Architecture of Edward & W. S. Maxwell' at the Montreal Museum of Fine Arts. The exhibition then travelled to several locations across Canada. It was 'conceived and planned by the Maxwell Project, a federally registered non-profit organization, which has undertaken research into the architectural practice of the brothers Edward and William Sutherland Maxwell in order to make their work known to a wide audience. All directors of the Maxwell Project contributed to the exhibition and catalogue.'[18] The directors consisted of architectural professors and historians from McGill University, Université de Montreal, Concordia University and the Montreal Museum of Fine Arts. Most of the paperwork, plans, drawings and book collections of the Maxwell brothers' architectural firm now resides at the Blackader-Lauterman Library of Architecture and Art at McGill University.

Art, antique and book collections

European

Once William returned to Montreal from his studies in Paris, he began educating himself in fine art and antiques by visiting dealers (most notably W. Scott & Sons) and regularly attending auctions at Fraser Brothers. He would make notations in the catalogues about works that interested him and marked down their selling price. His daughter has

---

17 Interview by Professor John Bland with Mary Maxwell Rabbani at McGill University, Montreal, 19 November 1980. From the files of Mary Maxwell Rabbani, Haifa, Israel.
18 *The Architecture of Edward & W. S. Maxwell*, p. 9.

said of him that 'He subscribed to a great many magazines such as furniture and interior decorating from England and America, and he cut
them up, including the major articles of interest to him such as porce-
lain, on architecture, on finials, on Chinese antiques etc.'[19] He was an
ardent believer in increasing one's knowledge and his love of art and
architecture led him to zealously read books and periodicals on these
subjects. His daughter spoke of him: 'He'd come home, shut himself up
in the library, and study and study and study. He knew more about art,
if I may say so, than any person I have met in my entire life, and I've
been brought up in that environment.'[20] He was known to read books
and clip articles and images from periodicals for his files until twelve
every night. He also bought postcards everywhere he went and acquired
an extensive collection of some 4,500 images from around the world of
architectural buildings and art works.

It wasn't long before he started collecting works for his own home,
which he designed and built between 1908 and 1910 at 716 Pine
Avenue (in mid-1929 the address was changed to the well-known 1548
Pine Avenue West). His daughter said of him, 'he had an infallible good
taste'.[21] He was very fond of 17th and 18th century Dutch painting
and once wrote about these works that, as 'story telling was the theme
and had the right of way . . . the pictorial quality seldom suffered at the
expense of the human relationships shown in their work.'[22] He had four
Dutch works in his collection, one by Jan Steen titled 'A Birthday Party'
which he purchased at the Anderson Galleries in New York in 1914. He
also owned a marine scene by Willem van der Velde, a village scene by
Peter Snayers, and the visitation of Christ by Simon de Voss.

He highly regarded the brushwork and finesse of the British water-
colourists from the 18th and 19th centuries. He owned several works,
but the most important was by J. S. Cotman (1782–1842), a marine
scene of Yarmouth, which he loaned to the Art Association of Montreal
for an exhibit in 1939.

In a panel over the mantelpiece in the living room of William's home
he placed an Impressionist-inspired mural painting by the French artist

19 Interview by Professor John Bland with Mary Maxwell Rabbani at McGill University,
    Montreal, 19 November 1980. From the files of Mary Maxwell Rabbani, Haifa, Israel.
20 ibid.
21 ibid.
22 W.S. Maxwell, 'Fifty-first annual exhibition, Royal Canadian Academy of Arts', article,
    1930. From the collection of Mary Maxwell Rabbani, Haifa, Israel.

Henri Martin (1860–1943). He also owned several other works by Martin.

His tastes in furniture leaned toward English and Continental European carved oak pieces, mostly chairs, side tables, dining tables and a sofa. Almost all the pieces he owned were made in the 19th century in the styles of the 16th, 17th or 18th centuries. Oak furniture tends to have a heavy feel to it as the wood is dark and the pieces can be chunky. This must have appealed to William, as they would have had the feel and look of the carved wood decoration he often designed for the interior of buildings.

He also had an extensive collection of European prints, including a few works by Albrecht Dürer (1471–1528), many 17th–19th century British and European works by various artists, along with several little-known French artists working during the early 20th century that he would visit in their studios during his travels to France.

Canadian

Being a great supporter and proponent of artists and the art community in Canada, he had a large collection totalling 70 paintings, watercolours, drawings and prints by Canadian artists. Many of these artists were his friends and fellow members of The Arts Club, Pen and Pencil Club or the Royal Canadian Academy. The Arts Club and the Royal Canadian Academy regularly held member art shows where William would purchase works.

His most important pieces are three paintings by James Wilson Morrice (1865–1924), which he purchased from the dealers W. Scott & Sons in 1925, just after the artist's death. Morrice is one of the most important Canadian painters. He travelled to Paris in 1889, and there befriended a large circle of artists exploring the trends developed after the Impressionists. He then returned to Canada and often painted with Maurice Cullen in an Impressionistic style. He spent the rest of his life travelling throughout Europe, North Africa and later the Caribbean. He met Matisse in 1909 and adopted his brightly coloured palette. Upon his death in 1924 Matisse said of him, in a letter to a friend, that he was an 'artist with a sensitive eye, who with a moving tenderness took delight in rendering landscapes in closely related values'.[23] The

---

23 Newlands, *Canadian Art from its Beginnings to 2000*, p. 224.

American painter John Sloan described him as 'one of the greatest landscape painters of the time'.[24] He was one of the Canadian artists who achieved international success during his lifetime, which was an inspiration to artists working in Canada during the first quarter of the 20th century. The three pieces owned by William are all small oils on panel depicting European scenes in a post-Impressionistic style. One work shows a group of people sitting in an outdoor café in a palazzo, another depicts bathers on a beach and the third shows sailing ships at dock.

He also owned paintings, watercolours and prints by several other renowned Canadian artists, who were also his friends, such as: William Brymner (1855–1925), who studied in Paris and was one of the first Canadian artists to paint atmospheric landscapes in the style of the French Barbizon School; Maurice Cullen (1866–1934), who was in Paris while William was studying there and was one of the first Canadian artists to paint in the Impressionistic style; and Clarence Gagnon (1881–1942), who studied in Paris in 1904 and specialized in depicting Quebec farm and village life in his works. His style was Impressionistic and he was known for his brightly coloured canvases; he also distinguished himself abroad as a printmaker, winning awards in the United States and France for his picturesque engravings of villages and towns. William owned several Gagnon prints and one of his works is inscribed: 'To my friend W. S. Maxwell'. And as well, Robert Pilot (1898–1967), the stepson of Maurice Cullen, who was influenced by Claude Monet after studying in Paris and is best known for painting historic buildings which include atmospheric elements such as fog, snow or the subtle colours of twilight.

It seemed natural that William would be friends with these Canadian artists, for most of them had studied in Paris around the same time that he did and they all shared a similar view on painting, as can be seen in their similar styles – not unlike William's personal painting style.

He also owned works by the three artists who had studio space above Edward and William's architectural firm. Laura Muntz Lyall (1860–1930) studied in Paris and exhibited frequently at the Paris salon to critical acclaim. She painted in the Impressionistic style and her works have a luminescence about them. She returned to Canada in 1898 where she made a living on portrait commissions. George Horne Russell (1861–1953) painted in Montreal and St Andrews, New Brunswick

---

24 Reid, *A Concise History of Canadian Painting*, p. 201.

(where Edward Maxwell had a summer home). He was known for his seascapes and he, too, painted in an Impressionistic style. Berthe des Clayes (1877–1968) was best known for her watercolour and pastel wooded landscapes.

Asian

At the end of the 19th century the Western art world was introduced to Oriental art through world fairs, beginning in London in 1862 and in the United States at the Chicago international exposition of 1893. Porcelains, lacquerware, fans and prints, from Japan in particular, were displayed in the West for the first time, to much acclaim. The Western world became a great admirer of what was to be known as the 'Oriental aesthetic'. Parisian artists were particularly influenced by all things Japanese – Pissarro, Manet, Monet and Whistler adopted Japanese subjects or motifs in their works, and all Impressionist and modern art was stylistically influenced by Japanese prints – their colours, outlines, foreshortened perspective and asymmetrical compositions. Vincent Van Gogh said of himself and his contemporaries, 'Japanese Art – we all had that in common.'[25] William became a great admirer himself of Japanese art and the largest group of works in his collections was Asian.

He was most likely exposed to Asian works while studying in Paris where the Exposition Universelle of 1900 had a Japanese Pavilion. On his return to Montreal he must have been studying Japanese art and architecture as there is a notebook dated 1904 in which William took detailed notes and drew sketches from a book entitled *Japanese Houses and their Surroundings* by Edward S. Morse, published in 1889. He continued making detailed notes from books throughout his lifetime and in 1942 he wrote extensively from *Fine Japanese Colour Prints* by E. F. Strange (1931).

His great love was Japanese prints, which he collected (more than 300) with abandon, to the point at which he possessed the second finest collection in North America after J. P. Morgan in New York. He purchased prints from dealers and auctions in Canada, New York and London. The first known dated invoice is the purchase of 'Old Japanese colour prints by Toyokuni 1st, Yeishi, Utamaro, Yeizan, Yeisen', dated

---

25 Quoted in Atkins, *Art Spoke: A Guide to Modern Ideas, Movements, and Buzzwords, 1848–1944*, p. 127.

29 March 1909, from the dealer Shozo Kato in London. He also purchased from Yamanaka Galleries and The Art Shop in New York. His collection consisted of works by the best artists of the Ukiyoye School of the 17th to 19th centuries, such as Harunobu, Kiyonaga, Utamaro, Eishi, Toyokuni, Hokusai and Hiroshige, among others. He described the Ukiyoye School – which literally translated means 'The Transient World of Daily Life' – thus:

> The moral idealism of the classic schools has been abandoned, and a frank acceptance of the joy of the world and its enthralling lures took its place. Rather flippant in style, it achieved by a novel use of the clear hard outline, an unrestrained sweep of line, and the use of brilliant fresh colour, a distinction of design and a decorative beauty worthy of comparison with the work of contemporary classic masters.[26]

One of the best pieces in his collection was by Hiroshige (1797–1858), who was a master of atmospheric landscape prints. William said of him, 'He succeeded in rendering the tenderness of dawn and sunset, the wind over the rice fields, the half light of a village street in the evening time, the beat of rain, the silence of deep sorrow, and the beauty of winter scenes.'[27] His print was titled 'A Shower on Nihonbashi' and depicted figures hurrying across a bridge with Mt Fuji faintly seen through the rain beyond the bankside warehouses and the wooded hills in the middle distance. It was one of the series Toto Meisho (celebrated views of Toto) and was a masterpiece from the set. In 1935 William exhibited a selection of Japanese prints from his collection at The Arts Club. He also gave a lecture on the subject.

Not only did he collect Japanese prints but he also had a very fine collection of over 150 Japanese netsukes, several Japanese and Chinese paintings and many Japanese ceramics, mostly from the 19th century. His most important piece was a beautiful Japanese oribe earthenware water pot and lid from the 16th century with a cream and green raku-style glaze and hand-painted brown bamboo leaves. He also had an interesting group of 32 iron and mixed metal Japanese Tsuba (metal work hand protectors) from the 18th century.

---

26 W. S. Maxwell, article titled 'Exhibition of Japanese Colour Prints of the 18th century, lent by Mr. Sidney Carter and Mr. W. S. Maxwell, May 18th to June 7th, 1935', The Arts Club, Montreal. From the collection of Mary Maxwell Rabbani, Haifa, Israel.
27 ibid.

Books

William was a true bibliophile and could not resist buying books on subjects he loved, such as architecture, art and antiques, to add to his library. His collection, acquired in Canada, New York and Europe and amassed throughout his lifetime, numbered between 3,500 and 4,000 volumes, and was one of the best in Canada. 'He had the true spirit of a student with all the interest and patience that implies and this characterized him until the end of his life,' writes his daughter, Mary Maxwell Rabbani; 'All my own feelings for and knowledge of art began when he would show me pictures in his wonderful books . . .'[28]

His most prized books were his art books, numbering more than 800. He also collected a similar number of literary books illustrated by modern artists such as Andre Derain and Raoul Dufy, mostly printed in limited editions. Many first editions and rare books were part of his collection, such as the first edition of Sir John Soane's *Designs in Architecture* (1778) and the 1716 London edition of Palladio's *The First Book of Architecture*. His book collecting was so outstanding that he was elected to serve on the Library and Prints Committee of the Art Association of Montreal from 1919–1929.

William's brother, Edward, acquired an extensive library as well, and book buying was a great love and activity the two brothers shared by visiting dealers or attending auctions of fine books.

Artistic endeavours: Paintings, watercolours, drawings and prints

Although William was very busy with the architectural firm and his own collecting, he never lost his love for painting and creating his own artwork. The top floor of his home was his painting studio, a refuge for him from the hubbub of his household. He not only painted at home, but his many trips throughout Canada, the United States and Europe can be traced through his paintings, watercolours and drawings capturing the places he visited. He was quite an extensive traveller, as noted through his dated and signed artwork and sketchbooks.

A list of his travels for which artwork exists is as follows:

---

28 Letter from Mary Maxwell Rabbani from the Philippines to Irena Murray, Montreal, 23 July 1989 in Murray, 'The Old Craze of Buying Books: The Libraries of Edward and William Maxwell', p. 40.

1899	Edinburgh, Scotland
1900	Dinan, France ~ Venice, Italy
1907	Portsmouth, New Hampshire
1908	Amiens and St Eustache, France ~ Burlington, Vermont ~ St Andrews, New Brunswick
1909	Southampton, England ~ Cherbourg, France ~ Jaffa, Palestine ~ St Andrews, New Brunswick
1912	Pompeii, Italy
1916	Edgartown, Massachusetts
1918	Sault a la Puce, Quebec
1919	Goodground, Long Island ~ Green Acre, Maine
1922	New York City, New York
1924	Green Acre, Maine
1929	Bermuda
1931	Baie St Paul, Quebec ~ St Jean Isle d'Orleans, Quebec
1933	Zurich, Switzerland ~ Grand Manan, New Brunswick ~ Toronto, Ontario
1934	Ogunquit, Quebec
1935	London, Paris, Brussels, Munich
1936	St Andrews, New Brunswick
1937	France ~ Nazareth, Palestine
1940	France ~ South Africa ~ Nazareth, Palestine
1941	Talpoith
1945	'Akká, Palestine
1947	Kyrenia, Cyprus

Zest for scholarship took him on six trips to Europe throughout his lifetime to admire the architecture and art of England, France, Belgium, Italy, Switzerland and Germany. His great love of France, which developed during his days as a student in Paris, never left him and he made a point of visiting his favourite country on each of his European trips. A list of his trips is as follows:

Feb.1899–Dec.1900	Studying in Paris and travelling in France, Switzerland and Italy
May 1902	Trip to London and Paris to marry May Bolles
Feb.–April 1909	France en route to pilgrimage in Haifa

Sept.–Nov. 1925	England (to visit the British Empire Exhibition in London) and Paris
Aug.–Oct. 1935	London, Brussels (to visit the International World Fair), Paris, Germany (Bremen, Munich, Nuremburg, Rothenburg, Dinkelsbuhl, Nordlingen, Stuttgart)
June–Sept. 1937	Paris (to visit the International World Fair) and southern France (Aix-en-Provence, Marseilles and Lyon) trip home from Haifa after the marriage of his daughter to Shoghi Effendi
May 1940	Moved to Haifa, Palestine until 1951

In 1935 he wrote an article for the *Journal of the Royal Architectural Institute of Canada* entitled 'Souvenirs de Voyage, Europe, 1935' in which he describes his ten-week trip to Europe visiting Germany, Brussels, Paris and London. He also gives advice on how to plan a European trip to view buildings by one's favourite architects:

> Due to the promptness with which European and American magazines publish the newer and better works, it is desirable to browse through them and approximately decide on an itinerary. Fundamentally, the general appearance and character of European cities remains unchanged. Without guidance a search for modern buildings that are distinguished is almost fruitless. It is desirable, on arriving in a city, to call on a professional confrere; one is invariably cordially received, the needed assistance given and usually esteemed friendships result from such contacts.[29]

He was quite a prolific and talented artist, with a great love of drawing. His daughter has said of him, 'He drew beautifully and his sketches are really exquisite. He had a fairy-like touch.'[30] His existing works consist of 27 paintings, 104 watercolours, 110 drawings and 17 sketch books. He was especially influenced by the art in France and was studying in Paris during the Exposition Universelle of 1900 which celebrated the achievements of the past century and exhibited new trends in the

---

29 Vol. XIII, no. 6 (June 1936), Toronto. From the Collection of Mary Maxwell Rabbani, Haifa, Israel.
30 Interview by Professor John Bland with Mary Maxwell Rabbani at McGill University, Montreal, 19 November 1980. From the files of Mary Maxwell Rabbani, Haifa, Israel.

arts and industry. It was one of the largest exhibitions ever held, with a record 50 million people attending. Two great Beaux-Arts buildings were constructed especially for the Exposition and each had its own exhibits, which would have been of great interest to William. The Petit Palais, later to become the permanent home of the art collection of the city of Paris, showed a retrospective exhibit of French decorative art, and the Grand Palais held an exhibit promoting the glory of French art, showing Impressionist artists such as Cezanne, Pissarro, Manet and Monet. William would most likely have visited the exhibition and seen the Impressionist art on exhibit. Due to his exposure to these artists and their paintings and his growing love of French art, he embraced the colourful, light-filled and loosely painted style of the French Impressionists. His painting technique was to build up paint on the canvas until it attained a loose, open and vibrant texture. The textured quality makes possible the absorption of light and suggests the presence of atmosphere. This was also very similar to the style of his friend, the Canadian Impressionist painter Maurice Cullen, who also studied in Paris. Due to his drawing training in the academic style and his innate sense of composition, his works could be described as the Impressionistic style applied to academic and traditional compositions. Almost all his paintings are small seascapes or landscapes and were most probably sketched out of doors, as was the preferred method among painters working in this style. His fine sense of composition was due in part to his training as a draftsman, but he also had a natural eye for proportion. His talent for choosing rich colour combinations, which he might have described as 'pleasing colour',[31] leaves a very positive impression on the viewer. One of his paintings that he considered worthy of exhibition was titled 'Beaupre Wharf' and depicts a schooner in dry dock in St Anne de Beaupre, Quebec. He entered it in the Royal Canadian Academy Montreal exhibitions of 1907 and 1915. Beaupre, near Quebec City, was a scenic location frequented by Maurice Cullen and other Canadian artists painting in the Impressionistic style.

His watercolours are more numerous and depict scenes from his travels to Europe, Palestine, Canada and the United States. He took his nieces (Edward's two daughters) on a painting trip to St Andrews, New Brunswick in 1933 and created a beautiful watercolour titled 'Harbour

---

31 From an article, 'Fifty-first annual exhibition, Royal Canadian Academy of Arts', by W. S. Maxwell, 1930. From the collection of Mary Maxwell Rabbani, Haifa, Israel.

Scene, Seal Cove, Grand Manan, New Brunswick'. The subtle capturing of the reflection of light across the water is technically brilliant or, as he might describe it, 'well analysed and indicated'.[32] This work was in the show of selected works by the Royal Canadian Academy 1933–34 that was exhibited in Canadian cities by the National Gallery of Canada. His watercolours also consist of ornamental designs of floral and leaf motifs, possibly for decorative elements to be used in buildings. There are also several designs for rugs and/or tapestries.

His drawings consist mostly of sketches of buildings, furniture designs, carpet border designs, sculptural motif designs and numerous sketches of members of the Pen and Pencil club that he would draw to pass the time during meetings. One of his most finely executed drawings is titled 'Large Shop Scheme I' depicting the façade of an ornate building and dated December 1897. He was only 23 and living in Boston when he executed this work and it shows the development of his fine drawing skill at an early age.

He had a fascination with prints and stencilling due in part to his love of Japanese prints, and he was quite astute in the art of print making. He was able to design and execute woodblock, steel engraving, linocut and stencil prints himself by carving the wood, making the steel plate and cutting the linocut and paper stencils. Most of his designs are oriental in theme, mixing geometric patterns with leaves, flowers and birds. He was known to spend evenings in his painting studio in his home working on his printmaking.

His other artistic endeavours included designing picture frames and experimenting with different colours and textures of paint on paper to make borders and matting for frames. He was also quite a good photographer. Among his works is an adorable photograph of kittens taken in 1895. In addition, he turned his hand to making his own furniture, in particular side tables, which he decorated on the top with his stencils.

Art associations and the artistic community

William was very active in art associations and clubs in Montreal throughout his lifetime. His earliest club membership was with the Renaissance Club, which consisted of a group of Montrealers who all shared a love of the arts and wished to share their interest by giving

---

32 ibid.

lectures of general interest to the public. In 1907 he was invited to become a member of the Pen and Pencil Club of Montreal (1890–1966). This was an elite club of Canada's top artists, writers and musicians, never numbering more than 30, where membership was by invitation only. 'Its carefully selected membership produced many lifetime friendships whose intensity must have influenced the creative work of many a painter and writer destined, in a few cases at least, to become famous.'[33] The purpose of the club was 'social enjoyment and promotion of the arts and letters'.[34] The group met every Saturday night in the studio of the painter Edmond Dyonnet. Members would bring an artistic or literary sketch on a subject decided at the previous meeting, to be discussed and criticized by fellow members. William had a habit of sketching other members of the Club during these meetings. Several of these sketches exist in his collection. Upon his death one of the members wrote of him: '. . . remembering as I do my first meeting with Mr Maxwell, when I was a draftsman with the old Bromsgrove Guild. Since then I came to know him well, with an ever growing respect for his character, abilities and kindliness . . . Minute books (of the Club) bear frequent testimony to his intense interest in all the various mediums of art.'[35]

At various times, members of the Pen and Pencil Club tried to find a permanent club premises, but without success. This eventually led to the foundation of The Arts Club in 1912, with William being one of its founders. He helped buy the building at 51 Victoria Street, designed its alterations, additions, fittings and furnishings and contributed generously in time and money to the establishment of this institution. He was the first president from 1912–13 and again in 1925–6, and chairman of the exhibition committee in 1935. The Club was open to both professionals and amateurs interested in art, and held monthly exhibitions of Canadian, European and Asian fine and decorative arts that were open to the public. The arts at this time were enjoying renewed appreciation, as new wealthy leaders of trade and industry were acquiring art and antiques, mostly from abroad but also gaining an interest in Canadian art as well. The Arts Club became a place for artists, architects, craftsmen and their patrons to meet and for ideas to be exchanged. It also

33 Cox, 'Fifty Years of Brush and Pen: A Historical Sketch of the Pen and Pencil Club of Montreal'. From the collection of Mary Maxwell Rabbani, Haifa, Israel.
34 ibid.
35 Letter to Miss Parent from Thurstan Topham, Verdun, Quebec, 2 April 1952. From the collection of Mary Maxwell Rabbani, Haifa, Israel.

helped set standards for excellence in the arts along with promoting modernism and the new Canadian artists. In the booklet *Portrait of a Club* is the following statement:

> The Club undoubtedly owes its very existence to the spirit and benevolent vision of William S. Maxwell, then one of Canada's most outstanding architects. This eminent citizen took its founding into his characteristically vigorous stride; soon it was a going concern physically and intellectually – a new and vital force in the cultural life of Montreal. He became its first president. An artist to his fingertips, and a collector as well, he greatly enjoyed the company of his fellow members; he was described as being 'neither a high-brow nor a mixer, but something in between which commanded respect as well as affection'.[36]

Every Friday William went to The Arts Club to mingle with his artist friends and would spend 'the whole evening in a cloud of blue (cigar) smoke. There he talked of the subjects that interested him, played poker and billiards'.[37] One of the Club's members recalled William's participation in the Club:

> W. S. Maxwell always took a great interest in club matters, always unruffled and courteous. He took delight in arranging suppers, such as a Chinese supper all done in proper atmosphere. He printed notices of exhibitions of works of art. He was versatile, enjoying his billiards, poker and even learned to play chess. He was always one of our most enthusiastic and valued members from the inception of the Club.[38]

Many of the leading Canadian artists of the time were members of the Club including Maurice Cullen, William Brymmer, George Horne Russell, Clarence Gagnon and Robert W. Pilot. William also gave lectures on Japanese prints, French books and book illustration, and he

---

36 Cox, *Portrait of a Club*, p. 14. From the collection of Mary Maxwell Rabbani, Haifa, Israel.
37 Interview with Mary Maxwell Rabbani, 1 April 1989, in Yates, 'The Lives of Edward and W. S. Maxwell', p. 22.
38 Letter to H. A. Valentine, President of the Arts Club, from Herbert T. Shaw, 19 March 1960 (Arts Club Archive, Montreal Museum of Fine Arts) in *The Architecture of Edward & W. S. Maxwell*, p. 161.

exhibited his own paintings, as noted in the 1935 summer exhibition catalogue, a work titled 'Seal Cove–Grand Manan, New Brunswick', along with an exhibition of his Japanese colour prints of the 18th-century Ukiyoye School, also in 1935. In homage to his friend Maurice Cullen he organized an exhibition of his works as well, in the same year.

He was a well liked and respected member of the Club whose friendship was cherished. After his passing the Club's newsletter wrote of him, 'Those fortunate to have known Willie Maxwell will carry a fragrant memory of his charming manner, unfailing consideration for others and swift will to assist with advice or effort whenever opportunity arose.'[39] In 1960 a plaque placed on the mantel over the fireplace in the main room was unveiled by Mary Maxwell Rabbani in honour of her father. The plaque reads: 'A distinguished architect who designed this room was a leading spirit in the formation of The Arts Club and became its first president. May he long be remembered and future generations appreciate his quality and his outstanding contribution to the Arts.'[40]

Another art institution that William was involved with was the Royal Canadian Academy of Canada. It was the oldest and leading institution of its kind in Canada, founded in 1880. He was elected an associate in 1909, an academician in 1914, and in the 1930 catalogue is listed among the 'Officers for 1929–30' as Vice-President, with E. Wyly Grier as President. In 1932 he was on the committee to arrange for a series of illustrated articles on Canadian painters, sculptors, designers and architects to appear in Canadian publications. The Royal Canadian Academy of Canada held annual vetted member exhibitions in different cities each year for the public to see the latest works by the top artists, sculptors and architects in Canada. A list of works exhibited by William is as follows:

1907   Beaupre Wharf (watercolour)
       Beaupre at Ebb Tide (watercolour)
1915   Beaupre Wharf (watercolour)
1916   Street Scene, Dinan, Brittany, France (pastel)
1931   The Old Shipyard, St Jean, Island of Orleans (watercolour)
       The Church at St Jean, Island of Orleans (watercolour)
       Water Lot Inn, Bermuda (watercolour)

---

39 *The Easel* (April 1952), vol. 1, no. 5. From the collection of Mary Maxwell Rabbani, Haifa, Israel.
40 Cox, *Portrait of a Club*, p. 24.

Little Ship Yard, Hamilton, Bermuda (watercolour)

1933   Harbour Scene, Seal Cove, Grand Manan, New Brunswick (watercolour)

Old Courtyard, Seal Cove, Grand Manan, New Brunswick (watercolour)

The firm of Edward and William Maxwell, and after 1923 Maxwell and Pitts, regularly showed examples of their architectural work in the annual exhibitions.

In 1938 William was the joint chairman for an exhibition of 76 photographic enlargements and several paintings by Clarence Gagnon and Robert Pilot of old buildings of the province of Quebec titled 'Vieux Quebec Exhibition'. This was an endeavour of the Province of Quebec Association of Architects and was held at the Art Association of Montreal (later to become the Montreal Museum of Fine Arts). It highlighted the glories of historical Quebec architecture and was to be the last exhibition in Montreal in which William would participate prior to his moving to Haifa in 1940, at the age of 66.

In May 1951 he returned to Montreal after spending 11 years in Haifa. He was very ill at the time and wanted to spend his last days at his home. A letter to his daughter, Mary Maxwell Rabbani, from a family friend, recounts William's homecoming: '. . . he went right into the living room. The first thing he picked up was a photograph of the monument on May's grave [May Bolles Maxwell, his wife] . . . He held it, nodding his head, then he touched each object giving its date and period.'[41] This must have been a very touching moment, showing the sweet and endearing nature of the man expressing his great love for his family and the arts as represented by his art collection. Even after being away for so long and being so ill he still had the encyclopedic memory to recount the history and significance to him of all the objects in his home which gave him so much pleasure. His great-nephew Edward Yates (the son of Elizabeth Maxwell) had lunch with him in his garden that summer and recounted how he was reminiscing about the old times in Montreal and how wonderful it had been. He passed away on 25 March 1952 in his 78th year.

---

41   From a letter to Mary Maxwell Rabbani from Rosemary Sala, Montreal, May 1951. From the collection of Mary Maxwell Rabbani, Haifa, Israel.

* * *

He was one of the first architects in Canada to acquire a through training abroad, not only apprenticing with one of the top firms in the United States, but also being one of the first to study in Paris. William's training in Paris brought the ideals of the Beaux-Arts style to his brother's architectural firm, shifting the design from medievalism to Beaux-Arts classicism. His outstanding talent as a skilled draftsman executing beautiful drawings and plans as emphasized by his teacher in Paris, helped the firm in winning many design competitions. His training, knowledge and design skills made the firm one of the most significant in Canadian history, and its most prosperous time was during his partnership with his brother from 1902–1923. Although he was to be considered a master among architects in Canada and worked on many commissions for powerful and elite clients, he had a strong sense of character and always stood true to his beliefs, never betraying what he considered to be the canons of his art.

He was a pioneer in being one of the first architects in Canada to highly value craftsmen/artisans and their contribution to enriching the designs and workmanship of architectural commissions. He thoroughly enjoyed the companionship of the craftsmen and artists with whom he collaborated and many became his personal friends.

His great love and passion for the arts was reflected in his art, antique and book collections which, due to his wonderful eye and good taste, were among some of the finest in Canada. He embraced all the arts. This is clear as seen from the broad range of his collections with works from Europe, Canada and Asia, ranging in time from the 15th century up to the 1940s.

His own artworks were an outlet for his creativity and a way to record the sights and scenes around him on his many trips in Canada, the United States and Europe. He was a very skilled and talented artist who had one foot in modernity, with his adoption of the Impressionistic style, and one foot in the past, with his love of classical, traditional composition.

He had the good fortune of living at a very interesting time historically in the development of the arts, with many new movements and breakthroughs taking place. He was an integral part of the development of the arts in Canada and generously made great contributions to its progress. He was well known and well liked in the arts community and made a lasting impression on everyone he met. He was a great proponent of furthering the arts and the careers of artists in Canada by making them accessible to the general public through his work with the Royal Canadian Academy and The Arts Club.

He was a unique man in his time, not only due to his many artistic talents but also his insatiable quest for knowledge in all things related to the arts. He was not a scholar who studied for his own benefit; he wanted to share this knowledge with his family, friends, fellow architects and artists, to further their appreciation and understanding of the arts. He had a great belief that the arts can play an important role in the world by promoting what is good and being a unifier among men.

A member of The Arts Club said of him, 'In manner he was modest and generous, with a wisdom tempered with humour. A host of friends devoted to him over many years testifies to his personal charm and integrity of character. In conversation he was serious without being pedantic. Counselling a young painter to strive for originality, he once said, "And remember, Nature is a good book with most of the leaves uncut".'[42]

In September 1952 William's Montreal home was declared a Bahá'í Shrine by Shoghi Effendi Rabbani, the world Head of the Bahá'í Faith, owing to the fact that 'Abdu'l-Bahá, the Son and successor of the Founder of the Faith, Bahá'u'lláh, had stayed there in 1912. It is now open to the public and well worth a visit to step into a piece of Canadian history and get a sense of the great man who lived there.

---

42 Cox, *Portrait of a Club*, p. 16.

BIBLIOGRAPHY

Alexander, Agnes. 'May Maxwell – A Tribute', unpublished enclosure in a letter of 28 May 1940. Research Department of the Universal House of Justice; from the Hawaii Bahá'í National Archives.

Allien, Berthalin. 'The Luminous Hour – Remembrance of an Early Believer', in *Bahá'í News* (United States), no. 407 (February 1965), pp. 10–11.

The Architecture of Edward & W. S. Maxwell. Exhibition Catalogue. Montreal, QC: The Montreal Museum of Fine Arts, 1991.

Atkins, Robert. *Art Spoke: A Guide to Modern Ideas, Movements, and Buzzwords, 1848–1944.* New York: Abbeville Press, 1993.

The Bahá'í World. Wilmette, IL: Bahá'í Publishing Trust. Vol. VII (1936–1938); vol. VIII (1938–1940); vol. XII (1950–1954).

Chaffee, Richard. *The Architecture of the École des Beaux-Arts.* Essays edited by Arthur Drexler. New York: Museum of Modern Art, 1977.

Collard, Edgar Andrew. 'All Our Yesterdays', in *The Montreal Gazette* (May 1962).

Cox, Leo. *Portrait of a Club.* Montreal: The Arts Club, May 1962.

—'Fifty Years of Brush and Pen: A Historical Sketch of the Pen and Pencil Club of Montreal'. From the collection of Amatu'l-Bahá Rúḥíyyih Khánum, Haifa, Israel.

The Easel. Newsletter of The Arts Club, Montreal (April 1952), vol. 1, no. 5.

Hogenson, Kathryn Jewett. *Lighting the Western Sky: The Hearst Pilgrimage and the Establishment of the Bahá'í Faith in the West.* Oxford: George Ronald, 2010.

Houston, Florence Wilson; Blaine, Laura Cowan; Mellette, Ella Dunn. *Maxwell History and Genealogy.* Indianapolis, Indiana: C. E. Pauley & Co., Indianapolis Engraving Co., 1916.

Maxwell, May. *An Early Pilgrimage.* Oxford, London: George Ronald, 1953, 1970.

Maxwell, W. S. 'Fifty-first annual exhibition, Royal Canadian Academy of Arts', 1930. From the collection of Amatu'l-Bahá Rúḥíyyih Khánum, Haifa, Israel.

— 'Souvenirs de Voyage, Europe, 1935', in *Journal of the Royal Architectural Institute of Canada* (Toronto), vol. XIII, no. 6 (June 1936).

Metelmann, Velda Piff. *Lua Getsinger: Herald of the Covenant.* Oxford: George Ronald, 1997.

Murray, Irena. *Edward & W. S. Maxwell: Guide to the Archive.* Montreal: Canadian Architecture Collection, McGill University, 1986.

— 'The Old Craze of Buying Books: The Libraries of Edward and William Maxwell', in *The Architecture of Edward & W. S. Maxwell*.

Newlands, Anne. *Canadian Art from its Beginnings to 2000*. Toronto: Firefly Books, 2000.

Pepall, Rosalind M. *Construction d'un musée Beaux-Arts: Montreal 1912*. Montreal Museum of Fine Arts, 1986.

— 'The Education and Training of William S. Maxwell', in *The Architecture of Edward & W. S. Maxwell*.

— 'Craftsmen and Decorative Artists', in *The Architecture of Edward & W. S. Maxwell*.

— 'City Houses', in *The Architecture of Edward & W. S. Maxwell*.

Phelps, Myron. *Life and Teachings of Abbas Effendi*. New York and London: G. P. Putnam's Sons, 1903.

Reclaiming the Everglades, a collaborative digital library project of the University of Miami, Florida International University, and the Historical Museum of Southern Florida libraries and special collections.

Reid, Dennis. *A Concise History of Canadian Painting*. Toronto: Oxford University Press, 1973.

Remey, Charles Mason. *Reminiscences and Letters*. Typed multi-volume autobiography, copy 8, United States Bahá'í National Archives.

Ruhe-Schoen, Janet. *A Love Which Does Not Wait: The Stories of Lua Getsinger, May Maxwell, Martha Root, Keith Ransom-Kehler, Hyde Dunn, Susan Moody, Dorothy Baker, Ella Bailey and Marion Jack*. Riviera Beach, FL: Palabra Publications, 1998.

Shoghi Effendi. *Messages to America 1932–1946*. Wilmette, IL: Bahá'í Publishing Committee, 1947.

Star of the West: The Bahai Magazine. Periodical, 25 vols. 1910–1935. Vols. 1–14 RP Oxford: George Ronald, 1978. Complete CD-ROM version: Talisman Educational Software/Special Ideas, 2001.

Sweeny, Robert. 'Building for Power: The Maxwell Practice and the Montreal Business Community', in *The Architecture of Edward & W.S. Maxwell*.

Thompson, Juliet. *The Diary of Juliet Thompson* (1947). Los Angeles: Kalimát Press, 1983.

The Universal House of Justice. *Century of Light*. Haifa: Bahá'í World Centre, 2001.

Yates, Henry B. 'The Lives of Edward and W. S. Maxwell', in *The Architecture of Edward and W. S. Maxwell*.

INDEX